Qualitative Studies of Silence

Qualitative Studies of Silence brings together influential qualitative researchers from across the social sciences and humanities who have sought to understand the power of what remains unsaid, both psychologically and socially. Each chapter identifies one or more signs of silence and explains how these can form the basis of a rigorous qualitative investigation. The authors also demonstrate how silences operate in our private and collective lives by fulfilling psychological, relational, institutional, and ideological functions. The book contains multiple disciplinary perspectives and presents analyses of wide-ranging topics, such as medical consultations, whistleblowers, silence in court, omission-as-propaganda, trauma survivors, the silence of war museums, racism in the Americas, gendered silences, paid domestic labour, the undocumented student movement, and the Nazi past. This collection shows how such qualitative studies can reveal and contribute to understanding the unsaid as social action.

Amy Jo Murray is a researcher based in the psychology department at the University of KwaZulu-Natal, South Africa. She is exploring creative ways of understanding social justice and inequality through qualitative research.

Kevin Durrheim is Professor of Psychology at the University of KwaZulu-Natal, South Africa, where he runs a research lab and teaches social psychology and research methods.

Qualitative Studies of Silence

The Unsaid as Social Action

Edited by

Amy Jo Murray
University of KwaZulu-Natal, South Africa

Kevin Durrheim
University of KwaZulu-Natal, South Africa

CAMBRIDGE
UNIVERSITY PRESS

#10844 98 039

CAMBRIDGE
UNIVERSITY PRESS

University Printing House, Cambridge CB2 8BS, United Kingdom

One Liberty Plaza, 20th Floor, New York, NY 10006, USA

477 Williamstown Road, Port Melbourne, VIC 3207, Australia

314–321, 3rd Floor, Plot 3, Splendor Forum, Jasola District Centre,
New Delhi – 110025, India

79 Anson Road, #06-04/06, Singapore 079906

Cambridge University Press is part of the University of Cambridge.

It furthers the University's mission by disseminating knowledge in the pursuit of
education, learning, and research at the highest international levels of excellence.

www.cambridge.org
Information on this title: www.cambridge.org/9781108421379
DOI: 10.1017/9781108345552

First published 2019

Printed in the United Kingdom by TJ International Ltd. Padstow Cornwall

A catalogue record for this publication is available from the British Library.

ISBN 978-1-108-42137-9 Hardback

For all children, who should be seen and heard

Contents

Figures

Contributors

C. FRED ALFORD is Professor Emeritus at the University of Maryland, College Park. He is the author of more than fifteen books on moral psychology, including *Whistleblowers: Broken Lives and Organizational Power* and *Trauma, Culture, and PTSD*.

KYLA ALLISON is a PhD candidate in the School of the Arts and Media at the University of New South Wales. Her research interests include affect and gender theory, with a particular focus on sexual abuse in politics, media, literature, and culture.

MICHAEL BILLIG retired in 2017. He previously worked at Loughborough University in the Department of Social Sciences. He has published books on a variety of subjects, including fascism, nationalism, psychoanalysis, and the overuse of technical language. His latest book, written with Cristina Marinho, is *The Politics and Rhetoric of Commemoration*.

GREGORY COLES is a PhD graduate in English at the Pennsylvania State University, where he teaches rhetoric, composition, and civic engagement. His rhetorical scholarship has been published in *College English* and *Rhetorica*.

KEVIN DURRHEIM is Professor of Psychology at the University of KwaZulu-Natal, where he teaches social psychology and research methods and runs a research lab. He writes on topics related to racism, segregation, and social change.

MICHELLE FINE is Distinguished Professor of Critical Psychology, Women's Studies, American Studies and Urban Education at the Graduate Center, City University of New York. Fine is a university teacher, educational activist, and researcher who works on social justice projects with youth, women and men in prison, educators, and members of social movements on the ground.

ROBYN FIVUSH is the Samuel Candler Dobbs Professor of Psychology at Emory University. She is a fellow of both the American Psychological

Association and the Association for Psychological Science. Her research focuses on the social construction of autobiographical memory and the relations among memory, narrative, identity, trauma, and coping.

STEPHEN FROSH is Professor in the Department of Psychosocial Studies at Birkbeck, University of London. He is the author of many books and papers on psychosocial studies and on psychoanalysis. He is a fellow of the Academy of Social Sciences, an academic associate of the British Psychoanalytical Society, a founding member of the Association of Psychosocial Studies, and an honorary member of the Institute of Group Analysis.

CHERYL GLENN is Distinguished Professor of English at The Pennsylvania State University, where she is Director of the Program in Writing and Rhetoric. Her publications include *Rhetoric Retold: Regendering the Tradition from Antiquity through the Renaissance*; *Unspoken: A Rhetoric of Silence*; *Silence and Listening as Rhetorical Arts*; *Rhetoric and Writing Studies in the New Century: Historiography, Pedagogy, and Politics*; and *Rhetorical Feminism and This Thing Called Hope*.

TOM HUCKIN is Professor Emeritus of Writing and Rhetoric Studies at the University of Utah, Salt Lake City. He specializes in critical discourse analysis and the study of contemporary propaganda.

EMESE ILYES is a researcher, educator, and PhD candidate at The Graduate Center, City University of New York. Her research is focused on tracing the process of moral exclusion. She is committed to lifting and envisioning radical possibilities where the incarceration of people with intellectual disabilities is replaced by justice.

CLARE JACKSON is Senior Lecturer in the Department of Sociology at the University of York, UK. She uses conversation analysis to study interaction in both ordinary and workplace settings, including family telephone calls, maternity units, and neurology clinics. She is particularly interested in applying conversation analysis to examine interactional practices of joint decision making.

NICOLE LAMBERT is Assistant Professor of Sociology at MassBay Community College. She earned her PhD in sociology at the University of Colorado, Boulder. Her current research project takes an intersectional approach to understanding the experiences of undocumented 1.5-generation Latinx immigrants in the United States.

CRISTINA MARINHO is Teaching Fellow at The University of Edinburgh in the School of Philosophy, Psychology and Language Sciences. With Professor Michael Billig, she has investigated political discourse at the Parliamentary Commemoration of April Revolution. This collaborative work resulted in the book *The Politics and Rhetoric of Commemoration*.

AMY JO MURRAY is a researcher based at the University of KwaZulu-Natal. She is exploring creative ways of understanding social justice and inequality through qualitative research. She is studying how the unsaid naturalizes and maintains the status quo within racialized relationships, specifically within the context of paid domestic labor.

SUSAN OPOTOW is Professor of Sociology (John Jay College of Criminal Justice) and Psychology (Graduate Center) of the City University of New York and publishes on the psychology of justice, conflict, exclusion, and inclusion.

MONISHA PASUPATHI is Professor of Psychology and Associate Dean of the Honors College at the University of Utah. She studies the way that storytelling shapes memory, self and self-regulation, and social development across the lifespan, with a particular emphasis on adolescence and early adulthood.

MICHAEL RICHARDSON is ARC DECRA Research Fellow and Senior Lecturer in the School of the Arts and Media at the University of New South Wales. He researches the intersection of affect and power in media, literature, politics, and culture and is the author of *Gestures of Testimony: Torture, Trauma and Affect in Literature* (2016).

MARY ROBERTSON is Assistant Professor of Sociology at California State University, San Marcos. She is the author of *Growing Up Queer: Kids and the Remaking of LGBTQ Identity* (2019). Her areas of teaching and research expertise include the sociology of sexualities, sex and gender, feminist and queer theory, and qualitative methods.

MELANI SCHRÖTER is Associate Professor in German Linguistics at the University of Reading, UK, author of *Silence and Concealment in Political Discourse* (2013) and co-editor of *Exploring Silence and Absence in Discourse* (2018). Research interests include political discourse, silence and absence in discourse, comparative discourse analysis, discourses of resistance.

CHRISTINA A. SUE is Associate Professor of Sociology at the University of Colorado, Boulder. Her research interests are in the areas of race and ethnicity (particularly ideology, identities, and multiracialism) and immigration, with a regional focus on the United States and Latin America, as well as in qualitative methodology.

MERRAN TOERIEN is Senior Lecturer in the Department of Sociology at the University of York, UK. She primarily uses conversation analysis to study interaction in workplace settings, including beauty salons, Jobcentres, recruitment to medical trials, and neurology clinics. She is particularly interested in joint decision making in institutional and ordinary conversations.

JAY WINTER is the Charles J. Stille Professor of History Emeritus at Yale University. He is the author of *Sites of Memory, Sites of Mourning: The Great War in European Cultural History* (1995). He holds honorary doctorates from the University of Graz, the Katholik University of Leuven, and the University of Paris.

EVIATAR ZERUBAVEL is Board of Governors Distinguished Professor of Sociology at Rutgers University. He is the author of twelve books, including *The Fine Line*, *Social Mindscapes*, *The Clockwork Muse*, *The Elephant in the Room*, *Hidden in Plain Sight*, and *Taken for Granted*.

Acknowledgments

We are very grateful to all of the contributors for participating in this project and from whom we have learned so much about the field of silence and about what it is to embody scholarly integrity. We would like to thank the following people for their generous academic spirit by helping in the conceptual crystallization of the book: Martha Augoustinos, Annette Becker, Michael Billig, Brita Bjørkelo, Diane N. Bryen, Ronald Cohen, Robert T. Craig, Jennifer L. Croissant, Heidi Kevoe Feldman, Scott Frickel, Stephen Frosh, Susan Gal, Olga Gonzalez, Debra Gray, Azriel Grysman, Rosalind Gill, Phil Hammack, Derek Hook, Klaus Humpert, Alistair Nixon, Jane Parpart, Brian Rappert, John Richardson, Juliet Rogers, Todd Schoepflin, Robin Sheriff, Paul Stenner, Cristian Tileaga, Patricia Von Munchow, Margaret Wetherell, Kevin Whitehead, and Deidre Wicks. We are appreciative of Cambridge University Press for giving us the opportunity to publish the collection, especially to Janka Romero and Emily Watton for their support and patience. The support of the DST-NRF Centre of Excellence in Human Development toward this research/activity is hereby acknowledged. Opinions expressed and conclusions arrived at, are those of the author and are not necessarily to be attributed to the Centre of Excellence in Human Development.

Finally, we would like to thank our parents, friends, and colleagues for their support, but especially our families: Adrian Murray (along with Michaela Faith, Gabriella Lee, Genevieve Reese, Jesse Lewis, and Ezekiel Elliot Murray) and Aleks Durrheim (along with Ružica Jovanovic and Shea Blue Durrheim). To leave you unacknowledged would truly be a case of significant absence!

Introduction: A Turn to Silence

Amy Jo Murray and Kevin Durrheim

Every society lives with silence and the tensions created by absence. We choose to notice some aspects of our world, allowing others to fade into the background. Then there are moments when we speak out about what was once silent, bringing into social life topics that had been unspoken or were unspeakable. The slogans of our time ring out to mark the silences that have made us what we are: #MeToo, #BlackLivesMatter, #RhodesMustFall, and even #AmericaFirst. These slogans are self-conscious unsilencings and can be powerful mobilizing devices.

Silences come to define the society that keeps them, and its future depends on how these silences are identified, broken, or maintained. This is nowhere more evident than in the transformation to democracy in South Africa that both editors of this volume have lived through. Apartheid was a state of silence, built upon geographic partition (Cell, 1982) that kept the pain and violence of what Fanon (1963) called the "colonized sector" out of sight and out of mind of those living in the "European sector." Whites could live in relative ease, consumed by ordinary concerns of day-to-day life while cultivating mundane and even exceptional pleasures and aspirations. White privilege was hardly viewed as privilege at all, but as justly earned success or as the product of a natural order or an unfortunate history. Certainly, rumblings of discontent could be heard. Daily news broadcasted dehumanizing representations of black people in angry crowds, throwing stones amid the flames of burning tires (Posel, 1990). But the topics of injustice, white privilege, and state violence were routinely made absent from national public discourse by banning, censorship, imprisonment, and exile, on the one hand, and by a cultivated and enacted sense of ordinariness, on the other, naturalizing white privilege and silencing oppression and black pain. These silences became the social action that maintained the apartheid regime, allowing it to continue in a business-as-usual fashion.

The Truth and Reconciliation Commission (TRC) played a central role in the transition to democracy. It broke the silence between the oppressed and the privileged by allowing victims of apartheid to tell the

1

truth about their experiences. All of those goings on that had been hidden and silenced – in the townships, on the streets, in schools, in private homes, in police cells, on the country's borders, and in exile – were to be spoken about. The silenced were given a platform that humanized the suffering of apartheid and that called the perpetrators to account. The Human Rights Violations Committee gathered a total of 21,296 statements, narrating a staggering 46,696 violations involving 28,750 victims (Truth and Reconciliation Commission Report, vol. 3, chap. 1, 1998, pp. 2–3). There was much to be said and, as one survivor stated, the TRC ensured that "we are no longer living under the tyranny of silence" (cited in Krog, 1998, p. 145). The TRC catalogued events, moments, and figures of the struggle through testimonies that spoke to the violence of apartheid: burnings and bombings, shootings, torture, forced removals, gendered violence, police custody, detention without trial, exile, disappearances, and attempts to disrupt the status quo. These stories needed – and still need – to be told and retold. Progress depended on an ability to break the great silence that had held South Africa in its grip.

However, as important as the TRC was for breaking silence, it also preserved silence. Not all utterances in TRC hearings were heard and accepted. For one, testimony fell on deaf ears when listeners refused to engage with utterances that fell outside of the preferred discourses of the TRC, discourses that focused on building the Rainbow Nation and were based on Christian ideology (Statman, 2000; Verdoolaege, 2005). TRC Commissioners redirected expressions of anger, calls for vengeance, and outraged reactions toward moments of forgiveness and reconciliation (Statman, 2000). Also, by focusing on discrete events and figures – namely victims and perpetrators – the TRC hearings presented a "reduction and flattening" (Wright, 2017, p. 175) of apartheid experiences. This focus on the extremes of apartheid meant that the harrowing effect of the daily grind – what Motsemme (2004, p. 922) calls the "material and political lived conditions" – of apartheid was effectively made absent. In choosing to say and hear some things, others were left unsaid and unheard, constituting a form of social action.

These silences have reverberated into the new order, which remains haunted by the past (cf. Frosh, 2012; Stevens, Duncan, & Hook, 2013). The TRC represented an important unsilencing moment in South African history, but it "contained contradictions, ambiguities and generated contestations and conflicts" (Robins, 2007, p. 126). It even serves as a "reference point for leaving the past 'behind'" (Gobodo-Madikizela, 2012, p. 253), burying apartheid in history, allowing the beneficiaries of apartheid – white South Africans – to forget about the injustice upon which their ongoing privilege rests (Gobodo-Madikizela, 2012). Yes, the "Rainbow Nation" still has its silences, some of which originate in the unsilencing project of the TRC. These silences have come to define the current order and struggles, which have their own unsilencing slogans (e.g., #FeesMustFall and #RhodesMustFall), curse words (white privilege, white monopoly capitalism), and political projects (e.g., decolonization, Black First Land First). Yet, as was the case with the TRC, these voicings and the social actions they inform cast a veil of silence that will haunt future generations.

This book seeks to focus attention onto the silences and absences of our social worlds. The chapters will show how the unsaid can become the object of qualitative analyses in a wide range of contexts, and they will demonstrate how the maintaining and breaking of silences can be treated as social actions.

Qualitative Studies of Silence

The work of the South African TRC shows the centrality of discourse for the setting up, securing, undoing, and at times maintaining of silence. No doubt, the silences and invisibilities of apartheid were established by violence, forced removals (Platzky & Walker, 1985), and imprisonments and torture (Foster & Davis, 1978) and cemented in law (Horrell, 1978), economics (Lipton, 1989), and the geography of partition (Christopher, 1994). However, all these practices and structures were informed by a pervasive discourse of apartheid (Norval, 1996). Consent for apartheid policies and practice was entrenched by a discourse of control and normalization (Posel, 1987).

Qualitative methods of ethnographic and archival research as well as discourse, narrative, and conversation analysis have been invaluable tools for studying the legitimizing powers of discourse. Critical scholarship in South Africa was part of a colossal global body of work that has been inspired by the turn to language in the social sciences and humanities, a turn that attempts to give voice to the oppressed and to tackle all manner of inequality and injustice. This work pivoted on the idea that language constructs reality (Berger & Luckmann, 1966). Critical qualitative studies straddled and cut through and across disciplinary boundaries: linguistics, history, psychology, education, political studies, cultural studies, feminism, sociology, anthropology, gender studies, and many others (Denzin & Lincoln, 1994). Inspired by the crisis of representation and legitimation, qualitative researchers showed how discursive routines and conventions – including those in the social sciences – worked to legitimate the status quo – patriarchy, racism, anti-Semitism, Islamophobia, sexism, heterosexism, classism, and so on – and silence alternative possibilities.

This turn was itself thoroughly discursive. It drew on the language of poststructuralism, ethnomethodology, and pragmatism, and it made thunderous challenges to the positivist traditions of inquiry and the traditional criteria for evaluating research (Denzin & Lincoln, 1994), including its central adherence to "objectivity." The breaking of silence in qualitative research was a noisy and political activity of debate and contestation that challenged and reestablished the boundaries of legitimacy and attempted to give voice to the voiceless. While an invigorated qualitative tradition sought to challenge these layers of silence in scholarship and in society at large, it did so by focusing on the said rather than the unsaid, and on presences rather than absences.

This focus is built into the very definition of its terms. For example, the concept of discourse was defined as social practices (Fairclough, 1992; Foucault, 1972) or a "group of statements" (Dreyfus & Rabinow, 1982, p. 107); and the fecund concept of interpretive repertoires was defined as "a lexicon or register of terms and metaphors" (Potter & Wetherell, 1987, p. 138) and as "building blocks ... constituted out of a restricted range of terms" (Wetherell & Potter, 1988, p. 172). Qualitative research focused attention on what people were saying and doing and on the representations that circulated in the media, among elites, and in everyday discourse. Absences were seldom treated as social actions.

Qualitative research was underpinned by the "authenticity of presence" (Atkinson, 1988, p. 454) that was accomplished through techniques such as thick description (Geertz, 1973) and literally transcribed conversation (Hepburn & Bolden, 2013). This work presented social interactions and routines for analysis and highlighted the expressive functions of language, including its powers for constructing speaker identities and the subjects and objects of talk. Silence was indicated (if it was) by audible gaps and pauses in the spoken word, whereas the focus of analysis was on the content and enactment of what was said and done instead of what was left unsaid and undone.

Nonetheless, even as they focused on talk, action, and other presences, qualitative researchers brushed up against the unsaid. They encountered conspicuous absences that appeared to incite, constrain, and naturalize forms of social action. The presence of the unsaid in the noisy world of discourse became evident in three layers of silence: social exclusions, traces of avoidance, and conversational expectations.

Social Exclusions

In a widely cited essay, Spivak (1988) posed the question, "Can the subaltern speak?" to highlight the "epistemic violence" that prevents marginalized and oppressed peoples from representing themselves. Poststructuralist, postcolonial, and feminist scholars had criticized the way positivist social science presumed to speak for the people who were the subjects of their investigations – often in the interests of governmentality, colonial administration, and patriarchy. Being sensitive to the crisis of representation and legitimation, critical scholars sought instead to create a space for marginalized and oppressed peoples to speak for themselves and to build an alliance politics rooted in the conditions of their own lives.

For Spivak, the problem with this impulse was the disjuncture between the discourses and texts of liberation that were articulated by leftist intellectuals in Europe and the United States and "on the other side of the international division of labor, the subject of exploitation [who] cannot know and speak the text of female exploitation, even if the absurdity of the nonrepresenting intellectual making space for her to speak is achieved" (1988, p. 288). The interview and other methods were "flood[ed] ... with social science agendas and categories" (Potter & Hepburn, 2005, p. 291) that were alien to the people who were invited to speak. Thus as qualitative research moved from the European/imperialist center to the margins of the third world, researchers encountered the "silent, silenced center" of humanity – "men and women among the illiterate peasantry, the tribals, the lowest strata of the urban subproletariat" (Spivak, 1988, p. 283) – who might have been given space to speak, but who remained as "mute as ever." The subaltern was silenced, and even if they could speak, they could not be properly heard. Rather than focus on speaking, Spivak recommends that we attend to silence, as we seek to understand who does and does not speak, whose voice gets to be represented, and how epistemic violence is exercised on the voice of the marginal and oppressed.

There was a silence at the heart of the turn to language and discourse. The texts of investigation were often the texts of the privileged and powerful. True, these were subjected to a critical deconstruction and analysis. But this work left in its wake a conspicuous absence, an absence of the themes, topics, and concerns of the subaltern – in their own voice.

Traces of Avoidance

The second way in which absences became evident in qualitative studies of texts and talk was when speakers could be seen as actively avoiding something. In a series of influential writings, Billig (1997, 2004, 2006) has brought the repressive functions of language into view. These were evident at occasions where speakers could be seen steering conversations away from certain topics and toward others. Speakers routinely avoided moral violations by maintaining polite conversation and circumnavigating rude, embarrassing, or troubling topics. Although transcripts could not reveal what people do not say, "traces of avoidance" (2004, p. 52) were evident in discursive activities and tactics that gestured toward and gave shape to repressed topics.

Avoidance is often signaled by discontinuity markers such as "yes, but … " or "anyway" that allow speakers to turn conversation away from a particular topic and toward another (Billig, 1997, 2004, 2006). These small words mark a gap, not in the audible flow of talk, but in topic, specifically away from that which is personally or collectively troubling to that which is polite, comfortable, civilized. Of course, these same arts of indirection can also be used to undo repression, unsilencing topics, for example, "Yes, we know X already, but you haven't said anything about Y."

Avoidance is a dialogical accomplishment whose success depends on hearers playing their part, allowing the unstated topic to slide past without notice to be replaced with another, more acceptable one. In this way, "what is customarily said may also routinely create the unsaid, and, thus, may provide ways for accomplishing repression" (Billig, 2004, p. 67). These absences become psychologically and ideologically significant because they allow individuals and collectives to skirt around troubling topics that are left to remain unresolved. Social actors may then become invested in their silences and the violation of the routines of repression may occasion personal and collective upheaval (Zerubavel, 2006).

Conversational Expectations

Many have commented on the "miraculous" coordination of social interaction (Levinson, 2000). Seamless turn taking; conversational relevance; laying down and picking up of topical threads; and the logic, beauty, and passion of conversation are staggering. Yet all this coordination occurs in the absence of rules, directions, and central organization. How?

The self-organizing and generative quality of conversational activity is made possible by the expectations that regulate participation and allow each individual to join and contribute to social life in a way that is deemed appropriate or relevant. Interaction is "governed" by expectations (Grice, 1975; Levinson, 2000). A rich vein of scholarship in pragmatics and conversation analysis has argued that expectations are not fully determined by semantic meaning. For example, the meaning of the sentence "It will be finished soon" depends on context, not semantics. If "it" is tea that is brewing, being "finished" could mean being served and "soon" would be a matter of minutes. However, the job of packing boxes of tea (it), would be finished when the container is full, which might take hours. Or it might be the negotiation of a contract to import tea, which would be finished by signing a contract that might take weeks to conclude, "soon," after months of negotiation (Levinson, 2000). The pragmatic meaning – how to respond – is specified in silence in the space between speaker and hearer. Pragmatic implication sometimes only has a "most tenuous relationship to the semantic content of what is said" (Levinson, 1983, pp. 39–40). Nonetheless, the relevance of implicit meanings and expectations to participants can become evident in features of context to which they orient in social interaction (Whitehead, 2017).

The Turn to Silence

Qualitative researchers have come to appreciate that silence is an important force in shaping social order and social action. The constructive powers of *what is said* are matched by the power of *what is not said*. Social scientists from a variety of disciplines have recognized the potential and importance of focusing on what is missing in conversation and society. Major publications – such as Deborah Tannen and Muriel Saville-Troike's (1985) edited collection (*Perspectives on silence*), Adam Jaworski's (1993) systematic conceptualization of silence (*Power of silence: Social and pragmatic perspectives*) and his (Jaworski, 1997) edited collection (*Silence: Interdisciplinary perspectives*) – declared that silence was no longer a study on the peripheries of academic interest. Instead, silence had become a legitimate, productive, and promising area of inquiry in its own right. This is even truer today when silence research has started to become a central concern for many qualitative researchers. There is growing interest in the influences, causes, implications, experiences, affect, and ideology wrapped up in various forms and features of silence (see, e.g., Achino-Loeb, 2006b; Ben-Ze'ev, Ginio, & Winter, 2010; Billig, 2004; Schröter & Taylor, 2018a; Zerubavel, 2006). We might say that the social sciences and humanities have taken a turn toward silence.

Just as the discursive turn invigorated qualitative inquiry, the turn to silence and the focus on the meaningfulness and activity of the unsaid has reignited interest in the functioning of language and ideology (Achino-Loeb, 2006a; Billig, 2004; Schröter & Taylor, 2018b). This scholarship has broadened the focus and expanded the boundaries of what the business of qualitative research can – and should – include (Mazzei, 2007). Following this trend, this book situates studies of silence and the unsaid within the general ambit of discourse analysis. While there have been many fruitful and influential investigations into the unsaid in disciplines such as linguistics and pragmatics (see, e.g., Ephratt, 2008, 2011; Kurzon, 2007), this collection is primarily interested in how silence – like discourse more generally – can be treated as a variety of social action (see also Schröter & Taylor, 2018b).

The Unsaid

Jaworski (1993) states that silence "can be graded from the most prototypical, (near) total silence of not uttering words to the least prototypical cases of silence perceived as someone's failure to produce *specific* utterances" (p. 73, emphasis in original). While a great deal of energy has gone into studying forms of silence such as pauses, delays, hesitations, gaps in talk, and other audible and measurable silences, more recently attention has turned to the less prototypical forms of silence that Jaworski mentions. These silences are the focus of this volume. We will use the terms "silence" and the "unsaid" interchangeably to refer to discursive absences that have been described as "what is not said, but could easily have been, and, indeed, on occasions is almost said but then removed from the conversation" (Billig, 1997b, p. 152) or discursive spaces that "are inhabited by so much more that could be said" (Carpenter & Austin, 2007, p. 671).

Noticing the Unsaid

Some essential elements of the unsaid deserve our attention. These characteristics of absence are central to our conceptualization of the unsaid and provide an umbrella for understanding the contributions to this collection. Qualitative studies are ideally suited to embracing an understanding of the unsaid as (1) slippery, (2) multilayered, and (3) a form of social action. We have purposely kept these orientations broad to allow for the wide scope of possibilities and approaches that exist in noticing and studying the unsaid. As Rappert and Bauchspies (2014, p. 2; cf. Jaworski, 1993, p. 34) argue:

[T]he more forcefully we try to analytically get a grip on what is not there, the greater the risk that something slips through our fingers. Rather than grasping more tightly or pointing more vigorously, it is necessary to investigate the missing with a sense of openness and receptivity.

Slipperiness

Qualitative studies of silence face significant analytic challenges. Johnstone (2008, p. 70) states, "noticing silences, things that are not present, is more difficult than noticing things that are present." Rappert and Bauchspies (2014, p. 2) describe silences as being "diffuse and wily," and Frickel (2014, p. 89) says that silence is "an exceptionally slippery subject."

There are two related reasons for this slipperiness. First, noticing, recording, and demonstrating absences are difficult tasks because they have "no clear boundaries, no hard analytical edges of definition" (Mazzei, 2003, p. 355). They are "non-occurrences" (Zerubavel, 2006, p. 13) and "non-conversations" (Bischoping et al., 2001, p. 156) that have no concrete identifying markers such as an audible, timeable lack of speech (Ephratt, 2011; Kurzon, 2007). This leaves the analyst with "fewer formal cues to work with" to determine "what *could* have been said yet *wasn't*" (Huckin, 2002, p. 353, emphasis in original). In his seminal work on silence, Jaworski (1993, p. 85) notes that silence is "a highly ambiguous form of communication ... it is more open for the audience to speculate about which assumption(s) the communicator had in mind to make manifest ... in his or her use of silence."

Different audiences (including researchers) are able to speculate in this way because each is able to "read" the context individually to make a determination about what is relevantly absent. Such contextual readings of social actions are themselves deeply affected by sociopolitical, cultural, and rhetorical factors that direct attention to contextual cues of relevance, intentionality, and expectation (see excellent discussions by Jaworski, 1993; Schröter, 2013; Schröter & Taylor, 2018b). In addition, silence can be utilized and interpreted as "both strategies and impositions" (Carpenter & Austin, 2007, p. 669), making possible and plausible a variety of readings into their intentionality and implications. This leads Bilmes (1994, p. 85) to note, "this kind of silence is, in some cases, noticeable to whoever looks with a competent eye. In other cases, it is created by arguing plausibly that something is missing." As such, different audiences – including different participants and observers of the interaction and different researchers and research readers – may reach different conclusions about the nature and content of discursive absences and their implications. Analysis is slippery when researchers attempt to look at the unsaid from these different points of view.

In addition to this ambiguity, there is a second reason that the unsaid can be appropriately described as being slippery. If – as the chapters in this volume will show – every expression leaves something else out that could have been said but was not, then analyses and diagnoses of silences and absences are themselves silencing. Billig (2004, p. 223) explains it this way:

As one matter is spoken (or written) about, so others are kept from immediate dialogic attention. Where topics of conversation become ritual, what is habitually spoken about may be dialogically functioning to prevent, as a matter of routine, other matters from coming to conscious, conversational attention. . . . Not only might such dialogues reveal, or express, what is elsewhere repressed, so they might also create their own silences.

Bringing one silence into view can have the effect of silencing other features of context and the perspectives that could make them visible. Silence is thus a slippery object. The more pressure you apply to a slippery object, the more likely you are to lose your grasp of it. The same is true of silence research. The more we try to pin the unsaid down, the more our own silencing may come into view, along with the criticism and challenge that it occasions.

This slipperiness has the potential to lead qualitative researchers into a number of ditches. On one side of the road is the ditch of naïve valida-tion. This occurs when analysts treat their hearings of silence uncritically, without considering alternative hearings and (especially) supplying evi-dence to show that participants have read the context and heard a silence in one way or another. On the other side of the road is the ditch of discouragement. There are many voices of skeptical reception: "How can you know something in particular is absent? How can you prove that something is missing?" Researchers might begin their study of absence excited about its nuances and possibilities but eventually aban-don the endeavor because the challenges of proving – and publishing about – the unsaid seem insurmountable.

Although slipperiness is a challenge, it also offers rich opportunity. It is precisely this slipperiness that gives the unsaid its power and its unique rhetorical and ideological functions. The ambiguity of the unsaid, the cultivated reading of contexts that make the unsaid apparent, and the potential silences produced by speaking about the unsaid all work together to make for a powerful form of communication. Silences can speak without being spoken, they can implicate without being implicated, and they can account without being drawn to account for themselves. Slipperiness gives the unsaid its vitality.

Multilayered

The unsaid is multilayered in its nuances and its implications. This is largely because silence is "always a joint production" (Tannen, 1985,

p. 100). It is produced by individuals, but always in interactional contexts and in concrete situations, and its roots and effects are in institutions, ideologies, and other broad social systems. In short, silence is distributed across multiple units and levels of analysis and can be approached from these different points of view.

Billig (2004, p.100) reminds us that the unsaid is present within and across a range of "different, but interrelated, levels, whether in the mind of the isolated individual or in shared practices of discourse." We leave troubling things unsaid in our conversations within ourselves and with others regarding troubling topics and identities (Bhattacharya, 2009; Marshall, 2014; Murray & Durrheim, 2018; Norgaard, 2011); utterances about and with privileged groups and social elites, but also the disadvantaged and dispossessed (Billig, 1997a; Sheriff, 2000; Sue, 2015); institutional practices (O'Malley, 2005; Ward & Winstanley, 2003); literature (Schlant, 1999); our public and political speeches (Crenshaw, 1997; Schröter, 2013); the media (Huckin, 2002; Schröter, 2013; Sue, 2015); the (lack of) commemoration of historical events and places (Mack, 2009; Winter, 2010); and in our research (Mazzei, 2003, 2007; Miller, 2017; Poland & Pederson, 1998; Warin & Gunson, 2013). Although we have just offered these topics in a neat and orderly list, the truth is that many of these absences are happening at the same time on multiple levels. Some topics are so personally, interpersonally, and societally troubling that they are absent in how we speak of them on multiple levels and in multiple contexts (Billig, 2004; Sheriff, 2000; Sue, 2015).

To complicate matters further, the unsaid is not only about what we do and do not say, but it can also incorporate what we do not hear and see, as is so well illustrated by the three wise monkeys who collectively "see no evil, hear no evil, speak no evil" (see Zerubavel, 2006). To be unheard or unseen can be the equivalent of being unvoiced. And we can extend silence to other senses too: we may be untouched or untouchable, cast in a prison of loneliness and isolation. Much of what becomes absent may be so because we collectively do not want to see, feel, smell, hear, and speak (about) something that is troubling or distasteful. This is powerfully captured by the narrator of Ralph Ellison's book *Invisible Man* (1952, p. 3), who states the following:

I am an invisible man. . . . I am a man of substance, of flesh and bone, fiber and liquids – and I might even be said to possess a mind. But I am invisible, understand, simply because people refuse to see me. . . . When they approach me they see only my surroundings, themselves, or fragments of their imagination – indeed, everything and anything except me.

As competent members of various social worlds, we learn which topics are troubling or toxic – what should be unseen, untouched, unheard, and unsaid – and how such topics may be avoided, ignored, and rendered invisible on collective and individual levels (Billig, 2004; Zerubavel, 2006). We develop habits, routines, and skills for reproducing the unsaid in private and in concrete contexts of social interaction. Collectively and over time, some topics may fall from direct awareness, becoming almost invisible in our thoughts, talk, and social action, what we refer to as repressed silences – where we are not talking about not talking about a topic. These are topics about which "everyone understands that it is risky to speak the truth, but this fact itself is 'undiscussable'" (Morrison & Milliken, 2000, p. 721). Repressed silences allow us to go about our daily lives disregarding the terrible facts and implications of threats such as climate change (Marshall, 2014; Norgaard, 2011) or racialized inequality (Murray & Durrheim, 2018; Sheriff, 2000; Sue, 2015). Silences may thus become deeply entrenched in our society, psychology, and our collective lives, slippery and resistant to change (Alford, 2001). Even acts of unsilencing – speaking out – can maintain old silences and birth new ones (cf. Carpenter & Austin, 2007).

The multilayering of silence also offers challenges and opportunities to the qualitative researcher. Obviously, no analysis can hope to uncover everything that could or should be said, so it is even more important to situate silences in concrete contexts, but also to look for the ways in which social action here is "articulated" with actions and interests at other levels of analysis (cf. Doise, 1986).

Social Action

The slippery and multilayered nature of the unsaid makes it a powerful tool for social action. As we speak of some things, other significant topics can fade into the background, making the unsaid "particularly well suited for political manipulation of others, on a personal level, as well as on a societal level" (Jaworski, 1993, p. 109). In essence, our social world and its politics are established and maintained as much by what we do not say as by what we do say. For example, marginalized peoples such as economic migrants can be silenced by being locked out of wealthy countries, but their interests, concerns, and humanity can also be silenced by representations of them as thronging masses, potential terrorists, or racial others – as was done in campaigning for Brexit (see Durrheim et al., 2018).

The unsaid is accomplished as social action across the various levels of analysis. It may be primarily an interactional accomplishment, achieved by coordinated actions of speakers and hearers or actors and audience but can gain psychological purchase as repression when individuals routinely direct private thoughts away from particular topics (Billig, 2004); it can come to define relationships when couples or families avoid certain issues (Kidron, 2009; Zhang & Siminoff, 2003); and it can be a system justifying naturalization that keeps the status quo from being questioned or noticed (Murray & Durrheim, 2018; O'Malley, 2005). Silences then "don't just appear or happen out of nothing"; they are social actions that are "produced in response to the dominant reality of our communities and our attempt to maintain that which we wish to preserve" (Mazzei, 2011, p. 664). But silence can also be a form of resistance, a way of subverting hegemony and creating alternative forms of action (Bhattacharya, 2009; Ward & Winstanley, 2003). As Sheriff (2000, p. 114) notes, "while silence tends to penetrate social boundaries it is not seamless; different groups, whether constituted by class, ethnicity, racialized identities, gender, or language, have markedly divergent interests at stake in the suppression of discourse." The vitality and complexity of the unsaid makes it a powerful personal, interpersonal, and ideological resource that needs to be carefully interpreted, especially by those who aim to speak about silence, such as qualitative researchers.

Because the unsaid is a form of social action, commentary on the unsaid in general – and qualitative studies of silence, in particular – are also forms of social action. Thus, studies of the unsaid are not only about what is verifiable, trustworthy, credible, defensible, or convincing; they are also about politics, ethics, and morality; about what is right and wrong, good and bad, virtuous and evil; and all of the grey areas in between. At times, topics and silences that deserve attention are ignored because "what we ignore or avoid socially is often also ignored or avoided academically" (Zerubavel, 2006, p. 13). At other times, speaking about silence and researching the unsaid can reproduce, reinforce, or intensify the very silences that such action attempts to unsilence (Carpenter & Austin, 2007).

We are reminded therefore that studying the unsaid is a way of participating in our social world and involves taking sides and mobilizing voices and actions. It is our hope that by providing a variety of perspectives, approaches, and methods for studying the unsaid, this collection will further increase the momentum of an exciting turn to silence and will itself be a form of social action within the social sciences.

Overview of Qualitative Studies of Silence

This collection is diverse in terms of style, focus, and disciplinary background, which is why we have resisted the temptation to become overly restrictive in our guiding conceptual commitments. We showcase some of the diverse range of qualitative studies of the unsaid. Yet each chapter will answer two broad but fundamental questions. The first question, "What is the unsaid?" will focus attention on methods, practices, and perspectives for identifying absence. Each chapter will show how silences can be identified and validated and will provide some "helpful hints" for conducting rigorous qualitative studies of the unsaid. The second question, "What is the unsaid *doing* (here)?" focuses attention on the ideological significance of absence. The chapters are not dry considerations of methods; they are moving invitations to study silenced worlds. Each chapter shows how actions are produced, constructed, constrained, justified, made accountable, or naturalized through the unsaid.

Since absence is such a slippery and multilayered phenomenon and the contributions to this collection represent varied perspectives on the unsaid, it would be oversimplistic – and possibly misrepresentative – to sort the chapters strictly according to themes or units of analysis. There are too many cases where chapters fit multiple categories, cross traditional boundaries, and land in grey areas of categorization. We have thus arranged the chapters according to an ebb and flow of emphases and lessons to be learned.

The opening chapters locate the unsaid in sequences of interaction. They describe fundamental methodologies for situating and studying actions in their context, and for identifying significant or relevant absences.

Billig and Marinho (Chapter 1) show how interacting speakers and audiences who were left- and right-wing parliamentary members in the Portuguese parliamentary commemorations of the April 12, 1975, Revolution produce silences. They analyze the rhetorical and ideological work done by significant presences and absences such as unapplause and partial criticism.

Toerien and Jackson (Chapter 2) use techniques of conversation analysis, namely sequence organization, preference organization, and turn design, to show how the unsaid is relevantly absent in talk-and-interaction. Their study is located in the institutional context of medical consultation, and they show how doctors and patients manage the (potentially troubling) diagnosis of non-epileptic seizures.

Zerubavel (Chapter 3) shows how small, seemingly insignificant words gain currency and convey social norms that often go unquestioned or unnoticed. The details of social labels, semiotic inclusion (and exclusion), euphemism, hesitations, the taken-for-granted, and generics can all work through the unsaid to produce and maintain hegemony. Zerubavel advocates learning to notice the taken-for-granted as a means of challenging unsaid assumptions of normality and power.

As the collection progresses, some of the lessons learned in the early chapters are fleshed out in chapters that foreground the ideological structuring of the unsaid and its implications. Sue and Robertson (Chapter 4) demonstrate the pervasive – and at times state-sponsored – silence about race in the Americas. They show how this absence has a structuring effect in society and how an ethnographic approach can be used to investigate collective social silence.

Murray and Lambert (Chapter 5) investigate the way intimate silences embedded in structural factors such as race, sexuality, class, gender, and citizenship can maintain inequality. They use case studies from South Africa and the United States to advocate for the use of multiple data sources and a form of triangulation that uses dissonances in data as layers that can make absences apparent.

Opotow, Ilyes, and Fine (Chapter 6) study the intersections of sexuality, race and disability in their analysis of silences, exclusions, and the dehumanizing, even violent, machinery of a high-profile court case. This chapter explores how qualitative research can become a force for social justice as it brings to light and questions that which is taken for granted in the justice system and in society more broadly.

Fivush and Pasupathi (Chapter 7) focus on how gendered ways of narrating simultaneously create voice and silence in interactions and how such socialized silences may affect how we understand our own story and the story of others. Coles and Glenn (Chapter 8) also concentrate on gender, but instead conceptualize gender as power differentials through which the dynamics of the unsaid are shaped and gain their import. They show how the unsaid occurs in rhetorical spaces that are necessarily gendered as silence perpetuates, is subjected to, and resists hegemony.

Schröter (Chapter 9) examines how "language ideologies" that equate silence with repression may be used to achieve political objectives. In particular, she shows how anti–political correctness discourse of the New Right in Germany has been used to revive values of the Nazi past. Huckin (Chapter 10) also looks at how silence works in the media, using a case study of US news coverage of the US–North Korean conflict. He provides a methodology for identifying the omission of certain content and argues that such absences constitute propaganda that feeds into and is fed by national myths.

Alford (Chapter 11) demonstrates how whistleblowers can become silenced to the point of being pushed to the edges of society by organizations. He shows how organizations work to destroy whistleblowers' voices by refusing to listen, creating voices unheard, and a silencing that can call into question all that the whistleblowers once believed about the world.

The concluding set of chapters provides warnings against facile attempts to speak for, of, or about the unsaid. Winter (Chapter 12) shows how the passage of time can produce silences that affect future generations. His moving chapter argues that the sounds of the Great War are forever lost and must then remain absent and unheard in museums, as they do in the Historial de la Grand Guerre.

Richardson and Allison (Chapter 13) take us from war into the experiences of trauma, which are improperly representable, beyond words, and overshot with silences. They use affect theory and case studies of torture and sexual abuse to conceptualize the unsaid as rupture and impasse, and to look for ways of listening to survivors.

Frosh (Chapter 14) presents a reading of the psychoanalytic studies of trauma, arguing that although traumas may be "beyond words," they produce unconscious murmurings, and returns. He offers an ethics for speaking and silence and suggests alternative methods for witnessing silences and accompanying the silenced.

Finally, in the conclusion, we (Durrheim & Murray, Chapter 15) draw on these contributions to propose a topography of the said and the unsaid. Discursive presences and absences are mutually constituted and as social beings, we move together through the terrain of the said and the unsaid, avoiding that which is collectively troubling and keeping to the paths of what can be said. In this sense, the unsaid is a form of joint action with profound implications for how we produce, experience, understand, change, exist, speak, and listen in our social world.

Acknowledgments

The support of the DST-NRF Centre of Excellence in Human Development toward this research/activity is hereby acknowledged. Opinions expressed and conclusions arrived at are those of the author and are not necessarily to be attributed to the Centre of Excellence in Human Development.

References

Achino-Loeb, M.-L. (2006a). Silence as the currency of power. In M.-L. Achino-Loeb (Ed.), *Silence: The currency of power* (pp. 1–22). New York: Berghahn Books.
Achino-Loeb, M.-L. (Ed.). (2006b). *Silence: The currency of power*. New York: Berghahn Books.

Alford, C. F. (2001). *Whistleblowers: Broken lives and organizational power.* Ithaca, NY: Cornell University Press.

Atkinson, P. (1988). Ethnomethodology: A critical review. *Annual Review of Sociology, 14,* 411–465.

Bhattacharya, H. (2009). Performing silence: Gender, violence and resistance in women's narratives from Lahaul, India. *Qualitative Inquiry, 15*(2), 359–371.

Ben-Ze'ev, E., Ginio, R., & Winter, J. (Eds.). (2010). *Shadows of war: A social history of silence in the twentieth century.* Cambridge: Cambridge University Press.

Berger, P. L., & Luckmann, T. (1966). *The social construction of reality: A treatise in the sociology of knowledge.* London: Allen Lane.

Billig, M. (1997a). Keeping the white queen in play. In M. Fine, L. Weis, L. C. Powell, & L. Mun Wong (Eds.), *Off white: Readings on race, power and society* (pp. 149–157). New York: Routledge.

Billig, M. (1997b). The dialogic unconscious: Psychoanalysis, discursive psychology and the nature of repression. *British Journal of Social Psychology, 36,* 139–159.

Billig, M. (2004). *Freudian repression: Conversation creating the unconscious.* Cambridge: Cambridge University Press.

Billig, M. (2006). A psychoanalytic discursive psychology: From consciousness to unconsciousness. *Discourse Studies, 8,* 17–24.

Bilmes, J. (1994). Constituting silence: Life in the world of total meaning. *Semiotica, 98,* 73–87.

Bischoping, K., Dodds, C., Jama, M., Johnson, C., Kalmin, A., & Reid, K. (2001). Talking about silence: Reflections on "race" in a university course on genocide. *Reflective Practice 2*(2), 155–169.

Carpenter, L., & Austin, H. (2007). Silenced, silence, silent: Motherhood in the margins. *Qualitative Inquiry, 13*(5), 660–674.

Cell, J. (1982). *The highest stage of white supremacy.* Cambridge: Cambridge University Press.

Christopher, A. J. (1994). *The atlas of apartheid.* London: Routledge.

Crenshaw, C. (1997). Resisting Whiteness' rhetorical silence. *Western Journal of Communication, 6*(3), 253–278.

Denzin, N. K., & Lincoln, Y. S. (Eds.). (1994). *Handbook of qualitative research.* Thousand Oaks, CA: Sage.

Doise, W. (1986). *Levels of explanation in social psychology.* Cambridge: Cambridge University Press.

Dreyfus, H. L., & Rabinow, P. (1982). *Michel Foucault: Beyond structuralism and hermeneutics* (2nd ed.). Chicago: University of Chicago Press.

Durrheim, K., Okuyan, M., Twali, M. S., García-Sánchez, E., Pereira, A., Portice, J. S. . . . & Keil, T. (2018). How racism discourse can mobilize right-wing populism: The construction of identity and alliance in reactions to UKIP's Brexit "Breaking Point" campaign. *Journal of Applied and Community Social Psychology, 28,* 385–405.

Ellison, R. (1952). *Invisible man.* New York: Random House.

Ephratt, M. (2008). The functions of silence. *Journal of Pragmatics, 40,* 1909–1938.

Ephratt, M. (2011). Linguistic, paralinguistic and extralinguistic speech and silence. *Journal of Pragmatics*, *43*, 2286–2307.

Fairclough, N. (1992). *Discourse and social change*. Cambridge: Polity Press.

Fanon, F. (1963). *The wretched of the earth*. New York: Grove Press.

Foster, D. H., & Davis, D. (1978). *Detention and torture in South Africa: Psychological, legal & historical studies*. Cape Town: David Philip.

Foucault, M. (1972). *The archeology of knowledge and the discourse on language*. Trans. A. M. Sheridan Smith. New York: Harper and Row.

Frickel, S. (2014). Absences: Methodological note about nothing, in particular. *Social Epistemology*, *28*, 86–95.

Frosh, S. (2012). Hauntings: Psychoanalysis and ghostly transmission. *American Imago*, *69*(2), 241–264.

Geertz, C. (1973). Thick description: Towards an interpretive theory of culture. In C. Geertz (Ed.), *The interpretation of cultures* (pp. 3–30). New York: Basic Books.

Gobodo-Madikizela, P. (2012). Remembering the past: Nostalgia, traumatic memory and the legacy of apartheid. *Peace and Conflict: Journal of Peace Psychology*, *18*(3), 252–267.

Grice, H. P. (1975), Logic and conversation. In P. Cole & J. L. Morgan (Eds.), *Syntax and semantics 3: Speech acts* (pp. 41–58). New York: Academic Press.

Hepburn, A., & Bolden, G. B. (2013). The conversation analytic approach to transcription. In J. Sidnell & T. Stivers (Eds.), *The handbook of conversation analysis* (pp. 57–75). Malden, MA: Blackwell Publishing Ltd.

Horrell, M. (1978). *Laws affecting race relations in South Africa, 1948–1976*. Johannesburg: South African Institute of Race Relations.

Huckin, T. (2002). Textual silence and the discourse of homelessness. *Discourse and Society*, *13*(3), 347–372.

Jaworski, A. (1993). *Power of silence: Social and pragmatic perspectives*. Newbury Park: Sage.

Jaworski, A. (Ed.). (1997). *Silence: Interdisciplinary perspectives*. Berlin: Mouton de Gruyter.

Johnstone, B. (2008). *Discourse analysis* (2nd ed.). Oxford: Blackwell Publishing.

Kidron, C. A. (2009). Toward an ethnography of silence: The lived presence of the past in the everyday life of Holocaust trauma survivors and their descendants in Israel. *Current Anthropology*, *50*, 5–27.

Krog, A. (1998). *Country of my skull: Guilt, sorrow and the limits of forgiveness in the New South Africa*. New York: Three Rivers Press.

Kurzon, D. (2007). Towards a typology of silence. *Journal of Pragmatics*, *39*, 1673–1688.

Levinson, S. C. (2000). *Presumptive meanings: The theory of generalized conversational implicature*. Cambridge, MA: MIT Press.

Levinson, S. C. (1983). *Pragmatics*. Cambridge: Cambridge University Press

Lipton, M. (1989). *Capitalism and apartheid South Africa, 1910–1986*. Cape Town: David Philip.

Mack, S. (2009). Black voices and absences in commemorations of abolition in North East England. *Slavery and Abolition*, *30*(2), 247–257.

Marshall, G. (2014). *Don't even think about it: Why our brains are wired to ignore climate change*. London: Bloomsbury Publishing.

Mazzei, L. A. (2003). Inhabited silences: In pursuit of a muffled subtext. *Qualitative Inquiry, 9*(3), 355–368.

Mazzei, L. A. (2007). *Inhabited silence in qualitative research: Putting poststructural theory to work*. New York: Peter Lang.

Mazzei, L. A. (2011). Desiring silence: Gender, race and pedagogy in education. *British Educational Research Journal, 37*(4), 657–669.

Miller, L. (2017). Telling the difficult things: Creating spaces for disclosure, rapport and "collusion" in qualitative interviews. *Women's Studies International Forum, 61*, 81–86.

Morrison, E. W., & Milliken, F. J. (2000). Organizational silence: A barrier to change and development in a pluralistic world. *Academy of Management Review, 25*, 706–731.

Motsemme, N. (2004). The mute always speak: On women's silences at the Truth and Reconciliation Commission. *Current Sociology, 52*(5), 909–932.

Murray, A. J., & Durrheim, K. (2018). "There was much that went unspoken": Maintaining racial hierarchies in South African paid domestic labour through the unsaid. *Ethnic and Racial Studies*, https://doi.org/10.1080/01419870 .2018.1532096.

Norgaard, K. (2011). *Living in denial: Climate change, emotions and everyday life*. Cambridge, MA: MIT Press.

Norval, A. J. (1996). *Deconstructing apartheid discourse*. London: Verso.

O'Malley, M. P. (2005). Silence as a means of preserving the status quo: The case of ante-natal care in Ireland. *Multilingua, 24*, 39–54.

Platzky, L., & Walker, C. (1985). *The surplus people: Forced removals in South Africa*. Johannesburg: Ravan Press.

Poland, B., & Pederson, A. (1998). Reading between the lines: Interpreting silences in qualitative research. *Qualitative Inquiry, 4*(2), 293–312.

Posel, D. (1987). The language of domination, 1978–1983. In S. Marks & S. Trapido (Eds.), *The politics of race, class and nationalism in twentieth-century South Africa* (pp. 419–44). London: Longman.

Posel, D. (1990). Symbolizing violence: State and media discourse in TV coverage of township protest, 1985–7. In N. C. Manganyi & A. du Toit (Eds.), *Political violence and the struggle in South Africa* (pp. 154–171). Basingstoke: Macmillan.

Potter, J., & Hepburn, A. (2005). Qualitative interviews in psychology: Problems and possibilities. *Qualitative Research in Psychology, 2*(4), 281–307.

Potter, J. & Wetherell, M. (1987). *Discourse and social psychology: Beyond attitudes and behavior*. London: Sage Publications.

Rappert, B., & Bauchspies, W.K. (2014). Introducing absence. *Social Epistemology, 28*, 1–3.

Robins, S. (2007). "Can't forget, can't remember": Reflections on the cultural afterlife of the TRC. *Critical Arts, 21*, 125–151.

Schlant, E. (1999). *The language of silence: West German literature and the Holocaust*. New York: Routledge.

Schröter, M. (2013). *Silence and concealment in political discourse*. Amsterdam: John Benjamins Publishing Company.

Schröter, M., & Taylor, C. (Eds.). (2018a). *Exploring silence and absence in discourse: Empirical approaches*. London: Palgrave Macmillan.

Schröter, M., & Taylor, C. (2018b). Introduction. In M. Schröter & C. Taylor (Eds.), *Exploring silence and absence in discourse: Empirical approaches* (pp. 1–21). London: Palgrave Macmillan.

Sheriff, R.E. (2000). Exposing silence as cultural censorship: A Brazilian case. *American Anthropologist, 102*(1), 114–132.

Spivak, G. (1988). Can the subaltern speak? In C. Nelson & L. Grossberg (Eds.), *Marxism and the interpretation of culture* (pp. 271–313). Chicago: University of Illinois Press.

Statman, J. M. (2000). Performing the truth: The social-psychological context of TRC narratives. *South African Journal of Psychology, 30*, 23–32.

Stevens, G., Duncan, N., & Hook, D. (Eds.). (2013). *Racism, memory and the Apartheid Archive: Towards a psychosocial praxis*. Johannesburg: Wits University Press.

Sue, C. A. (2015). Hegemony and silence: Confronting state-sponsored silences in the field. *Journal of Contemporary Ethnography, 44*, 113–140.

Tannen, D. (1985). Silence: Anything but. In D. Tannen & M. Saville-Troike (Eds.), *Perspectives on silence* (pp. 93–111). Norwood: Ablex Publishing Corporation.

Tannen, D., & Saville-Troike, M. (Eds.). (1985). *Perspectives on silence*. Norwood: Ablex Publishing Corporation.

Truth and Reconciliation Commission Report. (1998). *Truth and Reconciliation Commission of South Africa Report*. Cape Town: CTP Printers.

Verdoolaege, A. (2005). Managing reconciliation at the Human Rights Violations Hearings of the South African TRC. *Journal of Human Rights, 5*, 61–80.

Ward, J. & Winstanley, D. (2003). The absent presence: Negative space within discourse and the construction of minority sexual identity in the workplace. *Human Relations, 56*(10), 1255–1280.

Warin, M. J., & Gunson, J. S. (2013). The weight of the word. Knowing silences in obesity research. *Qualitative Health Research, 23*(12), 1686–1696.

Wetherell, M., & Potter, J. (1988). Discourse analysis and the identification of interpretative repertoires. In C. Antaki (Ed.), *Analysing everyday explanation: A casebook of methods* (pp. 168–183). Thousand Oaks: Sage Publications.

Whitehead, K. A. (2017, February). Conversation analysis, context, and membership categories: How far can participant orientations go? Presentation for the Department of Sociology, University of California, Santa Barbara.

Winter, J. (2010). Thinking about silence. In E. Ben-Ze'ev, R. Ginio, & J. Winter (Eds.), *Shadows of war: A social history of silence in the twentieth century* (pp. 3–31). Cambridge: Cambridge University Press.

Wright, T. (2017). Justice, silence and complexity: Recent forays into the reconstitution of apartheid experience. *African Studies, 76*, 163–176.

Zerubavel, E. (2006). *The elephant in the room: Silence and denial in everyday life*. Oxford: Oxford University Press.

Zhang, A. Y., & Siminoff, L. A. (2003). Silence and cancer: Why do families and patients fail to communicate? *Health Communication, 15*(4), 415–429.

1 Literal and Metaphorical Silences in Rhetoric: Examples from the Celebration of the 1974 Revolution in the Portuguese Parliament

Michael Billig and Cristina Marinho

This chapter examines the role of silences and significant absences in formal rhetoric, particularly parliamentary speech-making. We shall be arguing that it is important to distinguish between different types of silences and also to avoid assuming that silences are the same as significant absences. At first glance, it might appear to be unduly restrictive to examine such issues in the context of formal speeches rather than analysing them within ordinary, informal conversations. However, the context of formal rhetoric offers analysts two distinct advantages. First, the very formality of the situation enables analysts to distinguish clearly between different types of silences and absences, because they will be observing the use of rhetoric in what is quite literally a controlled environment (Ilie, 2010b). Second, there is a case for arguing that human thinking is itself deeply rhetorical (Billig, 1991, 1996). If that is accepted, then the interaction between speakers and audiences in situations of formal rhetoric will not be insulated from wider psychological processes, most notably those of persuasion and social display; instead, formal rhetoric will reflect those wider processes. In consequence, we can gain methodological and theoretical insights about silences and absences in general by looking closely at instances of formal rhetoric; in addition, any such insights, at least potentially, should not be confined only to contexts of formal speech-making.

We will be concentrating on the type of rhetoric that ancient rhetorical theorists called 'epideictic'. This refers to the moral rhetoric that predominates at ceremonies designed to praise or berate persons, places or events (Pernot, 2005, 2015a). In the modern world, ceremonies that commemorate past events, whether tragic or triumphant, are typical epideictic occasions (Billig & Marinho, 2017; Sheard, 1995; Vivian, 2006; Wodak & de Cillia, 2007). Modern rhetorical theorists have suggested that during such ceremonies, customary social divisions are put aside as speakers stress the collective identity of their community, culture or nation (Condit, 1985; Sheard, 1995; see also Perelman & Olbrechts-Tyteca, 1969). Our examples come from the annual ceremony in the Portuguese parliament to celebrate the 25 April revolution of 1974, when the right-wing authoritarian dictatorship, which António Salazar established in 1932, was finally overthrown. This ceremony does not conform to theoretical expectancies: the members of the Portuguese parliament do not put aside partisan politics, but they regularly make politically divisive speeches (Billig & Marinho, 2017).

Nevertheless, some matters cannot be openly expressed, but speakers by deploying meaningful patterns of rhetorical absences and presences can indirectly express what cannot be said directly. We will here be concentrating on right-wing speakers and will be showing why they might be ambivalent towards the ceremony and the event that it celebrates – and, most importantly, why they cannot openly voice these ambivalences. As we have shown in our book *Politics and Rhetoric of Commemoration*, the speeches of the left also contain significant absences, especially as the left reduces the complexities of history into the simplicities of myth (Billig & Marinho, 2017).

Metaphorical and Literal Silences

At the outset, two distinctions need to be made. First is the distinction between literal and metaphorical silences. Second is the distinction between the silences of speakers and those of audiences. Silences can be literal when there is an absence of speech or other rhetorical noise, such as a minute's silence to remember the dead within a formal ceremony. We will not be discussing this sort of respectful, literal silence, although such silences are not entirely literal for they possess rhetorical meaning. Silences can be metaphorical in another way. If speakers are silent about a particular theme that they might have been expected either by custom or by specific circumstances to speak about, this is not because they have literally remained silent. They will speak about matters other than the one expected by observers both within the audience and outside it. To discover whether there have been metaphorical silences within a particular speech or series of speeches, we will show why analysts would benefit from comparing what has not been said with what has been said.

Most rhetorical analysts have concentrated their attention on speakers: they have paid less attention to the sounds of the audience and even less to the audience's literal silences. Audiences can show their approbation or dissatisfaction by making noises, such as shouting comments, cheering, applauding and booing. Or they can remain silent. Whereas we will not be discussing the literal silences of speakers, we will be considering what the literal silences of audiences can indicate, and how the sounds and silences of an audience can interact with the metaphorical silences of a speaker.

Literal Silences of Audiences

We will begin right at the beginning with a case of literal silence. The first ceremony, when the Portuguese parliament celebrated the 1974 Revolution, occurred on 25 April 1977. The core of the ceremony, then as now, consists of speeches delivered by a representative from each political party that has a deputy in the assembly. The order in which each party's chosen speech-maker delivers their oration is strictly determined. The speaker from the party with the fewest deputies speaks first, then the next smallest party all the way up to the party with the most deputies, typically the party of government. In 1977, the tiny Marxist party, the UDP (People's Democratic Union), had only one elected representative who, accordingly, had the honour of delivering the first speech at the first ceremony.

When that first speaker completed his speech, the audience was silent. No one applauded, cheered or booed. Did this silence indicate disapproval of the speaker's extreme Marxism? Had the new Portuguese parliament, like some established parliaments, established a code that forbade applause (Ilie, 2010a, 2010b)? Or did this silence represent the first example of what would become a unifying code for the ceremony – as if the solemnity of the occasion demanded silent, non-partisan reactions? There is another possibility. Analysts, such as Atkinson (1984), Bull (2006) and Heritage and Greatbach (1986), have demonstrated how political speakers can elicit applause from their audiences by signalling through intonation and rhetorical devices that they are leaving a micro-moment of silence for applause. Had the UDP speaker shown his rhetorical incompetence by failing to signal that he was drawing his speech to an end?

It is implausible that the audience's silence may have resulted from the speaker's failure to signal the end of his speech. When the audience members saw the speaker gather up his papers and start to leave the podium, they could have started to applaud. In any case, the UDP speaker had finished with the sort of stirring statement that classical rhetorical theorists such as Quintilian called *sententiae* and that they recommended speakers use at the end of speeches (see Billig & Marinho, 2017, p. 54, for details). Moreover, the audience had not been totally silent during the speech. When the speaker criticised the government's foreign policy, deputies from right-wing parties voiced disapproval. So, the silence at the end of the speech was unlikely to reflect a general code of non-political silence during the ceremony.

We can only understand the meaning of that first silence by examining the UDP speech in context. By the end of the first ceremony, it was clear what had happened. Each of the other political speakers had been applauded when they finished their speeches. Unlike the president of the Republic and the president of the Assembly, who also gave speeches, none of the representatives of the parties were applauded by the whole audience. Only the deputies from their own party had applauded them. It was clear why the UDP speaker had been met with total silence: he had no party colleagues to applaud him. No one else in the audience was going to clap.

The final applause was, and remains to this day, a means for listening deputies to demonstrate their partisan identity. Their applause is not a response to the content of the final words of speakers who often use virtually identical *sententiae*. The audience was unwittingly delivering a blow to those theorists who claim that in formal ceremonies of national remembrance, partisan division gives way to national unity. To show partisan loyalty, party members must do more than merely applaud their own speaker; they must also not applaud speakers of other parties. This is why none of the other deputies put their hands together to applaud when the UDP member finished his speech.

The decision not to applaud could not have been a spontaneous reaction to the final words of the first speech. It was an established habit taken from the normal sessions of the Portuguese parliament. As coalition politics has developed in modern Portuguese politics, so have coalitions of applause in the ceremony of remembrance. Formal and informal coalition partners – whether governmental or campaigning coalitions – will applaud the speeches of their partners. Even so, they can publically demonstrate their specific partisan loyalty. Today party members will often stand to applaud speakers from their own party, while remaining seated when applauding those of coalition partners.

Here we can see the importance of significant absences for understanding presences. The applause that occurs takes its meaning from the applause that significantly does not occur. Non-applause is more than the absence of applause: it is a significant absence with its own rhetorical meaning and is an act that has to be performed by non-performance. In this respect, deliberate non-applause resembles the reaction of those who specifically do not laugh when they wish to indicate their disapproval of a joke that has just been told in their company. Thus, Billig (2005) devised the term 'unlaughter' to draw attention to this type of not laughing. Unlaughter is more than an absence of not laughing. It has to be performed. The unlaughing recipients of a joke have to indicate, whether by posture, gesture or facial expression, that they have heard the joke, recognised it as a joke but consider it too unworthy, inappropriate or immoral to be accepted as a joke, even a bad joke. Similarly, audiences at the Portuguese ceremony and also in ordinary sessions of the parliament typically meet the speeches delivered by representatives of rival parties with collective unapplause – a deliberate, meaningful and demonstrably performed absence of applause. This type of significant absence is more than a lack of presence: it has to be meaningfully performed and in consequence is itself a form of presence.

Physical Absence

The silence produced by an unapplauding audience is based upon a physical absence – the absence of the noise made by hands being clapped together, or the absence of the noise of cheering. There is a quiet moment between the end of one verbal action (the speech that has been completed) and the start of the next verbal action (the president of the Assembly calling the next speaker to the podium). Of course, there was not total silence following the end of the UDP speech, as members of the audience shuffled papers, coughed, stretched, whispered to their neighbours and so on. These movements were not sufficiently significant to be recorded in the official parliamentary record. This was a moment of rhetorical, rather than simply literal, silence.

Rhetorical meaning can also be indicated physically through the non-display of significant symbols. In every parliamentary celebration of the 1974 Revolution, right-wing deputies have displayed a significant physical absence. The symbol of the 1974 Revolution has been the red carnation: indeed, the revolution is often called 'the revolution of carnations'. The flower represents the moments on 25 April when people flocked onto the streets of Lisbon carrying red carnations in support for those members of the military who at dawn had taken command of those streets. Some of these supporters were photographed placing carnations in soldiers' rifles; these images were to become famous across the world.

For the official ceremony, the assembly hall is bedecked with red carnations. From the very first ceremony, members of left-wing parties have worn carnations pinned to their clothing. The members of the two main right-wing parties – the centre-right Social Democratic Party (PSD) and the traditionalist right Social Democratic Centre (CDS or CDS-PP as it is now called, having added 'Popular Party' to its name) – have not worn carnations. Whereas an empty buttonhole on any other parliamentary day would be insignificant, the absence of a carnation during the 25 April celebration is a significant absence. The empty buttonholes of the right physically demonstrate reservations about the ceremony and about the events that the ceremony celebrates. These reservations cannot be expressed too openly without appearing to offend the ceremony in which they were participating, or even appearing not to support the revolution itself. That would expose the right-wing parties to charges that they were not democratic; the CDS, founded by ex-supporters of the Salazarist regime, would be especially vulnerable to the charge (Marinho & Billig, 2013).

In recent years, some members of the PSD have begun to wear carnations for the ceremony, but CDS-PP members have stubbornly remained carnation-free. The ceremony of 2010 was the first time that a PSD speaker had worn a carnation, and it matched the political message of his speech: he was accusing the centre-left government of the Socialist Party (PS) of being exactly like the pre-1974 totalitarian government of Portugal. The flower in his buttonhole wordlessly supported his credentials as an opponent of totalitarianism, while the words of his speech concentrated upon the supposed totalitarian nature of the current democratically elected government and its policies to protect trade union rights and raise income tax (see Billig & Marinho, 2017, pp. 148ff).

In his speech, the PSD speaker drew attention to his carnation, claiming that it was a mistake to allow the left to control the ceremony and its symbols. His words were greeted by support from members of his own party. The CDS-PP members sat silently in their flower-free clothing. Previously no PSD speaker had commented on the lack of carnations pinned to their clothing. Not only had the carnations been physically absent, but also the meaningfulness of this absence was rhetorically absent from PSD speeches. Thus, the physical absence had been accompanied by a rhetorical silence. Only when the physical absence had been replaced by a physical presence did it also become a rhetorical presence.

The wordless awkwardness which PSD members can display towards the celebratory carnation was illustrated during the 2016 ceremony. The Portuguese president, Marcelo Rebelo de Sousa, belonged to the PSD. The president of the Republic is not a member of the parliament but is formally invited to participate in the ceremony and is part of the procession that enters the assembly at the start of proceedings. In the tradition of his party, Rebelo de Sousa was not wearing a carnation. However, in the days before the ceremony a national youth organisation had publically offered him a carnation to wear. This presented the president with a dilemma: if he refused the carnation, he would be rejecting a national symbol, but if he wore the carnation he would be rejecting his own and his party's custom. A deal was struck in the days before the ceremony: he would carry but not wear the carnation.

So Portugal's president was depicted in the official parliamentary film of the occasion holding the flower awkwardly before him as he entered the assembly in the formal procession. As soon as he reached his seat, de Sousa divested himself of the flower, unobtrusively placing it in the general display of carnations. Significantly, he did not place it among the carnations in front of his own seat, but he leaned over to place it in front of the seat next to his, thereby silently enacting a dissociation from the revolutionary symbol – a dissociation that would have been too controversial to express in words. Not only must modern politicians possess the rhetorical skills to deliver political speeches, but they must also know when to act silently, even stealthily.

The Metaphorical Silences of Speakers

Metaphorical silences that speakers accomplish rhetorically are very different from physical silences. Speakers have speeches to deliver. If a speaker is silent on one theme, then this silence must be filled by the sounds of words uttered about other themes. Not all thematic, metaphorical silences are significant absences. A lecturer who is delivering a formal lecture on particle physics would probably not discuss Freudian theory. Under normal circumstances, one would not claim this to be a significant absence. However, if the lecturer, while discussing controversies in the world of particle physics, omitted to mention the ideas of a long-standing rival theorist, then listeners might suspect that here was a significant absence. This is the absence of a theme that knowledgeable others might expect to be present but that the speaker knowingly omits. If a speaker does not mention 25 April 1974 on the solemn occasion whose purpose is to celebrate that day, then listeners and analysts might suspect that the absence carries significance. The speaker, if questioned afterwards, could not convincingly claim to have forgotten about it. Any defence that 'I wanted to talk of other things' would imply that the event to be celebrated was less important than these other matters. So the metaphorical silence would be implicitly downgrading the event whose importance was being taken for granted by the ceremony itself. In this context, it should be mentioned that some PSD speakers claim that 'we' should concentrate on the present rather than talk about the past. In this way, they neither criticise the old regime nor explicitly give unqualified praise to April (for details, see Billig & Marinho, 2017, chap. 6).

Laurent Pernot (2015a, 2015b) gives examples of significant absences in classical, epideictic oratory when he analysed speeches given by Greek orators living under the rule of the Roman Empire. It was customary at public epideictic ceremonies that speakers would praise the nobility, culture and political wisdom of Rome. It would be politically dangerous for any Greek orator to criticise Rome openly; certainly they could not outwardly declare that Greek culture was superior to that of Rome. According to Pernot, Greek orators such as Aristides and Dio typically omitted to laud Rome in the customary way, or they praised unimportant, and even less laudable, aspects of Roman culture. In this way, they used 'figured' or indirect speech that involves 'saying one thing to mean another' (Pernot, 2015b, p. 132).

The absence of the standard praise of Rome in the speeches of Greek orators was not haphazard. The patterns of thematic presences and absences enabled the speakers to convey indirectly what they could not openly express: namely that Greek culture was superior to Roman culture. Pernot, as an analyst, could only demonstrate this unexpressed meaning because he knew about the background politics of the time and he was familiar with the standard formats of epideictic oratory in the Roman Empire. If he had only analysed the rhetorical composition of the individual speeches, he would have been unable to demonstrate the absences, let alone their political and rhetorical significance. Ruth Wodak makes a similar point when she argues that critical linguists must be more than linguists; they require a deep historical knowledge if they are to understand what particular texts are expressing and, most importantly, what they might be omitting (Wodak, 2011; Wodak & Meyer, 2010). This is certainly the case with analysing the celebratory texts of the Portuguese parliament.

The situation of the Greek orators in the time of the Roman Empire was an extreme one. To avoid serious punishment, they needed to either keep silent about their views on Roman culture or employ indirect methods to convey their perilous meanings. There are, nevertheless, parallels with the less extreme situation of the Portuguese parliamentary celebration. Even in this democratic ceremony, there are limits to what the participants believe that they can directly say without transgressing the norms of the occasion. The example of the absent carnations illustrates this. When both major right-wing parties avoided wearing the carnation, their speakers did not say why they had pinned no flowers to their clothing: they silently demonstrated their apartness from the ceremony.

The parliament celebrates the ending of the previous dictatorship, whose overthrow had largely, but not exclusively, been accomplished by the left, especially by left-wing junior officers within the army (Rezola, 2007, 2010). By and large, those who formed the right-wing parties after the Revolution had not been involved in the Revolution itself.

The celebration has been particularly problematic for members of the CDS/CDS-PP who may have formally supported the old regime and whose party had been founded by such supporters. To take part in the ceremony of celebration, their speakers would have to suppress any praise for the old regime that they might privately have believed it deserved. On the other hand, CDS/CDS-PP speakers might believe that they could not disappoint their supporters by celebrating without reserve or by criticising Salazarism too strongly.

Just like the Greek orators studied by Pernot, speakers from the CDS have often needed to convey their feelings implicitly rather than explicitly, using significant silences of a metaphorical nature. Right-wing speakers, especially those from the CDS/CDS-PP, are much less likely to use critical terms, such as 'dictatorship', 'fascist' or 'totalitarian' when referring to the old regime than are speakers from the left (Marinho, 2012). They can also use the sort of 'figured' rhetoric that Pernot identified in Greek orators. They can appear to comply with the norms of the occasion whilst actually remaining thematically silent or ambivalent on the characteristics of the regime whose overthrow is being overtly celebrated. In this way, they can use rhetoric to convey what they do not and cannot say directly.

Like the Greek rhetoricians who omitted praising Roman values when they might have been expected to do so, so CDS/CDS-PP orators can omit the sort of customary criticisms of the Salazarist years. To give one example: in 2001 the CDS-PP speaker paid homage to those who had been killed by the far left after 25 April. He made no mention in his speech to the far greater number of victims who had been killed during more than forty years of Salazarism. The imbalance was clear. It would be expected that in a ceremony celebrating the end of Salazarism that homage might be paid to its victims. The absence of such homage becomes significant when a speaker pays homage to political victims but only to those whose deaths followed 25 April. The speaker was following an established pattern of his party's speakers: they talk of the suffering endured by their party after 25 April, but they mitigate or downplay the wider, fiercer and more lasting suffering of opponents under Salazar and under his successor Caetano.

Another tactic employed by the Greek orators to express the inexpressible was to praise Roman culture for unimportant or irrelevant virtues. CDS/CDS-PP speakers can praise 25 April in ways that are so qualified that they can be heard as criticisms. In 1979, the CDS speaker praised 'the ideal of 25 April'. In appearing to praise 25 April, the speaker implied that he was not praising the actual 25 April. The implication became clearer when he declared that 'we still need to construct this [the ideal]

25 April', as if the actual 25 April had not been good enough. The statement elicited cries of *muito bem* ('very good') from his party's deputies.

Similarly CDS/CDS-PP speakers have criticised Salazarism for comparatively minor faults. A number of the party's speakers have claimed that the old regime needed to be replaced, but their reasons are rhetorically interesting. In 1980, the CDS speaker declared that the old regime had been unable to find 'the necessary paths of evolution' and that it 'blocked itself to itself' and was 'walking in big steps to sclerosis'. Four years later, the CDS speaker said the regime was overthrown because it was unable to respond to changes. The CDS-PP speaker of 2004 claimed that the old regime had come to situations of 'impasse' and 'blockage'. He said that 25 April was necessary 'precisely to exceed a situation of impasse'.

Over the years such comments have been a continual theme in CDS/CDS-PP speeches (see Billig & Marinho, 2017, chap. 6). Speakers appear to criticise the old regime and to praise the Revolution. However, their balance of criticism and praise is 'figured', in that it resembles the Greek orators praising Rome for unimportant qualities. Unlike the left-wing speakers, these CDS/CDS-PP speakers are not condemning the old regime for being inherently totalitarian and persecutory throughout its time in power. The criticism is reserved for the later years when supposedly the regime had been unable to evolve, had become sclerotic and had created an impasse. There is an unspoken implication – an implication that cannot be openly expressed in this context. If it had become necessary over time to overthrow the regime, to unblock the blockage, as CDS/CDS-PP speakers assert, then this necessity had not always been necessary. Before sclerosis had set in, the regime did not need overthrowing. But this is not expressible during the celebration, certainly not by a party that regularly claims to be democratic.

At most, CDS/CDS-PP speakers imply a criticism of the old regime, rather than directly stating it. Moreover, they do so when criticising the left and its contribution to the April Revolution. For example, in 2015 the CDS-PP speaker, when talking of the first elections of 1975, claimed that the country could have lapsed into 'a new authoritarianism'. The phrase implies a similarity with an old authoritarianism (and other CDS/CDS-PP speakers refer to a new 'totalitarianism' or new 'dictatorship'). However, when explicitly talking of the old, pre-1974 regime, the 2015 CDS-PP speaker did not use the critical words 'totalitarian' or 'authoritarian' or 'dictatorship', which he had used when speaking of the left. Instead, he used the term that Salazar himself had used to describe his own regime: the 'New State'. What is significant is that generally CDS-PP speakers do not explicitly call the old regime authoritarian or totalitarian, although occasionally they may seem to give the impression that they do when they are directly criticising the left for being totalitarian.

Within such partial criticisms, there is a significant absence: the absence of total political condemnation. CDS/CDS-PP speakers do not apply unqualified condemnatory terms such as 'dictatorial', 'fascist' or 'totalitarian' to the previous regime. To adapt Aristotle's distinction, they are criticising the accidental nature of the regime, rather than its essential nature – as if the regime had happened to become sclerotic and blocked, rather than that it had always been dictatorial by its very nature. This is the mirror image of the Greek orators' absence of unqualified praise for Roman culture. Just as the Greek audiences would have understood the significant absences and figured presences, so the CDS/CDS-PP members of the audience would understand and appreciate what their party speakers were doing. Typically, the CDS/CDS-PP deputies in the audience respond to the words of their party's speakers with regular cries of approval: *muito bem!* They are demonstrating support for what their party's speakers openly convey and also for the absent messages that are silently implied.

Jointly Creating Presences and Absences

Accomplishing thematic absences and figured presences is not necessarily a task for the speaker alone. What cannot be spoken directly can be enacted, rather like the not-wearing of carnations enacts what cannot be spoken. Speakers can recruit their supporters in the audience to create patterns of applause and silence that, taken together, enact themes that cannot be spoken. The speakers from the CDS/CDS-PP and to a lesser extent the PSD praise the events of 25 November 1975, when the far left was defeated after its supporters in the military took to the streets (for details, see Billig & Marinho, 2017, pp. 29f). Sometimes speakers compare the overthrowing of a left-wing dictatorship which had not actually been established with the overthrowing of Salazarism's actual forty-two year rule. What cannot be directly said, especially during the celebration of 25 April, is that 25 November is a more important and praiseworthy event than 25 April.

However, the unspoken thought can be enacted by a skilful orator leading compliantly supportive party members in the audience to applaud the phrase '25 November' but not the phrase '25 April'. In 2004, the CDS/CDS-PP speaker spoke in praise of 25 November. He began by praising the April Revolution, saying that it had a democratic and patriotic dimension. Then he added: 'Nevertheless, it had another dimension of perversion and totalitarian temptation, which only ended on 25 November.' As he talked about 25 April and its democratic dimension, he left no slot for the audience to applaud. By contrast, he ended his statement about April's totalitarian dimension with the words '25 November'. In the build-up to the phrase, the speaker was giving conventional cues of intonation and gesture that he was about to leave a slot for the audience to applaud (for details, see Billig & Marinho, 2017, pp. 138f; Marinho, 2012, pp. 159f). The parliamentary record indicates that CDS-PP and PSD deputies duly obliged with applause.

Thus, the right-wing deputies applauded after '25 November' when they had been rhetorically invited to do so. The speaker gave them no analogous opportunity to applaud the phrase '25 April'. In this way, speaker and audience combined to enact a thought that had to remain unspoken. The applause following 'November 25' on its own was not sufficient to convey that 25 November was more praiseworthy than 25 April. It was part of a wider pattern that included the absence of applause for '25 April' – a phrase which the speaker had placed in positions, such as at the beginnings of sentences, where applause was not possible. The result was not that silence literally followed '25 April', but that after the phrase the speaker's words ran on without a break or signal for applause.

In this way, the enactment of an inexpressible thought can be complex especially when accomplished by speaker and audience together. In such a case, the 'figured' rhetoric does not rest in the speaker's words alone but also in intonation and gesture and, of course, in the reactions of the audience, or rather parts of the audience, to the combination of words, intonation and gesture.

However, figured rhetoric can be involved in the unbalanced pattern that is created. CDS/CDS-PP speakers can on occasion place '25 April' at the end of an utterance that is formatted to elicit a reaction from supporters. Typically, this is not done to elicit general, unqualified support for the day, but to elicit support for the figured qualification of the day. We have already mentioned one such example. The speaker in 1979 talked of the ideal of 25 April and ended an utterance with '25 April' when he declared, to the vocal support of his party members, that we still need to 'construct this [the ideal] 25 April'. He did not place a non-figured reference to the actual 25 April at the end of any utterance that was rhetorically designed for displays of support. The result is a pattern of support that indicates but does not state that the celebrated historical day is not to be unequivocally praised.

Deliberate Awareness

The enactment of inexpressible thoughts raises the issue whether the performance has occurred with or without conscious awareness. Perhaps speakers and supporters are unaware of the biased pattern that they combine to create. Of course, analysts cannot see into the minds of the social actors, whom they are observing, to determine whether or not there is conscious awareness. Nevertheless, this does not mean that analysts cannot take a position on the question of awareness.

Our methodological stance resembles that taken by Krebs and Jackson (2007). An analyst has no privileged access to the minds of speakers when preparing their speeches or to the minds of audiences when reacting to those speeches. That does not mean that an analyst cannot comment on the likeliness of an action being consciously performed. By examining in detail the nature of the rhetorical acts that are being performed, the analyst can reveal that some acts are so rhetorically complex, involving intricate judgements and decisions, that they are highly unlikely to have been accomplished by accident (Billig & Marinho, 2014). A proficient speaker who successfully formats the intonation of their phrases and leaves a precise gap for applause is unlikely to have done this accidentally. The CDS-PP speaker who produced the intonation and gesture that led to the phrase '25 November' being placed at the end of an utterance, together with the micro-pause following the phrase, is performing such a precisely choreographed action that it could hardly have been performed by chance. The speaker might have been aware that he was inviting his supporters to applaud at that precise moment.

This, however, does not mean that, when planning his speech, that particular orator specifically said to himself 'I must make certain that I don't do the same for "25 April" because I want to deliver a speech that will enable us to display collectively what I cannot express individually.' Although the overall pattern of applause and lack of applause might not have been uppermost in his mind, his ideological habits may have led him to combine his deliberate seeking of applause with a habit of not putting the phrase '25 April' as the final words of an uplifting, carefully formatted utterance. In consequence, the resulting gestalt depends upon deliberate planning and upon ideological habits that in the particular instance are practised rather than systematically planned in detail.

Similarly the supporters in the audience may not have reacted with conscious awareness of the overall pattern of applause and unapplause that they were creating. They would have reacted immediately and spontaneously to the rhetorically formatted statement ending with '25 November'. As Heritage and Greatbach (1986) demonstrated, such

applause is too concerted and too spontaneous to be the sum of individually taken decisions. The audience members may not have noticed that
their speaker had not invited them to applaud '25 April'. On the other
hand, the pattern of this spontaneous pattern of applause and lack of
applause does not rest on unthinking reactions alone. It too is the product
of an ideological position whose elements are consciously held, together
with an awareness that there are certain elements of this ideological
position that it is unwise to express too overtly in public. And this background finds expression within the patterns of spontaneous reactions that
an audience can display.

Thus the ideological background must involve some conscious awareness especially in a speaker's rhetorical preparation and delivery. But the
precise pattern that is built up in the particular situation may not be
completely deliberate, certainly not on the part of the audience. It is likely
that there is a combination of awareness and unawareness. This analytic
judgement cannot be verified by accessing the minds of speakers and
audience members. It depends upon closely examining what speakers
and audience are doing to produce particular patterns of rhetorical presences and absences. The analyst needs to study carefully the rhetorical
details and micro-details of delivery and response and also to interpret
such details. Methodologically there can be no alternative to
interpretation.

Ideological Assumptions

By being sensitive to what is not said, the analyst can gain insights into the
general norms of a social situation. As we have already noted, rhetorical
theorists often presume that political partisanship is set aside for the
duration of national epideictic ceremonies. From the very first speech at
the first ceremony, this was clearly not the case for the ceremony in the
Portuguese assembly. Not only did the Marxist speaker deliver a speech
that was highly political, but also other deputies, who might have objected
to the speaker's specific politics, did not complain that he was being
inappropriately political; nor most significantly did the president of the
Assembly. Thus the absence of a norm against being political is confirmed
by the absence of censure when speakers are overtly political.

It is the same with general ideological assumptions. These are different
from the specific assumptions of particular ideological positions of the
sort which we have been discussing so far. General ideological assumptions refer to beliefs that people in particular times and places tend to take
for granted. These are assumptions that enable the current social world to
be experienced as if it were the natural world. Accordingly, such

assumptions are to be revealed by absences of queries or criticisms. For example, in the Portuguese ceremony, no one outwardly questions the often uttered and applauded cries of 'Viva Portugal!'

Nationalism encompasses more than attachments to a specific nation. It is an international ideology, whose assumptions are shared by particular, even mutually hostile, forms (Billig, 1995). Each particular nationalism assumes the naturalness of a world of nation-states, which itself is a product of a specific historical epoch rather than a universal fact. Within the Portuguese ceremony, even extreme left-wing speakers use nationalist language, praising the people of Portugal (Billig & Marinho, 2017). The fact that left-wing Marxists do not question the idea of nation-states shows how deep-rooted the assumptions of nationalism are.

Here is a general lesson. If we want to uncover the assumptions of our own times – the assumptions that lead us to take our world as the natural order – then we must try to notice beliefs that are generally used but not defended because they are generally left unquestioned. It is the absence, rather than the presence, of questioning that can be so significant. This, of course, is not confined to the realms of political oratory.

This leads to a further implication. Case histories, if conducted correctly, are always more than case histories, because processes from the wider world flow through the specific cases (Billig & Marinho, 2017). Accordingly the rhetorical features observed in the specific example of the Portuguese parliament's celebration of the 25 April Revolution are not confined to that particular occasion. The deputies' ways of responding, such as their ways of showing approval and disapproval, have been transferred from the customs of non-celebratory parliamentary sessions. In addition, the rhetoric of parliamentary debate cannot be totally distinct from the rhetoric of ordinary conversations – if it were, then it would be completely, not just intermittently, incomprehensible to outsiders.

This implies that the distinctions made in this chapter – such as that between metaphorical and literal silences – may have wider applications than formal oratory, let alone formal epideictic oratory. Most can also be observed in informal conversations. The notion of unapplause, used here to describe responses of Portuguese deputies, is taken from the concept of unlaughter, which in its turn comes from analyses of conversational joke telling. There can be metaphorical silences in everyday life. Conversationalists might combine to skirt around particular topics by talking about other matters, rather than leaving literal silences. By their joint talk, conversationalists can combine to create an unspoken 'elephant in the room' (Zerubavel, 2006). Also speakers in ordinary conversations can use figured language to criticise others while appearing to praise them. Thus, it is to be expected that the sort of silences discussed here will also be found in informal situations, although there may be differences of detail between formal and informal situations. Therefore, analyses of silences within formal oratory can contribute to understanding silences more generally.

References

Atkinson, J. M. (1984). *Our masters' voices*. London: Methuen.

Billig, M. (1991).*Ideology and opinions*. London: Sage.

Billig, M. (1995). *Banal nationalism*, London: Sage.

Billig, M. (1996). *Arguing and thinking*. Cambridge: Cambridge University Press.

Billig, M. (2005). *Laughter and ridicule*. London: Sage.

Billig, M., & Marinho, C. (2014). Manipulating information and manipulating people: Examples from the 2004 Portuguese parliamentary celebration of the April Revolution. *Critical Discourse Studies*, *11*(2), 158–174.

Billig, M., & Marinho, C. (2017). *The politics and rhetoric of commemoration*. London: Bloomsbury.

Bull, P. (2006). Invited and uninvited applause in political speeches. *British Journal of Social Psychology*, *46*(3), 563–578.

Condit, C. M. (1985). The functions of epideictic: The Boston Massacre orations as exemplar. *Communication Quarterly*, *33*(4), 284–299.

Heritage, J., & Greatbatch, D. (1986). Generating applause: A study of rhetoric and response at party political conferences. *American Journal of Sociology*, *92*(1), 110–157.

Ilie, C. (2010a). Strategic uses of parliamentary forms of address: The case of the U.K. Parliament and the Swedish Riksdag. *Journal of Pragmatics*, *42*(4), 885–911.

Ilie, C. (Ed.) (2010b). *European parliaments under scrutiny*. Amsterdam: John Benjamins.

Krebs, R. R., & Jackson, P. T. (2007). Twisting tongues and twisting arms: The power of political rhetoric. *European Journal of International Relations*, *13* (1), 35–66.

Marinho, C. (2012). *Celebrating the April Revolution in the Portuguese parliament: Discursive habits, constructing the past and rhetorical manipulation*, PhD dissertation, Loughborough University, Loughborough.

Marinho, C., & Billig, M. (2013). The CDS-PP and the Portuguese Parliament's annual celebration of the 1974 Revolution: Ambivalence and avoidance in the construction of the fascist past. In R. Wodak & J. E. Richardson (Eds.), *Analyzing fascist discourse* (pp. 146–162). London: Routledge.

Pernot, L. (2005). *Rhetoric in antiquity*. Washington DC: Catholic University Press.

Pernot, L. (2015a). *Epideictic rhetoric*. Austin: University of Texas Press.

Pernot, L. (2015b). Greek 'figured speech' on imperial Rome. *Advances in the History of Rhetoric*, *18*(2), 131–146.

Perelman, C., & Olbrechts-Tyteca, L. (1969). *The new rhetoric*. London: University of Notre Dame Press.

Rezola, M. I. (2007). *25 de Abril*. Lisbon: A Esfera dos Livros.

Rezola, M.I. (2010). The Portuguese transition to democracy. In R. Herr & A. C. Pinto (Eds.), *The Portuguese Republic at one hundred* (pp. 83–99). Berkeley: University of California Press.

Sheard, C. M. (1995). The public value of epideictic rhetoric. *College English, 58* (7), 765–794.

Vivian, B. (2006). Neoliberal epideictic: Rhetorical form and commemorative politics on September 11, 2002. *Quarterly Journal of Speech, 92*(1), 1–26.

Wodak, R. (2011). Suppression of the Nazi past, coded languages and discourses of silences: Applying the discourse-historical approach to postwar anti-Semitism in Austria. In W. Steinmetz (Ed.), *Political languages in the age of extremes* (pp. 351–379). Oxford: Oxford University Press.

Wodak, R., & de Cillia, R. (2007). Commemorating the past: The discursive construction of official narratives about the 'Rebirth of the Second Austrian Republic'. *Discourse & Communication, 1*(3), 337–363.

Wodak, R., & Meyer, M. (2010). Critical discourse analysis: History, agenda, theory and methodology. In R. Wodak & M. Meyers (Eds.), *Methods of critical discourse analysis* (pp. 1–33). London: Sage.

Zerubavel, E. (2006). *The elephant in the room: Silence and denial in everyday life*. Oxford: Oxford University Press.

2   Seeing Silenced Agendas in Medical Interaction: A Conversation Analytic Case Study

Merran Toerien and Clare Jackson

Although it is possible for speakers to disagree with each other in injurious ways, a significant body of evidence indicates that 'there is a "bias" intrinsic to the organization of talk which is generally favourable to the maintenance of bonds of solidarity between actors and which promotes the avoidance of conflict' (Heritage, 1984, p. 265). When disagreement occurs, then, conflict may routinely be kept 'beneath the surface' of interaction, present but unsaid. Accordingly, speakers may 'silence' themselves to keep the conflict implicit but may also have quite subtle interactional strategies for 'silencing' others, nevertheless, to pursue their own agendas.

Critical scholars have long pointed to the tendency for conflict to be present in the specialised domain of medical consultations. For instance, Mishler (1984) described 'lifeworld' vs 'biomedical' concerns to capture routine discrepancies in how patients and doctors approach the clinical encounter in Western medicine. Although such conflicts may become 'spectacular' (e.g. leading to legal action), in our data set of recorded consultations, they almost always remain subtle. These interactions thus offer a useful site for exploring how we might uncover the 'unsaid' in an analytically defensible way.

In this chapter, we present a single-case analysis (Schegloff, 1987), taken from ongoing work on UK neurology outpatient consultations (Reuber et al., 2015, 2018), to demonstrate how conversation analysis (CA) might address the aims of this edited collection. Specifically, we propose that three key analytical tools from CA – sequence organisation, preference organisation and turn-design – can provide a way in to identifying, and making sense of, the unsaid. We start by summarising what is meant by each of the three tools. We then introduce our case study. The main body of the chapter presents our analysis, focusing on how the three tools may be used to reveal (1) what is *relevantly* absent in a sequence of talk, (2) the unsaid in what *is* articulated and (3) the (often subtle) silencing of another through particular interactional 'moves'.

Three Powerful Tools for Exploring the Unsaid in Interaction

Recognising that talk (and accompanying non-vocal elements) is fundamentally used to *do* things – greet, invite, apologise, complain and so on – CA is a method for studying how social action is accomplished through talk-in-interaction (Schegloff, 1996). CA has shown that interaction is 'highly organised and orderly and, indeed, that specificities of meaning and understanding in interaction would be impossible without this orderliness' (Drew & Heritage, 1992, p. 2). Accordingly, CA has cumulatively developed analytical resources derived from extensive empirical work. We introduce three of these, with a focus on how they provide ways to ground our claims that something specific is being done – and *not* done – in a given interaction.

Sequence Organisation

CA demonstrates the power of some turn types to place pressure on a recipient to respond in a particular way (Stivers & Rossano, 2010). For instance, remaining silent in the face of another's question is extraordinarily difficult. Such actions can be described as *initiating* turns or 'First Pair Parts' (FPPs), because they set in motion a course of action that needs (at least) one type-related *responsive* turn or 'Second Pair Part' (SPP) to complete the sequence. Schegloff and Sacks (1973) identified such two-turn units – termed 'adjacency pairs' – as the most basic form of sequential organisation in talk. In so doing, they highlighted the powerful fact that (meaningful) turns at talk do not occur randomly or merely serially but are structured by reference to one another, 'in some before and after relationship' (Sacks, 1987, p. 54). The adjacency pair is the simplest form of before and after relationship, consisting only of two turns that are adjacently produced by two speakers, and relatively ordered, such that there is an initiating and responsive turn, which are 'pair-type' related. This basic pairing may be expanded through further, related talk (Schegloff, 2007), but for our purposes, the analytic machinery afforded by the notion of an adjacency pair is sufficient.

Such technical terminology may seem like a complex way of stating that greetings get returned, questions get answered and so forth. However, by meticulously spelling out this conversational organisation, Schegloff and Sacks (1973) showed that specific turns at talk (FPPs) can place *a normative constraint* on the next speaker to produce a *particular kind* of next turn. That is, FPPs set up the *conditional relevance* for what should come next. Thus, the absence of a relevant next turn becomes noticeable and morally accountable. Speakers of initiating turns will typically pursue a response if it is not forthcoming (Davidson, 1984), thereby maintaining the interactional force of their FPP, and recipients of initiating turns will typically make some move other than simple non-response when attempting to evade the constraints imposed by the FPP.

Furthermore, in what Sacks, Schegloff and Jefferson (1974, p. 729) term the 'next turn proof procedure', the production of a particular SPP demonstrates the kind of action a recipient of a FPP figures is underway. A question, for instance, makes an answer conditionally relevant next, and the production of an answer shows that the recipient of the FPP has understood that the first speaker initiated a question-answer sequence. Thus, the basic organisation of two-turn sequences is central to achieving intersubjectivity in interaction (Heritage, 1984).

Clearly, sequence organisation captures something that matters for us as participants in interaction. It also gives us, as analysts, a powerful tool: by looking back in the talk to identify what was made relevant next, and ahead in the talk to see how participants handled whatever was just said, we can show (among many other things) that a particular something was *relevantly* present or absent for the participants themselves.

Preference Organisation

The organisation of adjacency pairs does not imply that speakers have few options in selecting responses to FPPs. Even within the constraints of conditional relevance, FPPs set up a range of possibly relevant SPPs (Pomerantz, 1984). An invitation might, for instance, be relevantly followed by an acceptance, a declination, or some form of hedge. Hence, the production of any particular, relevant SPP is always a selection from alternatives. However, these alternatives are not equivalent; some responses are 'preferred' over others (ibid.). *Preference* does not refer to 'personal, subjective, or "psychological" desires' (ibid., p. 53) but instead to a distinction between preferred SPPs that forward the action of the FPP (e.g. accepting an invitation) and dispreferred SPPs that block it (e.g. declining an invitation) – regardless of what the individual speaker personally wants (Heritage, 1984).

Preferred and dispreferred responses are typically shaped differently (Pomerantz, 1984). Preferred responses tend to be straightforward, produced without delay and are regularly the default expected response. In contrast, dispreferred responses tend towards complexity, involving, for example, delay, softening, apology and explanation. It is in these delays and elaborations that we see what Heritage (1984, p. 265) was referring to in the quote at the start of this chapter: that interaction is biased in favour of maintaining social solidarity. That is, in producing a dispreferred SPP, speakers design their turn so as to ameliorate possible disaffiliation; they tend to 'just say yes' but not to 'just say no', thereby working to avoid (overt) conflict (Kitzinger, 2000). Moreover, because dispreferred turns are routinely delayed, speakers of FPPs may hear even short silences after their turns as heralding some kind of socially delicate next action and may opt to amend their own FPP before the dispreferred SPP is even produced (Pomerantz, 1984). Preference, then – together with the notion of conditional relevance – points to the interactional import of literal silences.

Furthermore, the operation of preference allows for consideration of the selection and design of the SPP relative to the FPP and warrants comparison of what was produced in second position with the relevant alternatives that were not. Thus, when a conditionally relevant next action is produced, we can ask: given the design of the FPP, what was not said that could, relevantly, have been said in the responsive turn? Together with sequence organisation, then, preference organisation gives us a resource for grounding claims that something, specific, was left, *relevantly*, unsaid.

Turn-Design

Analysis of the relationship between turns is inextricably intertwined with the analysis of the design of the individual turns. Turn-design refers to the components of a turn-at-talk – words selected, intonation, timing, grammatical format, what sort of slot (if any; Stivers & Rossano, 2010) the turn sets up for the next speaker (e.g. yes/no vs narrative), use of non-vocal features (e.g. eye gaze), breathiness or laughter and so forth. Analysis of turn-design involves examining the way a turn is constructed to accomplish a particular action (Drew, 2012).

The term 'design' does not imply that speakers select every component in a reflexive fashion before speaking. However, there is extensive evidence to show both that speakers do not use different formats for doing the same action randomly or interchangeably (Curl, 2006; Curl & Drew, 2008) and also that alternative turn-designs can lead recurrently to different types of responses (Heritage et al., 2007). Analysis of individual turns is thus always comparative: the analyst considers the alternative ways that a turn might have been designed as a means of understanding what this particular turn-design is doing interactionally. This comparison is grounded in at least two ways. First, by coupling the analysis of turn-design with a sequential analysis, the analyst makes use of what came immediately before and what occurred immediately afterwards as resources for seeing what the participants made of the turn under study (i.e. next turn proof procedure; Sacks, Schegloff & Jefferson, 1974). Second, by drawing on the cumulative, empirically generated understanding of how particular actions are typically done, the analyst can make comparisons between the turn under study and larger relevant collections (Schegloff, 1987, 1996, 1997). In these ways, the analyst is reined in from purely imagining the alternative things that *might* have been said.

Introducing Our Case Study

Our study of UK neurology outpatient consultations was funded by the UK's National Institute for Health Research (see Reuber et al., 2015, 2018) and included 223 recorded consultations plus self-report data collected from participants before and after consultations. Participants opted-in to the study following an informed consent discussion with a research assistant and could choose whether to be audio- or videorecorded. The consultation we discuss here was videorecorded.

In our focal case, an adult patient – accompanied by her mother – attends the clinic because she experiences as-yet undiagnosed seizures, which may (or may not) be epileptic in origin. It becomes apparent early in the consultation that she has already undergone diagnostic testing, on the basis of which the neurologist was unable, as Mum puts it, to 'pick up' anything. The gold standard for differential diagnosis of seizures is to capture the patient's 'events' on video, whilst recording their electrical brain activity using an electroencephalogram (EEG). The aim is to distinguish between epileptic seizures and events that are not epileptic in origin. The key distinction between epileptic and non-epileptic seizures (NES) is that the former are caused by abnormal electrical activity in the brain (capturable by EEG) and the latter – understood to be psychological in origin – are not. This matters for treatment, since epilepsy can often be well controlled with anti-epileptic drugs, whereas NES requires specialised psychotherapy (Dickson et al., 2017).

The distinction between epileptic and non-epileptic seizures has been shown to be troubling for patients in that they (1) are often resistant to the idea that they have psychological 'problems', (2) may hear the diagnosis as implying that they are malingering and (3) may resist psychotherapy (Monzoni & Reuber, 2015; Robson & Lian, 2016). Reciprocally, neurologists reportedly find it difficult to deliver a diagnosis of NES, struggle to explain their cause (Monzoni & Reuber, 2015; Robson & Lian, 2016) and construct the treatment recommendation as a delicate matter even when there is no resistance from the patient (Monzoni et al., 2011).

Neurologists in our study commented that they often face extensive resistance to a diagnosis of NES and consider it important to get the patient's buy-in to the diagnosis as a prerequisite for successful treatment. Thus, the underlying agendas for the neurologist and patient may be at odds, with the patient pursuing a diagnosis of, and treatment for, epilepsy, while the neurologist pursues acceptance of a psychological diagnosis and treatment programme (Monzoni & Reuber, 2015).

In our focal case, we will show how these divergent agendas play out between a patient's mum and neurologist. The consultation lasts for more than thirteen minutes, making it impossible to analyse in full here. We thus focus on three key extracts, which occur during the opening of the consultation and the verbal examination. Our aim is to demonstrate how three of CA's principal tools can be utilised to identify and explicate the unsaid in a variety of ways.

Analysis Part I: Setting up Conflicting Agendas in the Consultation's Opening

The recording opens with the neurologist, patient and patient's mum establishing that they've met before at a specialist centre for diagnosing seizures (data not shown). We join them less than a minute into the consultation, with Mum summarising the neurologist's report regarding a previous inpatient investigation (Extract 1, lines 2–3).

Extract 1: G00604[1]

```
01 Neu:   Oh here's the report of course. Yes, I remember now.
02 Mum:   Yeah. You said there was nothing (0.2) th↑a:t
03        [you picked u(h)p,
04 Neu:   [(Mm:)
05        (0.5) ((Neu turning pages of patient's notes))
06 Neu:   So:: here we go: (neh neh neh) ((as if talking to self))

((approximately 46 seconds elapses, while neurologist reads
   patient's notes))

07 Neu:   So how's things [with you at the moment?
08 Mum:                    [((gearing up to speak – mouth opens
          across the silence at line 9. Neurologist still audibly
             turning
          pages in the notes))]
09        (0.8)
10 Mum:   .hhh They'r- (0.4) getting mo::re like epileptic
11        seizures.
```

```
12           [.hh      [I've go::t
13 Neu:      [In what  [sense do you (mean.)
14 Mum:      .HHHH I've got it on::: (0.9) >someone suggested put
15           it< on camco:rder,=
16 Neu:      =Oh let's have a look
```

Medically, the failure to pick up abnormal electrical activity in the brain does not rule out epilepsy, but it leaves open the possibility that the patient's seizures are psychogenic in origin. Thus, Mum's characterisation of what's known thus far justifies the visit – there's diagnostic uncertainty – and orients to the possibility that the patient may not have epilepsy. In its design, however, Mum's turn subtly indicates that she does not (at this point) endorse this possibility. She describes the lack of evidence from the previous investigation as something simply 'said' by the neurologist and implies failure on the part of the institution to capture abnormal electrical activity. Consequently, she minimises the status of the test results, constructing them as non-definitive. This can be best appreciated by contrasting '**you said** there was nothing that **you picked up**' with a more factual version, such as 'the tests were negative'. Hence, even as she, ostensibly, merely summarises the neurologist's report, she subtly conveys scepticism towards the results.

Sequentially, the neurologist has several options in responding to Mum. Given that she has summarised something the neurologist has primary rights to know (i.e. what he said about the results of a medical test; see Heritage, 2012), confirmation (preferred) or disconfirmation (dispreferred) of this report is relevant next. Alternatively, he could treat this as a topic-proffer (Button & Casey, 1984) by expanding on his report. In so doing, one relevant option would be to articulate what the non-finding means for the likely diagnosis. At most, however, he produces only a minimal acknowledgement (see possible hearing on line 4) and then focuses on the patient's notes. In this way, he demonstrably engages with (by reading) the matter of what he said in his report. Thus, the audible silence at line 5 is not an outright lack of response to the substance of Mum's turn, despite the absence of talk. Nevertheless, given the types of responses that could have relevantly come next, the neurologist's focus on the notes and subsequent shift to asking a standard opening question (line 7) amount to an evasion. Precisely what he might be evading is not yet clear. We know it's common for doctors to avoid dealing with a patient or accompanying other's initiatives early in the consultation, particularly when this might entail handling diagnostic questions pre-emptively before further history taking or examination (Gill & Maynard, 2006).

So it would be going too far to claim that we see, in the evasion, some move to silence Mum's scepticism. However, we can (defensibly) say that his silence entails not performing some very particular actions that could relevantly have come next – all of which would have risked engaging with the question of his current opinion regarding the implications of the test results.

Mum further pursues her sceptical position vis-à-vis a non-epilepsy diagnosis in how she responds to the neurologist's opening question (line 7). This turn – 'so how's things with you at the moment' – seeks an update from the patient on her condition (Heritage & Robinson, 2006; Robinson, 2006). Yet, not only does Mum reply (in probable place of her daughter; Stivers, 2001), but her response also provides a candidate diagnosis for the patient's seizures rather than just an account of her current symptoms (Stivers, 2002). This is cast in terms of a change since the patient was last seen: 'They'r- getting more like epileptic seizures' (line 10–11). Hence, Mum simultaneously fits her response to the terms of the neurologist's question (she is offering an update), while also advancing her view that her daughter has epilepsy.

Although making a bid for a biomedical diagnosis, Mum's turn is worded cautiously ('getting more like' is downgraded relative to something like 'they're epileptic seizures'). Consequently, she avoids an explicitly argumentative move. Sequentially, her candidate diagnosis is also positioned *responsively*; ostensibly, she is just answering the neurologist's opening question. Her turn does not place as much pressure on the neurologist for a confirming/disconfirming response as an interrogatively formatted turn would have done in first position (e.g. 'Do you think these are epileptic seizures?'; see Gill & Maynard, 2006). Moreover, while the design of her response implicitly contrasts the current seizures with those the neurologist might have observed at the centre – thereby casting doubt on the previous non-finding – this is done at one remove. Had she positioned the candidate diagnosis differently – e.g. by saying at lines 2–3, 'you said there was nothing that you picked up but since then they've been getting more like epileptic seizures' – she would have overtly foregrounded the way in which her recent observations seem to be at odds with the neurologist's previous report.

Reciprocally, the neurologist evades either endorsing or contradicting Mum's candidate diagnosis by, instead, asking a follow-up question, seeking Mum's explanation for her claim: 'In what sense do you (mean)' (line 13). This treats the prior observation as simply launching what routinely comes next in a medical consultation: history taking and verbal examination building on the prior problem presentation

(Robinson, 2003). So, while the neurologist's question treats Mum's turn as requiring probing – thus balancing scepticism with openness to hearing more – it avoids engaging in explicit debate about the candidate diagnosis itself. Likewise, Mum evades producing a response – in so many words – to this follow-up question. Although the production of a video of her daughter's seizures could well serve as an answer (potentially demonstrating a seizure that was 'more like' epilepsy), it is notable that Mum appears to be restarting a turn at line 14 that was already begun at line 12 (see repetition of 'I've got'). Thus, in proffering the video evidence, she simultaneously holds onto her own turn, even as she may thereby offer a kind of response to the neurologist. This enables her to avoid having to subjectively justify her claim that the patient's seizures are 'getting more like epileptic' ones, while creating a slot to provide objective evidence that might do that work most effectively.

Thus, across this short bit of talk, a sequential analysis reveals a range of moments in which the neurologist and Mum could relevantly have said things they did not. Occasionally this results in actual silence (e.g. line 5). However, for the most part, we see the production of turns that – when analysed with respect to their design and their sequential position – are avoiding engaging with elements of the prior talk and/or demonstrably avoiding making certain claims more explicitly. Taken together, sequence organisation, preference organisation and turn-design allow a way in to seeing the work that is going on below the surface of this interaction. Virtually from the start of the consultation, a kind of battle is set in motion: the mother subtly conveys her view that the patient likely has epilepsy, a position that the neurologist is demonstrably not (yet) willing to endorse. However, neither of them articulates what the alternative(s) might be, and there is no directly oppositional talk. It is only by considering the interactional moves each participant makes that we start to get a handle on what is unsaid but nevertheless palpably in the room.

Analysis Part II: Maintaining Conflicting Agendas across the Verbal Examination

Having established that there's footage of the seizures, the focus shifts, for more than six minutes, to trying unsuccessfully to play this video, and they're left no nearer to a diagnosis. Over the course of the next extract, the patient largely absents herself by concentrating on the phone. We know from later in the interaction, when she is more wholly participating, that the patient shares her mother's agenda to seek a definitive diagnosis of epilepsy and treats further testing as unnecessary. For now, though, we see Mum handling the neurologist's questions, in a fashion akin to Stivers's (2001) observations of paediatric consultations, where parents might speak on behalf of their children, although here, of course, the patient is an adult.

We rejoin the consultation as the neurologist reinitiates diagnostic questioning (FPP, line 1). His indexical reference – 'that sort of thing' – refers back to the event apparently captured by the video, while avoiding naming or characterising it. Given previous findings that neurologists tend to avoid explicit labels when delivering a diagnosis of NES, but not when diagnosing epilepsy (Reuber & Monzoni, 2015; Robson & Lian, 2016), this vague reference again hints at a possible scepticism towards the latter diagnosis. Moreover, his turn-design avoids even the general term – seizures – which is commonly used when both doctors and patients talk about epilepsy rather than NES (Plug, Sharrack & Reuber, 2009).

Extract 2: G00604 {08:12}

```
01 Neu:   So >anyway< that sort of thing, how: often does that
02        happen?
03 Mum:   It can happen any ti:me. [Uhm   ]
04 Neu:                            [How of]ten though.
05        (1.3) ((Mum opens mouth to speak but gestures
          indicate she can't find the words))
06 Mum:   Uh:::m (0.7)
07 Neu:   Every day, every week?
08 Mum:   It can happen (0.8) three times in one day. .hh ().
09        Her face comes up like this ((uses hand to scrunch
          the side of her face))
10 Neu:   Mm:mm:
11 Mum:   Like Hunchback of Notre [Da::me.
12 Neu:                           [Yeah.
13 Mum:   .hh (0.5) Her ha[nd   ] ((curls hand to face)) is:- I can=
14 Neu:                   [Yeah]
15 Mum:   =only- (1.9) ((she scrunches one side of her face))
16        go like that.
17 Neu:   Mm hm,
18 Mum:   And (). She has- she's taken tumble- .h two
19        tumbles down my stairs,
20 Neu:   Mm hm,
21 Mum:   But she's only come off with brui::ses.
22        (0.4)
23 Mum:   .hh But it's more like a grand mal seizure she takes.
24 Neu:   Mm hm,
25 Mum:   Takes the little ones, .hh which I can get her out of.
26 Neu:   Yeah.
27 Mum:   And then when she takes the big ones::,
28 Neu:   Mm hm.
```

```
29 Mum:   She doesn't remember any of it.
30        (3.0)
31 Neu:   Ri::ght,
32        (11.0) ((Neurologist reads notes, patient
          continues to focus on getting the video to work))
```

The neurologist treats Mum's initial response to his query (SPP; 'It can happen anytime', line 3) as ill-fitted to his FPP, as seen in his pursuits of the kind of answer he was seeking (lines 4 and 7): some measure of frequency. Mum first offers a less specific kind of answer, which may be a way of accounting for her difficulty in producing one (see the hesitation markers on lines 3 and 6). More speculatively, it may be that by opting to respond in terms of when the symptoms can occur rather than how often, she is tacitly providing grounds for a diagnosis of epilepsy by implying that the seizures are not 'fake' (i.e. that they don't only happen when somehow 'useful' to the patient). Mum does address the question of frequency at line 8 but even then emphasises a worst case ('it can happen three times in one day') rather than an indication of general frequency. Moreover, she then moves beyond the terms of the question – 'breaking the sequential mold' (Stivers & Heritage, 2001, p. 151) – to provide an extensive observational account of what happens when the patient has seizures, thereby providing unsolicited evidence for epilepsy. Her evidence takes several forms: (1) she dramatically embodies a portrayal of the seizures (lines 9–16), invoking brain-related events in the manner of a stroke; (2) she describes things that happen to the patient that are observably beyond her control (i.e. not 'put on') and that might result in injury (lines 18–21) and loss of consciousness (line 29); (3) she uses the medical term 'grand mal seizure' to explicitly index epilepsy (line 23); and (4) she makes a distinction between big and small seizures, thereby potentially warranting the previous non-finding – that her daughter had small seizures only at that time (lines 23–29). In the round, Mum's response pushes back against the implied scepticism in the neurologist's question and subtly advances her agenda of establishing that her daughter has epilepsy.

Faced with this unsolicited information, the neurologist does nothing more than acknowledge its content (lines 10, 12, 14, 17, 20, 24, 26, 28, 31). Whilst he shows himself to be attentive (Gardner, 1997) to this complex mix of life world and biomedical evidence, he does not opt to express an opinion or seek further information. Yet these are relevant options at several points in Mum's extended telling. Notably, line 23 ('But it's more like a grand mal seizure') is a parallel to Mum's response to the neurologist's opening question – 'They're getting more like epileptic seizures' (line 10–11 Extract 1) – again offering a candidate diagnosis, this time with a more specialised term, implicitly indicating her own expertise in the matter (although still with some caution). Mum can thus be said to be pursuing her candidate diagnosis here. Relevant responses to candidate diagnoses include endorsing (preferred) or rejecting (dispreferred) these (Gill & Maynard, 2006) and, as we saw in response to the previous version, another way to indicate engagement without expressing an opinion is to ask a follow-up question. Here, the neurologist simply issues a continuer (line 24), treating Mum's turn as still in progress and thus passing up the opportunity to take a full turn. He thereby evades the normative constraints imposed by Mum's turn.

Throughout this extended telling, Mum's gaze is towards the neurologist, but as she completes her turn on line 29, her gaze shifts sideways towards her daughter (who is still focused on the phone). During the silence at line 30, she also drops her left hand – with which she has been gesturing – back to her lap. She thus indicates that her extended turn is fully done. Yet the neurologist still produces nothing but a minimal acknowledgement (line 31). In maintaining near silence, he treats Mum's turns merely as part of the information gathering that is warranted in the early phase of medical consultations (Robinson 2003). Again, then, we see Mum proposing a diagnosis of epilepsy, and the neurologist avoiding endorsing this – but without any overt disagreement rising to the surface of the interaction.

The previous sequence ends with a fairly extended period of silence, whilst the neurologist is engaged with the medical notes (Extract 2, line 32). Following a short interaction relating to the non-functioning video (lines 33–37), Mum launches a description of another set of observed symptoms (lines 39–41).

Extract 3: G00604 (continues from Extract 2)

```
33 Pat:    It's not ()° ((said to herself))
34         (2.4)
35 Mum:    See (female name) transferred [it on-] from her phone
36         onto mi:ne.
37 Neu:                                  [Mmhm]
38         (7.0)
39 Mum:    And she still kinda- (2.7) she makes a funny noise.
40         And she'll
41         go into like what I term as .hh the snory sleep.
42 Neu:    Mm hm.
43 Mum:    But my daugh- >other daughter< has already looked it
44         up on the comp[uter,] .hh (.) and she picked it up as:
45         cryptogenic.
```

```
46 Neu:          [Mm hm]
47 Neu:          Are you- have you- are you on any medication
48               [at the moment for these   ]
49 Pat:          [((pat looks up at neu and then shakes head))]
50 Neu:          No I didn't [think so.] (alright)
51 Mum:                      [No:.      ]
52               (0.4)
53 Neu:          Okay
54 Mum:          .hh (.) 'Cause we don't know:- () 'cause cryptogenic
55               uh:::m (1.5) ((during this silence, mum gestures
                 that she can't find the word))
56 Neu:          Well let's not [worry about that] at the moment.
57 Mum:                         [Ri::ght.        ]
```

Although now at some distance from her original descriptions, following a lapse in the sequential trajectory, Mum uses an 'and'-prefaced formulation to build her new turn as continuing and expanding her previous utterances (line 39; Jefferson, 1972; Local 2004). Jefferson (1972) distinguishes between *continuing* a sequence and *resuming* a sequence following some form of break, arguing that a resumption makes overt a return to the previous sequence, whereas a continuation glosses over whatever break there's been. Using the 'and'-preface Mum simply continues with her description of the seizures without overtly acknowledging the intervening lapse; she silences the silence. Consequently, she once again provides a slot where the neurologist might engage with the diagnostic import of her observations. However, the neurologist treats her turn again as merely informational by acknowledging but not elaborating on its content (line 42). Faced with his continued minimal responses, Mum produces the most explicit statement of her candidate diagnosis: that her daughter likely has 'cryptogenic' epilepsy (line 43–45) – epilepsy without a known cause.

Hitherto, Mum has presented her diagnostic reasoning – based on her own experience as a witness to her daughter's seizures – rather cautiously, so that even when she uses medical terminology, she does not assert that the seizures are epileptic but rather are 'more like' epilepsy. This contrasts with what she is doing at lines 43–45. Here she uses the term 'cryptogenic' to offer a candidate diagnosis based on her other daughter's Internet search. Hence, she provides a possible basis for the previous non-findings, whilst maintaining that the patient's symptoms are consistent with epilepsy, as defined by an 'objective' third party (a website with no stake in her daughter's diagnosis).

When Mum mentions the Internet search, the neurologist merely acknowledges it – notice the overlap on lines 44–46. However, importantly, he makes no response to the term 'cryptogenic'. Instead, he disattends it (Mandelbaum, 1991), moving on to produce a new question about medication (line 47–48). Sequentially, he manages the accountability of this non-response to the candidate diagnosis by doing ongoing history taking. The new question is notably directed to the patient, thereby also subtly evading the line of reasoning initiated by Mum's extensive response to his previous, constrained question about frequency of symptoms.

The neurologist's question about medication initiates a new sequence and occasions the first relevant but non-verbal response from the patient; she looks up from the phone and shakes her head. This response is confirmed by Mum (line 51) and acknowledged by the neurologist (line 50 and 53); hence, the sequence is possibly complete. Mum opts to keep open the sequence by using a 'because'-prefaced formulation (line 54), which might have been headed for an account of why the patient is not on medication. We can't hear quite what she says next, but she goes on to repair her turn, restarting with 'because' and repeating her earlier use of 'cryptogenic' to refer to her daughter's seizures. Although she doesn't manage to complete this turn (see line 55), she thus re-invokes the previously ignored candidate diagnosis, showing that she has noted the lack of uptake (despite no actual silence) and treats it as relevantly absent by pursuing a response. Here, for the first time, the neurologist uses an explicit silencing technique: 'Well let's not worry about that at the moment' (line 56). While leaving open the possibility of returning to it later, he thus overtly refuses to pursue this line of reasoning at present.

We don't have space to follow the conflict through to its conclusion, but Mum and neurologist subsequently employ similar interactional moves. Each silence (or disattend) the other's agenda by maintaining a different 'line': Mum pursues her candidate diagnosis while the neurologist keeps returning to the business of history taking/verbal examination.

Discussion

In this final section, we return to the key questions of this edited collection – (1) What is the unsaid? (2) What is the unsaid doing (here)? – to highlight the implications of our analysis for how CA may be used to answer them.

What Is the Unsaid?

Across our analysis, we've argued that what is going unsaid can be identified in actual silences and in the detail of what is said. Specifically, we have sought to demonstrate how CA can reveal the following:

(1) What is *relevantly* absent in a sequence of talk. This relies on an understanding of sequence organisation, with its core notion of conditional relevance, which allows us to ground claims that a particular type of social action is relevantly missing.

(2) The unsaid in what *is* articulated. This relies on all three of the core tools we introduced at the start of this chapter. By considering how a given turn is designed and how it relates to the turn before and the turn that follows, we can get a handle on what was relevantly not said even if no silence occurs. This entails comparative analysis, considering the range of possible actions (and how each might be designed) that were made relevant by a particular FPP. In this sense, speakers may be said to silence themselves, opting not to say things that could, relevantly, have been said.

(3) The silencing of another through particular interactional 'moves'. We have shown one instance of a participant explicitly seeking to silence the other. However, neurologist and Mum far more regularly pursue their conflicting agendas subtly. Across our analysis, we identified several interactional moves for doing so: (a) responding to a candidate diagnosis (which makes relevant a confirmation/disconfirmation) with a question or (b) a continuer; (c) avoiding answering a question in the terms set by the question's design; (d) building further talk as if it were just a continuation of what had already, ostensibly, been brought to a close; and (e) treating such talk as doing nothing more than 'information provision', thereby evading the constraints that would arise if it was treated as doing some other social action (such as pursuing an underlying disagreement). Through such moves both parties seek to silence (or disattend) the other's agenda by subtly maintaining a different interactional trajectory.

What Is the Unsaid Doing (Here)?

Monzoni and Reuber (2015) argue that delivering a diagnosis of NES is interactionally delicate, regularly met by patient resistance and routinely handled indirectly by neurologists whether or not they encounter resistance. Our analysis extends these findings by showing that even before a diagnosis is made, the parties orient to this delicacy. This is starkly evident in the complete absence of reference, across our consultation, to what the alternative to epilepsy might be. Yet the neurologist listed NES, in his post-consultation questionnaire, as the other possibility under consideration. Thus, the physical health diagnosis is named within the interaction, but not the mental health diagnosis. It is fascinating to note that epilepsy was once considered a highly stigmatising condition (Schneider & Conrad, 1980). Yet here we see NES being constructed as the stigmatised alternative – too face-threatening to name (Goffman 1955). And we see the efforts Mum goes to in order to pursue the 'least bad' diagnostic outcome (rather epilepsy with no known cause than NES).

Our analysis thus suggests that the unsaid in our focal case is accomplishing two things: (1) enabling the participants to pursue their conflicting agendas without the conflict rising to the surface of the interaction and (2) keeping the possibility of a psychiatric diagnosis off the record (it's the proverbial elephant in the room). These things are closely intertwined, since the conflict entails Mum's pursuit of a neurological diagnosis and the neurologist's maintenance of an apparently more neutral stance, which treats the diagnostic process as incomplete. Keeping this conflict below the surface has interactional benefits, maintaining the 'bonds of social solidarity' (Heritage, 1984, p. 265) between neurologist and Mum (and, by extension, neurologist and patient) and allowing them to occupy conflicting positions without overtly threatening each other's 'face' or formally challenging the norms of the doctor-patient relationship.

Furthermore, Monzoni and Reuber (2015) argue that use of 'avoidant practices' when diagnosing NES serves the institutional goals of the neurology clinic. We agree. By keeping the conflict covert, Mum and neurologist are able to pursue (from their own perspectives) what amounts to a compatible goal: diagnosing the patient's condition as a precursor to appropriate treatment. To this end, Mum succeeds in voicing her candidate diagnosis and, crucially, her supporting evidence, which could be consequential for the neurologist's diagnostic reasoning (Gill & Maynard, 2006). At the same time, the neurologist keeps the interaction focused on the standard diagnostic procedure (with history taking and examination, including any recommended tests, typically preceding talk about the diagnosis; Robinson, 2003), thereby facilitating evidence gathering of his own. All this would be disrupted if the interaction became overtly about the conflict. What remains unknown, as Monzoni and Reuber (2015) acknowledge, is whether neurologists' avoidant practices serve the longer-term goal of gaining NES patients' acceptance of a psychiatric diagnosis and psychotherapeutic treatment – or whether they have the paradoxical consequence of enhancing patients' resistance by subtly pointing to the stigmatised nature of NES.

Conclusion

Although not often framed as a study of the unsaid per se (for exceptions, see Bolden, 2010; Chevalier & Moore, 2015; Schegloff, 1996), CA has much to offer, empirically and methodologically, to our understanding of the unsaid in interaction. It provides an inductive, disciplined approach, which demands that we ground claims in evidence from the interactions themselves. This is crucial, as it is easy – with respect to absences in particular – to claim that someone failed to say a huge range of things that they *might* have said. But this is unavoidably true, given that speakers are always choosing to say one thing rather than many others, and to say it in some particular way. The analytic tools of CA give us a defensible basis for justifying our claims (as analysts) that something was *relevantly* missing or said in one way when it could, relevantly, have been said in another (Schegloff, 1988). Importantly, this does not restrict us to focusing only on things participants explicitly do. CA demands that we point to the evidence, but it furnishes us with the tools to identify subtle interactional moves – to 'see' the things that interactants do below the surface of the interaction and to ground our claims that there is, indeed, sometimes an elephant lurking, unremarked upon, but making its presence very much felt.

Acknowledgements

This chapter arises out of a wider project funded by the UK's National Institute for Health Research (NIHR), Health Services and Delivery Research (HS&DR) programme. Project numbers 10/2000/61 (published; further details available at www.journalslibrary.nihr.ac.uk/hsdr/h sdr03070#/abstract.) and 14/19/43 (published; further details available at www.journalslibrary.nihr.ac.uk/programmes/hsdr/141943/#/).

The views and opinions expressed in this chapter are the authors' and do not necessarily reflect those of the NHS, NIHR, MRC, CCF, NETSCC, Health Services and Delivery Research programme or Department of Health.

We acknowledge the invaluable contributions of the full project team: Markus Reuber, Rod Duncan and Rebecca Shaw (project co-applicants) and Zoe Gallant and Fiona Smith, the research assistants responsible for recruitment and data collection. Special thanks to the patients and neurologists who made this study possible. Finally, we are very grateful to the editors and two anonymous reviewers for their thoughtful and constructive comments on a previous version of our chapter.

References

Bolden, G. B. (2010). 'Articulating the unsaid' via and-prefaced formulations of others' talk. *Discourse Studies*, *12*(1), 5–32.

Button, G., & Casey, N. (1984). Generating topic: The use of topic initial elicitors. In J. M. Atkinson & J. Heritage (Eds.), *Structures of social action: Studies in conversation analysis* (pp. 167–190). Cambridge: Cambridge University Press

Chevalier, F. H., & Moore, J. (Eds.). (2015). *Producing and managing restricted activities: Avoidance and withholding in institutional interaction* (Vol. 255). Amsterdam; Philadelphia: John Benjamins Publishing.

Curl, T. S. (2006). Offers of assistance: Constraints on syntactic design. *Journal of Pragmatics*, *38*(8), 1257–1280.

Curl, T. S. & Drew, P. (2008). Contingency and action: A comparison of two forms of requesting. *Research on Language and Social Interaction*, *41*(2), 129–153.

Davidson, J. (1984). Subsequent versions of invitations, offers, requests, and proposals dealing with potential or actual rejection. In J. M. Atkinson & J. Heritage (Eds.), *Structures of social action: Studies in conversation analysis* (pp. 102–128). Cambridge: Cambridge University Press.

Dickson, J. M., Peacock, M., Grünewald, R. A., Howlett, S., Bissell, P., & Reuber, M. (2017). Non-epileptic attack disorder: The importance of diagnosis and treatment. *British Medical Journal: Case Reports, 2017*. Retrieved from http://casereports.bmj.com/content/2017/bcr-2016-218278.abstract

Drew, P. (2012). Turn design. In J. Sidnell, & T. Stivers (Eds.), *The handbook of conversation analysis* (pp. 131–149). Chichester: John Wiley & Sons.

Drew, P., & Heritage, J. (1992). Analyzing talk at work: An introduction. In P. Drew & J. Heritage (Eds.), *Talk at work* (pp. 3–65). Cambridge: Cambridge University Press.

Gardner, R. (1997). The listener and minimal responses in conversational interaction. *Prospect*, *12*(2), 12–32.

Gill, V., & Maynard, D. (2006). Explaining illness: Patients' proposals and physicians' responses. In J. Heritage & D. W. Maynard (Eds.), *Communication in medical care: Interaction between primary care physicians and patients* (pp. 115–150). Cambridge: Cambridge University Press.

Goffman, E. (1955). On face-work: An analysis of ritual elements in social interaction. *Psychiatry*, *18*(3), 213–231.

Heritage J. (1984). *Garfinkel and ethnomethodology*. Cambridge: Polity Press.

Heritage, J. (2012). Epistemics in action: Action formation and territories of knowledge. *Research on Language & Social Interaction*, *45*(1), 1–29.

Heritage, J., & Robinson, J. D. (2006). The structure of patients' presenting concerns: Physicians' opening questions. *Health Communication*, *19*(2), 89–102.

Heritage, J., Robinson, J. D., Elliott, M. N., Beckett, M., & Wilkes, M. (2007). Reducing patients' unmet concerns in primary care: The difference one word can make. *Journal of General Internal Medicine, 22*(10), 1429–1433.

Jefferson, G. (1972). Side sequences. In D. Sudnow (Ed.), *Studies in social interaction* (pp. 294–338). New York: Free Press.

Jefferson, G. (2004). Glossary of transcript symbols with an Introduction. In G. Lerner (Ed.), *Conversation analysis: Studies from the first generation* (pp. 13–31). Philadelphia: John Benjamins.

Local, J. K. (2004). Getting back to prior talk: And-uh(m) as a back-connecting device in British and American English. In E. Couper-Kuhlen & C. E. Ford (Eds.), *Sound patterns in interaction: Crosslinguistic studies of phonetics and prosody for conversation* (pp. 377–400). Amsterdam: John Benjamins.

Kitzinger, C. (2000). Doing feminist conversation analysis. *Feminism & Psychology, 10*(2), 163–193.

Mandelbaum, J. (1991). Conversational non-cooperation: An exploration of disattended complaints. *Research on Language & Social Interaction, 25*(1–4), 97–138.

Mishler, E. G. (1984). *The discourse of medicine: Dialectics of medical interviews* (Vol. 3). London: Greenwood Publishing Group.

Monzoni, C. M., Duncan, R., Grünewald, R., & Reuber, M. (2011). How do neurologists discuss functional symptoms with their patients: A conversation analytic study. *Journal of Psychosomatic Research, 71*(6), 377–383.

Monzoni, C., & Reuber, M. (2015). Linguistic and interactional restrictions in an outpatient clinic: The challenge of delivering the diagnosis and explaining the aetiology of functional neurological problems. In F. H. G. Chevalier & J. Moore (Eds.), *Producing and managing restricted activities: Avoidance and withholding in institutional interaction* (pp. 239–270). Amsterdam; Philadelphia: John Benjamins Publishing.

Plug, L., Sharrack, B. & Reuber, M. (2009). Seizure, fit or attack? The use of diagnostic labels by patients with epilepsy or non-epileptic seizures. *Applied Linguistics, 31*(1), 94–114.

Pomerantz, A. (1984). Agreeing and disagreeing with assessments: Some features of preferred/dispreferred turn shapes. In J. M. Atkinson & J. Heritage (Eds.), *Structures of social action: Studies in conversation analysis* (pp. 57–101). Cambridge: Cambridge University Press

Reuber, M., Chappell, P., Jackson, C., & Toerien, M. (2018). Evaluating nuanced practices for initiating decision making in neurology clinics: A mixed-methods study. *Health Services and Delivery Research, National Institute for Health Research Journal's Library*.

Reuber, M., Toerien, M., Shaw, R., & Duncan, R. (2015). Delivering patient choice in clinical practice: A conversation analytic study of communication practices used in neurology clinics to involve patients in decision-making. *Health Service Delivery Research, National Institute for Health Research Journal's Library, 3*(7). Retrieved from http://nets.nihr.ac.uk/data/assets/pdf_file/0017/1 24901/FLS-10-2000-61

Robinson, J. D. (2003). An interactional structure of medical activities during acute visits and its implications for patients' participation. *Health Communication*, 15(1), 27–59.

Robinson, J. D. (2006). Soliciting patients' presenting concerns. In J. Heritage & D. Maynard (Eds.), *Communication in medical care: Interactions between primary care physicians and patients* (pp. 22–47). Cambridge: Cambridge University Press.

Robson, C. M. & Lian, O. S. (2016). 'Are you saying she's mentally ill then?' Explaining medically unexplained seizures in clinical encounters. *Forum Qualitative Sozialforschung/Forum: Qualitative Social Research*, 17(1). Retrieved from https://doi.org/10.1080/17482631.2017.1392219

Sacks, H. (1987). On the preferences for agreement and contiguity in sequences in conversation. In G. Button & J. R. E. Lee (Eds.), *Talk and social organisation* (pp. 54–69). Clevedon: Multilingual Matters.

Sacks, H., Schegloff, E. A., & Jefferson, G. (1974). A simplest systematics for the organization of turn taking in conversation. *Language*, 50, 696–735.

Schegloff, E. A. (1987). Analyzing single episodes of interaction: An exercise in conversation analysis. *Social Psychology Quarterly*, 50(2), 101–114.

Schegloff, E. A. (1988). Goffman and the analysis of conversation. In P. Drew & A. Wootton (Eds.), *Erving Goffman: Exploring the interaction order* (pp. 89–135). Cambridge: Polity Press.

Schegloff, E. A. (1996). Confirming allusions: Toward an empirical account of action. *American Journal of Sociology*, 104(1), 161–216.

Schegloff, E. A. (1997). Whose text? Whose context? *Discourse & Society*, 8(2), 165–187.

Schegloff, E. A. (2007). *Sequence organization in interaction: Vol. 1: A primer in conversation analysis*. Cambridge: Cambridge University Press.

Schegloff, E. A., & Sacks, H. (1973). Opening up closings. *Semiotica*, 8(4), 289–327.

Schneider, J. W., & Conrad, P. (1980). In the closet with illness: Epilepsy, stigma potential and information control. *Social Problems*, 28(1), 32–44.

Stivers, T. (2001). Negotiating who presents the problem: Next speaker selection in pediatric encounters. *Journal of Communication*, 51(2), 252–282.

Stivers, T. (2002). Presenting the problem in pediatric encounters: 'Symptoms only' versus 'candidate diagnosis' presentations. *Health Communication*, 14(3), 299–338

Stivers, T., & Heritage, J. (2001). Breaking the sequential mold: Answering 'more than the question' during comprehensive history taking. *Text–Interdisciplinary Journal for the Study of Discourse*, 21(1–2), 151–185.

Stivers, T., & Rossano, F. (2010). Mobilizing response. *Research on Language and Social Interaction*, 43(1), 3–31.

Appendix 1
Transcription Key (Jefferson, 2004)

A. Aspects of the relative timing of utterances

[square brackets	Overlapping talk
= equals sign	No discernible interval between turns
(0.5) time in parentheses	Intervals within or between talk (measured in tenths per second)
(.) period in parentheses	Discernible interval within or between talk but too short to measure

B. Characteristics of speech delivery

Punctuation symbols are designed to capture intonation, not grammar, and are used to describe intonation at the end of a sentence or some other shorter unit:

. period	Downward intonation
, comma	Slightly rising intonation
? question mark	Fully rising intonation
- dash	Abrupt cut-off of sound
: colon	Extension of preceding sound – the more colons the greater the extension
here underlining	Emphasised relative to surrounding talk
.tch or .t	Tongue click
hhh.	Audible outbreath (number of h's indicates length)
.hhh	Audible inbreath (number of h's indicates length)
>Talk<	Speeded up talk
#	Croaky/creaky voice
Hah hah or huh huh etc.	Beats of laughter
() empty single brackets or words enclosed in single brackets	Transcriber unable to hear or uncertain of hearing
((word)) words enclosed in double brackets	Transcribers' comments

---

Note

1. Please see Appendix A for a key to CA transcription conventions.

3   Listening to the Sound of Silence: Methodological Reflections on Studying the Unsaid

Eviatar Zerubavel

In the 2000 Argentinian film *Waiting for the Messiah*, a young man asks his father what they should do about their family's mounting financial problems. The father answers, "*Not tell* Mother. That's all we can *do*.*" By the same token, wonders a Holocaust survivor's daughter about her ever-silent mother, "What is she *not saying?*" (Wajnryb, 2001, p. 31).

In a somewhat similar vein, writing about American liberal discourse, Mica Pollock considers the notable absence of explicit race labels such as *black* or *African American* a product of a conscious effort to suppress race awareness. Such "race silence," in other words, is the result of actively *"refusing* to use the word 'black,'" *"deleting* race labels," *"eras[ing]* specific race words" (Pollock, 2004, pp. 46, 206, 79, 240, emphases added. See also pp. 73, 171, 174–75, 184, 188, 193, 217, 237).

The idea that remaining silent is an activity (Jaworski, 1993, p. 81) is also exemplified by *non-statements*, as evidenced by the media coverage of Donald Trump's "failure to mention" Jewish victims on the 2017 international Holocaust Remembrance Day (Jacobs, 2017) or Article 5 of the NATO treaty (which commits each member state to consider an armed attack against one member state to be an armed attack against them all) at the organization's meeting in Brussels that year (Gray, 2017). Equally notable have been references to what he failed to say in his response to the violence surrounding the August 2017 far-right rally in Charlottesville, Virginia. One newspaper article was explicitly titled "Trump *Conspicuously Avoids Condemning* White Supremacists in Virginia" (Koronowski, 2017, emphasis added). Another one noted his *"refusal to denounce* far-right extremists," effectively blaming him for *"failing to explicitly condemn* the role of white supremacists" (Jacobs & Murray, 2017, emphases added).

Such instances clearly imply deliberate *avoidance*. So do efforts to remain "tactfully" silent, as when actively refraining from commenting on someone's rather obvious stutter (Zerubavel, 2006, pp. 29–32). Remaining silent, in other words, thus entails not just simply the absence of speech but also the presence of *non-speech*!

No wonder silence can actually be heard (Andreyev, 1971 [1910], p. 131. See also pp. 135, 140, 142, 144; Kern, 1983, p. 170). As Paul Simon has famously suggested, it has an unmistakable "sound." In fact, as the images of a "thick," "heavy," "resounding," or even "deafening" silence (Wajnryb, 2001, pp. 75, 143; Barnes, 2017; Ephratt, 2017) seem to imply, it often "speaks" louder than words.

Silence, in short, is "part of [our] communicative system" (Jaworski, 1993, p. xii, see also pp. 81–82; Bird, 1996, pp. 34–48; Cheung, 1993, p. 1; Pinder & Harlos, 2001, p. 334; Samarin, 1965, p. 115). A pronouncedly active performance, it entails "neither muteness nor mere absence of audible sound" (Dauenhauer, 1980, p. 4), as it "fills the pauses and cracks and crannies of our discourse" (Wajnryb, 2001, p. 25, see also p. 35).

That explains the common use of an elephant to figuratively represent the object of "conspiracies" of silence (Zerubavel, 2006). The image of "the elephant in the room" is metaphorically evocative of a hard-not-to-notice object, the presence of which everybody is privately aware yet nobody is willing to publicly acknowledge by actually mentioning it. It was thus repeatedly invoked, for example, in efforts to capture Bill Clinton's almost surreal delivery of his presidential State of the Union address to the US Congress only days after the Monica Lewinsky scandal broke out in 1998, as well as in the very midst of his congressional impeachment trial in 1999:

There was an elephant in the room, but the man at the podium didn't mention it. The allegations about a White House sex scandal sat in the House Chamber like an uninvited pachyderm. Everyone in the room knew it was there, but President Clinton did not ... talk about it. In a 72-minute speech, Clinton discussed everything from Social Security to the Internet, but there wasn't a word about Monica Lewinsky. (Adair and Gazella, 1998, p. 8A).

Television cameras never picked up the elephant in the room, and President Clinton surely didn't mention it. But that figurative elephant, Clinton's impeachment trial, was everywhere during the president's State of the Union speech Tuesday. (Bauder, 1999)

[Having] the impeachment trial and the president's speech hours apart is like having an elephant in the room. ... It's huge, it's undeniable, yet people pretend it's not there. (Harper, 1999, p. A11)

Silence is particularly "deafening" in situations where we not only avoid even mentioning something (as when explicitly saying "Let's not discuss this now") but also remain silent about the fact that we remain silent. Writing about homosexuality in the Catholic Church, for example, Mark Jordan offers a most compelling portrayal of such *meta-silences* (Zerubavel, 2006, p. 53):

The tense silence about sex was perhaps nowhere more noticeable than after dismissals. When someone was sent away for failing to demonstrate a vocation to celibacy, little or nothing was said. Seminarians just disappeared. The assigned place in choir closed up. The room or dorm bed was cleaned and someone else was moved into it. . . . The seriousness of the sexual fall was underscored precisely by saying nothing about it. (Jordan, 2000, p. 165)

Needless to say, it is much easier to study what people do say than what they do not, let alone tell the difference between simply not talking about something and deliberately avoiding it, since acts of commission are far more noticeable than ones of omission (Zerubavel, 2006, p. 13; Zerubavel, 2018, p. 9). Nevertheless, study-ing the latter has already proved doable. After completing her study of "colormute" liberal discourse, Pollock, for example, claimed that she "was now perfectly positioned" to discern when people "were delib-erately *not talking* about race" (Pollock, 2004, p. 11, emphasis added), that is, actively avoiding it. Indeed, as Ruth Wajnryb describes the skills involved in studying the silence pervading Holocaust survivors' homes,

[y]ou learn to probe at the gap that separates what is said and what is meant . . . . [To] know what is hinted at, alluded to . . . . [T]o recognise . . . the disallowable, the taboo . . . . [T]o recognise and read avoidance strategies. Finally, cumulatively and perhaps most importantly, *you learn to identify . . . what is absent. You learn to read the silence.* (Wajnryb, 2001, pp. 21–22, emphasis added)

Focusing on *discursive absences*, I hereby present some of the ways that allow us to listen to the sound of silence and thereby hear what is left unsaid.

Hesitations and Euphemisms

Hearing silence is much easier in retrospect, after it has already been broken (Zerubavel, 2006, pp. 61–72). Thus, for example, if I am sitting at a ninety-minute meeting listening to an inexplicably long discussion of some rather trivial matter, it may very well be only when the next, particularly difficult topic is finally introduced when there are only fifteen minutes left to discuss it that I may realize that it had in fact been actively avoided. In a somewhat similar vein, we retrospectively hear silence by becoming aware of being surprised that some rather expected piece of information was actually not mentioned earlier. In other words, silence "occurs and is perceived as . . . meaningful when talk . . . is expected by the hearer [yet] withheld by the speaker" (Jaworski, 1993, p. 79).

Yet silence can also be heard not only in retrospect. After all, in cases where we try to avoid even mentioning what we are silent about, "[i]t is as if a ten-ton boulder were in the middle of the living room with no one being allowed to mention it. One always must walk around it . . . . A series of conversational topics increasingly becomes forbidden" (Bloch, 1987, p. viii). As so suggestively implied by the image of walking on broken glass or eggshells, that figurative room feels more like a minefield, as all the participants "gingerly skirt the perimeter" of every topic of conversation, well aware that at any moment they might "step on a land mine" (Wajnryb, 2001, p. 249, see also p. 46).

To hear the silence, one must therefore be particularly alert to any possible sign of *hesitation*. Any pause in a conversation can thus be tacitly indicative of an effort to actively avoid saying something. A "person stuttering and hesitating before describing an individual . . . as 'black'" (Pollock, 2004, p. 174, see also pp. 175, 205), for instance, clearly dramatizes such momentary silences.

Furthermore, silence can also be heard whenever *euphemisms* (*restroom, passed away*) are being used. A euphemism, after all, allows its user to actually allude to something without explicitly mentioning it. Using the seemingly innocuous term *escalation*, for instance, "provide[s] a way of talking about nuclear weapons without really talking about . . . billions of human beings incinerated or literally melted" (Lifton, 1982, p. 107). By the same token, by using "code" phrases such as *the inner city* or *at-risk populations*, one can actually invoke people's race without referring to it explicitly (Pollock, 2004, p. 125). Using the somewhat vague term *the war* likewise allows Holocaust survivors to only allude to (without getting more deeply into) the actual horrors of their experience in the death camps (Stein, 2007, p. 86; see also Stein, 2014, pp. 24–25).

It therefore comes as no surprise that an abundance of euphemisms are indeed used in America in the context of race (*the N word*), sex (*the F word*), and death (*gone*), three of Americans' most taboo topics, thereby indicating that something is in fact being veiled. As such, they actually help reveal silences by tacitly foregrounding (Zerubavel, 2006, pp. 65–68; 2015, pp. 82–89; 2018, pp. 63–85) the unmentionable. Effectively constituting a "code of silent omissions" functionally equivalent to the "preliminary shower-bath that renders anti-perspirants unnecessary," they are indeed "the deodorant of language" (Adams, 1985, p. 48).

Euphemisms reveal the subtle yet unmistakable avoidance of things about which their users, whether fearful or embarrassed, choose to remain silent (Zerubavel, 2006, pp. 5–8). Were it not for such avoidance, after all, there would be no need to use them! Thus, whenever I hear a euphemism being used, I also hear the silence surrounding the discursive object it is consciously designed to avoid.

Generics

As exemplified by the US Department of Homeland Security's effectively vague and thus also somewhat euphemistic slogan "If You See *Something*, Say Something," the use of *generics* can also help unveil silences. After all, as evidenced by the public outcry over Trump's response to the violence in Charlottesville ("We condemn in the strongest possible terms this egregious display of hatred, bigotry, and violence *on many sides, on many sides*" [Koronowski, 2017], emphasis added), being vocal about a generic phenomenon often also implies remaining silent about a specific one! Using the generic and therefore semiotically more inclusive greeting *Happy Holidays* thus also implies not using its indisputably Christian-specific and therefore more exclusive counterpart *Merry Christmas* (Lewis & Djupe, 2016; McGill, 2016; Petulla, 2016; Stack, 2016). And when hearing an allusion to *all*, one can also hear a tacit avoidance of mentioning members of specific ethnoracial groups (Pollock, 2004, pp. 74–86).

In fact, such use of generics also constitutes a form of actual silencing, as exemplified by the cultural battle between advocates of the specific and therefore explicitly particularistic slogan *Black Lives Matter* and its supposedly generic and thus purportedly universalistic counterpart *All Lives Matter*. Rejecting the latter's seemingly inclusionary veneer, members of the Black Lives Matter movement foreground the often silenced police killings of African Americans. As both Judith Butler and Donna Brazile, for example, have put it,

When some people rejoin with "All Lives Matter" they misunderstand the problem …. It is true that all lives matter, but … not all lives are understood to matter which is precisely why it is most important to name the lives that have not mattered, and are struggling to matter …. If we jump too quickly to the universal formulation "all lives matter," then we miss the fact that black people have not yet been included in the idea of "all lives" …. [T]o make that universal formulation … one that truly extends to all people, we have to foreground those lives that are not mattering now, to mark that exclusion, and militate against it. (Yancy & Butler, 2015)

Of course ALL lives matter. But there is no serious question about the value of the life of a young white girl or boy. Sadly, there is a serious question … about the value of the life of a young black girl or boy. So those who are experiencing the pain and trauma of the black experience in this country don't want their rallying cry to be watered down with a *generic* feel-good catchphrase. (Brazile, 2015, emphasis added)

As Van Jones has so eloquently put it, "When you have a specific pain, you want a specific slogan" (Van Jones quotes in ibid.).

"It Goes Without Saying"

Yet silence surrounds not only what we actively avoid but also what we tacitly assume by default and thereby take for granted as a self-evident "given" (Garfinkel, 1967, pp. 24–30). Unlike the culturally marked regions of our phenomenal world, which are considered socially "abnormal" and, as such, are typically labeled, the unmarked ones are taken for granted (Zerubavel, 2018) and, as such, usually "go without saying" (see also Bourdieu, 1977 [1972], pp. 166–67; 1984 [1979], p. 424; Tannen, 1993).

That explains why bearers of culturally marked identities are expected to "announce" their social "abnormality," whereas bearers of unmarked ones (on marked and unmarked identities, see Brekhus, 1996, 2003; Mullaney, 1999; Zerubavel, 2018) can usually expect their "normality" to be taken for granted. Personal information merely confirming default cultural assumptions is therefore rarely considered notifiable (Ryan, 2006, p. 241). While gays and lesbians, for instance, often feel compelled to come out, straights, by contrast, are rarely expected to announce their sexual orientation, which is conventionally presumed. By the same token, unlike vegetarians and vegans, other dinner guests are not expected to proactively notify their hosts in advance that they *do* eat meat. And since it is conventionally presumed that one is not terminally ill, one is likewise rarely expected to proactively volunteer such non-information. Yet the silence surrounding what is considered normal is even more remarkable when there are no words to even allude to it. The very lack of such vocabulary thus helps reveal culture-wide silences.

Such realizations led me more than twenty years ago to ask why adding a slice of cheese culturally transforms a hamburger into a "cheeseburger" whereas adding some ketchup does not transform it into a "ketchupburger" (Zerubavel, 1997, p. 1). Effectively regarded as ordinary and therefore literally un-remark-able, what we consider normal does not need to be explicitly articulated. As such, it "goes without saying."

Hence the inverse relation between *labeling* and normality. Whereas the abnormal is explicitly labeled, the normal needs no mentioning. The term *Black English* has therefore no equivalent racialized counterpart such as *White English*, a term that, given the presumed normality of whiteness in America, would most likely be considered *culturally redundant* and, as such, *semiotically superfluous*. The glaring asymmetry between the term *homoerotic* and its nominally equivalent yet rarely used counterpart *hetero-erotic* likewise underscores the presumed normality of different-sex desire.

Indeed, note the glaring paucity of terms designed to denote phenomena we conventionally consider normal and thereby assume by default and take for granted. Since they are effectively presumed, the terms that would denote them thus seem semiotically superfluous.

The taken-for-grantedness of what we conventionally consider normal, in other words, is evidenced in its semiotic superfluity, as manifested in the paucity of cultural labels designed to denote it. We might therefore try to compare the actual vocabularies culturally available for denoting "normal" versus "abnormal" phenomena. Indeed, the relation between such vocabularies is pronouncedly asymmetrical, with terms denoting the latter being much more widely available than ones denoting the former, about which we therefore remain culturally silent.

Given the historical closetedness of homosexuality in America, the term *openly gay* is therefore far more widely used than its nominally equivalent counterpart *openly straight*. Heteronormativity also explains the sharp disparity between the term *same-sex marriage* and its nominally equivalent yet culturally redundant and therefore semiotically superfluous counterpart *different-sex marriage*. Such striking disparity implies that the former term denotes an abnormal and therefore literally remark-able phenomenon, in sharp contrast to the normal, culturally expected form of marriage denoted by the latter (see also Heath, 2013, p. 574).

By the same token, the term *male nurse* reflects the culturally abnormal status of male nurses relative to the "normality" of female nurses. Conventionally assumed by default and thereby taken for granted, the latter require no special marking. Given that nurses tend to be female, in other words, the term *female nurse* would thus be considered culturally redundant and therefore semiotically superfluous. Hence the methodological usefulness of *lexical gaps*. As I encounter the terms *openly gay* and *male nurse*, I also hear the absence of their nominally equivalent counterparts *openly straight* and *female nurse*!

All this can be empirically demonstrated by measuring actual lexical usage through frequency counts of words and phrases we use, with glaring disparities between nominally equivalent lexical pairs exemplifying the semiotic asymmetry between the normal and the abnormal. After all, conventional standards of normality tend to remain nameless, since only what deviates from them is considered remark-able enough to actually be labeled, as evidenced in various Google searches I conducted recently (Zerubavel, 2018). Whereas a search for the term *polyamory*, for example, yielded 2,230,000 hits, a parallel search for its nominally equivalent yet nonetheless assumed-by-default and therefore conventionally taken-for-granted counterpart *monoamory* yielded only 2,490 (Google search done on December 13, 2016), thereby exemplifying the culturally presumed normality of single-partner romantic relations. By the same token, whereas a search for the term *biracial* yielded 6,350,000 results, a parallel search for its nominally equivalent counterpart *monoracial* yielded only 42,300 (Google search done on December 17, 2016), not to mention that my automatic spell-checker immediately flagged it as a typo, thereby tacitly exemplifying its semiotic superfluity!

To further appreciate the glaring asymmetry between the lexical manifestations of normality and abnormality, consider again our conventional default assumptions regarding sexual orientation. Whereas a search for the term *openly gay* yielded 3,740,000 hits, a parallel search for its nominally equivalent counterpart *openly straight* yielded only 32,800 (Google search done on August 20, 2015). While the former denotes what is conventionally considered abnormal and, as such, literally remark-able, the latter denotes a normal, culturally un-remarkable phenomenon conventionally assumed by default and thereby taken for granted. By the same token, whereas a search for the term *the LGBT community* yielded 4,360,000 results, a parallel one for its nominally equivalent yet culturally redundant and therefore semiotically superfluous counterpart *the straight community* yielded only 38,900 (Google search done on March 9, 2016). And whereas searches for the terms *gay marriage* and *gay-friendly* yielded 22,200,000 and 19,400,000 results, respectively, parallel searches for their nominally equivalent yet culturally redundant and thereby semiotically superfluous counterparts *straight marriage* and *straight-friendly* yielded only 89,500 and 65,400, respectively (Google searches done on March 15, 2016, and May 3, 2016).

Studying Absence

Although specifically addressing discursive absences, this chapter also calls for studying absence in general, whether manifested in the form of "tactful" disattention (Goffman, 1963, pp. 84–87; Zerubavel, 2006, pp. 29–31; 2015, pp. 60–61), abstinence (Mullaney, 2006), the artistic production of effaced vulvas (Kaplan, 2017), commemorating the absence of Poland's prewar Jewish population (Zubrzycki, 2017), or "gaps in the literature" waiting to be filled with academic attention. Ever since realizing that by watching doctors and nurses consult hospital wall clocks, I was in fact also observing them *not* consulting their own watches (Zerubavel, 1979, p. 95), I have been deeply interested in such "not-doings" (Mullaney, 2006), having actually written about silence

(Zerubavel, 2006), the "background" (Zerubavel, 2015), as well as the taken for granted (Zerubavel, 2018). After all, as famously implied in the exchange between the police inspector and Sherlock Holmes about the dog that did *not* bark on the night the horse Silver Blaze disappeared, "non-occurrences" may very well constitute actual occurrences:

> "Is there any point to which you would wish to draw my attention?"
> "To the curious incident of the dog in the night-time."
> "The dog did nothing in the night-time."
> "That was the curious incident," remarked Sherlock Holmes.
>
> (Doyle, 1986 [1892]), p. 540)

In other words, as manifested in the change from a passive to a pronouncedly active definition of consent in American sexual ethics (Zerubavel, 2018, p. 94) or the fact that we culturally characterize vegetarians and vegans by what they do not eat, even non-action can be seen as action. As Senate Majority Leader Mitch McConnell characterized his refusal to hold confirmation hearings for President Obama's Supreme Court nominee Merrick Garland "[t]he most important decision I've made in my political career was *the decision not to fill* the Supreme Court vacancy created by the death of Justice Scalia" (Stolberg, 2017, p. 20, emphasis added). And when announcing after the 9/11 attacks that countries "will be held *accountable for inactivity*. You're either with us or against us in the fight against terror" ("Bush says it is time for action," 2001, emphasis added), President Bush was actually saying that any country that would not actively side with the United States would in fact be considered as being against it (see also Zerubavel, 2018, p. 93).

As such, we should study not only what is present but also what we consider "conspicuous by its absence." As Bing Crosby wryly notes while watching his wife and his best friend in the film *The Country Girl*, "there is only one thing more obvious than two people looking longingly at each other and it's two people avoiding it." We therefore need to develop our ability to "see" the conventionally invisible and "hear" the conventionally inaudible. This chapter constitutes a first step in that direction.

References

Adair, B., & Gazella, K. (1998, January 28). It lasted 72 minutes without a mention. *St. Petersburg Times*, p. A8.

Adams, R. M. (1985). Soft soap and the nitty-gritty." In D. J. Enright (Ed.), *Fair of speech: The uses of euphemism* (pp. 44–55). Oxford: Oxford University Press.

Andreyev, L. N. (1971 [1910]). Silence. In *The little angel and other stories* (pp. 121–147). Freeport, NY: Books for Libraries Press.

Barnes, B. (2017, October 9). "Almost radio silence": Movie producer is the (whispered) talk of Hollywood. *New York Times*, p. A13.

Bauder, D. (1999, January 19). For TV networks, big coverage day. *Associated Press Online*.

Bird, F. B. (1996). *The muted conscience: Moral silence and the practice of ethics in business*. Westport, CT: Quorum Books.

Bloch, D. A. (1987). Foreword. In D. S. Greenwald & S. J. Zeitlin (Eds.), *No reason to talk about it: Families confront the nuclear taboo* (pp. vii–x). New York: W. W. Norton.

Bourdieu, P. (1977 [1972]). *Outline of a theory of practice*. New York: Cambridge University Press.

Bourdieu, P. (1984 [1979]). *Distinction: A social critique of the judgement of taste*. Cambridge, MA: Harvard University Press.

Brazile, D. (2015, July 22). Why "All Lives Matter" misses the point. *CNN*. Retrieved, from www.cnn.com/2015/07/22/opinions/brazile-black-lives-matter-sl ogan/.

Brekhus, W. H. (1996). Social marking and the mental coloring of identity: Sexual identity construction and maintenance in the United States. *Sociological Forum*, *11*, 497–522.

Brekhus, W. H. (2003). *Peacocks, chameleons, centaurs: Gay suburbia and the grammar of social identity*. Chicago: University of Chicago Press.

"Bush says it is time for action." (2001, November 6). *CNN*. Retrieved from http://edition.cnn.com/2001/US/11/06/ret.bush.coalition/index.html.

Cheung, K-K. (1993). *Articulate silences: Hisaye Yamamoto, Maxine Hong Kingston, Joy Kogawa*. Ithaca, NY: Cornell University Press.

Dauenhauer, B. P. (1980). *Silence: The phenomenon and its ontological significance*. Bloomington: Indiana University Press.

Doyle, A. C. (1986 [1892]). Silver blaze. In *Sherlock Holmes: The complete novels and stories* (vol. 1, pp. 521–546). New York: Bantam Books.

Ephratt, M. (2017). The silence address: Silence as it emerged from media commentators and respondents following Prime Minister Netanyahu's 2015 address at the UN. *Israel Studies*, *22*, 200–229.

Garfinkel, H. (1967). What is ethnomethodology? In *Studies in ethnomethodology* (pp. 1–34). Englewood Cliffs, NJ: Prentice Hall.

Goffman, E. (1963). *Behavior in public places: Notes on the social organization of gatherings*. New York: Free Press.

Gray, R. (2017, May 25). Trump declines to affirm NATO's Article 5. *The Atlantic*. Retrieved from www.theatlantic.com/international/archive/2017/ 05/trump-declines-to-affirm-natos-article-5/528129/.

Harper, J. (1999, January 19). Media highlights surreal day with trial, State of the Union. *Washington Times*, p. A11.

Heath, M. (2013). Sexual misgivings: Producing un/marked knowledge in neoliberal marriage promotion policies. *Sociological Quarterly* 54, 561–583.

Jacobs, B. (2017, January 27). No mention of Jews in White House's Holocaust Remembrance Day tribute. *The Guardian*. Retrieved from www.theguardian .com/us-news/2017/jan/27/white-house-holocaust-remembrance-day-no-jews.

Jacobs, B., & Murray, W. (2017, August 12). Donald Trump under fire after failing to denounce Virginia white supremacists. *The Guardian.* Retrieved from www.theguardian.com/us-news/2017/aug/12/charlottesville-protest-trump-condemns-violence-many-sides.

Jaworski, A. (1993). *The power of silence: Social and pragmatic perspectives.* Newbury Park, CA: Sage.

Jordan, M. (2000). *The silence of Sodom: Homosexuality in modern Catholicism.* Chicago: University of Chicago Press.

Kaplan, A. (2017). *Effacing the vulva: Producing the West.* Unpublished manuscript, Rutgers University.

Kern, S. (1983). *The culture of time and space 1880–1918.* Cambridge, MA: Harvard University Press.

Koronowski, R. (2017). Trump conspicuously avoids condemning white supremacists in Virginia, blames "many sides" for violence. Retrieved from https://thinkprogress.org/trump-charlottesville-statement-6624f029 b0e0/.

Lewis, A. R., & Djupe, P. A. (2016). Where to say "Merry Christmas" vs. "Happy Holidays" – 2016 edition. Retrieved from http://fivethirtyeight.com/features/where-to-say-merry-christmas-vs-happy-holidays-2016-edition/.

Lifton, R. J. (1982). Imagining the real. In R. J. Lifton & R. Falk (Eds.), *Indefensible weapons: The political and psychological case against nuclearism* (pp. 3–125). New York: Basic Books.

McGill, A. (2016, December 20). Merry Christmas vs. Happy Holidays, round 2,016: The perennial debate gets a new coat of cheers from Donald Trump. *The Atlantic.* Retrieved from www.theatlantic.com/politics/archive/2016/12/merry-christmas-vs-happy-holidays-round-2016/511115/.

Mullaney, J. L. (1999). Making it "count": Mental weighing and identity attribution. *Symbolic Interaction, 22,* 269–283.

Mullaney, J. L. (2006). *Everyone is NOT doing it: Abstinence and personal identity.* Chicago: University of Chicago Press.

Petulla, S. (2016, December 24). "Merry Christmas" versus "Happy Holidays": Why Trump may prefer the former. *NBC News.* Retrieved from www .nbcnews.com/news/us-news/merry-christmas-versus-happy-holidays-why-tru mp-prefers-former-n699611.

Pinder, C. C. & Harlos, K. P. (2001). Employee silence: Quiescence and acquiescence as responses to perceived injustice. *Research in Personnel and Human Resources Management, 20,* 331–369.

Pollock, M. (2004). *Colormute: Race talk dilemmas in an American school.* Princeton, NJ: Princeton University Press.

Ryan, D. (2006). Getting the word out: Notes on the social organization of notification. *Sociological Theory, 24,* 228–254.

Samarin, W. J. (1965). Language of silence. *Practical Anthropology, 12,* 115–119.

Stack, L. (2016, December 19). How the "War on Christmas" controversy was created. *New York Times.* Retrieved from www.nytimes.com/2016/12/19/us/war-on-christmas-controversy.html?_r=0.

Stein, A. (2007). Trauma stories, identity work, and the politics of recognition. In J. M. Gerson & D. L. Wolf (Eds.), *Sociology confronts the Holocaust: Memories* and identities in Jewish diasporas (pp. 84–91). Durham, NC: Duke University Press.

Stein, A. (2014). *Reluctant witnesses: Survivors, their children, and the rise of Holocaust consciousness.* New York: Oxford University Press.

Stolberg, S. G. (2017, November 12). Bannon paints a target on McConnell's back. His response? "Ha-ha." *New York Times*, p. 20.

Tannen, D. (1993, June 20). Marked women, unmarked men. *New York Times Magazine* (pp. 18, 52, 54).

Wajnryb, R. (2001). *The silence: How tragedy shapes talk.* Crows Nest, Australia: Allen & Unwin.

Yancy, G., & Butler, J. (2015, January 12). What's wrong with "All Lives Matter"? *New York Times.* Retrieved from http://opinionator .blogs.nytimes.com/2015/01/12/whats-wrong-with-all-lives-matter/?_r=0.

Zerubavel, E. (1979). *Patterns of time in hospital life: A sociological perspective.* Chicago: University of Chicago Press.

Zerubavel, E. (1997). *Social mindscapes: An invitation to cognitive sociology.* Cambridge, MA: Harvard University Press.

Zerubavel, E. (2006). *The elephant in the room: Silence and denial in everyday life.* New York: Oxford University Press.

Zerubavel, E. (2015). *Hidden in plain sight: The social structure of irrelevance.* New York: Oxford University Press.

Zerubavel, E. (2018). *Taken for granted: The remarkable power of the unremarkable.* Princeton, NJ: Princeton University Press.

Zubrzycki, G. (2017). The politics of Jewish absence in contemporary Poland. *Journal of Contemporary History*, 52, 250–277.

4   Social Silences: Conducting Ethnographic Research on Racism in the Americas

Christina A. Sue and Mary Robertson

Social Silences, Hegemony, and Race

Socially silenced topics such as racism can be of important social significance. Yet this significance can drive a topic underground, making it resilient and resistant to exposure and difficult for fieldworkers to observe as a phenomenon. Based on our experiences conducting ethnographic research (including participant observation, interviews, and focus groups), along with the published reflections of others, we discuss the broader significance and purpose of race-related silences and the various manifestations of racialized social silence, and then we propose strategies for addressing them. Although we focus on race in the Americas, our discussion and suggestions are intended to inform ethnographers encountering various forms of social silence across different contexts.

Social silences are ubiquitous and can represent powerful forms of social control. They can affect and infiltrate multiple levels of society, including state, institutional, and popular discourse. They are embedded in everyday language use; in learning to speak, people also learn what not to say or what to repress and how to repress through discursive interaction (Billig, 1997, 1999). Through the absence of talk and other silencing dynamics, social silences can morph into conspiracies of silence – social phenomena in which a topic becomes unmentionable at all levels of society, and all societal members are expected to maintain the silence. In such social conspiracies, "a group of people tacitly agree to publicly ignore something of which they are all personally aware" (Zerubavel, 2007, p. 181). Silences of this nature can be particularly impenetrable as the larger the number of people participating, the more resounding the silence (Zerubavel, 2007). Conspiratorial forms of silence have been referred to as "public secrecy" (Taussig, 1999), "cultural censorship" (Sheriff, 2000), and "the unmentionable" (Hirschauer, 2007). In some cases, these silences serve as a mechanism for maintaining hegemony – a form of domination in which elites and non-elites participate in reproducing systems of power (Gramsci, 1971) – by concealing the underlying mechanisms used to reproduce hegemonic processes; the undetectable nature of these processes renders them an effective and powerful form of domination.

Social silences are fascinating and necessary topics of inquiry; however, they can be problematic to study. Silences result in "nonoccurrences" and are thus rather difficult to observe (Zerubavel, 2007, p. 182). As Zerubavel (2007, p. 184) notes, what makes silences so insidious is that

the silence itself is never actually discussed among the conspirators. Unlike when we explicitly agree not to talk about something ("Let's not get into that"), the very fact that they avoid it remains unacknowledged and the subtle social dynamics underlying their silence are thus hidden from view.

Scholars concerned about the failure of investigators to attend to the unspoken and obscured (e.g., Billig, 1997; Sheriff, 2000) critique traditional social science methods for focusing too much on what is said, rather than what is *not* said.

A major point of theorization surrounding race-related silences specifically has been the concept of color-blind racism, which Eduardo Bonilla-Silva (2003) defines as an ideology that "explains contemporary racial inequality as the outcome of nonracial dynamics" (p. 2). Scholars have identified how this ideology operates at the micro level, working to purposefully and actively silence race talk in everyday speech (van Dijk, 1992), in institutional settings (Pollock, 2004), and via psychological processes and norms (Sue, 2015). Van Dijk (1992) has noted that a central component of racism is its denial and has illustrated how this denial operates through the use of discourse, including the concealing of negative attitudes toward ethnic and racial minorities (for additional discussions of denial of prejudice, see Augoustinos & Every, 2007; Durrheim, Quayle, & Dixon, 2016). Tying the micro to the macro, van Dijk argues that such discourses have broad social, cultural, and political functions. Similarly, others have highlighted how silences on race have the effect of reproducing or even exacerbating racial inequality (Augoustinos & Every, 2007; Pollock, 2004; Warren & Sue, 2011). For scholars to better expose the inner workings of structural systems of social control – like color-blind racism – more discussion is needed on the methodological aspects of studying race (Bulmer & Solomos, 2004; Twine, 2000), and specifically, the intersection of race and silence.

Historical, Cultural, and Emotional Aspects of Silence

In the process of investigating social silences, the ethnographer needs to be prepared for the potential strength of people's emotional attachment to the silence and their investment in maintaining it. This is especially true in situations where silence serves as a mechanism for maintaining hegemonic structures, such as those related to racial inequality. Race talk has been identified as eliciting strong emotions associated with guilt, fear, anxiety, betrayal, and defensiveness (Sue, 2015). However, to fully appreciate and understand these reactions, fieldworkers need to reflect on *why* something is being silenced, what this silence *means* to people, and what may be the potential *consequences* for breaking the silence. In the words of Bulmer and Solomos (2004, p. 8), "the meanings of race and racism need to be located within particular fields of discourse and articulated to the social relations found within that context."

We argue that understanding the social and historical processes underpinning a particular silence in one's field site is essential to being able to understand and navigate it. Over the course of her research, Sue came to understand why engaging the topic of racism in Mexico was so problematic in her field site. Not only does discussion of racism challenge the belief held by Mexico's leaders, cultural institutions, and citizens that racism does not exist in the country, but it also stirs sentiments of national pride. Mexico's national ideology asserting a lack of racism stems from efforts by government leaders in the wake of the Mexican Revolution (1910–1921), Mexico's civil war. To draw attention away from inequalities in the country, strengthen nationalist sentiment and unity, and solidify their rule, post-revolutionary leaders argued that the mixed-race nation of Mexico was free of the racist virus. Over time, the Mexican populace embraced this message. Today, Mexican nationalism is deeply intertwined with the vision of a racist-free Mexico. Consequently, if individuals challenge this ideology, their patriotism is called into question (Sue, 2013).

Fieldworkers also need to recognize and consider the potential consequences for treading on socially silenced topics. As Zerubavel (2007) points out, "breaking the silence violates not only some individuals' personal sense of comfort but a collectively sacred social taboo, thereby also evoking a somewhat heightened sense of fear" (p. 186). Breaking a social silence may result in strong repercussions, emotional and otherwise. On this topic, Warren (2001) relayed his experience with interviewing an Indigenous woman in Brazil. Her husband became infuriated, fearing that local landowners would find out that his wife had spoken about race and Indigenous identities with Warren. The man explained, "I know we are Indians, but this talk of recognition will only bring us trouble" (p. 96). In another case, when Sheriff (2001) discussed her findings on race and police brutality during a radio interview, she was told by locals: "The police are not going to like what you said . . . you must be very careful what you say in Brazil" (p. 27). While we understand that all fieldwork involves risk, trespassing on social silences warrants a particular kind of care and sensitivity. We discuss this in the following sections, which are organized around various forms of silence, including government and institutional silence, interpersonal silence, and interview or focus group silence.

Government and Institutional Silence

The Mexican case represents a clear example of government silencing. In 1921, government officials removed the race question from the Mexican census, arguing that the question was not necessary given the absence of racism, a rationale that has also been used in other Latin American countries (Loveman, 2014). Much more recently, in the 1990s, in reports submitted by Mexico to the UN International Convention on the Elimination of All Forms of Racial Discrimination, the Mexican government argued that it did not need to enact legislation to combat racism because "the phenomenon does not arise in our country, nor is it even a subject of national debate" (Committee on the Elimination of All Forms of Racial Discrimination [CERD]/C/260/Add.1). Not only did the Mexican government assert that racism does not exist, but it also cited the *silence* surrounding the topic as proof of its nonexistence.

In subsequent exchanges with the UN committee, Mexican officials steadfastly maintained their position, even after the committee rejected Mexico's stance, pointing to evidence of Indigenous and black marginalization. The UN's position is consistent with recent research, showing black and Indigenous educational and socioeconomic inequality, as well as inequality related to skin tone (e.g., Martínez et al., 2014; Villarreal, 2010). Within Mexico, there has also been a silence surrounding the very existence of Mexico's population of African descent (Sue, 2013), despite the fact that Mexico was the destination for at least 200,000 African slaves (Aguirre Beltrán, 1944). This silence manifests in national narratives of *mestizaje*, which only acknowledge the Spanish and Indigenous contributions to the formation of the Mexican populace, as well as the historical omission of a question about Mexico's black population on the decennial census.

Other examples of state silencing are well documented in the literature. For example, in 1890, the Brazilian Minister of Finance ordered the burning of the federal slave registration archives, destroying records documenting Brazil's long history of African slavery (Twine, 1998). After independence, Cuban government officials suppressed racial movements, along with any discussion of racism (Sawyer, 2006). Later, the communist regime further entrenched the state's silence on racism. Dominguez (1978) elucidates this point: "The revolution has claimed to have solved the race problem; it has therefore become subversive to speak or write about its existence" (cited in Sawyer, 2006, p. 68). In this context, racial projects were perceived as being destructive to Marxist national projects (Sawyer, 2006). Government and/or elite silences on race and the banning of racial categories have been documented in the Americas (Loveman, 2014; Warren & Sue, 2011) as well as in Europe (e.g., Body-Gendrot, 2004; Essed, 2004; Simon, 2017; van Dijk, 1992) and other Western societies (Augoustinos & Every, 2007).

Social silences can also exist in various institutions. While acknowledgment of institutionalization of oppression has become commonplace, it can be difficult to demonstrate *empirically* how this institutionalization functions when it is silenced. Castagno (2008) conducted ethnographic research in predominately white US schools and found that teachers routinely silenced or avoided critical race talk, despite students' inquiries on the topic. For example, when students would reference inequality or racism, teachers would silence their comments, saying things like "I don't want to hear it again," signaling that such comments were unworthy of discussion. Pollock (2004) found similar dynamics occurring in her ethnographic study of race labeling in US schools. She documented how teachers are often "colormute" and suppress the use of racial labels. These examples illustrate various ways in which social silences manifest in government and institutional spheres.

Interpersonal Silence

A powerful illustration of the interpersonal silence surrounding racism comes from an interaction described by John Burdick (1998, pp. 25–26) regarding his ethnographic work in Brazil:

I was sitting in the kitchen of a poor working-class home on the outskirts of Rio de Janeiro, talking to Dona Maria, a woman who called herself *preta* [black]. I had known Dona Maria for just over six months, during which time we had spoken of religion and politics and death and the best way to prepare rice and beans. The one subject we had not broached was color. I was unsure how to introduce the subject, or whether it was a subject to be introduced at all. At the table that hot morning, I had just finished off a glass of water. I was still thirsty, but there was no more cool water to be had. Except for Dona Maria's own glassful.

"I'm so thirsty, Dona Maria, would you mind if I had some of yours?"

She made as if to pour some from her glass into mine, but it was too late: I had already seized her glass and was quickly draining it. When I looked up, I could see her eyes were moist.

"What's wrong, Dona Maria?"

A few seconds passed before she regained her composure.
"No one has done that before."
"Done what, Dona Maria?"
"No one who is white – has put their lips there, where mine have been."
After that, as the day drew on, and the week, and the year, Dona Maria drew me into spaces of pain and longing and silent earthquakes. These are the small everyday spaces where the pain of color prejudice occur in Brazil. She told me of the moment when her goddaughter refused to say in public that she was her godmother; of the time in her twenties when the boy she loved left her for a girl with softer hair than hers; of the supercilious looks she used to get from her cousins, who were from a lighter-skinned family; of having to take her meals apart from the family in the house where she worked as a maid for ten years. These things were not supposed to bother her; she was a magnificently faithful Catholic, and all adversity was supposed to rest lightly upon her shoulders. But bother her they did, and mightily. Her tears testified to that.

As with Mexico, a major force contextualizing this interaction was the state silence on racism in Brazil. Not only was color prejudice not supposed to bother Dona Maria but, according to Brazilian national ideology, it was not supposed to exist at all. Even though Burdick had a well-established relationship with Dona Maria, she only inadvertently breached the silence on racism when she could not contain her dismay and emotions surrounding this particular incident.

In her fieldwork, Twine (1998) also found that the government silence had trickled down to the populace. In the town where Twine conducted her research – a region with a history of planation slavery – many of the residents denied that slavery had ever operated there. However, several conversations with dark-skinned Afro-Brazilians suggested that they *chose* not to retain memories of African slave ancestors since they revealed some knowledge about their African slave origins. Twine interpreted their denial not as ignorance but as "willful forgetting."

A common way in which interpersonal silence is reinforced is through the "policing" of those who break the silence. One of Sue's more outspoken respondents, a 21-year-old university student, addressed this directly in a private conversation:

Do you really want to know about racism in Mexico? First things first, people don't talk about it. . . . It is like a topic that does not exist, as if it did not exist in this country. But deep down, everyone knows that it exists . . . you even sound bad talking about it. The people believe that if you talk about it that you are being difficult or too intense.

Jessica's interpretation of the silence on race mirrored Sue's experience in the field – if someone breaks the silence, they receive criticism and are frequently silenced.

As with government and institutional silence, in the rare instance in which the topic surfaces in everyday talk, it can be quickly re-disguised. One of Sue's respondents, a 57-year-old middle-class homemaker, immediately worked to re-conceal race talk when it became exposed in her own family. Her son, who has dark brown skin and eyes, came home one day and told his mom that he was rejected for a job at a local McDonald's because they were looking to hire employees who were "very light with blue or green eyes." She recalled, "I told him to not pay much attention, that maybe it was not the job that he deserved. . . . I calmed him down and invited him out to eat and it passed. And ever since, I haven't liked to bring it up because I feel that he was hurt, right? I continued on as usual and he forgot about it." According to Sue's respondent, they have never revisited what happened that day. This case can be understood as an illustration of collaborative avoidance (Durrheim et al., 2016) involving interpersonal policing.

Twine (1998) experienced being policed as a researcher. In both informal conversations and while conducting interviews, her respondents silenced her and accused her of being racist for calling attention to racial disparities in Brazil. Referencing a similar dynamic in the context of Cuba, one of Sawyer's (2006) respondents explained: "because racism is officially illegal but widely practiced, there is a taboo about talking about race. If you bring up racial issues, many will accuse you of being racist and the cause of the problem" (p. 129). Across these examples, we can see how the lack of discussion of silenced topics in popular discourse is partially the result of censoring and community policing. Needless to say, these dynamics pose serious obstacles to data collection.

Interview or Focus Group Silence

Despite the benefits of naturalistic methods (Potter & Hepburn, 2005), sole reliance on these methods may not be feasible in contexts where naturally surfacing discourse on a silenced topic is exceedingly rare. That said, when asked to discuss a silenced issue in a more artificial setting such as an interview or focus group, people are oftentimes reluctant to engage. And if they do, the conversation can become ripe with discomfort, tension, and insecurity. An illustration of this comes from an interview Sue conducted with a 63-year-old working-class Mexican homemaker. During their conversation, the woman's husband (who has dark brown skin) was in the next room with only a doorframe separating them. When Sue introduced the topic of racism, the woman's demeanor instantly changed from calm and relaxed to alert and tense. When Sue gently asked if she had witnessed any specific instances of racism, the woman resorted to fervent eye signals and hand motions in the direction of her husband, to convey that he had suffered discrimination. However, she refused to verbalize her thoughts beyond a quick whisper of "they look down on him because of his color." Now that we have discussed various contexts in which social silences can manifest and the challenges they pose for researchers, we will turn to a discussion of potential strategies for navigating, understanding, and collecting data on the unsaid.

Strategies for Studying Silence

The following strategies for studying silence include both naturalistic and direct methods. We use the term "naturalistic" to mean that the "activity being [observed] would have happened as it would have anyway" (Potter & Hepburn, 2005, p. 16) regardless of the presence of the researcher. In contrast, "direct" methods are those that involve researcher intervention such as the use of interviews or focus groups and lead to data being gathered and actions occurring as a direct result of researcher intervention. When observing social phenomena via naturalistic methods, we suggest researchers be attuned to natural breaches, pay attention to humor, and listen for code words.

Be Attuned to Natural Breaches

Naturalistic methods, such as paying attention to breaches in a silence, are an ideal way to study the unsaid (for a discussion of the strength of naturalistic methods, see Potter & Hepburn, 2005). Even the most entrenched silences are periodically ruptured. Here we discuss two noteworthy breaches Sue encountered in the field, analysis of which significantly informed her research. First, she came across an editorial published in a Mexican newspaper titled "The Next Benito Juárez Will Not be President of Mexico . . . but of the United States" (Zapata, 2004). Juárez is the twenty-sixth president of Mexico who is revered among Mexicans. Among other things, he is known for being the first (and only) Indigenous president of Mexico. In the editorial, the author, César Fernando Zapata, a Mexican national working in the United States, proclaimed that racism is rampant in Mexico and that the Mexican strain of racism is even worse than that of United States. The article seemed destined to provoke controversy as it violated the treaty of silence on racism.

In an effort to better understand the consequences of breaking the silence, Sue contacted Zapata, inquiring about the reaction he had received from readers. In a personal email communication, Zapata characterized the feedback as representing the "extremes" – he was either congratulated for his sincerity, and for being "right on the mark," or insulted for being pro-Yankee, anti-Mexican, and a sellout. These responses are telling and largely encapsulate the complications and ironies that surround social silences. The "right on the mark" kind of comment suggests there is a latent, unspoken truth about racism in Mexico that is known to Mexicans but not discussed. Summing up this position, Zapata wrote: "[Racism] is something that all of us Mexicans know. An 'open secret' as it is called. Few, however, dare to say it in public or recognize it, for fear of being pegged as anti-patriotic." Unfortunately, the social consequence of which Zapata wrote became his own reality. In breaking the silence on racism, his own patriotism and moral standing were called into question. Only in understanding what is at stake when disrupting Mexico's state-sponsored silence on racism can one appreciate and understand *why* Mexicans so actively enforce the silence. In this particular case, it was only through Zapata's breach in the silence that Sue was able to fully understand and appreciate the social norms and consequences surrounding the silence on racism.

A breach on a much larger scale occurred when the Mexican government issued a commemorative stamp series of Memín Pinguín, a popular black Mexican comic book character. This attracted negative attention from a number of high-profile African Americans who saw Memín as a negative black stereotype. The controversy intensified when the administration of President George W. Bush issued a statement condemning Mexico's endorsement of what it perceived to be a racist image. In response, Mexican government officials and members of the populace collectively defended Memín, reaffirming the national stance that Mexico is not racist. This controversy represented a highly visible breach in the traditional silence on race in Mexico. Consequently, Sue was able to gather an abundance of conversational data on the topic, data that spoke not only to how Mexicans understand and interpret racism but also to how silence is restored post-rupture.

Pay Attention to Humor

Humor can become a socially acceptable way of communicating about a silenced subject and is thus a kind of breach, but a subtler version. Jokes can serve as a channel for covert communication in contexts where discussion of the topic is unacceptable if conducted in a serious tone (Emerson, 1969). Humorous talk can thus open up "a discursive space within which it becomes possible to speak about matters that are otherwise naturalized, unquestioned, or silenced" (Goldstein, 2003, p. 10).

From a Freudian perspective, humor can become an outlet for the enjoyment of what is normally repressed in discourse (Billig, 1997). Therefore, attention to and analysis of humor can provide privileged access to socially silenced topics.

An illustration of this comes from Sue's observations in schools. She witnessed in classrooms different instances of racial humor, which not only exposed her to racial discourse but also provided her with naturally surfacing conversation prompts. For example, after observing the classroom of a 43-year-old teacher, Sue asked him about some of the joking she had witnessed. He explained:

If a black student arrives, someone always begins to make jokes about them, but it never goes beyond joking. I mean it is nothing cruel like hitting them or keying their car. . . .

CS: And how would that black student react? Would they be laughing and everything?
BERNARDO: On some occasions, they are upset because everything depends on the kind of mood they are in when they come to class.
CS: And do you think this is okay?
BERNARDO: I think it is not okay when the comment is made cruelly or to attack or belittle someone but when it is done in a joking manner . . . it is not a problem.

Sue's observations of racial jokes provided her with an opening to talk about race and better understand how race talk is expressed in society. However, she also noted that people perceived race humor differently, depending on their positionality. Nevertheless, because racial humor is generally not publicly acknowledged as a form of racism in contexts such as Mexico and Peru (Sue & Golash-Boza, 2013), it is not censored in the same way. Racial humor thus provides an opportunity to uncover local meanings associated with race talk and local understandings of prejudice (see Durrheim et al., 2016).

Listen for Code Words

Although coded speech is not the direct equivalent of silence, it is one of the ways people talk around a silenced topic without being overt. Therefore, we argue that being attuned to code words or terms used for the purpose of concealment is an effective tool for identifying and studying silence. In Mexico, as with other contexts (e.g., Pollock, 2004; Twine, 1998), Sue found that many non-racial terms are coded with racial meaning, providing a language with which people can indirectly talk about race (e.g., some job advertisements included the phrase "good appearance," which can refer to light skin and European features, among other things). These code words are connected to conceptual associations with race, such as economic status – lightness and European features signify wealth, whereas darkness and Indigenous or African heritage signal poverty. The effect is that race talk is frequently coded in class terms. Sue was able to identify this through attentiveness to discursive "slips." For example, a 54-year-old day care worker described a hypothetical job situation as follows:

> Two people are going to look for a secretary position. Two young ladies, let's say. One goes all fixed up in a suit and the other one, even though she has the same level of skills, has a humble appearance and is not well-groomed like the other one. Even though *the ind – the most humble one* [emphasis added] will be accepted, the one that goes nicely dressed will be accepted first.

Here, the respondent was going to use a racial term ("Indian") but then switched to a class term ("humble," meaning poor). Slippages such as these alerted Sue that, in some cases, race talk *was* occurring but in covert forms.

In her ethnographic research at a lesbian, gay, bisexual, transgender, and queer (LGBTQ) youth drop-in center in the United States, Robertson found that paying attention to code words helped her understand the tensions she had observed between white youth and youth of color, which were not openly discussed. She became attuned to how the silence on race was subtly breached through encoded language. For example, in a conversation she had with the program director about low attendance after a recent relocation of the facility, the director explained that he had overheard a white youth complaining that the new space is "too ghetto." This reference was unlikely to be related to class as the new facility was in an entirely renovated building in an upscale neighborhood. It was much more likely to be a reference to black and brown youth, thus alluding to race without directly mentioning it (see Durrheim et al., 2016 for discussion). Picking up on the subtle ways that white youth used code words to implicitly talk about race helped Robertson recognize breaches in the silence that were taking place under the radar. Finally, Penglase's (2009) work on drug trafficking in Brazilian shantytowns also highlights the importance of understanding ambiguous terms when researching silenced topics or "public secrets." He found shantytown residents use "indirection in comments that seem to be talking about no one in particular, but which are, in fact, describing drug traffickers" (p. 57). Being able to identify the subtle linguistic ways in which individuals talk about silenced topics is crucial to studies of the unsaid. Although the use of naturalistic methods such as these is ideal in many ways, relying solely on such methods may result in an abundance of nonoccurrences in the field. We therefore also recommend the use of more direct methods such as conducting interviews or focus groups. When using these methods, particular techniques can help facilitate discussions of the silenced topic, like removing individuals from particular settings, using hypothetical debates or scenarios, using local prompts, and using a direct approach to stimulate conversation on the silenced topic.

Remove Individuals from Settings That Enforce Silence

Another strategy for minimizing risks and discomforts associated with discussing silenced topics is to have conversations outside of settings in which the silence is being actively maintained. For example, in cases in which silences are perpetuated by the government or particular institutions, the researcher should avoid talking about the silenced topic in affiliated settings, especially with representatives or employees of these organizations/institutions, to avoid any concern of being overheard, and to minimize the organizational/institutional aspects of respondents' identities. When in the field, Sue noticed a significant difference in the willingness of a 40-year-old teacher to discuss delicate issues in his school environment compared to outside of it. In the school, when discussing Catholicism, he shared his belief that the Virgin of Guadalupe – a beloved Mexican symbol – was a Spanish invention designed to control the Indigenous masses. But as he was doing so, he lowered his voice and looked around, apparently concerned with being overheard even though the building was clearly empty. Sue did not push the conversation but referenced it at another time, when at her apartment, in which the teacher followed up, speaking at length with confidence and self-assurance. Similarly, Pollock (2004) found that her respondents were much more likely to "de-race" their public talk in educational settings compared to private settings. These examples illustrate how settings representing silences can stifle conversations about silenced topics as well as impede the ability of the researcher to provide a safe and comfortable environment that is conducive to discussion.

Use Hypothetical Debates or Scenarios

Another useful tool for encouraging discussion about silenced topics in an interview or focus group setting is the introduction of hypothetical scenarios or debates. During her interviews, Sue described a hypothetical scenario for discussion: "Two individuals apply for a manager position. They are both well spoken, have similar educational backgrounds, and meet the qualifications for the job. However, one has very light skin and the other has dark brown skin." People generally opined that the light-skinned applicant would be given preference, a response that then served as an entrée into a broader conversation about race in Mexico. One of the reasons that the hypothetical scenario strategy is effective is that it allows respondents to talk *around* a silenced topic in a depersonalized way, thus enabling a less-threatening and lower-risk conversation.

Ethnographer Patricia Adler has adopted a similar strategy, introducing debates into her interviews (Adler, personal communication, September 12, 2013). She presents a sociological debate to her participants (e.g., "some sociologists think ... while others believe ... ") and then asks for their opinion. With this approach, it is important to present both sides so that respondents are not "led" toward one position. This tactic works well in silenced situations because it takes the burden off the researcher and respondent from having to directly breach the silence since the debate is already on the table. The abstract nature of this approach allows respondents to assert an opinion at less personal risk, as they are simply weighing in on an extant controversy.

Use Local Prompts

The use of a prompt such as a local cultural reference, which introduces the silenced topic, can stimulate informal, interview, or even focus group conversation. In a focus group setting, Sue screened the Mexican film classic – *Angelitos Negros* [Little Black Angels] – which presents a rare engagement with the topic of racism. She then asked her participants to discuss the film without having to introduce the topic of racism or provide terms for the discussion, since the film was on the silenced theme. This technique is advantageous not only because conversation on a silenced issue is not contingent on an individual breaching the silence but also because it comes from the local context, thus minimizing external categories and frameworks.

Use a Direct Approach

Lastly, Sheriff (2000) advocates the use of a technique that she calls "metadiscursive" data collection; "metadiscursive" data are those that are "constituted by informants' elicited statements about their silence, rather than silence and/or unmediated linguistic behavior itself" (p. 115). Employing this technique in Brazil, she asked informants explicitly about why race and racism are silenced in Brazil. A similar approach could be to ask participants: "Have you ever witnessed the silence being broken? If so, what happened? If not, what do you think might happen? How might you or others react?" This approach "calls out" the silence, but in a way aimed to facilitate understanding of the reasons, meanings, and emotions behind it.

Taken together, we offer these suggestions as potential tools that may assist researchers in studying the unsaid. However, their usefulness will ultimately be determined by the sensitivity of the researcher to the local contexts, as well as other issues such as researcher positionality. In particular, researchers must use caution when employing direct methods, especially when one is an outsider to the environment being studied.

On Silence and Positionality

Researchers' classed, gendered, and raced positions, among others, always affect the research experience, and the study of silence is no exception. In this section, we provide a few examples to illustrate how researcher positionality interacts with the study of silence in various ways. Beginning with the main substantive theme addressed in this article – racism in the Americas – US investigators of this topic have retrospectively noted that nothing in the literature or their academic training prepared them for studying race cross-culturally (Stanfield II, 1993; Twine, 1998, 2000), much less in environments where talk of racism is silenced. For example, without much methodological advice available to her, Twine (2000) went into the field anticipating that Afro-Brazilians would be more willing to open up about racism with her, compared to a white researcher. However, she found this was not the case. Instead, she was treated with suspicion and distrust, likely related to her position as a national outsider and a black person, given the lack of feelings of solidarity among those of African descent. Sue's experience as a mixed (white/Chinese) "American" also affected her interactions with participants. While being a light-skinned American gave her authenticity as a researcher and access to a variety of people and social settings, she still encountered a number of barriers when trying to study the silence on racism.

When reflecting on the effect of one's positionality, it is important to recognize that researchers' identities interact with a *preconditioned environment*. In other words, the social context of research is shaped by "the historical, cultural, and political structures and discourses that frame the meanings and experiences of researchers and research participants within the research interaction" (Gunaratnam, 2003, p. 159). In the case of Mexico, not only is light skin valorized, but the post-Revolutionary ideology used the United States as an explicit comparative reference for its assertion that Mexico did not suffer from the racist virus. This preconditioned environment not only silences discussion of racism, but also the silencing mechanisms are strengthened in the presence of anything or anyone representing the United States. Sue's Americanness thus became a point of reference in her field interactions, similar to what happened with Lamont (2004) when she interviewed people in very different positions in terms of nationality and class. Lamont found that her respondents "made me part of their script, and used my identity as a prop to define who they are, by opposition or otherwise" (Lamont, 2004, p. 166). Along these lines, Roth (2012) notes that people have multiple schemas in their cognitive portfolios that can be triggered by particular situations. This is related to the importance of the positionality of the informant, whose reasons and motivations for silences around race and racism may have much to do with their own racial and class positions, in addition to those of the researcher. Ultimately, the positionality of the respondent, the researcher, and the situational and interactional nature of the research-participant interaction need to be taken into account when studying silence.

Conclusion

Although there are many barriers to studying social silences such as those surrounding race, the endeavor is a worthy one. Inquiry into social silences is important because topics are oftentimes buried, censored, or stigmatized *because of their significance*. In addition to shedding light on the substantive aspects of silenced topics, such as racism, studies of silence can also illuminate dynamics related to hegemony, culture, and inequality. Yet social scientists have not fully taken advantage of the opportunity to understand hegemonic processes through the study of silence. We believe ethnographic methods are particularly well suited to study the unsaid and the underlying mechanisms through which hegemony is achieved.

In placing the spotlight on silenced issues, especially those related to race, we hope to call attention to the relative paucity of research that exists on such topics, despite their importance. As Zerubavel (2007) notes: "What we ignore socially is also ignored academically, and conspiracies of silence are therefore still an under-theorized as well as understudied phenomenon" (p. 182). Consistent with Zerubavel, we believe that the academy as an institutional gatekeeper is often complicit in perpetuating particular silences via a lack of attention. We hope that the strategies for studying social silences proposed in this chapter will prove useful for researchers attempting to study the unsaid.

References

Aguirre Beltran, G. (1944). The slave trade in Mexico. *The Hispanic American Historical Review, 24*(3), 412–430.

Augoustinos, M., & Every, D. (2007). The language of "race" and prejudice: A discourse of denial, reason, and liberal-practical politics. *Journal of Language and Social Psychology, 26*(2), 123–141.

Billig, M. (1997). The dialogic unconscious: Psychoanalysis, discursive psychology and the nature of repression. *British Journal of Social Psychology, 36,* 139–159.

Billig, M (1999). *Freudian repression: Conversation creating the unconscious.* Cambridge: Cambridge University Press.

Body-Gendrot, S. (2004) Race, a word too much? The French dilemma. In M. Bulmer & J. Solomos (Eds.), *Researching race and racism* (pp. 150–161). London: Routledge.

Bonilla-Silva, E. (2003). *Racism without racists: Color-blind racism and the persistence of racial inequality in the United States.* Lanham: Rowman & Littlefield.

Bulmer, M., & Solomos, J. (Eds.). (2004). *Researching race and racism.* London; New York: Routledge.

Burdick, J. (1998). *Blessed Anastacia: Women, race, and popular Christianity in Brazil.* New York: Routledge.

Castagno, A. E. (2008). 'I don't want to hear that!': Legitimating whiteness through silencing in schools. *Anthropology & Education Quarterly, 39*(3), 314–333.

Durrheim, K., Quayle M., & Dixon, J. (2016). The struggle for the nature of 'prejudice': 'Prejudice' expression as identity performance. *Political Psychology, 37*(1), 17–35.

Emerson, J. (1969). Negotiating the serious import of humor. *Sociometry, 32*(2), 169–181.

Essed, P. (2004). Naming the unnameable: Sense and sensibilities in researching racism. In M. Bulmer & J. Solomos (Eds.), *Researching race and racism* (pp. 119–133). London: Routledge.

Goldstein, D. (2003). *Laughter out of place: Race, class, violence, and sexuality in a Rio shantytown.* Berkeley: University of California Press.

Gramsci, A. (1971). *Selections from the prison notebooks.* New York: International Publishers.

Gunaratnam, Y. (2003). *Researching 'race' and ethnicity: Methods, knowledge and power.* London: Sage Publications.

Hirschauer, S. (2007). Puttings things into words: Ethnographic description and the silence of the social. *Human Studies, 29*(4), 413–441.

Lamont, M. (2004). A life of sad, but justified, choices: Interviewing across (too) many divides. In M. Bulmer & J. Solomos (Eds.), *Researching race and racism* (pp. 162–171). London: Routledge.

Loveman, M. (2014). *National colors: Racial classification and the State in Latin America.* New York: Oxford University Press.

Martínez Casas, R, Saldívar, E., Flores R. D., & Sue, C. A. (2014). The different faces of Mestizaje: Ethnicity and race in Mexico. In E. E. Telles & the Project on Ethnicity and Race in Latin America (PERLA) (Eds.), *Pigmentocracies:*

Ethnicity, race, and color in Latin America (pp. 36–80). Chapel Hill: University of North Carolina Press.

Penglase, B. (2009). States of insecurity: Everyday emergencies, public secrets, and drug trafficker power in a Brazilian favela.*PoLAR: Political and Legal Anthropology Review, 32*(1), 47–63.

Pollock, M. (2004). *Colormute: Race talk dilemmas in an American school.* Princeton: Princeton University Press.

Potter, J., & Hepburn, A. (2005). Qualitative interviews in psychology: Problems and possibilities. *Qualitative Research in Psychology, 2,* 281–307.

Roth, W. (2012). *Race migrations: Latinos and the cultural transformation of race.* Stanford: Stanford University Press.

Sawyer, M. (2006). *Racial politics in post-revolutionary Cuba.* Cambridge: Cambridge University Press.

Sheriff, R. E. (2000). Exposing silence as cultural censorship: A Brazilian case. *American Anthropologist, 102,* 114–132.

Sheriff, R. E. (2001). *Dreaming equality: Color, race and racism in urban Brazil.* New Brunswick: Rutgers University Press.

Simon, P. (2017). The failure of the importation of ethno-racial statistics in Europe: Debates and controversies. *Ethnic and Racial Studies, 40*(13), 2326–2332.

Stanfield II, J. H. (1993). Methodological reflections: An introduction. In J. H. Stanfield & R. M. Dennis (Eds.), *Race and ethnicity in research methods* (pp.3–15). Newbury Park: Sage Publications.

Sue, C. A. (2013). *Land of the cosmic race: Racism, race mixture, and blackness in Mexico.* New York: Oxford University Press.

Sue, C. A., & Golash-Boza, T (2013). 'It was only a joke': How racial humour fuels colour-blind ideologies in Mexico and Peru. *Ethnic and Racial Studies, 36* (10), 1582–1598.

Sue, D. W. (2015). *Race talk and the conspiracy of silence: Understanding and facilitating different dialogues on race.* Hoboken, NJ: Wiley.

Taussig, M. (1999). *Defacement: Public secrecy and the labor of the negative.* Palo Alto, CA: Stanford University Press.

Twine, F. W. (1998). *Racism in a racial democracy: The maintenance of white supremacy in Brazil.* New Brunswick: Rutgers University Press.

Twine, F. W. (2000). Racial ideologies and racial methodologies. In F. W. Twine & J. W. Warren (Eds.), *Racing research, researching race: Methodological dilemmas in critical race studies* (pp. 1–34). New York: New York University Press.

Van Dijk, T. A. (1992). Discourse and the denial of racism. *Discourse and Society, 3*(1), 87–118.

Villarreal, A. (2010). Stratification by skin color in contemporary Mexico. *American Sociological Review, 75*(5), 652–678.

Warren, J. W. (2001). *Racial revolutions: Antiracism and Indian resurgence in Brazil.* Durham: Duke University Press.

Warren, J. W. & Sue, C. A. (2011). Comparative racisms: What antiracists can learn from Latin America. *Ethnicities, 11*(1), 32–58.

Zapata, C. F. (2004, June 25.) The next Benito Juárez will not be president of Mexico . . . but of the United States. *Desde las Entrañas del Monstruo.* Retrieved from http://cesarfernando.blogspot.com/2004/06/el-prximo-benito-jurez-no-s er.html.
Zerubavel, E. (2007). The social structure of denial: A formal sociological analysis of conspiracies of silence. In I. Reed & J. C. Alexander (Eds.), *Culture, society and democracy: The interpretive approach* (pp. 181–189). Boulder: Paradigm Publishers.

5 Intimate Silences and Inequality: Noticing the Unsaid through Triangulation

Amy Jo Murray and Nicole Lambert

Silence permeates intimate spaces. For years, intimate silences such as sexual abuse and harassment – in Hollywood and in less glamorous or public places such as the office or the home – have shaped social action. In the wake of the Harvey Weinstein scandal, powerful Hollywood actresses began speaking out about the abuses they have suffered in the entertainment industry. Now, with movements like #MeToo and Time's Up, people are talking about violence and exploitation in intimate relationships (Langone, 2018). These slogans that encourage people to speak out about sexual harassment testify to the existence of the silence in the first place. Abuses were happening. Violations were taking place. Women – and in some cases men as well – were being victimized. Yet nothing was said: silence. The unsaid lurks in the background as we go about our lives, especially when these silences implicate intimacies that are uncomfortable and maintain inequality.

Social scientists have long been concerned with addressing social inequality and the impacts of inequality in society. Inequality impacts all facets of society and exists between groups with differing social power (such as between whites and other racial groups), but also within members of the same group (for example, between men and women of the same race). Inequality impacts income, quality of education, where we live, whom we marry, whom our friends are, our health, our daily interactions, our chances to improve our lives and the lives of our families, and much more (Beeghley, 2008). Researchers have uncovered how structural policies, cultural stereotypes, and daily microaggressions maintain and perpetuate social inequality (Mandel, 2009; Sue et al., 2007; Tatum, 2003).

More recently, attention has been paid not only to what *is* said or done but also to how silence – or what *is not* said or done – perpetuates social inequalities to maintain the status quo. In this sense, we use the terms "silence," "absence," and the "unsaid" to indicate that "a person *when speaking* does not relate to a particular topic" (Kurzon, 2007, p. 1677, emphasis in original), as opposed to audible silences such as pauses,

89

hesitations, or other gaps in speech. The unsaid can produce inequality when individuals remain silent about marginalizing, unjust talk, actions, or politics that affect them and their community (Bhattacharya, 2009; Carpenter & Austin, 2007; Sheriff, 2000); organizations and institutions maintain silence about power structures, social practices, and official policies that might require inclusivity, change, and costs (Macalpine & Marsh, 2005; O'Malley, 2005; Ward & Winstanley, 2003); and governments and politicians might foreground certain topics while backgrounding others that would threaten vested interests and existing hegemonic ideology (Crenshaw, 1997; Jaworski, 1993; Sue, 2015). What we can-(not) do and say to and about each other can produce and maintain inequality. In the broadest sense, the unsaid obscures social inequalities by driving them underground, thus making them resistant to change and ensuring the continuation of extant power structures (Hirschauer, 2006; Murray & Durrheim, 2018; Sue, 2015).

Irvine (2011) likens the unsaid with the act of ignoring so obvious a presence as an 800-pound gorilla. He argues, "the way we tiptoe around the 800-pound gorilla in the room can be precisely the way we acknowledge, and reveal its presence" (p. 32). This metaphor is useful for two reasons. First, it highlights the collective nature of the unsaid. It is always a collective process because silence "demands collaboration and the tacit communal understandings that such collaboration presupposes" (Sheriff, 2000, p. 114). In other words, people agree collectively – most often without saying – that something should go unsaid (Billig, 2004; Zerubavel, 2006). Second, our avoidance of something reveals that something is being avoided, and "in this way, the unsayable will be present, even if marked by its absence" (Billig, 1997a, p. 151).

But how can we know that something is absent? How can we see that which is made invisible, ignored, denied, omitted, or skirted around? These are difficult issues, especially since the unsaid is extremely – and necessarily – ambiguous and context dependent (Jaworski, 1993; Schröter, 2013). Because absences can take different forms (Ward & Winstanley, 2003); can be viewed as "both strategies and impositions" (Carpenter & Austin, 2007, p. 669); and do not have clear, defined analytical boundaries (Huckin, 2002; Mazzei, 2004), they can be difficult to pin down.

This chapter will discuss the possibilities for using triangulation to analyze absence – as a way of seeing who "tiptoes" around what – and will then situate that discussion using two case studies. The case studies show how absences – what Mazzei (2004, p. 1130) refers to as those "unspoken silences that speak volumes" – maintain gendered, racial, class, and immigrant hierarchies in two locations – South Africa and the

United States. Both studies found that intimate topics such as sexuality and interpersonal violence were kept silent in particular contexts or by particular groups. These silences allow hegemonic social action to continue unquestioned, thereby maintaining fundamental inequalities (Murray & Durrheim, 2018). While the content and context of the case studies were very different, both studies relied on layered data and triangulation to reveal absences and the social actions they produced in deeply charged, divided, and unequal societies. Based on the discussion, we will conclude with some suggestions for studying the unsaid in qualitative research.

Noticing the Unsaid through Triangulation

In our separate research studies, we found that the tiptoeing that Irvine (2011) suggests was made clearer when layered data – referring to multi-method and/or dyadic research – were examined "in conversation with one another by interrogating the dissonant findings ... to uncover new knowledge" (Hesse-Biber, 2012, p. 144) through triangulation. Triangulation allows for comparisons to be made between layers of data and for their meanings and achievements to be interrogated as participants tiptoe in different ways for particular audiences (Perlesz & Lindsay, 2003). Triangulating multiple sources of data can assist in noticing when people tiptoe and why, comparing how the tiptoeing takes place across participants and contexts. It might be useful to clarify our use of the term "triangulation," especially since it can potentially bring a fair amount of baggage to the discussion (Denzin, 2010; Flick, 2017). This is echoed by Hesse-Biber's (2012, p. 137) statement: "the concept of triangulation takes on a broad spectrum in its definition and praxis over decades of usage within the social sciences – from a tool of convergence with the goal of validation, to one that seeks divergence in the service of complexity and richness of understanding".

Triangulation has been used to make sense of "silences and discrepancies" (Nightingale, 2003a, p. 81) in research across various contexts (see Nightingale, 2003a, 2003b, 2006; Perlesz & Lindsay, 2003; Vikström; 2003, 2010). In all of these cases, the researchers emphasize "the importance of going after conflicting results as a way to reveal new avenues of understanding and new research questions" (Hesse-Biber, 2012, p. 145). A prime area of research that can emerge from dissonant layered data is the study of the unsaid. Triangulation allows qualitative researchers to demonstrate the presence of an absence – often a difficult task – by comparing sets of data, not to discount or minimize discrepancies but rather to look for and value discrepancies (Vikström, 2010). In this approach, silences and discrepancies are not faults in the data and do not discount each other but instead inform each other and, when looked at in relation to each other, can provide a new way of interpreting the data. Researchers can become more aware of the unsaid, noticing absences that are made present by looking across types and sources of data, and their differences (Nightingale, 2003a).

Once such absences have been noticed, perhaps we can learn more about what absences are doing in, through, and around us. In the case studies that will be presented, we used triangulation as an "analytical tool for looking at dissonant data and revealing new information that can further social change" (Hesse-Biber, 2012, p. 145). Noticing what is missing is the first step to understanding what those absences accomplish (Zerubavel, 2006). Triangulation can assist the researcher in stepping outside of taken-for-granted knowledge to notice social action that is being achieved, protected, or avoided through absence (Billig, 2004; Zerubavel, 2006). Once the silence has been noticed and acknowledged – as in the case of the #MeToo movement – possibilities for wider social change have the potential to emerge.

In the following case studies, Murray uses a dyadic research approach to examine silences around black sexuality and intimate spaces within the context of paid domestic labor in post-apartheid South Africa and how these silences protect racialized and gendered power and control. Lambert examines silences around intimate partner violence and child abuse in the undocumented student movement in the United States and how these maintain gendered inequality in the family. While these case studies exist in specific sociopolitical contexts and in distant geographical spaces and focus on different kinds of intimacies, both case studies deal with intimate silences that exist in society and are played out by the participants. However, it was only through the triangulation of layered data that we could notice these absences at all. In addition, bringing these two "distant" case studies together into a single chapter becomes a form of triangulation as well.

Post-Apartheid Paid Domestic Labor (Murray)

Paid domestic labor is a site of fundamental inequalities. According to Statistics South Africa (2017), there are around 996,000 female domestic workers, making this sector a major source of income for black South African women. Domestic labor is an important site of contact between poor black women and middle- to upper-class households, many of which are still predominantly white. This is largely because domestic work is an entanglement of race, class, gender, ethnicity, citizenship, and the fundamentally informal nature of the labor (Ally, 2010; du Toit 2010; Romero 1992).

Domestic labor exposes uncomfortable troubles regarding inequality, largely through the intense and intimate nature of the relationship, which takes place in the private spaces of elite households (Archer, 2011; Murray & Durrheim, 2018). In her seminal work on intimacy within the colonial empire, Stoler (2002, p. 133) notes that domestic workers become "subaltern gatekeepers of gender, class and racial distinctions that by their very presence they [transgress]." Boundaries are protected, reinforced, or transgressed in the domestic sphere as expectations, roles, and power play out between people, in both what is said and what is unsaid and unspeakable (Dickey, 2000; Stoler, 2002).

One such boundary that is particularly intimate is sexuality – black women are viewed with racist stereotypes such as being sexually promiscuous, adulterous, and uncivilized (Collins, 2004; Jenkins, 2007; Whisson & Weil, 1971). This construction leads to the imagined need for monitoring and control (Jenkins, 2007), namely by her female employer (Hansen, 1990). Various routines in domestic labor ensure that the fantasy of the domestic worker as chaste, virginal, and civilized is maintained. She wears a uniform instead of her own clothes. She is rarely allowed into private spaces or left alone with the employer's husband (Hansen, 1990; Nyamnjoh, 2005), intimacies that would be "uncomfortable, risky, and to be discouraged" (Nyamnjoh, 2005, p. 188). Furthermore, visitors – especially male visitors – are routinely not allowed onto the employer's property. All of these practices serve to naturalize her separation from men.

Yet this need for rules, monitoring, and restrictions creates a problem in the domestic labor relationship. The domestic worker is denied her rights to express her sexuality, especially if she is not allowed visitors onto a property where she is living. It is troubling to have such a right denied; despite her legal empowerment as a laborer and a citizen of post-apartheid South Africa, her sexuality remains under the gaze and control of her employer. For the employer, this level of power can also be troubling, especially since many white employers espouse liberal, non-racist ideals. Thus many employers exercise power in unwritten, ambiguous expectations so as to protect their power without allowing it to seem hierarchical or abusive (Archer, 2011).

This dynamic took shape as Murray conducted a dyadic research study involving black workers and white employers. The majority of research about this relationship involves only employers, only workers, or a third party such as a labor broker. However, by only looking at one side of the same story, we might overlook discrepancies and absences. In this study, diaries and interviews were used together (see Alaszweski, 2006) with five domestic labor employment pairs composed of a white employer with a black domestic worker who lived on the employer's property. In the diary, participants were asked to focus specifically on "conversations; things that they felt were left unsaid, things that they wish they could have said; topics that seemed salient but were not spoken about; and understandings of and feelings regarding such interactions." After three weeks of daily diary recording, each participant took part in an individual interview to explore their accounts and perceptions of the silences within their own diary and to debrief regarding the diary-keeping process. After the interviews were conducted, the dyads and events were matched to map the moments and accounts that had been expressed in the diaries and the individual interviews – for both the employers and the workers.

Silence about Intimate Spaces and Activities

By including both parties, this research was able to see how troubling issues were constructed from each point of view. Issues around male visitors, their legitimacy, and participants' orientations toward "inherent" dangers of male visitors occurred again and again. Yet some conspicuous discrepancies appeared when the employer and worker data were compared. Employers' and workers' talk about male visitors was oriented differently, creating different absences that reflect their unequal positions as classed and racialized citizens of post-apartheid South Africa.

In discussing the possibility of males visiting the domestic worker on the employer's property, employers avoided talking about their worker's sexuality. Instead, employers noted the dangerous, predatory nature of black men, as in the case of Rachel, who noted that "people thought we were crazy because we had a little girl as well. And how were we gonna let this black man live on our property?" foregrounding black male sexuality but leaving his sexual activity with the domestic worker as an absence. At other times, the very notion of sexual contact between a worker and her male visitor was viewed as mortally dangerous, as in the case of Tracy who "didn't want a repeat of the last situation" where the worker had a boyfriend who would visit but "she later contracted a disease and subsequently passed away," an utterance that a socially competent member of South Africa would hear as implying HIV/AIDS and its dangerous sexual origins. Yet sex as such remained implied but unspoken. Alternatively, some employers invoked identities of their workers that revolved around essentially maternal and asexual feminine features such as being a caregiver, nurse, or helper (as in the case of Judith, who is responsible for her daughter with cerebral palsy) or as "cute" and elderly (as in the case of Yoliswa, who lived with her elderly husband on the employer's property).

All of the employers acknowledged the lonely existence of being a domestic worker, but many still noted that their property, their family, and even the domestic worker needed to be protected from male visitors. In all of the cases in this study, the employers monitored the comings and goings of the worker and regulated – and in some cases prohibited – visitor access, such as when Tania's husband told Eunice, "We gave you a rule [that no visitors were allowed] and we'd like you to stick by that." These constructions avoided the topics of sexuality and sexual intimacy between male visitors and the workers and instead foregrounded issues related to the health, safety, and security of the employer household and their worker who needed to be monitored and regulated. Her right to engage in sexual activity and to express her sexuality with a partner were never mentioned. They are absences that haunt polite, protective, paternalistic conversations about safety and security.

For many workers in this study, the topic of (the restriction of) visitors is not mentioned at all, possibly implying that such regulations are natural and to be expected. Expressions of isolation and loneliness were framed as longing for family members, such as children or grandchildren, leaving the possibilities of romantic loneliness as a silence. However, two workers did discuss their male visitors. Both focused on the moral uprightness of their man, like Eunice who noted that her boyfriend "is not drinking. Is not smoking. Only is drinking tea," orienting away from the racist stereotype of the dangerous black male toward a construction of a docile, teetotaler. Eunice also referred to her partner as her husband, although they were not married, giving the relationship a more stable and virtuous gloss. Lindiwe worried that if her employer knew about her boyfriend, "maybe she gonna look me like I'm not a good girl. Maybe I'm a slut." In her interview, Lindiwe stated, "I am not planning to have another child. That is why I am using contraceptives and condoms to prevent infections." By stating that she is avoiding both pregnancy and a sexually transmitted disease such as HIV/AIDS, Lindiwe presents herself as a responsible, controlled woman and worker, thereby countering stereotypes of her sexuality that she imagines her employer might hold.

These constructions clearly orient away from stereotypes of black sexuality and its connotations of disease, immorality, and lack of control in the racist imagination (Jenkins, 2007). However, the purpose of constructing themselves and their male visitors as morally virtuous and sexually responsible is left unsaid. Why is it important to present oneself and one's sexual partner as "good" and for whose benefit? While there is a sense in which participants generally present themselves favorably in research interactions, the ultimate audience exists beyond the conversation between the researcher and participant, an audience that is invisible in these interactions but is ever-present in the paid domestic work relationship: the employer. The final moral judge of domestic workers and their visitors is the employer, who can deem such visits as dangerous or undesirable. Interestingly, none of the workers in this study highlight the power of their employer to refuse to admit male visitors onto the employer's property. The restriction of visitors or the complete lack of visitors is never questioned or challenged.

When the topic of male visitors is compared across employers and workers, a clear dissonance emerges. The issue of black sexuality forms the background against which the topic of male visitors is discussed. Employers do not speak about the rights of workers to engage in sexual activity with their partner but instead focus on the need to monitor and control visitations onto the property. Workers, while proclaiming the uprightness of themselves and their partner, do not mention the rights of employers to restrict access to intruders or intrusions onto their property. The rights of the counterpart regarding intimate spaces remain unspoken. Tiptoeing abounds! The effect is the naturalization and legitimation of privileged white control over the intimate activities of subaltern black women. While talking in certain ways about intimacies and intimate spaces, stereotypes that remain toxic within both black and white imaginations continue to maintain the gendered and racialized inequality of domestic labor, which reflects wider inequalities within post-apartheid South Africa. It is hearable, gestured toward, and oriented to but only made visible when we examine how each side (does not) talk about themselves and their counterpart. The dyadic nature of the research provided opportunities to notice the unsaid. The unsaid and its implications become present when the dissonances and slippages in the dyadic data are heard in relation to each other, revealing a new understanding of this issue.

The Undocumented Student Movement (Lambert)

There are an estimated 11.3 million undocumented immigrants in the United States of America, approximately 3 million of whom are 1.5-generation (Gonzales-Barrera & Krogstad, 2017). Although exact definitions of "1.5-generation" immigrants differ, the term broadly refers to anyone born in another country who migrated to the United States before the age of 16 (Rumbaut, 2004). The terms "undocumented youth," "1.5-generation undocumented immigrants," and "undocumented students" are used interchangeably throughout the chapter. Restrictive immigration policies construct the "illegal alien" as a *"legal and political subject* whose inclusion within the nation was simultaneously a social reality and a legal impossibility – a subject barred from citizenship and without rights" (Ngai, 2004, p. 4, emphasis in original). Undocumented immigrants are physically present within the boundaries of the nation but legally, socially, and culturally invisible (Coutin, 2002). Illegality enables the arbitrary rescinding of rights by citizens and makes undocumented immigrants reliant on convincing those who can vote to act on their behalf (De Genova, 2002).

For undocumented youth, their school experiences prior to university education are in many ways similar to their peers. In the 1980s, the Supreme Court ruled a proposed ban on providing K-12 education for undocumented children unconstitutional. Thus, across the United States, undocumented youth intermingle with their documented classmates without having to reveal their documentation status. However, they find their desires for continued education and better-paying jobs than those their parents have stifled by their legal status (Ábrego, 2006; Gonzales, 2011). Undocumented youth realize that they cannot work certain jobs or apply for college scholarships because of their legal status (Gonzales, 2011). Knowledge of the American political system and newly intensified consequences of illegality in adulthood inspires many 1.5-generation undocumented immigrants to protest for their legal and cultural inclusion (Ábrego, 2011; Pallares & Flores-González, 2010). Undocumented youth activists have learned to make compelling rights claims, lobby politicians for immigration forms, and undertake "die-ins" and other public protests to bring attention to their cause (Nicholls, 2013).

A key element of undocumented student activism is "telling your story": Fiorito and Nicholls (2016) argue that the undocumented student narrative is three pronged: (1) youth came to the country at a young age without a say in the migration decision, (2) they face many challenges due to documentation status, and (3) they work hard to overcome the challenges they face. The different struggles undocumented youth describe – educational obstacles, financial struggles, fear of deportation, and family separation – are told in particular contexts in particular ways that serve to maintain or deconstruct the hegemonic undocumented student narrative, as outlined earlier. However, this narration is always undertaken in a broader political and cultural context that restricts available discourses. It is not as simple as deliberately silencing one type of narrative or thinking some experiences are more important than others; rather, gender, immigration status, racialization, and fear of potential negative consequences shape which narratives get told, which do not, and why.

Over the course of six years, Lambert used a combination of semi-structured in-depth interviews and participant observation to study the undocumented student movement in the Mountain West region of the United States. The interviews asked broad, open-ended questions about participants' migration history; racial, ethnic, and national identities; why they got involved in activism; and the challenges they face in their lives. Combining participant observation and interviewing enabled the observation of, and interaction with, undocumented 1.5-generation immigrants in a variety of settings. These settings included one-on-one interviews, organizational meetings, conferences, testimony given at legislative hearings, information sessions on policies, invited presentations on college campuses, protests, and community theater presentations. With a variety of data at her disposal, Lambert felt well prepared to analyze the intricacies of undocumented student activism; however, an unexpected finding emerged: the role of family violence in the lives of undocumented youth.

Silence about Intimate Violence

The reoccurring interview narrative of family violence was unexpected for several reasons: (1) violence is scarcely mentioned in existing literature on the 1.5-generation (and, when mentioned, is almost always in the context of violence occurring *prior* to migration), (2) violence was an infrequent public narrative, and (3) there were no interview questions about violence and trauma. The narratives of violence emerged while asking participants why/how they first came to the United States and to "Describe your family." Family members, mainly fathers, committed the bulk of violence discussed by interviewees. The question about family – originally intended to give background information – provided insight into topics left unsaid. Interviewees spoke of child abuse, having family members hold their legal status over their heads to convince them not to tell anyone about the abuse they experienced, and witnessing their mother's being abused by boyfriends or husbands. The quote that follows is from Guadalupe, whose narrative perfectly illustrates the issues discussed earlier. After she remarked that she thinks of her dad as an "angry man" when asked about her family, she responded to a request to provide further details by saying the following:

The first thing that comes to mind is that he would physically abuse my brother and me a lot growing up. . . . For a long time, my dad would tell us that we couldn't say anything to anyone because if we called the cops on him we were all going to get deported so that was really how he held us under; that all the things we had worked for would go down the drain and we would get deported if we said anything.

Later on in the interview, she came back to discussing family violence and talked about how her mother never got involved to stop the violence, so when she was old enough she moved out to stop it. Guadalupe's narrative demonstrates how silence operates in multiple ways – not talking to anyone about the violence she experienced out of fear of deportation and silence in her own family regarding the violence (i.e., her mother). In addition to the interpersonal silence, she has not talked about her experiences publicly because to do so would break the larger cultural taboos surrounding family violence in US society.

In limited cases, violence was discussed publicly; however, it was always in the context of violence that occurred before migration, providing a justification for migrating to the United States without authorization. In one instance, Ana describes how her mother brought her and her younger brother to the United States when Ana was 16 to escape her violent husband. She says that although it would mean that they would struggle financially, it was worth the dangers they incurred crossing the border using a *coyote* (human smuggler) to escape the violence. Ana believes that her mother made the right decision by leaving her father, even if it meant migrating without authorization. Similarly, Julie, a Mexican woman in her late twenties, explains that her mother left her father because he was emotionally abusive and tried to force her mother to abort her pregnancy with Julie. Although Julie has never met her father, he has refused to allow Julie's stepfather to adopt her. Thus, she has been unable to legalize her immigration status.

In both of these cases, women's decisions to leave their country of origin and come to the United States were influenced by men attempting to control women's decisions through violence or coercion. Although the content of these narratives is similar to that only spoken about in interviews, the previous examples were told publicly because they conform to existing stereotypes about Latino men and construct migration, even unauthorized migration, as necessary for the safety of their families. Additionally, experiencing and witnessing abuse are traumatic experiences, which makes talking about them publicly all the more challenging for undocumented students who are already grappling with potentially anti-immigrant audiences when talking to the media, legislators, and other community members.

Child abuse and intimate partner violence are underreported crimes, particularly among members of communities of color in the United States, who are often distrustful of police and other organizations with racist practices (Raj & Silverman, 2002). Family violence is an "open secret" – a topic understood to be happening but not to be discussed (Hirschauer, 2006). Official data on child abuse and intimate partner violence are sometimes metaphorically described as an "iceberg" – the reported cases represent only a small number of actual cases each year (Gracia, 2004). Sometimes this represents an absolute silence; however, research also suggests that in some cases abuse is known to people besides the victim, yet a culture of silence and victim blaming results in inaction (Gracia, 2004). Although this is a common facet of US society, undocumented immigrant Latinas' positionality in the social structure makes them more vulnerable to abuse due to their place in race, class, gender, and immigrant hierarchies, makes their abusers more likely to hold their (or their own) legal status over their heads as means of forcing silence, and creates cultural barriers to help seeking. The threat of deportation of *all* undocumented family members (not just the abuser) adds an additional layer of fear of discussing these issues. Furthermore, undocumented student activists are working toward immigration reform. Narratives that discuss negative community characteristics are silenced to avoid political setbacks.

Taken together, US society generally discourages conversations around family violence, the marginalized positionality of undocumented immigrant Latinas leads to a silence around family violence, and the broader immigrant rights movement avoids public discussions of violence. In terms of its impacts, undocumented youth learn that in exchange for the (still unmet) promise of immigration reform, certain narratives (such as those of family violence and other forms of criminal behavior) must be left unsaid. This silence maintains the "open secret" of family violence in undocumented immigrant families. The use of multiple data sources uncovered how family abuse was or was not talked about in different settings. The implications of this unsaid narrative in the lives of undocumented youth and their families only become visible when analyzing data sources in conjunction with one another.

Conclusions

In our separate studies, we had to grapple with how to show that an absence was present. Absence has been described as "an exceptionally slippery subject" (Frickel, 2014, p. 89) and "diffuse and wily" (Rappert & Bauchspies, 2014, p. 2). When studying absence, it is important to notice "what is not said, but could easily have been, and, indeed, on occasions is almost said but then removed from the conversation" (Billig, 1997b, p. 152). In both case studies, that which goes unsaid across contexts or participants became central to the maintenance of inequality, and triangulating layered data revealed meaningful slippages and absences that would have otherwise remained "unnamed, unnoticed, and unspoken" (Mazzei, 2008, p. 1129). It was possible to build a persuasive case for an absence through the triangulation of layered data or multiple sources and types of data to see how participants are tiptoeing and around which issues. Triangulation made absence within and between sources of data more apparent and, by focusing on dissonance and silence, a richer and more complex understanding of data was achieved – an understanding that would be less likely without triangulation (Hesse-Biber, 2012; Perlesz & Lindsay, 2003). By looking at what was (not) said in particular contexts or by particular participants and why this was the case, we became aware of issues, identities, or positionings that were kept invisible, subjugated, or marginalized as a form of social action (Hesse-Biber, 2012; Nightingale, 2003a; Perlesz & Linday, 2003; Vikström, 2003, 2010).

The issue of audience may be a particularly salient one when studying troubling topics, such as intimacies, in qualitative research because what is (not) said may be produced differently across specific settings or audiences. The use of layered data allowed us to notice that something was missing in some settings by particular social actors, that something was being omitted or only partially addressed here instead of there, or that something seemed to be crying out for attention and acknowledgment in one set of data but was, indeed, a non-topic in another. By understanding the situated nature of data and the specific context from which the data emerge, including the particular research dynamics at play, layers of data can be placed in mutual dialogue and understood not just in terms of what is present but to highlight what is absent and the social actions that those absences achieve (Perlesz & Lindsay, 2003).

Absences that are troubling within society and have the potential to cause disruption at various levels must be pushed aside, forced into the background of our everyday consciousness. They allow those who are vulnerable and marginalized to continue to bear the burdens of physical and psychological abuses and mistreatments. In the case of these research studies, such burdens included being abused by a family member or not being allowed to freely engage in sexual, romantic relationships. Silences also simultaneously allow others around the vulnerable to avoid talking about the foundations and implications of collective silences, avoiding an acknowledgment that may demand change and transformation. It is always a collective process because, as Sheriff (2000, p. 114) notes, "while silence tends to penetrate social boundaries it is not seamless; different groups, whether constituted by class, ethnicity, racialized identities, gender, or language, have markedly divergent interests at stake in the suppression of discourse." Such silences clearly shape inequality in subtle but important ways.

As qualitative researchers, we must realize that we are part of what goes unsaid. As researchers, we are both participants in and observers of the unsaid. We are participants in absence because we ourselves are members of particular groups, communities, and societies that deny, avoid, and repress issues that trouble us. We are part of the greater social world and "what we ignore or avoid socially is often also ignored or avoided academically" (Zerubavel 2006, p. 13). We cannot think that we have the moral high ground or that we are "above" oppressive silences simply because we research them.

Yet there are times when we observe and focus on absence as both citizens and qualitative researchers, attempting to speak about that which is often taboo or unspeakable. On the one hand, even this unsilencing may work to reproduce and reinforce the inequality and social action that we are investigating. On the other hand, the act of noticing silences in our research can, in and of itself, be a form of social action. By drawing attention to a silence, qualitative researchers can powerfully influence our social world in multiple and unexpected ways. As the #MeToo movement and others who speak out about abuse, harassment, and inequality in intimate spaces show, the first step in addressing silenced inequalities is to notice the unsaid and begin to talk about it. But, what comes next? Is talking about intimate silences enough to remedy the inequalities they reflect, or is there more to be done when researching and unsilencing inequalities that go unsaid in society? The #MeToo movement is voicing the unsaid in ways that might impact inequality in other sectors outside of Hollywood. The world noticed #MeToo, and other women are sharing stories of violence in their lives in the hopes of societal change. Much like raising awareness of intimate inequalities via social media hashtags, those researching the unsaid create an audience that begins the process of unsilencing inequalities. Beyond the academic knowledge produced by studies of the unsaid, researchers can take steps to bring silenced issues to light in the hopes that there will be broader action taken to challenge the inequalities we uncover.

Acknowledgments

The support of the DST-NRF Centre of Excellence in Human Development toward this research/activity is hereby acknowledged. Opinions expressed and conclusions arrived at, are those of the author and are not necessarily to be attributed to the Centre of Excellence in Human Development.

References

Ábrego, L. J. (2011). Legal consciousness of undocumented Latinos: Fear and stigma as barriers to claims-making for first and 1.5 generation immigrants. *Law & Society, 45*(2), 337–69.

Ábrego, L. J. (2006). "I can't go to college because I don't have papers": Incorporation patterns of Latino undocumented youth. *Latino Studies, 4,* 212–231.

Alaszewski, A. (2006). *Using diaries for social research.* London: Sage.

Ally, S. (2010). *From servants to workers: South African domestic workers and the democratic state.* Pietermaritzburg: University of KwaZulu-Natal Press.

Archer, S. (2011). "Buying the maid Ricoffy": Domestic workers, employers and food. *South African Review of Sociology, 42*(2), 66–82.

Beeghley, L. (2008). *Structure of social stratification in the United States* (5th ed.). New York: Taylor and Francis.

Bhattacharya, H. (2009). Performing silence: Gender, violence and resistance in women's narratives from Lahaul, India. *Qualitative Inquiry, 15*(2), 359–371.

Billig, M. (1997a). Keeping the white queen in play. In M. Fine, L. Weis, L. C. Powell, & L. Mun Wong (Eds.), *Off white: Readings on race, power and society* (pp. 149–157). New York: Routledge.

Billig, M. (1997b). The dialogic unconscious: Psychoanalysis, discursive psychology and the nature of repression. *British Journal of Social Psychology, 36,* 139–159.

Billig, M. (2004). *Freudian repression: Conversation creating the unconscious.* Cambridge: Cambridge University Press.

Carpenter, L., & Austin, H. (2007). Silenced, silence, silent: Motherhood in the margins. *Qualitative Inquiry, 13*(5), 660–674.

Collins, P. H. (2004). *Black sexual politics: African Americans, gender, and the new racism.* New York: Routledge.

Coutin, S. B. (2000). *Legalizing moves: Salvadoran immigrants' struggle for U.S. residency.* Ann Arbor: University of Michigan Press.

Crenshaw, C. (1997). Resisting Whiteness' rhetorical silence. *Western Journal of Communication, 6*(3), 253–278.

De Genova, N. P. (2002). Migrant 'illegality' and deportability in everyday life. *Annual Review of Anthropology, 31,* 419–437.

Denzin, N. K. (2010). Moments, mixed methods, and paradigm dialogs. *Qualitative Inquiry, 16*(6), 419–427.

Dickey, S. (2000). Permeable homes: Domestic service, household space and the vulnerability of class boundaries in urban India. *American Ethnologist, 27*(2), 462–489.

du Toit, D. (2010). Extending the frontiers of employment regulation: The case of domestic employment in South Africa. *Law, Democracy and Development, 14,* 205–230.

Fiorito, T. R., & Nicholls, W. J. (2016). Silencing to give voice: Backstage preparations in the undocumented youth movement in Los Angeles. *Qualitative Sociology, 39,* 287–308.

Flick, U. (2017). Mantras and myths: The disenchantment of mixed-methods research and revisiting triangulation as a perspective. *Qualitative Inquiry, 23,* 46–57.

Frikel, S. (2014). Absences: Methodological notes about nothing, in particular. *Social Epistemology, 28,* 86–95.

Gaitskell, D., Kimble, J., Maconachie, M., & Unterhalter, E. (1983). Class, race and gender: Domestic workers in South Africa. *Review of African Political Economy, 27,* 86–108.

Gilligan, C. (1977). In a different voice: Women's conceptions of self and morality. *Harvard Educational Review, 47*(4), 481–517.

Gonzales, R. G. (2011). Learning to be illegal: Undocumented youth and shifting legal contexts in the transition to adulthood. *American Sociological Review, 76* (4), 602–619.

Gonzales, R., & Chavez, L. (2012). "Awakening to a nightmare": Abjectivity and illegality in the lives of undocumented 1.5-generation Latino immigrants in the United States. *Current Anthropology, 53*(3), 255–281.

Gonzales-Barrera, A., & Krogstad, J. M. (2017). What we know about illegal immigration from Mexico. *Pew Research Center.* Retrieved from www .pewresearch.org/fact-tank/2017/03/02/what-we-know-about-illegal-immigra tion-from-mexico/

Gracia, E. (2004). Unreported cases of domestic violence against women: Towards an epidemiology of social silence, tolerance, and inhibition. *Journal of Epidemiology & Community Health, 58,* 536–537.

Hansen, K. T. (1990). Body politics: Sexuality, gender and domestic service in Zambia. *Journal of Women's History, 2,* 120–142.

Hesse-Biber, S. (2012). Feminist approaches to triangulation: Uncovering subjugated knowledge and fostering social change in mixed methods research. *Journal of Mixed Methods Research, 6*(2), 137–146.

Hirschauer, S. (2006). Putting things into words: Ethnographic description and the silence of the social. *Human Studies, 29*(4), 413–441.

Huckin, T. (2002). Textual silence and the discourse of homelessness. *Discourse and Society, 13*(3), 347–372.

Irvine, J. T. (2011). Leaky registers and eight-hundred-pound gorillas. *Anthropological Quarterly, 84,* 15–40.

Jansen, E. (2011). From Thandi the maid to Thandi the madam: Domestic workers in the archives of Afrikaans literature and a family photograph album. *South African Review of Sociology, 42*(2), 102–121.

Jaworski, A. (1993). *Power of silence: Social and pragmatic perspectives.* Newbury Park: Sage.

Jenkins, C. M. (2007). *Private lives, proper relations: Regulating black intimacy.* Minneapolis: University of Minnesota Press.

Kunda, Z., & Spencer, S. J. (2003). When do stereotypes come to mind and when do they color judgment? A goal-based theoretical framework for stereotype activation and application. *Psychological Bulletin, 129,* 522–544.

Kurzon, D. (2007). Towards a typology of silence. *Journal of Pragmatics, 39,* 1673–1688.

Langone, A. (2018, March 22). #MeToo and Time's Up founders explain the difference between the 2 movements – and how they're alike. *TIME*. Retrieved from http://time.com/5189945/whats-the-difference-between-the-metoo-and-times-up-movements/.

Macalpine, M., & Marsh, S. (2005) "On being white: There's nothing I can say": Exploring whiteness and power in organizations. *Management Learning, 36*(4), 429–450.

Mandel, H. (2009). Configurations of gender inequality: The consequences of ideology and public policy. *The British Journal of Sociology, 60*(4), 693–719.

Mazzei, L. A. (2004). Silent listenings: Deconstructive practices in discourse-based research. *Educational Researcher, 33*(2), 26–34.

Mazzei, L. A. (2008). Silence speaks: Whiteness revealed in the absence of voice. *Teaching and Teacher Education, 24*, 1125–1136.

Murray, A. J., & Durrheim, K. (2018). "There was much that went unspoken": Maintaining racial hierarchies in South African paid domestic labour through the unsaid. *Ethnic and Racial Studies*, doi: https://doi.org/10.1080/01419870.2018.1532096

Ngai, M. (2004). *Impossible subjects: Illegal aliens and the making of modern America*. Princeton: Princeton University Press.

Nicholls, W. J. (2013). *The DREAMers: How the undocumented youth movement changed the immigrant rights debate*. Stanford, CA: Stanford University Press.

Nightingale, A. (2003a). A feminist in the forest: Situated knowledges and mixing methods in natural resource management. *ACME: An International E-Journal for Critical Geographies, 2*, 77–90.

Nightingale, A. (2003b). Nature-society and development: Social, cultural and ecological change in Nepal. *Geoforum, 34*, 525–540.

Nightingale, A. (2006). The nature of gender: Work, gender, and environment. *Environment and Planning D: Society and Space, 24*, 165–185.

Nyamnjoh, F. B. (2005). Madams and maids in Southern Africa: Coping with uncertainties and the art of mutual zombification. *Africa Spectrum, 40*(2), 181–196.

O'Malley, M. P. (2005). Silence as a means of preserving the status quo: The case of ante-natal care in Ireland. *Multilingua, 24*, 39–54.

Pallares, A., & Flores-González, N. (2010). *¡Marcha!: Latino Chicago and the immigrant rights movement*. Chicago: University of Chicago Press.

Perlesz, A., & Linsay, J. (2003). Methodological triangulation in researching families: Making sense of dissonant data. *International Journal of Social Research Methodology, 6*, 25–40.

Power, J. G., Murphy, S. T., & Coover, G. (1996). Priming prejudice: How stereotypes and counter-stereotypes influence attribution of responsibility and credibility among ingroups and outgroups. *Human Communication Research, 23*, 36–58.

Raj, A., & Silverman, J. (2002). Violence against immigrant women: The roles of culture, context, and legal immigrant status on intimate partner violence. *Violence Against Women, 8*(3), 367–398.

Rappert, B., & Bauchspies, W. K. (2014). Introducing absence. *Social Epistemology, 28*, 1–3.

Romero, M. (1992). *Maid in the USA*. New York: Routledge.

Rumbaut, R. (2004). Ages, life stages, and generational cohorts: Decomposing the immigrant first and second generation in the United States. *International Migration Review, 38,* 1160–1205.

Schröter, M. (2013). *Silence and concealment in political discourse*. Amsterdam: John Benjamins.

Sheriff, R. (2000). Exposing silence as cultural censorship: A Brazilian case. *American Anthropologist, 102*(1), 114–132.

Statistics South Africa. (2017). *Quarterly Labor Force Survey* (Quarter 2, 2017). Pretoria: Statistics South Africa.

Stoler, A. L. (2002). *Carnal knowledge and imperial power: Race and the intimate in colonial rule*. Berkley: University of California Press.

Sue, C. A. (2015). Hegemony and silence: Confronting state-sponsored silences in the field. *Journal of Contemporary Ethnography, 44*(1), 113–140.

Sue, D. W., Capodilupo, C. M., Torino, G. C., Bucceri, J. M., Holder, A. M. B., Nadal, K. L., & Esquilin, M. (2007). Racial microaggressions in everyday life: Implications for clinical practice. *American Psychologist, 62*(4), 271–286.

Tatum, B. (2003). *Why are all the black kids sitting together in the cafeteria? And other conversations on race*. New York: Basic Books

Vikström, L. (2003). Different sources, different answers: Aspects on women's work in Sundsvall, Sweden, 1860–1893. *Interchange, 34,* 241–259.

Vikström, L. (2010). Identifying dissonant and complementary data on women through the triangulation of historical sources. *International Journal of Social Research Methodology, 13,* 211–221.

Ward, J., & Winstanley, D. (2003). The absent presence: Negative space within discourse and the construction of minority sexual identity in the workplace. *Human Relations, 56*(10), 1255–1280.

Whisson, M. G., & Weil, W. (1971). *Domestic servants; A microcosm of "the race problem."* Johannesburg: Institute of Race Relations.

Zerubavel, E. (2006). *The elephant in the room: Silence and denial in everyday life*. Oxford: Oxford University Press.

6   Silence in the Court: Moral Exclusion at the Intersection of Disability, Race, Sexuality, and Methodology

Susan Opotow, Emese Ilyes, and Michelle Fine

Silence audibly reverberated in the courtroom that held a sensationalized trial, which concluded in October 2015. This case revolved around the accusation that a 45-year-old white woman professor ("the woman") engaged in two counts of sexual assault with a 38-year-old African American man ("the man") who was neither a student nor a client but, in fact, had been a co-author with her on a series of professional papers. This accusation was rooted in the man's categorization by medical and institutional systems as cognitively disabled, unable to communicate, and therefore unable to consent to a sexual relationship. The woman, a professor of philosophy, disputes this categorization and has collaborated with him on academic presentations and published articles using an augmented form of communication. Messy, multilayered, and undeniably tragic, this provocative and disorienting case of sexual assault quickly attracted international attention and was a cover story in the *New York Times Magazine*. Today, there is an opera in the works, as well as multiple documentaries, books, and plays.

To explore whether and with what consequence the scope of justice (Opotow, 1990, 2018) may be expanded through taking silence seriously, this chapter is organized in three parts. We begin by briefly relaying the story of the man at the heart of the court case to dissect how race, disability, and sexuality intersect in a manner that science and vulnerability are evoked as a cover for dehumanization. This is followed by an empirical examination of the scientific and legal debate surrounding facilitated communication (FC), a form of assisted communication. The chapter concludes with a meditation on silencing as a deeply political project. Throughout this chapter, we emphasize that qualitative research can and should initiate conversations from differing perspectives, provoke new interpretations, and unsettle the taken for granted. Attention to multivocal discourse

(Bakhtin, 1981; Skinner, Valsiner, & Holland, 2001) for studying silence, we argue, makes visible the layered nature and echoes of silence and silencing.

The Trial

On the first day of the trial, the man was introduced – not in his wheelchair but held up by his mother – as a demonstrable exhibit. His mother walked him silently before the jury clasping both of his hands, speaking, "This is my son." After that brief moment of spectacle, he was absent from the trial. His *absence* and *silence* are as central to the case as the woman's actions. Indeed, absences and silences, we propose, perpetuate moral exclusion within the legal system. We define *moral exclusion* as positioning others as outside the scope of justice and therefore viewing them as undeserving of fairness and failing to protect them from harm (Opotow, 1990, 2018). Consistent with this, the man was not allowed to testify to ascertain his perspective. No one interviewed him to gather evidence of his consent or his experience of coercion. His voice and subjectivity were conveyed only through his mother and brother, his legal guardians, who had approved of this relationship until the woman told them they were falling in love and had been sexually intimate.

That was when the civil case for monetary damages first emerged, quickly followed by a criminal case investigating whether or not this was an instance of sexual assault. Though the man was allowed neither a voice nor a presence in the courtroom, expert witnesses – psychologists, physical therapists, and communication specialists – spoke of his long history of educational records that presumably confirmed, year after year, his cognitive disability. His mother and brother, who were suing the woman for rape, represented his everyday life and experiences. Loaded words, flung as a performance of outrage by the prosecutor, sketched the man as an animalistic bodily presence. In contrast, the woman spoke of the man as a thinker and writer, a person with desires, dreams, and ideas and as a person with the right to a life that includes intimacy and love. She said she had intended to marry him before she had been arrested.

Throughout their two-year relationship, she had communicated with him through a system of augmented communication called *facilitated communication,* a controversial method considered unscientific by the courts and therefore ruled as inadmissible. Fully absent during the dramatic three-week trial, the man was made voiceless through others' voices. Silence and silencing of the presumed victim translated into victimhood and objectification, reinforcing the man's position outside the scope of justice and naturalizing his moral exclusion.

Within three weeks, with many questions remaining in the shadows of silence, the jury came back with a guilty verdict for the woman on both counts after two and a half hours of deliberations. They agreed with the prosecutor that it was beyond a "reasonable doubt" that the woman was a rapist who had taken advantage of the "mentally defective" man, to use the language repeatedly reiterated by the judge and prosecutor in court.

In those three weeks, the assumption that an argument would be heard advocating for the man's humanity seemed increasingly naïve as psychological experts wielded vulnerability as an accusation – not as a signifier of oppression or an entitlement to justice – but as evidence of the man's incapacity, his inability to consent, and therefore his lack of entitlement to love or sexuality. Filling the space with accusations of vulnerability allowed the man's subjectivity to be silenced and a basic understanding of his humanity to remain among the unsaid. Throughout the trial, spectators had watched as the man was brought in – only once – as nothing more than a piece of evidence echoing the freak shows of the past. The courtroom silently witnessed a psychologist, an expert brought in from Michigan, draw a bell curve and point a giant arrow at the very end of its tail to position the man according to IQ tests. The stenotype operator noted with barely perceptible movements as every expert brought in by the prosecutor compared the man to an animal, a monkey reaching for a banana, or an infant in diapers.

A year and a half after the guilty verdict, an appellate court overturned the conviction, determining that the woman – who was serving time in prison for two counts of sexual assault – did not receive a fair trial. The woman won an appeal for a retrial with a new judge but ultimately did not proceed because she lacked financial resources and did not want to experience a wrenching legal process again. Instead, she and the prosecutors settled for time served in prison, with the stipulation that she would register as a sex offender for the rest of her life.

Silence and Vulnerability

This case draws the connection between vulnerability and silence, revealing how these constructs have been deployed to advocate for the disempowerment and segregation of populations that have, in a dizzyingly circular fashion, come to be defined almost exclusively by these constructs without interruption. This case calls attention to the way silencing and silences in the court room, framed as protection, perpetuate exclusion from the scope of justice. Attending to the production of silences allows these circuits of erasure and exclusion to be exposed.

This chapter begins to unfurl such knotted questions as the following: Does the court have an obligation to pay attention to silence? Can qualitative research examine silence to reveal overt and covert silencing as a symptom of moral exclusion and structural violence? Is vulnerability a path toward entitlement or toward disposability? Is denying a grown man with disabilities a sexual relationship an act of protection or a violation of human rights?

This case suggests a pattern toward pity that verges on disgust but not justice; protection but not voice; and persecution of those who dare to love, especially those who dare to love those who are not supposed to be love-able. This case reveals the curious pivot upon which "disability" has been draped over a body to presumably extend, but actually constrict, moral concern for human rights. Situating a single case within a legal, scientific, and historical context, it is possible to decipher how silence perpetuates moral exclusion, how silencing of the purported "victim" activates the ghosts of interracial sexuality where violence and love struggle, and the how the language of vulnerability rhetorically evacuates the nonnormative human subject, rendering suspect those who extend love to them. To make audible the moves that enable silencing, this chapter references various kinds of qualitative data to animate the psychological dynamics swirling in a courtroom, drowning in the unspoken and evocative history and effects of sexuality, race, disability, guilt, violence, and desire that hold powerful sway in US history.

In the analyses that follow, we take an ethical stance in our writing – perhaps an ironic use of silencing – to redirect attention from the particulars and, instead, lift up the dynamics embodied and litigated in court at the race/disability intersect. By not using names of people involved, we intend to avoid the specificities of blame, accusation, siding with, and also avoid muddying the waters of a case still in litigation. So, instead, our use of bland nouns, "the man" and "the woman," deflects attention from the idiosyncratic people involved to reveal how silencing, erasing, and conjuring the exiled spectacle are metabolized, and how race, disability, and sexuality intersect so that, in concert, legal procedure and science can become a cover for dehumanization and exclusion.

Technologies of Silencing

In this trial, the judge refused to accept expert testimony in the courtroom to explain facilitated communication (FC), the method of communication used by the defendant and the presumed victim, the only method of communication found accessible to the man, his only alternative to a lifetime of silence. Nor would the judge allow evaluations of the man conducted with FC or other kinds of evaluations conducted by FC experts, despite research on successful testimony in court using FC (Bryen & Wickham, 2011). The judge did permit classic psychological tests that classified the man as having an IQ of a preschooler.

An international expert on FC was not allowed to testify about the results of the assessment she conducted with the man, in which he displayed competence on a series of questions. The man's tutor for a Black Literature course at Rutgers University, who helped him write course papers, was removed as a witness, as was a mother whose child uses FC. Although no attempt was made to find a way for the man to represent himself in the courtroom, the judge did permit the man's mother to display him as an exhibit in the courtroom and did permit experts critical of FC to present their evaluations.

The only person permitted to speak to the efficacy of FC was the woman. Her attorney described a "message test" conducted a few years before in which the man, using FC, was asked questions and provided correct answers that his facilitator, the woman, could not have known. This message test indicated that the man had memories, relational knowledge, and could communicate. But at the trial and since, his capacity to communicate was quashed. Only the woman, the accused, could speak of love and consent, while the prosecutor spoke of rape and coercion.

There was a radical rejection of FC as well as the man's own testimony although the judge could have elicited information from the man, even if FC was exiled. Even though the man has significant motor impairments, everyone – including the prosecutor – agreed that he is capable of intentional and directed locomotion. Therefore, he could have given unassisted "yes" or "no" answers. In the courtroom or in a private room, the judge could have asked him: "Did you consent to sexual relations with woman?" and directed him: "If so, move your body toward the door."

In this inhospitable legal landscape, the relationship between the man and the woman was portrayed as one-sided. She was described by the prosecutor as aberrant, a "super-predator" in a "preposterous" and "ridiculous" relationship. When the woman's attorney countered these representations to describe a "loving relationship" between two people, what he described may have been inconceivable to the jury: a relationship in which closeness and intimacy breached boundaries of race, gender, socioeconomic status, and the seemingly inviolable boundary of ability status.

The defense attorney asked the jury to move beyond such categorical conventions to grasp, and even to appreciate, that people who are different can forge close and intimate bonds. He asked the jury to see the radical and compelling humanity and love in their relationship. The jury, however, deliberated for only two and a half hours without an understanding of the man's relationship with the woman from his perspective. They returned a verdict of guilty on two counts of rape. The exclusion of FC was the portal through which people, testimonies, evidence, relationality, and representations of competence and consent were exiled, revealing institutional processes of silencing, moral exclusion, and injustice perpetuated by the legal system.

Facilitated Communication

Facilitated communication is a form of augmentative, alternative, and assisted communication in which physical, communicative, and emotional support are provided by a *facilitator* to an individual with communication disabilities. People who utilize FC are heterogeneous with respect to their challenges and needs. With assistance from the facilitator, the individual may point to symbols, such as letters, pictures, or objects on a keyboard or typing device.

Introduced by Australian educator Rosemary Crossley (1994) in the 1970s–1980s, FC became popular in Australia, Europe, and Asia. It was introduced in the United States in the late 1980s–early 1990s by Syracuse University Professor Douglas Biklen (1990), who had observed Crossley's work in Australia in 1989.

Early adopters of FC praised its efficacy and simplicity. A 1992 *Los Angeles Times* article on the use of FC in special education reported, "An intriguing aspect of the technique is that the disabled individual must be touched by someone he or she trusts in order to type thoughts. The facilitator does not type out words but sometimes steadies the hand ... to overcome problems of getting started" (Kim, 1992). With some background support, students who were previously nonverbal became increasingly capable of communicative complexity, from responding "yes" or "no" to writing words (Kim, 1992).

Lauded as a miracle cure for silent and seemingly unreachable individuals (e.g., Hanf, 1993), FC has been controversial since its inception (Goleman, 1993). In the early 1990s, its reputation was sullied by claims of sexual abuse made by people communicating via FC that were widely reported in the media. Some of these allegations were later described as false but other studies found that allegations of abuse emerging via FC should be taken seriously in light of research indicating that children with disabilities are 3.4 times more likely to be maltreated than peers without disabilities (Botash, Babuts, Mitchell, O'Hara, Lynch, & Manuel, 1994; Sullivan & Knutson, 2000).

Professional Associations on Facilitated Communication: Controversy and Critique

Media reports on allegations of sexual abuse from people with communication disabilities in the early 1990s raised the profile of FC. It also raised concerns about what had initially been viewed as a miracle of found communicative capacity. Several professional associations with expertise on communication-related disabilities subsequently assessed the validity of FC and issued policy statements to guide professionals and the public. Their statements did not support FC as a valid technique.

A policy statement by the American Psychological Association (1994) entitled "Facilitated Communication Not a Scientifically Valid Technique for Individuals with Autism or Mental Retardation" described facilitated communication as controversial and unproven, stating: "It has been claimed that this process enables persons with autism or mental retardation to communicate; however, scientifically based studies have repeatedly demonstrated that this is not a valid technique for individuals with profound developmental disabilities" (also see American Psychological Association, 2003).

Though policy statements from the Association for Behavior Analysis International (1995), American Speech-Language-Hearing Association (1995), and American Academy of Child and Adolescent Psychiatry (1995) differ somewhat in their descriptions of facilitated communication, each describes FC as unproven, without scientific merit, and potentially harmful. They describe potential negative consequences of FC as impeding access to more effective treatment and warn that FC can lead to unsubstantiated allegations of abuse or mistreatment. They recommend further research on FC and advise that informed consent specifying risks and benefits of FC is essential. This unanimity among prominent associations has been countered by qualitative research, which we subsequently discuss, which shows how people, once labeled as autistic, retarded, and unable to speak, can produce thoughtful and insightful writing about their lives, relationships, and the world (Biklen et al., 2005).

Although the associations' policy statements concurred that facilitated communication is unproven, the empirical background is more complex. The associations' statements are brief, and they omit – indeed, silence – substantial disagreement about the efficacy of FC within their field, if the field is to be understood as more inclusive – that is, including practitioners as well as researchers – and utilizing non-experimental empirical approaches. For example, the American Speech-Language-Hearing Association's (ASHA) 1994 resolution advised: "When information available to facilitators is controlled and objective evaluation methods are used, peer-reviewed studies and clinical assessments find no conclusive evidence that facilitated messages can be reliably attributed to people with disabilities."

Yet in October 1994, a month before AHSA released its position statement that conclusive evidence for FC is lacking, an AHSA working group, the Subcommittee on Facilitated Communication of the ASHA Ad Hoc Committee on Auditory Integration Training and Facilitated Communication ("Subcommittee"), was completing an extensive, two-year evaluation of FC.[1] Convened to examine the validity and efficacy of FC, the Subcommittee intentionally included people with diverse perspectives and experiences: speech-language pathologists and parents, as well as researchers.

The Subcommittee's 1994 *Technical Report: Facilitated Communication* (*"Technical Report"*) analyzed an extensive literature on facilitated communications (90+ citations) that reported on research findings, the impact of facilitated communication, the scope of practice of speech-language pathologists, standards for implementation, preservice and in-service education of speech-language pathologists, ethical issues, and future research needs. The *Technical Report* was not intended to be an ASHA position statement but instead to describe facilitated communication as an intervention for persons with autism and other severe communication disorders. It advised that "the primary purpose of this report is to define and describe facilitated communication, present current research findings in facilitated communication, and offer suggestions for its use in clinical practice." The *Technical Report* evaluated questions of validity and authorship – such as facilitators' influence on message content – for qualitative and quantitative studies of facilitated communication.

Quantitative and Experimental Research on FC   The *Technical Report* noted that quantitative research primarily utilized experiments and blind procedures to test the validity of facilitated communication using simple response methods that included one-word responses and sentence completion tasks to assess communication ability. The *Technical Report* noted that experimental research provided minimal support for the validity of facilitated communication, reporting that "eleven of 143 subjects have 'passed' validation tests," and it documented instances of facilitators unwittingly authoring messages for communicators.

But the *Technical Report* also observed a noteworthy absence: "none of these subjects [in the experimental research] exhibited levels of communication skill that are consistent with their facilitators' reports." This raised questions about the appropriateness and validity of methods utilized by experimental researchers to investigate FC. These methods included the following:

(a) the use of confrontation tasks that may exacerbate word finding difficulties; (b) insufficient time for subjects to become familiar with tasks presented; (c) use of unnatural settings; (d) unfamiliar examiners; (e) stressful nature of the testing context; (f) use of conditions, such as distractors, that alter the facilitated communication process; (g) inappropriate use of the technique by facilitators; (h) failing to allow subjects sufficient time to respond; (i) lack of information about subjects' pre-existing communication and related skills; (j) lack of experience with test taking; and (k) failed confidence.

Just as the positive results for FC in the qualitative research have been subject to critical scrutiny, the *Technical Report* advises that the preponderance of negative outcomes in experimental research must also be subject to scrutiny.

Qualitative Research on FC   The *Technical Report* also critically surveyed qualitative research on FC, which differed markedly from quantitative studies in their methodological approach. Qualitative research predominantly utilized naturalistic studies that focused on the transition from silence to communication, the communicator's progression toward independent communication, a diminished need for physical support, and a growing sense of efficacy and well-being. The *Technical Report* summarized findings as follows:

As consistent as experimental studies have been in failing to support communicators' skills using this method, qualitative and naturalistic results have been compelling in the opposite direction. [Emphasis in original.] All of these studies have reported positive changes in the communication skills of individuals following the introduction of facilitated communication. . . . Qualitative and naturalistic studies have reported unexpected literacy and communication skills in facilitated communication users. These skills have been associated with a variety of positive outcomes, including enhanced perceptions by others, increased success including these students in regular education classes and curriculum, positive changes in behavior and generalized use to other forms of communication.

The *Technical Report* concluded that fundamental disparities between quantitative and qualitative findings hinge on how *success* is defined. It expressed concern about research findings based on studies in which "success rests on demonstrations of communication effectiveness under experimentally controlled conditions, without consideration of other changes in behavior and quality of life." Thus, as the *Technical Report* observed, it is not surprising when research findings from these differing methodological approaches are contradictory. This is unfortunate because it confuses the public and does not provide professionals with clear and helpful direction.

From this perspective, it is clear that the "gold standard" of experimental design and methods prevailed in professional associations' assessments of FC. As a result, qualitative studies, grounded in the knowledge and experience of practitioners and people with communicative disabilities, were disregarded in their assessments of FC's efficacy.[2]

Facilitated Communication in Court

Frye and *Daubert* are legal standards that address the admissibility of expert testimony in court. *Frye* evaluates the general acceptance of testimony in the field from which it originates (*Frye* v. *United States*, 1923), while *Daubert* relies on judges to evaluate the methods and principles upon which expert opinions are based (*William Daubert et al.* v. *Merrell Dow*, 1993). Both *Frye* and *Daubert* have been critiqued for shifting the responsibility for assessing scientific research from highly trained expert witnesses to judges who may lack the expertise to serve as gatekeepers for scientific evidence (Bernstein, 2007; Jasanoff, 2005).

In some states, *Daubert* superseded *Frye* in 1994 (cf., Rotgers & Barrett, 1996), but many states, including New Jersey where this trial was conducted, still utilize *Frye* (Jurilytics, 2017). Therefore, when novel or controversial methods – such as FC – are at issue, New Jersey courts are tasked with determining the reliability and general acceptability of the method. This positions judges as gatekeepers to ensure that expert testimony proceeds from knowledge that rests on reliable scientific methods. However, when "reliable" is defined narrowly to mean expertise gleaned from experimental hypothesis-testing methods, other informative evidence and testimony can be excluded from consideration.

A key contentious issue raised in court challenges involving FC is the authorship of statements: Who is actually speaking? Is it the communicator or facilitator? The *Technical Report* advised that courts have handled questions of authorship in two ways. Sometimes *Frye* has been applied to indicate that a method must be considered scientifically validated before evidence produced by its use can be admitted into evidence. At other times, rights have been awarded to use facilitated communication as a means of communication so that adult communicators can speak for themselves rather than through a guardian or parent (e.g., *Jerry & Diane B.* v. *Le Mars Community School District et al.*, 1992; also see Bryen & Wickham, 2011).

The *Technical Report* stated that the Subcommittee was not aware of any situations that had progressed to the courts in which facilitators had been accused of purposely controlling the output of facilitated communication users to make educational decisions, control their finances, speak for them, or mislead others about who was the author of FC messages.

Before the woman's trial began, the judge ruled that facilitated communication failed New Jersey's test for scientific evidence. After the trial's conclusion, noted ethics scholars Jeff McMahan and Peter Singer (2017) expressed their astonishment at the judge's refusal to admit evidence that could have exonerated the woman while admitting contrary evidence from the prosecution. They acknowledged that FC is controversial and some studies have indicated that facilitators believed they were enabling communication when they were not. McMahan and Singer argue, however, that these studies cannot prove that the woman was misled in this way, particularly because independent evidence – from professional papers, the man's course work in a Black Literature course, and his responses to a lengthy examination by Dr. Crossley – have suggested that he is literate and can communicate. In a *New York Times* op-ed, philosophers McMahan and Singer (2017) maintain that the man's wishes should have been established. Because the trial failed to do so, the woman was a "victim of grievous and unjust harms."

The Appeal Found guilty of two counts of first degree aggravated sexual assault and after serving time in a women's correctional facility in New Jersey, the woman appealed her conviction, arguing that she was unable to fully present evidence of sexual consent given the restrictive rulings of the trial court. On June 9, 2017, three judges in the Superior Court of New Jersey issued their decision on the appeal (*State of New Jersey* v. *Marjorie Anna Stubblefield*, 2017). The judges agreed with the woman. They stated: "the overly exclusionary ruling deprived defendant of an opportunity to present evidence supporting her defense" (Appeal, p. 20). They advised: "Although a trial court retains broad discretion in determining the admissibility of evidence, that discretion is abused when relevant evidence offered by the defense and necessary for a fair trial is kept from the jury" (Appeal, p. 15). They observed: "the four expert witnesses produced by the State, overwhelmed the lone witness to [the man] having the capacity to consent, the defendant, who did not have the expertise or objectivity to render such an opinion," depriving the defendant of a fair trial.

Thus, they argued, not only was the man silenced, but FC and all potential testimonies of successful FC sitting in the courtroom were also silenced. The judges emphasized that the court's prime responsibility is to ensure a fair trial. It should therefore have allowed some latitude to the defendant to present her defense. The judges reversed the woman's convictions and called for a new trial before a different judge who would allow various people who have evaluated or assisted the man's communication via FC to testify and the defended to fully explain her position.

Cumulative Damages of Silencing

This case clarifies that cumulative damages can ensue from silencing, including injustice, exclusion, and hardship. The legally justified silencing of FC testimony is an empirical study, utilizing data that includes a history of FC, particulars of a criminal trial, assessment-based policies of four professional associations, an empirical evaluation of quantitative and qualitative FC research, standards for inclusion of expert testimony in courtrooms, text of an appeal decision, media accounts, and our observations in the courtroom. Together, this information from this variety of sources allows us to study and trace the arc of silencing to understand what is often unnoticed and not well understood – the process by which the silenced, *the unsaid*, can ripple from the 1970s into the present to have deleterious effects on individuals and society. With one exclusion authorized by the judge, the court eliminated the man as a sexual subject, invalidated the woman's understanding of his capacity, deprecated FC as a technology appreciated by many banned witnesses (parents, children, and educators), and refused to hear evidence gathered through qualitative methods.

The case also reveals how prevailing stereotypes can justify the exclusion of people who are non-neurotypical from decisions affecting their lives. It describes the naturalization and enforcement of exclusionary processes by respected societal institutions that include the professional associations and the justice system, which are both charged with fostering societal well-being. Such exclusionary decisions and policies are effected naturally and invisibly and then labeled as fairness and following the rules.

The Appeal offers important commentary on how *Frye* and *Daubert* – rules for the admissibility of evidence – can be applied in ways that are unfair and, from the broader perspective of this book, can foster silencing and abet exclusionary processes and outcomes. In this case, the prosecutor mobilized a so-called scientific consensus to convict the woman of rape and violate the right of a 38-year-old man to testify on his own behalf, all in the name of protecting him. As this case reveals, silencing not only excludes; it actively conjures, distorts, and colonizes the exiled spectacle.

Silencing and Sexuality: Conjuring the Exiled Spectacle

Let us remember: the only reason that anyone learned about the sexual intimacy between this woman and this man is that she/they told his family. Silencing is, of course, about exclusion, but it is more than that; it is also about conjuring the apparition of the exiled spectacle. As in this case, silencing removes and inserts, occludes, and awakens the object of desire/repulsion. Particularly when tethered to sexuality and interracial sexuality, silencing, like most forms of prohibition, generates an ironically fertile space where fears, anxieties, stereotypes, and guilty desires wash in, invading, unchecked by real bodies, real relationships, encounters, or contestations. The apparition, the fantasy, the representation sketched by the white male prosecutor reframed the dynamic relationship between the woman and the man. We could only imagine. The prosecutor delivered to the jury twinned imaginaries – the rape victim and the rapist – in a kind of "facilitated communication" among the judge, prosecutor, and jury.

Even as silencing constricts, let us consider how orchestrated and officially sanctioned silencing unleashes the racialized and disability-infused imaginary.

At the opening of the trial, the man was literally introduced as an "exhibit" to the jury, while his mother explained, "This is my son" – not in a wheelchair but leaning on her for assistance. We learned from the prosecutor that he was able to "scoot away" to convey displeasure, and "scoot on the floor" to "eat a banana" with closed fists. Whisked away after the display, he reappeared only as a referent – the embodiment of an absence – in the opening statement of the prosecutor, who referenced him, just as the psychologists brought in by the prosecutor did, as "just not there." With these references, the man at the center of the case was routinely dismembered and evacuated, leaving behind a body but not a mind or a self, that is, judged by experts by nothing but a quick glance. The prosecutor peppered his arguments, accusations, and insinuations with lyrics from Tina Turner's "What's Love Got to Do With it?" and repeated references to the man's "phallus" and his diapers. A series of racist dog whistles, targeted at the jury, were sustained by the judge, dehumanizing the man, demonizing the woman, and "penetrating" the courtroom, even as the man, his story, and his capacities were banished.

Once FC was deemed pseudoscience by the judge, after being referenced by the prosecutor as "gobbledygook" with no other translation process introduced; once the man was removed physically from the courtroom and the films of his competence were deemed inadmissible, the stickiness of suspicion spread widely – delegitimizing the man, FC, and the papers he and the woman had presented together at professional conferences; throwing a shadow of naïveté on the young woman student who was his tutor for a class on Black Literature at the university, the internationally recognized psychologist from Australia who assessed him for more than thirty hours, the romance narrative offered by the woman, and the films of his correct answers.

A row of witnesses was supposed to testify about how FC helped their children gain academic skills and autonomy, but their tongues were clipped. As the case progressed, the viewing audience multiplied, and the shadow of invalidity seemed to stretch over the disabled disability rights activists wearing T-shirts saying "Just because I can't speak doesn't mean I don't have anything to say" or "People with disabilities have sex." Young adults using NEOs and other assistive communication technologies began to show up day after day, listening to the judge insist that their means of communication was ineffective in the eyes of the law. The man was never given a chance to tell his story, through FC, the films, or any other medium. Even very young children at the center of sex abuse cases have someone interview them, a *guardian ad litem*, to represent their perspectives to the court.

Silencing, as an active process of censorship, hollows out a discursive and psychic vacuum, but it also animates and sucks in stereotypes, anxieties, fears, and projections to fill the void. It is of course difficult to discern how these racial, class, and disability-infused dynamics swirled in the collective (un)conscious of the courtroom. But the racialized-classed-disability-infused assemblage was obvious. A predominantly African American female jury listened intently to an African American woman judge, a white male prosecutor, and an interracial (black and white) married defense team. A white, highly literate professor of philosophy and African American studies in her early forties, a mother who was recently divorced from an African American man, sat accused of master minding nonconsensual sex with a black, unemployed, and far less educated man in his late thirties, legally defined as a dependent in a guardianship relationship with his mother and brother – in her university office.

Master narratives swallow counter-stories, evidence, and complexity. Narrative domination requires silencing. As Gloria Anzaldua (1987) has written, "wild tongues cannot be tamed, they can only be cut out" (p. 53). Indeed, in this case, the man's tongue was cut out; he, his story, the qualitative stories of thousands of others catalogued in the 1994 ASHA Subcommittee *Technical Report,* the experience of the man's tutor, the findings of the psychologist from Australia, and the wisdom/desires of the people with disabilities who showed up to the trial to represent their humanity and sexuality with breathing machines, wheelchairs, dogs, and communication assistive devices were banished from the courtroom for the narrative of rape to prevail uncontested. One young woman, an activist using a wheelchair, attended most of the trial. On the very last day right before the closing statements were offered, the judge told her to move to the back of the room so that she was "not a fire hazard." This act of dismissal, voiced in a discourse of "protection," considering the content of the case, echoed in the chamber.

The Urgency of Fugitive Stories

Silencing is a deeply political project, engaged typically to bolster and seal a master narrative. Fugitive stories, released by wild tongues, provoke a more complex, troubling exposure; they leak the lurid hidden details denied by the master narrative.

The hermetically sealed, heavily guarded dominant narrative in that courtroom exploded one afternoon after the sentencing when the woman's 16-year-old daughter stood to speak before watching her mother marched out of the courtroom, in handcuffs, with a twelve-year sentence of two consecutive counts of sexual assault: "My mother is the nicest person in the world; she is just naïve – she doesn't see race or disability." In her bold oration, she turned to and challenged the man's family: "You loved my mother when they wrote articles together, but as soon as she told you they were having sex, you tried to sue the university," and she cursed the judge, "Fuck you, you are ruining my life," then burst into tears and fled the courtroom.

Within moments, a woman who had been attending the trial regularly, a well-known disability rights activist, released a deep scream upon hearing "guilty on two counts of sexual assault" – "Now no one will be able to touch me sexually without the threat of someone calling it rape."

This is of course a story of a single lawsuit, and yet we believe it speaks back, with a kind of theoretical generalizability, to a range of projects undertaken by critical psychologists who gather up fugitive stories, to offer what historian Nell Painter (2002) would call a "full accounting" of "soul murder" (p. 15). The videos, interviews, and surveys of black men and women being beaten, tortured, and killed by white police in the United States challenge the master story of policing as protection (Stoudt & Torre, 2014); the interviews with unemployed women, men, and children expose the embodied and cultural devastation of mass unemployment during the Great Depression (Jahoda, Lazarsfeld, & Zeisel,

2001); the testimonies of South Africans archived in the Apartheid Archive Project (Stevens, Duncan, & Hook, 2013); stories of black women who survived apartheid are stitched into the embroideries gathered by Puleng Segalo (2011) to reveal historic and contemporary wounds of state-inflicted violence; and "people's surveys" conducted by Ignacio Martín-Baró (1994) and colleagues in El Salvador documented the abuses wrought by the government militias. Critical psychologists have an obligation to gather these fugitive stories that pierce and contest the master story and refuse silencing (Scott, 1992).

Once voices and stories leave the larynx and circulate, however, there are no guarantees on if/how/whether they will be heard. In this case, we have no way of knowing how this trial would have unfolded were the man permitted to communicate his experience and capacity; perhaps his love, consent, desires would have been on display, or maybe his own sense of rage, exploitation, and betrayal. We will never know. We write not to take sides, to defend the woman, or to challenge the intentions of the mother and brother. We write to expose the violence enacted and occluded by the court once the judge reached for scissors to cut out the man's tongue and deny him the right to self-representation *as if she were protecting him.*

While the history of eugenics and anti-disability discrimination is long and ugly in the United States, persons with disabilities have over time been granted cumulative legal rights: to serve on juries, testify as witnesses, practice as lawyers, be represented as victims, preside as judges … but some are still denied the right to represent themselves as sexual beings.

Concluding Thoughts: Lessons for the Qualitative Researcher

This chapter is both about the silencing of qualitative research and itself a qualitative project that draws on science, history, and law to address what is said and unsaid. It describes qualitative research as uniquely situated to utilize multiple sources of data and perspectives to reveal silencing as a method of moral exclusion. Allowing the domination of a single narrative, in contrast, risks marginalizing already marginalized voices, leading to erasure and silencing. As this case reveals, it can eliminate the humanity of people as well as the unique knowledge we gain from collective wisdom. This case also reveals that when a single narrative is positioned as primary, it can circulate among various societal spheres, obscuring problematic and unresolved issues that affect individuals and ultimately affect society as a whole.

To be ethically grounded, research must be attentive to individuals situated in history and context (Weis & Fine, 2012). Qualitative research is uniquely positioned to be attentive to multivocal discourse (Bakhtin, 1981) that surfaces complexities, conflicts, and challenges that might otherwise remain silenced and unsaid. It can curate evidence that is readily available as well as hidden transcripts (Scott, 1992). It can be attentive to multiple kinds of data – in histories, cases, observations, transcripts, reports, and more – to hold multiple perspectives, reveal nuances, and provoke discussion about the messy in-betweens, without imposing a hierarchy on whose truth prevails. The layered approach we advocate allows researchers to work their way into the grounded particulars that are lived, and out toward the provisional generalizable echoes of shared experience.

References

American Academy of Child and Adolescent Psychiatry. (1995, reviewed 2008). *Facilitated communication*. Retrieved from www.aacap.org/AACAP/Policy_Sta tements/2008/Facilitated_Communication.aspx

American Psychological Association. (1994). *Facilitated communication not a scientifically valid technique for individuals with autism or mental retardation*. Retrieved from http://www.apa.org/about/policy/chapter-11.aspx

American Psychological Association. (2003). *Facilitated communication: Sifting the psychological wheat from the chaff*. Retrieved from www.apa.org/research/action/facilitated.aspx

American Speech-Language-Hearing Association. (1995). *Facilitated communication* [Position Statement]. Retrieved from www.asha.org/policy

American Speech-Language-Hearing Association's (ASHA) Subcommittee on Facilitated Communication of the Ad Hoc Committee on Auditory Integration Training and Facilitated Communication. (1994). *Technical Report: Facilitated Communication*. Retrieved from www.asha.org/policy/T R1994-00139.htm

Association for Behavior Analysis International. (1995). *Statement on facilitated communication, 1995*. Retrieved from www.abainternational.org/about-us/poli cies-and-positions/facilitated-communication,-1995.aspx

Anzaldúa, G. (1987). *Borderlands/La frontera*. San Francisco, CA: Aunt Lute.

Bakhtin, M. (1981). *The dialogic imagination: Four essays*. (Holquist, M., Trans.). Austin: University of Texas Press.

Bernstein, D. E. (2007). Expert witnesses, adversarial bias, and the (partial) failure of the Daubert revolution.*Iowa Law Review, 93*, 451.

Biklen, D. (1990). Communication unbound: Autism and praxis. *Harvard Educational Review, 60*(3), 291–315.

Biklen, D., with Attfield, R., Bissonnette, L., & Blackman, L. (2005*). Autism and the myth of the person alone* (Qualitative studies in psychology). New York: New York University Press.

Botash, A. S., Babuts, D., Mitchell, N., O'Hara, M., Lynch, L., & Manuel, J. (1994). Evaluations of children who have disclosed sexual abuse via facilitated communication. *Archives of Pediatric & Adolescent Medicine, 148*, 1282–1287.

Bryen, D. H., & Wickham, C. H. (2011). Ending the silence of people with little or no functional speech: Testifying in court.*Disability Studies Quarterly, 31*(4). Retrieved from http://dsq-sds.org/article/view/1711/1759

Crossley, R. (1994). *Facilitated communication training.* New York: Teachers College Press.

Daubert v. *Merrell Dow Pharmaceuticals*, 509 U.S. 579 (1993).

Frye v. *United States.* 293 F. 1013 (D.C.Cir. 1923).

Goleman, D. (1993). New treatments for autism arouse hope and skeptics. *New York Times.* Retrieved from www.nytimes.com/1993/07/13/science/new-treat ments-for-autism-arouse-hope-and-skepticism.html

Hanf, B. (1993). The autistic find doubters prevail [Letter to the Editor]. *New York Times.* Retrieved from www.nytimes.com/1993/07/28/opinion/l-the-autis tic-find-doubters-prevail-985893.html

Jacobson, J. W., Mulick, J. A., & Schwartz, A. A. (1995). A history of facilitated communication: Science, pseudoscience, and antiscience science working group on facilitated communication. *American Psychologist, 50*(9), 750–765.

Jahoda, M., Lazarsfeld, P., & Zeisel, H. (2001) *Marienthal: The sociography of an unemployed community.* London: Transaction Publications.

Jasanoff, S. (2005). Law's knowledge: Science for justice in legal settings. *American Journal of Public Health, 95*(S1): S49–S58. PMID 16030338.

Jerry & Diane B. v. *Le Mars Community School District et al.* (2017, March). *Daubert and Frye in the 50 states.* Retrieved from https://jurilytics.com/50-state-overview

Kim, R. (1992, June 17). The magic touch. *Los Angeles Times.* Retrieved from http://articles.latimes.com/1992–06-17/news/mn-480_1_severely-disabled-students

Martín-Baró, I. (1994). *Writings for a liberation psychology.* Cambridge, MA: Harvard University Press.

McMahan, J., & Singer, P. (2017, April 3). Who is the victim in the Anna Stubblefield case? *New York Times.* Retrieved from www.nytimes.com/2017/0 4/03/opinion/who-is-the-victim-in-the-anna-stubblefield-case.html

Opotow, S. (1990). Moral exclusion and injustice: An overview. *Journal of Social Issues, 46*(1), 1–20.

Opotow, S. (2018). Social justice theory and practice: Fostering inclusion in exclusionary contexts. In P. L. Hammack (Ed.), *The Oxford handbook of social psychology and social justice* (pp. 41–56). New York: Oxford University Press.

Painter, N. (2002) *Southern history across the color line.* Chapel Hill: University of North Carolina Press.

Rotgers, F., & Barrett, D. (1996). Daubert v. Merrell Dow and expert testimony by clinical psychologists: Implications and recommendations for practice. *Professional Psychology: Research and Practice, 27*(5), 467–474.

Scott, J. (1992). *Domination and the art of resistance: Hidden transcripts.* New Haven, CT: Yale University Press.

Segalo, P. (2011, October). *Gendered suffering and the complexities of keeping silent. Theological, Religious, and Ethical Voicelessness in the New Millennium* [Conference]. Pretoria, University of South Africa.

Skinner, D., Valsiner, J., & Holland, D. (2001). Discerning the dialogical self: A theoretical and methodological examination of a Nepali adolescent's narrative. *Forum Qualitative Sozialforschung/Forum: Qualitative Social Research*, 2(3). Retrieved from www.qualitative-research.net/index.php/fqs/article/viewArticl e/913/1994

Stevens, G., Duncan, N. & Hooks, D. (2013) *Race, memory and the apartheid archives*. London: Palgrave Macmillan.

State of New Jersey v. *Marjorie Anna Stubblefield*, Superior Court of New Jersey, Appellate Division, Docket No. A-02112-15T1, June 9, 2017.

Stoudt, B. G., & Torre, M. E. (2014). The Morris Justice Project. In P. Brindle (Ed.), *SAGE cases in methodology*. London: Sage.

Sullivan, P. M., & Knutson, J. F. (2000). Maltreatment and disabilities: A population-based epidemiological study. *Child Abuse & Neglect*, 24(10), 1257–1273.

Weis, L., & Fine, M. (2012). Critical bifocality and circuits of privilege: Expanding critical theory and design. *Harvard Educational Review*, 82(2), 173–201.

Notes

1. Work on the *Technical Report* began in 1992. Final comments on the report by dissenting committee members and a rebuttal to their comments were dated October 2,1994, and October 31, 1994, respectively. The appendices on dissent in the *Technical Report* surface conflictual perspectives about FC by the Subcommittee. It appears that the November 1994 FC Policy Statement by the American Speech and Hearing Association, which was unequivocally unsupportive of FC, was issued just after the *Technical Report* had been completed and dissent it elicited had been published.

2. Professional associations' policy statements, written in the early 1990s, have not been revised since. The American Academy of Child and Adolescent Psychiatry did revisit its statement in 2008 but did not revise it.

7   Silencing Self and Other through Autobiographical Narratives

Robyn Fivush and Monisha Pasupathi

We create our identities through narrating the experiences of our lives. How we narrate is intimately related to who we are and how well we are doing. Importantly, our autobiographical narratives are constructed in everyday social interactions in which we narrate to, with, and through others, and these interactions are nested within broader sociocultural and historical contexts (Fivush, Habermas, Waters, & Zaman, 2011; McLean & Syed, 2015). As a consequence, narratives are contested territory; they can be validated, but they can also be negated, negotiated, and reconstructed through social interactions that privilege both particular contents and particular ways of narrating those contents (Fivush, 2010; Pasupathi & Wainryb, 2018). What is *not* said becomes as important for identity as what is said.

In this chapter, we explore how what is left unsaid in narratives is shaped both implicitly and explicitly in how people tell their stories to and with others, and how these negotiated and imposed silences may have long-lasting impacts on what can later be remembered or, possibly, even subsequently experienced. Our argument is that silence is constructed in small moments of shared stories and has large implications for how we understand our past and our future selves. Within these broader arguments, we focus on gender as an example of voice and silence in personal narratives (Fivush & Marin, 2018). We emphasize that gender is a complex construct, encompassing genetic, biological, and sociocultural components (Perry & Pauletti, 2011). Moreover, recent theory and research have questioned the conceptualization of gender as a binary construct, underscoring the complexity of the biological and social construction of gender as a more continuous and/or dimensional way of being in the world both physically and psychologically (Richards, Bouman, Seal, Barker, Nieder, & T'Sjoen, 2016). In an interesting parallel, both gender and narrative are ways of constructing self that are negotiated and contested and, as we will argue, may be mutually constitutive of each other. At a broad level, personal narratives show substantial differences by gendered identity, at least in industrialized Western cultures, such that individuals who identify as biologically female and those who self-ascribe to stereotypically female characteristics generally tell more elaborated, emotionally expressive narratives than do individuals who identify as biologically male (Grysman, Fivush, Graci, & Merrill, 2016; Grysman & Hudson, 2013). Thus, an interrogation of how narratives construct voice and silence simultaneously, how this is negotiated in local interactions embedded within culturally mediated master narratives, and how these forms are socialized in development leading to multiple gendered ways of understanding the past, the present, and the future selves is a critical question.

Understanding Silence through Narratives

Narratives are fundamentally the way in which humans understand themselves and their world (Bruner, 1990). Narratives carve the flow of experience into meaningful units, creating beginnings, middles, and ends, and provide links between and among disparate experiences to create a coherent story of self through time (McAdams, 1992; Ricœur, 1991). Moving beyond a simple recount of what happened, narratives include thoughts and emotions of self and others, motivations, and intentions, creating a story of human drama (McLean, Pasupathi, & Pals, 2007). Narratives are ubiquitous in human interaction; they emerge approximately every five minutes in everyday conversations (Bohanek et al., 2009), and we tell about 90 percent of even mildly emotional everyday events to another within forty-eight hours (Rime, 2007; Pasupathi, McLean, & Weeks, 2009). Whether in the workplace or home, meeting new people or chatting with friends and family, we tell stories about what happened that day and the significant events of our lives. We tell stories with others to create and maintain social connections and positive emotional bonds (Beike, Brandon, & Cole, 2016; Pasupathi et al., 2009), and we tell stories to others to entertain, to connect, to teach, and very often to understand (Bluck & Alea, 2002; Pasupathi et al., 2009; Webster & Gould, 2007).

In telling our stories, we create meaning from these experiences, an interpretive framework that helps us understand why this event happened and what it means for who we are as a person, how we became this way, and what this means for our future. In hearing others' stories, we understand who they are as a person, building empathy and identification (Echtorhoff, Higgins, & Levine, 2009; Hammock, 2008), as well as understanding something about the world and about ourselves. But in the very act of narrating, voicing some aspects of experience, we, by necessity, silence others. We do this for ourselves, in terms of self-silencing; we do this due to others, as listeners shape what we say; and all of this is within cultural frames that provide accepted narrative arcs and disallow others. In the next section, we discuss the local and cultural context in more detail and then transition to how this process emerges developmentally as parents socialize their children into culturally mediated and accepted narrative forms that privilege the expression of some aspects of experience. Although our arguments are broad, we focus on gender as a case example of how voice and silence are socially and culturally mediated. In the last section, we bring these threads together and consider a more speculative assertion – that in silencing aspects of our past, we may actually change the way we experience our present and our future.

Silencing by Self and Other

Narrative co-construction is nested in local social and larger cultural contexts that lead to a nuanced conceptualization of silence as emerging in the interaction between narrator and listener (Fivush, 2010; Pasupathi & Billitteri, 2015). In the very moments of sharing a narrative, silence is being constructed against what is actually being said. Moreover, this process begins early in development, as children are surrounded by stories (Fivush, Haden, & Reese, 2006), stories of self, of others, and of shared experiences co-constructed to express certain ways of being in the world. Over time, as narratives are told across our lifetimes, certain ways of telling and not telling may become more stable. Thus, the very process of creating a coherent narrative of personal experiences in the moment and over time reflects a process of both voicing and silencing simultaneously. We see this process beginning in childhood, as we consider an excerpt from a conversation between a mother and her four-year-old daughter, Alice (all names in this chapter are pseudonyms). Alice's pre-school teacher (Susan) had died, and Alice begged her mother to take her to the wake. A few months after the wake, they engage in this conversation:

MOTHER: Well, I think what we're going to talk about next is going to Susan's wake.
CHILD: Uh, well I remember when they were crying and Sally, Sally (the teacher's daughter) started crying.
MOTHER: ... mmm hmmm. And it was very sad to see her so sick.
CHILD: Yes.
MOTHER: And then what happened?
CHILD: Well she, they, they, did everything but it didn't work and she died.

MOTHER: Yeah, and it was sad, wasn't it?
CHILD: Yeah (very softly)
MOTHER: And you begged Mommy and Daddy to take you to the wake.
CHILD: Yeah (very softly)
MOTHER: And what was the wake like?
CHILD: Well it had sadly music and it was really sad to talk about so I didn't want to talk about it.
MOTHER: ... Didn't we go talk to her daughter?
CHILD: Yeah (very softly)
MOTHER: And we gave her big hugs.
CHILD: ... Yeah ... but I don't want to talk about this because you're almost going to make me cry.
MOTHER: Okay, I won't, we won't talk about it anymore.

Although brief, this highly complex interaction illustrates multiple levels of voicing and silencing, at both the local and cultural contexts, as we now discuss.

The Local Context

Silencing within the immediate social context occurs at various points in the construction of a narrative. Individuals can withhold information deliberately to manage their self-presentations, as initially argued by the symbolic interactionists (e.g., Goffman, 1959), and also with less awareness, leading to a sense of self-silencing. We see this happening even this early in development; Alice is so distressed that she explicitly says she does not want to talk about it. She is self-silencing in the service of regulating her difficult emotions – in part through avoiding those emotions (Mancini & Bonanno, 2009). But the mother perseveres, at least for a bit, pushing Alice to explore more about the experience and her feelings, implicitly teaching Alice that it is important for her to talk about her emotions, even if uncomfortable. Thus, in a way, Alice's mother is negating Alice's silence, creating and perhaps even enforcing a form of voice onto this experience. But it is a specific form of voice, filtered through the mother's own personal narrative and through accepted internalized cultural narratives, leading to privileging certain content or interpretations over others. Thus, in helping Alice construct a coherent narrative of this event, the mother is simultaneously encouraging the voicing of sadness and the importance of sharing sadness, imposing this cultural narrative, while silencing other interpretations. So, the forms and content of emotional experiences that we choose to disclose and how others let us disclose them both construct how we experience those emotions and, perhaps, how we do not.

Similarly, although most emotional events will be narrated to others very soon after they occur (Rimé, 2007), events that evoke shame and guilt and entail transgressive content are more likely to remain undisclosed (Pasupathi et al., 2009), often for fear of social consequences and to avoid thinking about the events – evidence that broader cultural frames about transgression, morality, and identity shape the silencing of particular events in ways that are linked to concerns for the self and for audiences. We can see some of this happening in a second excerpt between a mother and her four-year-old son, Charlie, discussing how Charlie feels when his sister, Mandy, does not let him play with her and her friends:

M: How did you feel when Mandy wouldn't let you play the other day, when she was playing with Jess and she told you boys to go away? How did that make you feel?
C: Umm, sad.
M: And why does Mandy do that?
C: Because she's mean.
M: (laughing) Is she mean? Is she mean all the time? When she doesn't let you play, you're not very happy, are you?
C: ummm.

At this point, the mother simply changes topic and begins to talk about a different event. The mother silences Charlie's interpretation that his sister is mean by simply invalidating it through laughing at his comment and then, at least indirectly, contradicting his interpretation by saying she is not mean, at least not all the time. Rather than negotiating this interpretation, she simply switches topics. Thus, unlike Alice's mother, this mother does not try to explore this emotion in any meaningful way. Rather than imposing a particular story shape on sadness, she simply silences it.

Thus, when stories are told, both the narrator and listeners must agree that the story will be told and heard (Clark, 1996; Pasupathi & Billitteri, 2015). Charlie's mother essentially closes down the story, whereas Alice's mother insists the story be told. But in some sense, both mothers are imposing a certain form of silence on their child's experience. From this perspective, silence can be constructed through not allowing voice or through only allowing certain events or interpretations to be voiced. As another example, among married couples, events are silenced when the narrator introduces the event but the listener does not take up that particular event (Pasupathi, Lucas, & Coombs, 2002). Once the event is being narrated, telling a coherent and contextually appropriate narrative relies on selection of some information and thus non-inclusion of other information, and both narrators and their audiences shape what is and is not included based on subtle interplays of signals of comprehension, interest, support, or their opposites. Listeners can both implicitly silence aspects of the narrative by being inattentive or distracted or explicitly by actually negating or reinterpreting (McLean & Pasupathi, 2011; Pasupathi & Hoyt, 2009); narrators can, in turn, be more and less responsive to these signals, as well as silence aspects of the narrative based on their own concerns for emotion and self-regulation. When listeners provide a sense that an experience is heard and understood, and that an experience is accepted as valid and meaningful, they provide a space for people to have a voice, rather than be silenced (Bavelas, Coates, & Johnson, 2000; Pasupathi, Stallworth, & Murdoch, 1998; Pasupathi, et al., 2009). We see all of these processes at work in the conversation between Alice and her mother. Although Alice provides many details about what happened and includes her own feelings, it is the mother who provides the glue of the narrative, eliciting and validating information that provides a coherent temporal structure and causal fabric to the event. The mother also validates multiple times how sad the event was, but she also wants Alice to understand something about the importance of sharing those sad emotions to comfort others ("didn't we go talk to her daughter? ... and we gave her big hugs"). Thus, in this brief excerpt, we see the negotiation of voice and silence, what is allowed to be silent, how and what is allowed to be voiced, and how shared meaning is negotiated and constructed. In Charlie's narrative, we see only silencing – it is simply not acceptable to have these kinds of emotional evaluations about one's sister.

Such storytelling has implications for the way specific events come to be remembered (Tversky & Marsh, 2000). Elements of an event that are silenced on one occasion are less likely to be recalled when the event is remembered subsequently, even in different contexts (e.g., Pasupathi et al., 1998; Pasupathi & Hoyt, 2010; Pasupathi & Oldroyd, 2015). Experimental work that manipulates listener attention or distraction has shown that unresponsive listeners are particularly likely to silence meaning-laden, emotional aspects of stories (Pasupathi & Hoyt, 2009). And when certain aspects of shared experiences are not discussed by the group, the individual is subsequently less able to recall those details, suggesting that what remains unsaid may become unremembered (Cuc, Koppel, & Hirst, 2007). Thus, we are not only silenced in the telling; our subsequent memories may be shaped by what is said and not said in the moment.

The Cultural Context

In the process of constructing personal meaning through sharing stories, people draw on layers of social and cultural meaning that are available to them in the form of master narratives – widely shared and normatively validated understandings of how a life story and its associated events ought to unfold (Hammack, 2008; McLean & Syed, 2015), as well as related beliefs and attitudes propagated through the culture. For example, in the United States, a master narrative of redemption – that difficult and stressful experiences should be narrated in ways that convey both their negative nature and their positive aftermath – is widely evident in memoirs, fiction, and even in the country's founding historical narrative of the Pilgrims (McAdams, 2006). As narrators and listeners build specific stories that are interwoven with cultural frames, individual stories can incrementally feed into larger cultural and social narratives (McLean & Syed, 2015; Syed, Pasupathi, & McLean, in press). This interplay is of real consequence for individuals. At a minimum, using culturally available frames for one's particular stories promotes the comprehensibility of the experience and links the narrator to a collective identity. Thus, it is not surprising that using such frames can relate to positive outcomes – there is good evidence that, for many adults, using a redemption master narrative to structure their own difficult times may be generally linked to more positive outcomes (e.g., Bauer & McAdams, 2010; Lilgendahl & McAdams, 2011). At the same time, the available cultural frames can also be experienced as a kind of pressure for people narrating lives that do not fit the more culturally shared story frame (Fivush, 2010). This pressure may stem from an internalized sense that one's story needs to have a positive ending. This pressure may be both self-induced as a culturally appropriate narrative frame but may also be imposed by listeners who do not or cannot hear stories without a positive ending (Brison, 2003). Both listeners and narrators draw from culturally shared meaning-making frames to voice some aspects of experience (survival, resilience, hidden benefits) and to silence others (disintegration, loss of meaning, lasting damage).

We see these broader cultural narratives play out even in the everyday excerpts presented earlier. Alice's mother clearly wants a redemptive ending to her child's difficult experiences attending the wake – talking to the teacher's daughter and giving her big hugs provide a meaningful purpose to this event – but Alice does not want to accept this. When Alice again insists that she does not want to talk about it, the mother lets it go and the story essentially has no satisfying conclusion. Alice's silence does not allow the imposition of the culturally imperative redemption, that something good came from the experience. Thus again, even in this small excerpt, we see the complicated play of Alice silencing herself, Alice's mother wanting to voice a particular culturally acceptable story, and neither of them being completely satisfied with what gets said and how it is said.

Gendering Narratives

In principle, many features of experiences can be voiced or silenced within narration; thus, the implications of silencing and voicing are varied and numerous. One critical component of narrative voice and silence that we have already at least alluded to in our excerpts is gender. Gender is a highly complicated and sometimes contested construct that provides a lens through which we understand the world, both our own personal experiences and the experiences of others (Fivush & Marin, 2018). Here, we discuss how cultural constructions of gender and of narrative can mutually constitute each other.

At the broadest level, cultural narratives are often gendered in terms of culturally stereotypical ways of conceptualizing female and male, especially around emotion and vulnerability, providing gender-typical ways of expressing and not expressing personal experience that conforms to Western stereotypes (McLean & Syed, 2015). Psychological research has traditionally conceptualized gender as two broad categories, with participants self-identifying as either female or male. Using this definition, women are both stereotyped and self-report themselves to be more caring, emotional, and empathetic than men, especially around sadness, whereas men stereotypically express more anger than do women (Prentice & Carranza, 2002). In line with this, women generally tell more emotionally expressive, relationally oriented personal narratives than do males (Grysman & Hudson, 2013) and express more vulnerability in their personal narratives than do males (McLean, 2015). For example, Thorne and McLean (2003) found that when asked to narrate a traumatic experience, adolescent boys used a "John Wayne" cultural frame, narrating invincibility, whereas girls used a "Florence Nightingale" frame, narrating caring relationships. Thus, when narrating their own personal experience, men and women may draw on somewhat different master narratives and cultural tropes about masculinity and femininity in ways that result in voicing certain aspects of experience and silencing others (Fivush & Marin, 2018). In turn, listeners draw on that same cultural storehouse of narratives and tropes to hear and validate some aspects of narratives, and to silence others through inattention, distraction, or outright negation. Interestingly, gender of the listener matters; men are more emotionally expressive when narrating their experiences to a women listener than to a male listener (Grysman & Denney, 2017), suggesting that both narrating and listening occur in a larger cultural context that frames the local interactions, such that women both express and validate emotions more so than men. Critically, the argument is that this form of cultural gendering both defines and limits cultural constructions of self, reinforcing a binary female/male way of being in the world. How might these kinds of local interactions evolve over developmental time and what are the implications for what is voiced and silenced?

Developing Gendered Silences: Early Socialization

Silencing and voicing begin very early in development. From the moment of birth, infants are surrounded by stories and are quickly drawn into participating in these narrative retellings of daily life, heavily structured by parental elicitation (see Fivush, Haden, & Reese, 2006, for a review). The ability to tell a coherent story of self is a critical cultural skill (McAdams, 2015), and through these early parentally structured narratives, children begin to learn the forms and functions of narrative tellings, sharing their stories with others in more detailed, coherent, and culturally appropriate ways (Fivush et al., 2011). As our excerpts have illustrated, children learn what to express, and, just as importantly, what not to express.

Indeed, there are substantial individual differences in how children come to tell their own autobiographical stories, and these differences are largely due to stable individual differences in how parents structure these reminiscing conversations with their children (Fivush et al., 2006). More specifically, parents, and perhaps especially mothers, vary along a dimension of elaboration, such that some mothers provide richer, more detailed co-narrations of the past than other mothers. More elaborative mothers provide more connective tissue for the unfolding story, creating a more coherent account of the experience. Elaborative mothers also talk more about the inner world, connecting thoughts and emotions of self and others to external actions and behaviors, in ways that help children learn to understand and evaluate their own subjective experience (Fivush & Zaman, 2013).

Alice's mother excerpted earlier is a prototypically elaborative mother, asking many open-ended questions, negotiating experience and weaving together a coherent narrative account of a difficult emotional experience. Not all parent-child reminiscing is so coherent and evaluative. Charlie's mother opens a conversation and begins to explore Charlie's emotional experience, but as soon as Charlie expresses something "inappropriate" about his sister, the mother shuts him down. She does not try to negotiate or reweave a different story. Although she does elicit some narrative information about the causes of Charlie's sadness, unlike Alice's mother, Charlie's mother does not try to explore this emotion in any meaningful way. A still different approach can be seen in this example of a father and his four-year-old son, Andy, when asked to discuss a time Andy was sad:

FATHER: What about sometime when you're sad?
CHILD: (Unintelligible)
FATHER: When Sammie bites you, you're sad?
CHILD: Yes.
FATHER: What else makes you sad?
CHILD: I dunno.
FATHER: What about when you have to leave your friends? Does that make you sad?
CHILD: Yes.
FATHER: But then you get to see your friends again. Does that make you happy?
CHILD: Yes.
FATHER: So your friends make you happy and sad?
CHILD: Yes.
FATHER: What about when you go to bed? Are you sad at night when you have to go to bed?
CHILD: Uh huh.

Rather than a narrative, this dyad simply constructs a list, events that lead to sadness. Andy does not even nominate any of these events: the father does, and Andy simply acquiesces. There is no sense of shared emotion, or the value of sharing emotion, as we saw with Alice and her mother. And, of course, because there is no narrative, there is no narrative tension or movement, no evaluative framework, or working through of emotional experience. Andy is learning that emotions are like facts; a simple listing or accounting is all that is necessary. It is not that emotions are voiced or silenced; they are simply unimportant.

Thus, even in these quite sparse early parentally guided narratives, parents and children are beginning to navigate difficult narrative territory, negotiating not just what happened but also how the child felt, and why, and whether these feelings are valid or not, and how they should be expressed and explored. Moreover, such silencing and voicing is complex – in that the silencing of some aspects of experience can occur simultaneously with encouragement to voice other aspects of an experience, often in particular ways. What is silenced is always constructed against not just *what* is said but *how* it is said.

Gender Differences in Early Parent-Child Reminiscing

As these examples illustrate, the narrative socialization of emotional expression, in particular, may be gendered, both by gender of parent and gender of child. Although there are many sources of individual variability, empirical research that has used self-identified gender as a variable has found systematic effects of gender. For parents, mothers use more emotion words, a greater variety of emotion words, and elaborate more on emotional experience than do fathers when reminiscing about the past with their preschool children (see Fivush & Zaman, 2013, for a detailed review). In these ways, mothers are modeling that women express and elaborate on emotion to a greater extent than do men. Moreover, these patterns persist through adolescence (Fivush, Marin, McWilliams, & Bohanek, 2009).

Patterns based on gender of the child are more nuanced. Some studies find that both mothers and fathers mention emotion more frequently when reminiscing with daughters than with sons, whereas other studies do not (e.g., Fivush & Zaman, 2013). In addition, there is some suggestion that the type of emotion matters; both mothers and fathers talk more about sadness with daughters than with sons. More specifically, parents use the word "sad" more often with daughters, elaborate on what sadness feels like as an emotion, and talk more about the causes and consequences of sadness with daughters than with sons (Fivush, 1989; Fivush, Brotman, Buckner, & Goodman, 2000; Kuebli & Fivush, 1992). So, it is not simply mentioning sadness more frequently but also providing a more embellished account of sad emotional experiences with daughters than with sons, as we saw in the narrative examples provided earlier. In contrast, there is some suggestion that both mothers and fathers talk more about anger with sons than with daughters (Bird & Reese, 2006; Fivush, 1989); however, this tends to be simply in mentioning anger; parents do not elaborate very much on the experience of anger with either daughters or sons. Finally, the gender composition of the dyad seems to matter as well; mother-daughter reminiscing about emotional experiences tends to be the most elaborated, and father-son reminiscing seems to be particularly sparse in its emotional expressivity (Fivush & Zaman, 2013; Reese, Haden, & Fivush, 1996).

What we see in these early parentally guided reminiscing conversations is the embodiment of cultural stereotypes about gender and emotional expressivity that both models and socializes gendered narrative frames;

such frames become, in turn, internalized in expressed behavior in the next generation. Whereas there are few differences in how boys and girls express their past emotions in the preschool years, by middle childhood, girls are expressing more emotion and more elaborated emotional experience in their personal narratives than are boys, and this pattern continues through adolescence (Buckner & Fivush, 1998; Fivush, Bohanek, Zaman, & Grapin, 2012; Pasupathi & Wainryb, 2010). This is not to argue that the gendered expression of emotion is completely socially constructed; the socially constructed expression of emotion may very well build on early gender differences in temperament and emotionality (Else-Quest, Hyde, Goldsmith, & Van Hulle, 2006). Rather, we argue that the proclivity to express and elaborate on emotional experience is at least partly socialized and modeled in early reminiscing conversations. We emphasize important caveats. First, we are drawing broad conclusions on patterns within self-identified gender groups, but we acknowledge that this form of self-categorization is only one way of characterizing self, and that there is large variability within these groups as well. Second, most of this research has been conducted with individuals who are asked to self-categorize as female or male, and most are living in traditional gendered arrangements. These are important limitations that call for additional research.

The Silencing of Emotion

If early socialization experiences facilitate more elaborative expression of emotions for girls and constrain emotional expressivity for boys, does this mean that emotion is silenced for boys? And does silencing mean lack of ability, that boys are unable to express emotion in the same way as girls? The answer is complex. Boys are being exposed to multiple narrative models, as are girls, so both must be learning gendered ways of expressing self. That is, in the process of gendered socialization, all of us learn not just the gendered stereotypes and expectations of our own gender but also of other genders (Blakemore et al., 2008). And, indeed, both girls and boys can tell a narrative that reflects other genders. If boys were simply unskilled at narrative emotional expressivity, we would expect that narratives they tell about themselves and others would be more or less equally devoid of emotional content. But this is not the case. When asked to tell a story they know about their mother as a child and their father as a child, adolescents are easily able to tell these stories – but here, the stories reflect the gendered narrative style of the protagonist in the story (the parent), not the narrator. Both boys and girls tell stories about their mothers that are more emotionally expressive than stories about their fathers (Merrill,

Srivanis, & Fivush, 2017; Zaman & Fivush, 2011). Perhaps this reflects how the story had been told to them, but even so, this means that they are processing and retelling the story through the parents' gendered lens. More to the point, boys' stories about their mothers are more emotionally expressive than stories about themselves! Moreover, both boys and men tell more emotionally expressive narratives with a female listener, suggesting again that the local context modulates what is said and what is silenced. So, it cannot be completely a skill-based argument. Boys can tell emotionally expressive narratives. Rather, it must at least partly be some form of implicit or explicit selectivity, such that boys "choose" not to be emotionally expressive when talking about themselves in most contexts. It is in this sense that we argue that emotion is being silenced in boys – both by others, as is evident in the parent-child reminiscence work, and by boys themselves, as is evident in the adolescent and young adult data in which boys' and men's personal narratives are constrained in their emotional expressivity. In turn, such silencing is reciprocally intertwined with master narrative positions like the one Thorne and McLean (2003) dubbed the "John Wayne," in which a narrator constructs a story of heroic invulnerability in the face of trauma. The reinforcement of the "John Wayne" frame via all of the incremental personal stories constructed by boys and men, silencing emotions of vulnerability and having those emotions silenced, ensures that this frame stays present for the next generation of boys.

Consequences of Silencing: Beyond Self and Memory to Health and the Future

As we have shown, both the local and cultural narrative context privileges certain forms of narrative expression over others, and this may be socialized and modeled across development, in ways that influence how individuals come to tell their own stories. More specifically, cultural master narratives and early narrative interactions are gendered in ways that privilege the expression and elaboration of emotional experience for women and the silencing of emotional expressivity and vulnerability for men. But a critical question is if and how this narrative silencing matters. We address this question in two ways. First, we show how a history of narrative silencing influences how individuals come to experience new events as they are occurring – that is, that a history of silencing influences what we even notice about our ongoing experiential world. Second, we ask if and how narrative silencing influences self-understanding, both in terms of self-esteem and psychological well-being.

Encoding Ongoing Experience

Narrative researchers usually focus on how we reconstruct our past, but, of course, what we can remember must be at least partly based on what we noticed, or encoded, as the experience occurred. This is a difficult issue to address because, obviously, we cannot ever really know what someone actually encoded about an event as it was experienced. But we can ascertain immediate recall as a proxy for what is most salient about the event at time of occurrence and then assess if and how that influences subsequent recall. Two studies relevant to our arguments have used this approach. Wang (2013a) asked young adults to record exactly what was happening as they received a text prompt three times a day for a one-week period, essentially at time of encoding. A week later, participants received an unexpected recall task for a subset of the events recorded. At encoding, women recorded more elaborate details than men, and they rated their experiences as more emotionally intense. One week later, women recalled more accurate and elaborative memory narratives than men and, at recall, also included more relationship information than men, suggesting this gender difference emerged as women thought about and possibly talked about these experiences with others across the week. Grysman (2018) asked young adults to narrate significant life events that occurred the previous day (close to occurrence), the previous week, and the previous two years. Across all three time intervals, women narrated more emotionally expressive, elaborated, and relationally oriented narratives than did men. Interestingly, these differences were greater for events that were further in the past, either because these events were more personally significant or possibly because, over time, women think and talk more about these experiences (Bluck & Alea, 2002), and therefore the memories become even more elaborated and emotional. Although limited, the emerging research suggests that women and men may actually approach new experiences and encode them in gendered ways, and these gendered differences may increase from time of experience to recall. Together with other work that does not focus on gender per se (e.g., Philippe et al., 2011), these findings suggest that a history of privileging or silencing certain aspects of experience, such as emotion, may actually change the way in which individuals understand new experiences as they are occurring, with women noticing and encoding more elaborative detail and emotional and relational aspects of ongoing experiences than do men.

Psychological Well-being

The silencing of emotional experience may have real consequences for well-being – broadly defined to include relationships, self- and emotion regulation, motivation and interest, and distress. Blunting the expression of one's own emotions in narratives can, long term, be related to poorer awareness of one's own emotional experiences and, in turn, more limited capacities for emotional and self-regulation. Such blunting can come about both from self-silencing and from silences imposed by others' unresponsiveness, disinterest, or active rejection. In contrast, expressing and elaborating on emotional aspects of experience are related to the capacity for adaptive emotion regulation, self-regulation, and the ability to develop healthy relationships with other people (see Fonagy, Gergely, Jurist, & Target, 2002; Laible & Thompson, 2002). Minimizing the articulation and elaboration of emotional experience when narrating one's life to others has obvious costs for the development of intimate relationships and connections to others and even for physical health (e.g., Gross & John, 2003; Way, 2013). Beyond well-being, the capacity to voice one's experiences to listeners may also be linked to maintaining motivation and interest (Thoman, Sansone, Fraughton, & Pasupathi, 2012; Thoman, Sansone, & Pasupathi, 2007). Finally, a cultural silencing of distress and vulnerability can be conceptually related to male reluctance to seek out health care (e.g., Yousaf, Grunfeld, & Hunter, 2015) and to men's vulnerability to suicide (e.g., Canetto & Cleary, 2012).

Of course, throughout this chapter we have emphasized the value and importance of giving oneself voice, and the way listeners can enable one to voice experiences. That said, voicing by self and other can also create risks, such as a risk for co-rumination whereby conversational partners devolve into venting emotions with no reconstruction or resolution; rumination and co-rumination are critical risk factors for depression (e.g., Rose et al., 2014). Thus, it is not that silence is bad, and voicing is good. Rather, both operate together in ways that are important for constructing what happened in the past, as well as what that means for our present and future selves.

Conclusions

How we construct the narratives of our lives matters for our evolving sense of self and well-being. But, by definition, in voicing narratives in coherent and evaluative ways, we silence other parts of our experience. In this chapter, we explored how narrative voice and silence are constructed and constrained at multiple levels, in terms of cultural narrative frames, local narrative interactions, and across development, focusing on gender and emotional expressivity as an illustration. Voicing of emotion is privileged for women and silenced for men. Most provocative, histories of narrative voice and silence may influence how individuals process new experiences and create new memories and narratives. Thus, histories of voice and silence constrain the future, impacting our sense of self and well-being.

We want to reiterate several limitations of our arguments: most important, gender is a highly complicated biological and cultural construct, and gendered aspects of narrative silencing are just one example of how, in allowing certain voices, narratives silence other voices. And gender is just one factor among many that influence this process. We argue that gender and narrative mutually constitute each other, such that as narratives are negotiated so are ways of being gendered in the world. Voice and silence occur at multiple levels, in multiple ways, for multiple populations. Indeed, recent narrative negotiations around nonbinary conceptualizations of gender are already changing the master narratives available to individuals (Corwin, 2009). Thus, we view our arguments as a framework for understanding voice and silence in narrative construction more broadly. We also acknowledge that our arguments are based largely on research with Western industrialized cultures, and the ways in which master narratives, local narrative interactions, and narrative development vary by culture must be considered further (e.g., Wang, 2013b). Our goal was to provide a way of thinking about narratives as a dynamic interplay between what is privileged and what is silenced in our everyday conversations about our experiences across time, and, in this way, narratives provide a window into how voice and silence are constructed from small moments that build enduring identities. What our approach emphasizes is that what is voiced is itself a construction of silence in the moment of telling. Examining what is said is simultaneously examining what is left unsaid.

References

Bauer, J. J., & McAdams, D. P. (2010). Eudaimonic growth: Narrative growth goals predict increases in ego development and subjective well-being 3 years later. *Developmental Psychology, 46*(4), 761–772. doi:10.1037/a0019654

Bavelas, J. B., Coates, L., & Johnson, T. (2000). Listeners as co-narrators. *Journal of Personality and Social Psychology, 79*, 941–952.

Beike, D. R., Brandon N. R., & Cole, H. E. (2016). Is sharing specific autobiographical memories a distinct form of self-disclosure? *Journal of Experimental Psychology: General, 145*, 434–450.

Bird, A., & Reese, E. (2006). Emotional reminiscing and the development of an autobiographical self. *Developmental Psychology, 42*, 613–626.

Blakemore, J. E. O., Berenbaum, S. A., & Liben, L. S. (2008). *Gender development*. New York: Psychology Press.

Bluck, S., & Alea, N. (2002). Exploring the functions of autobiographical memory: Why do I remember the autumn. In J. D. Webster & B. K. Haight (Eds.), *Critical advances in reminiscence work: From theory to application* (pp. 61–75). New York: Springer.

Bohanek J. G., Fivush R., Zaman, W., Lepore, C. E., Merchant, S., & Duke, M. P. (2009) Narrative interaction in family dinnertime conversations. *Merrill-Palmer Quarterly*, *55*(4), 488–515.

Brison, S. (2003) *Aftermath: Violence and the remaking of a self.* Princeton, NJ: Princeton University Press.

Bruner, J. (1990). *Acts of meaning.* Cambridge, MA: Harvard University Press.

Buckner, J. P., & Fivush, R. (1998). Gender and self in children's autobiographical narratives. *Applied Cognitive Psychology*, *12*, 407–429.

Canetto, S. S., & Cleary, A. (2012). Men, masculinities and suicidal behaviour. *Social Science & Medicine*, *74*(4), 461–465. doi:10.1016/j.socscimed.2011.11.001

Clark, H. H. (1996). *Using language.* Cambridge: Cambridge University Press.

Corwin, A. I. (2009). Language and gender variance: Constructing gender beyond the male/female binary. *Electronic Journal of Human Sexuality*, *12*(4).

Cuc, A., Koppel, J., & Hirst, W. (2007). Silence is not golden: A case for socially shared retrieval-induced forgetting. *Psychological Science*, *18*(8), 727–733.

Echterhoff, G., Higgins, E. T., & Levine, J. M. (2009). Shared reality: Experiencing commonality with others' inner states about the world. *Perspectives on Psychological Science*, *4*(5), 496–521.

Else-Quest, N. M., Hyde, J. S., Goldsmith, H. H., & Van Hulle, C. A. (2006). Gender differences in temperament: A meta-analysis. *Psychological Bulletin*, *132* (1), 33.

Fivush R., Habermas, T., Waters, T. E. A., & Zaman, W. (2011) The making of autobiographical memory: Intersections of culture, narratives, and identity. *International Journal of Psychology*, *46*(5). 321–345. doi:10.1080/00207594.2011.596541.

Fivush, R. (1989). Exploring sex differences in the emotional content of mother-child conversations about the past. *Sex Roles*, *20*(11–12), 675–691.

Fivush, R. (2010). Speaking silence: The social construction of silence in autobiographical and cultural narratives. *Memory*, *18*, 88–98.

Fivush, R., Bohanek, J. G., Zaman, W., & Grapin, S. (2012). Gender differences in adolescents' autobiographical narratives. *Journal of Cognition and Development*, *13*(3), 295–319.

Fivush, R., Brotman, M. A., Buckner, J. P., & Goodman, S. H. (2000). Gender differences in parent-child emotion narratives. *Sex Roles*, *42*, 233–253.

Fivush, R., Haden, C. A. & Reese, E. (2006). Elaborating on elaborations: The role of maternal reminiscing style in cognitive and socioemotional development. *Child Development*, *77*, 1568–1588.

Fivush, R., & Marin, K. (2018). The development of a gendered narrative identity. In C. B. Travis & J. W. White (Eds.). *Handbook of the psychology of women* (pp. 473–487). Washington, DC: Psychology Press.

Fivush, R., Marin, K., McWilliams, K., & Bohanek, J. G. (2009). Family reminiscing style: Parent gender and emotional focus in relation to child well-being. *Journal of Cognition and Development, 10*(3), 210–235.

Fivush, R., & Zaman, W. (2013). Gender, subjectivity and autobiography. In P. J. Bauer & R. Fivush (Eds.), *Handbook of the development of children's memory*. New York: Wiley-Blackwell.

Fonagy, P., Gergely, G., Jurist, E. L., & Target, M. (2002). *Affect regulation, mentalization, and the development of the self*. New York: Other Press Professional.

Goffman, E. (1959). *The presentation of self in everyday life*. New York: The Overlook Press.

Gross, J. J., & John, O. P. (2003). Individual differences in two emotion regulation processes: Implications for affect, relationships and well-being. *Journal of Personality and Social Psychology, 85*, 348–362.

Grysman, A. (2018). Gender and gender typicality in autobiographical memory: A replication and extension. *Memory, 26*(2), 238–250.

Grysman, A., & Denney, A. (2017). Gender, experimenter gender and medium of report influence the content of autobiographical memory report. *Memory, 25*(1), 132–145.

Grysman, A., Fivush, R., Merrill, N. A., & Graci, M. (2016). The influence of gender and gender typicality on autobiographical memory across event types and age groups. *Memory & Cognition, 44*(6), 856–868.

Grysman, A., & Hudson, J. A. (2013). Gender differences in autobiographical memory: Developmental and methodological considerations. *Developmental Review, 33*(3), 239–272. doi:10.1016/j.dr.2013.07.004

Hammack, P. L. (2008). Narrative and the cultural psychology of identity. *Personality and Social Psychology Review, 12*(3), 222–247.

Kuebli, J., & Fivush, R. (1992). Gender differences in parent-child conversations about past emotions. *Sex Roles, 27* (11–12), 683–698.

Laible, D. J., & Thompson, R. A. (2002). Mother-child conflict in the toddler years: Lessons in emotion, morality, and relationships. *Child Development, 73*, 1187–1203.

Lilgendahl, J. P., & McAdams, D. P. (2011). Constructing stories of self-growth: How individual differences in patterns of autobiographical reasoning relate to well-being in midlife. *Journal of Personality, 79*(2), 391–428. doi:10.1111/j.1467-6494.2010.00688.x

Mancini, A. D., & Bonanno, G. A. (2009). Predictors and parameters of resilience to loss: Toward an individual differences model. *Journal of Personality, 77*(6), 1805–1832.

McAdams, D. P. (2006). *The redemptive self: Stories Americans live by*. New York: Oxford University Press.

McAdams, D. P. (2015). *The art and science of personality development*. New York: Guilford Publications.

McAdams, D. P. (1992). Unity and purpose in human lives: The emergence of identity as a life story. In R. A Zucker, A. I. Rabin, J. Aronoff, & S. J. Frank (Eds.), *Personality structure in the life course* (pp. 323–375). New York: Springer.

McLean, K. C. (2015). *The co-authored self: Family stories and the construction of personal identity.* New York: Oxford University Press.

McLean, K. C., & Pasupathi, M. (2011). Old, new, borrowed, Blue? The emergence and retention of personal meaning in autobiographical storytelling. *Journal of Personality, 79*(1), 135–164. doi:10.1111/j.1467-6494.2010.00676.x

McLean, K., Pasupathi, M., & Pals, J. (2007). Selves creating stories creating selves: A process model of self-development. *Personality and Social Psychology Review, 11,* 261–278.

McLean, K. C., & Syed, M. (2015). Personal, master, and alternative narratives: An integrative framework for understanding identity development in context. *Human Development, 58*(6), 318–349. doi:10.1159/000445817

Merrill, N., Srinivas, E., & Fivush, R. (2017). Personal and intergenerational narratives of transgression and pride in emerging adulthood: Links to gender and well-being. *Applied Cognitive Psychology, 31*(2), 119–127.

Pasupathi, M., & Billitteri, J. (2015). Being and becoming through being heard: Listener effects on stories and selves. *International Journal of Listening, 29,* 67–84. doi:10.1080/10904018.2015.1029363

Pasupathi, M., & Hoyt, T. (2009). The development of narrative identity in late adolescence and emergent adulthood: The continued importance of listeners. *Developmental Psychology, 45,* 558–574.

Pasupathi, M., & Hoyt, T. (2010). Silence and the shaping of memory: How distracted listeners affect speakers' subsequent recall of a computer game experience. *Memory, 18*(2), 159–169. doi:10.1080/09658210902992917

Pasupathi, M., Lucas, S., & Coombs, A. (2002). Functions of autobiographical memory in discourse: Long-married couples talk about conflicts and pleasant topics. *Discourse Processes, 34,* 163–192.

Pasupathi, M., McLean, K. C., & Weeks, T. (2009). To tell or not to tell: Disclosure and the narrative self. *Journal of Personality, 77,* 1–35.

Pasupathi, M., & Oldroyd, K. (2015). Telling and remembering: Complexities in long-term effects of listeners on autobiographical memory. *Applied Cognitive Psychology, 29,* 835–842. doi:10.1002/acp.3193

Pasupathi, M., & Rich, B. (2005). Inattentive listening undermines self-verification in personal storytelling. *Journal of Personality, 73,* 1051–1086.

Pasupathi, M., Stallworth, L. M., & Murdoch, K. (1998). How what we tell becomes what we know: Listener effects on speakers' long-term memory for events. *Discourse Processes, 26,* 1–25.

Pasupathi, M., & Wainryb, C. (2010). On telling the whole story: Facts and interpretations in memory narratives from childhood through adolescence. *Developmental Psychology, 46,* 735–746.

Pasupathi, M., & Wainryb, C. (2018). Remembering good and bad times together: Functions of collaborative remembering. In M. L. Meade, C. Harris, P. Van Bergen, J. Sutton, & A. Barnier (Eds.), *Collaborative remembering: Theories, research, and applications* (pp. 261–279). Oxford: Oxford University Press.

Perry, D. G., & Pauletti, R. E. (2011). Gender and adolescent development. *Journal of Research on Adolescence, 21*(1), 61–74.

Philippe, F. L., Koestner, R., Lecours, S., Beaulieu-Pelletier, G., & Bois, K. (2011). The role of autobiographical memory networks in the experience of negative emotions: How our remembered past elicits our current feelings. *Emotion*, *11*(6), 1279–1290. doi:10.1037/a0025848

Prentice, D. A., & Carranza, E. (2002). What women and men should be, shouldn't be, are allowed to be and don't have to be: The contents of prescriptive gender stereotypes. *Psychology of Women Quarterly*, *26*, 269–281.

Reese, E., Haden, C. A., & Fivush, R. (1996). Mothers, fathers, daughters, sons: Gender differences in autobiographical reminiscing. *Research on Language and Social Interaction*, *29*(1), 27–56.

Richards, C., Bouman, W. P., Seal, L., Barker, M. J., Nieder, T. O., & T'Sjoen, G. (2016). Non-binary or genderqueer genders. *International Review of Psychiatry*, *28*(1), 95–102.

Ricoeur, P. (1991). Life in quest of narrative. In D. Wood (Ed.), *On Paul Ricoeur: Narrative and interpretation* (pp. 20–33). London: Routledge.

Rime, B. (2007). The social sharing of emotion as an interface between individual and collective processes in the construction of emotional climate. *Journal of Social Issues*, *63*, 307–322.

Rose, A. J., Schwartz-Mette, R. A., Glick, G. C., Smith, R. L., & Luebbe, A. M. (2014). An observational study of co-rumination in adolescent friendships. *Developmental Psychology*, *50*(9), 2199–2209.

Syed, M., Pasupathi, M., & McLean, K. (in press). Master narratives, ethics, and morality. In L. Jensen (Ed.), *The Oxford handbook of moral development: An interdisciplinary perspective*. Oxford: Oxford University Press.

Thoman, D. B., Sansone, C., Fraughton, T., & Pasupathi, M. (2012). How students socially evaluate interest: Peer responsiveness influences evaluation and maintenance of interest. *Contemporary Educational Psychology*, *37*(4), 254–265. doi:10.1016/j.cedpsych.2012.04.001

Thoman, D. B., Sansone, C., & Pasupathi, M. (2007). Talking about interest: Exploring the role of social interaction for regulating motivation and the interest experience. *Journal of Happiness Studies*, *8*, 335–370.

Thorne, A., & McLean, K. C. (2003). Telling traumatic events in adolescence: A study of master narrative positioning. In R. Fivush & C. A. Haden (Eds.), *Autobiographical memory and the construction of a narrative self: Developmental and cultural perspectives* (pp. 169–184). New York: Psychology Press.

Tversky, B., & Marsh, E. J. (2000). Biased retellings of events yield biased memories. *Cognitive Psychology*, *40*(1), 1–38.

Wang, Q. (2013a). The cultured self and remembering. In P. J. Bauer & R. Fivush (Eds.), *The handbook of children's memory development*. New York: Wiley-Blackwell.

Wang, Q. (2013b). Gender and emotion in everyday event memory. *Memory*, *21* (4), 503–511.

Way, N. (2013). *Deep secrets: Boys' friendships and the crisis of connection*. Cambridge, MA: Harvard University Press.

Webster, J. D., & Gould, O. (2007). Reminiscence and vivid personal memories across adulthood. *International Journal of Aging & Human Development*, *64*(2), 149–170. doi:10.2190/Q8V4-X5H0-6457-5442

Yousaf, O., Grunfeld, E. A., & Hunter, M. S. (2015). A systematic review of the factors associated with delays in medical and psychological help-seeking among men. *Health Psychology Review, 9*(2), 264–276. doi:10.1080/17437199.2013.840954

Zaman, W., & Fivush, R. (2011). When my mom was a little girl . . .: Gender differences in adolescents' intergenerational and personal stories. *Journal of Research on Adolescence, 21*(3), 703–716.

8   Gendering the Unsaid and the Unsayable

Gregory Coles and Cheryl Glenn

In the wake of a mass shooting that killed seventeen people at Marjory Stoneman Douglas High School in Florida, survivor Emma Gonzalez delivered a moving speech at the March for Our Lives rally in Washington, DC, on March 24, 2018. Perhaps the most remarkable feature of the speech was that it was largely composed of silence. Gonzalez began by emphasizing how little time it had taken for the school shooter to silence seventeen voices forever:

> Six minutes and twenty seconds with an AR-15 and my friend Carmen would never complain to me about piano practice. Aaron Feis would never call Kyra "Miss Sunshine." Alex Schachter would never walk into school with his brother Ryan. . . . Martin Duque Anguiano would never, Peter Wang would never, Alyssa Alhadeff would never, Jaime Guttenberg would never, Meadow Pollack would never. (CNN, 2018)

After speaking for about one minute and fifty seconds, Gonzalez stood in silence on the stage for four and a half tense minutes. Then a timer sounded, and Gonzalez concluded her speech with these words: "Since the time I came out here, it has been six minutes and twenty seconds. The shooter has ceased shooting and will soon abandon his rifle, blend in with the students as they escape, and walk free for an hour before arrest. Fight for your lives, before it's someone else's job" (CNN, 2018).

While Gonzalez's use of silence in this speech clearly reflects her agency and empowerment as a rhetor, not all silence reflects such empowerment. The deeply meaningful, rhetorically incisive silence of Gonzalez's speech stands in stark contrast to the milieu of silence about sexual assault that was confronted – first in the United States and then globally – by the #MeToo movement. For many survivors of sexual assault, rhetorical situations and societal power differentials in the Harvey Weinstein era had made it impossible to speak of the assault, let alone the perpetrator. These survivors were *able* to speak, in the plainest physiological sense – in fact, some of them were public figures with enormous audiences listening to their words. Yet those who did try to address their experiences faced enormous consequences and remained mostly unheard by the world around them. Others with similar stories were thus dis-incentivized from speaking out. The words these survivors most needed to speak remained unsaid and unsayable within their world. Ultimately, they claimed agency for themselves by moving from an *imposition* of silence to a *position* of speaking and being heard. Whereas Gonzalez remained silent to communicate clearly the message she desired to be heard, vast numbers of sexual assault survivors before #MeToo felt silenced no matter how loudly their voices spoke, because no one had agreed to listen to them. Gonzalez's silence was purposefully chosen; the sexual assault survivors had been silenced by outside forces.

In both of these examples, a form of the unsaid is at work. That is, both discourses are marked by notable absences and can be retrospectively analyzed according to themes that remain tacit within them. In each case, something important has been left unspoken; and in each case, someone looking back on the silence can make defensible claims about its meaning and its importance. Yet the rhetorical implications of the two moments differ vastly. Gonzalez's unsaid boldly draws attention to itself, and Gonzalez marshals this attention strategically to enact a rhetorical performance of the silence and loss created by gun violence. By contrast, when sexual assault survivors left their experiences unspoken, their silence was subtler thus more easily overlooked by others, as indeed it was overlooked for decades. Whereas Gonzalez deploys the unsaid in a move to gain rhetorical power, the survivors represented by the #MeToo movement needed to escape the realm of the unsaid to gain power: they claimed agency by both speaking and being heard. How is it that the unsaid can function so differently – noticed or unnoticed, powerful or powerless – under different circumstances?

To be clear, in keeping with the rest of this volume, we are here defining "unsaid" not as mere silence but as a thematic absence within discourse, regardless of whether words are being spoken, written, signed, or otherwise communicated. We are concerned here with what is *left unsaid* in discourse, including both purposeful and incidental absences, both those noticed by others and those that escape notice. (For more on the rhetorical implications of silence beyond the realm of the unsaid, see Glenn's *Unspoken* [2004], as well as work by Acheson [2008], Ryan-Flood & Gill [2010], Booth & Spencer [2016], and many others.)

In this chapter, we argue that the meaning of the unsaid is always inflected by the power differential known as gender. As gender theory of recent decades has argued, being gendered "masculine" or "feminine" according to the rhetorical norms of society is markedly different from being biologically sexed or otherwise identified as "man" or "woman."

Gender is, writes Teresa de Lauretis, "the representation of each individual in terms of a particular social relation which pre-exists the individual" (1987, p. 5). In societal performance, à la Judith Butler (1993), rather than a biological inherency of domination or subordination – a *doing* written onto the human *being* (see also work by Joan Wallach Scott [1988], Cynthia Fuchs Epstein [1988], Susan Gal [1991], and Anne Fausto-Sterling [1993]). As Cheryl Glenn has observed, gender is now commonly understood by academics as both "a hierarchy of power relations" and "a horizontal axis of incommensurability (be it financial, academic, religious, physical)" (2004, p. 22). Thus, she argues, "the distinction between gender and sex is not as important [to the study of silence] as the distinctions people themselves might make between their so-called biological sex and their so-called social roles and the connections they might make between their social standing and their social roles" (2004, p. 23). The term "gender," after all, was aligned with grammatical inflection before being applied to the manner in which sexed bodies inhabit society. Hence Thomas Laqueur defines gender as a "primary way of signifying relations of power" (1990, p. 12).

If scholars are to locate and determine unsaid's import, we cannot do so without attending to the dynamics of the power differential that is gender. Considering the gender of the unsaid attunes us to what Glenn calls the grammar of rhetorical power: "who may speak, who may listen or who will agree to listen, and what can be said" (1997, pp. 1–2). Often the spoken remains the realm of power, and silence the realm of powerlessness – thus, Michelle Cliff admonishes us to realize "the alliance of speechlessness and powerlessness; that the former maintains the latter; that the powerful are dedicated to the investiture of speechlessness on the powerless" (1978, p. 5). Yet the relation of speech to power is not always so plain, as the examples in this chapter will elucidate. In other words, whether people are men or women, masculine or feminine, is not so important to their purposeful use of the unsaid or of speech as their willingness and ability to use the unsaid or speech to fulfill their rhetorical purpose. Rhetorical power is not limited to words alone; for this reason, the study of the unsaid has much to offer to the powerful and disempowered alike. Whether the unsaid calls attention to itself or goes unnoticed, it remains consequential. Absences both reflect and construct the power differentials of the spaces they fill. The decision to leave certain words or ideas unsaid might convey an imposition of authority, a begrudging submission, a fear agreement, or a means of resistance; ideas' ostensible absence in no way limits their potency.

Indeed, a number of scholars within rhetorical studies have argued that many women's rhetorical contributions in society have long been overlooked because they occurred in "silence" and that attending to these silences will thus open an undiscovered horizon of women's rhetoric (see, e.g., Glenn & Ratcliffe's 2011 collection, and also Bokser, 2006; Enoch, 2008; Farmer, 2001; Johnson, 2002). Jacqueline Jones Royster and Gesa Kirsch (2012) argue that one of the distinctive features of feminist rhetorical inquiry in the coming years must be "critical imagination," the discipline of thinking "between, above, around, and beyond" available evidence to consider the weight of what is missing from that evidence, including what has been left unsaid (p. 71). Other scholars have taken these insights of feminist inquiry and extended them to recover the unvoiced rhetorics of other historically subordinated, "feminized" groups, including non-Western rhetorics (Mao & Young, 2008; Wang, 2008) and sexual minority rhetorics (Brown, 2009; Fredriksen-Goldsen et al., 2009).

Yet all rhetorical absences are not created equal. In some cases, as with Gonzalez, the unsaid can be a purposeful strategy reflecting the agency of the rhetor. In other cases, as with the sexual assault survivors represented in the #MeToo movement, the unsaid can be the result of muting, the product of societal power structures that marginalize certain voices and render certain thoughts unsayable. As Aimee Carrillo Rowe and Sheena Malhotra (2013) have joined other scholars in noting, we are in error when we simply conflate voice with agency and silence with oppression. The reality is far more nuanced, especially where gendered power relations are at play – as they always are. Legal scholar Margaret Montoya (2000) posits by way of Mikhail Bakhtin that depending on the cultural contexts and identities of those who remain silent, the same silences may be either "centripetal" or "centrifugal": that is, the choice not to speak may center and maintain the status quo, or it may decenter and communicate resistance. According to Montoya, we can understand how the unsaid works in society only if we first understand how the unspeaking body is raced, cultured, and gendered in relation to societal expectation. Jean Mills's (2006) investigation bolsters this hypothesis when she notes that what bilingual women choose to speak or leave unsaid varies in different languages and cultural contexts. Although the women themselves have not changed, the possibilities afforded them by linguistic presence and linguistic absence are constantly under negotiation.

Conceptualized through gender theory, our chapter will demonstrate the ways that these various uses of the unsaid are gendered (as opposed to "sexed"). That is, we are not simply concerned with how bodies' biological sexes or gender identities are often mapped onto their enactments of the unsaid or with how male-identified and female-identified persons differ in their uses of the unsaid. Rather, we are concerned with how assignations of "masculinity" and "femininity," particularly as they relate to presumptions and performances of domination and subordination, impact the rhetorical function of the unsaid. Permitted-to-speak bodies are often already empowered, using the unsaid as a meaningful absence to maintain their power, while those able-to-speak weak bodies perform simply another iteration of a regulatory, disciplinary norm by their speech or silence. Yet the ways bodies are sexed or gendered, raced, abled, or classed (socioeconomically) matter less in the interpretation of the unsaid than their willingness and ability to speak or be silent about a particular matter to fulfill their rhetorical purpose: to maintain their position of power, simulate a subordinate position, or resist the domination of others.

The power dynamics of speech and silence – of mapping domination and subordination onto what is (or can be) spoken in discourse and what remains (or must remain) unsaid – are always imbricated with what linguistic anthropologists have called *language ideologies*: "sets of beliefs about language articulated by users as a rationalization or justification of perceived language structure and use" (Silverstein, 1979, p. 193). That is, a person's speech or silence about a given topic, or their speech or silence more generally, is always informed by communal presuppositions about what kinds of linguistic engagements are expected or allowed. If silence regarding a certain matter is expected – or enforced – then speech becomes a kind of violation. Where speech is demanded, however, the unsaid may have an equal capacity for resistance. The locus of power is thus not in the mere fact of speech or silence but in the way language ideologies inflected by gender are reaffirmed or violated in specific contexts.

In attempting to determine the meaning and impact of the unsaid and its methodological relevance, then, attention to gendering is indispensable. If the unsaid is gendered masculine, it is often assumed to be rhetorically purposeful and powerful, but its gendering alone does not make it so. Nor, if gendered feminine, is the unsaid always the result of muting or silencing altogether. On the contrary, the masculine unsaid may be subverted by the introduction of an alternative hierarchy that shifts the locus of power. Meanwhile, the feminine unsaid may become a tool that defies hegemonic power structures by using the unsaid as a tactic for conveying forbidden ideas, stubbornly communicating the unsayable. The boundaries of power are not static but slippery, constantly being renegotiated in relation to one another. Thus, attuning to gender as power differential reveals the specific ways the unsaid performs its rhetorical artistry, as a means to maintain or defy power or to admit subordination.

In the remainder of this chapter, we illustrate the centrality of gender in both locating the unsaid and determining its function. Using examples from politics, social life, academia, and literature, we discuss three broad categories of the unsaid as it plays out within gendered power differentials: (1) the "masculine" unsaid, as it perpetuates existing hierarchies; (2) the subordinate unsaid, borne from a place of "feminine" disadvantage; and (3) the resistant unsaid, which emerges from subordination and yet tactically subverts the status quo. In aligning the "masculine" with dominance and the "feminine" with subordination, to be clear, we are following the grammatical and poetical designations that align masculinity with linguistic "strength" and femininity with linguistic "weakness." While these traits have been historically ascribed as the respective ideals of male and female persons, we are certainly not suggesting that they are inherent beyond their cultural constructions as such. In addition, our assignation of "tactics" as emerging from a place of subordinate resistance is in keeping with Michel de Certeau's (1984) distinction between "strategies," which emerge from preexisting power structures, and "tactics," which are rooted in a response to subjugation.

These broad categories we propose are not intended to be discrete or exhaustive – all three have leakages into one another, and any given real-life example might bear traces of them all. What the categories offer, rather, is a means of beginning to codify common rhetorical spaces in which the unsaid can be located and interpreted according to its interplay with gender.

The Masculine Unsaid

On October 9, 2016, US presidential candidates Hillary Clinton and Donald Trump faced off in a town hall–style debate in St. Louis, Missouri. The format of the debate allowed candidates to wander the stage as they pleased, during both their own responses and their opponent's responses. Trump took advantage of this format to walk closely behind Clinton as she delivered some of her answers, his silent presence demanding her audience's attention even though he never spoke. Clinton (2017, p. 136) later reflected on the event:

"This is not okay," I thought.

It was the second presidential debate, and Donald Trump was looming behind me. Two days before, the world heard him brag about groping women. Now we were on a small stage, and no matter where I walked, he followed me closely, staring at me, making faces. It was incredibly uncomfortable. He was literally breathing down my neck. My skin crawled.

It was one of those moments where you wish you could hit Pause and ask everyone watching, "Well? What would *you* do?"

Do you stay calm, keep smiling, and carry on as if he weren't repeatedly invading your space?

Or do you turn, look him in the eye, and say loudly and clearly, "Back up, you creep, get away from me, I know you love to intimidate women but you can't intimidate me, so *back up*."

The importance of the debate's timing, just two days after the revelation of Trump's lewd comments about women in 2005, cannot be overstated in understanding this rhetorical moment. Trump had already verbally asserted his authority over women's bodies, his perceived right to "grab them by the pussy" with impunity. Now, he asserted that same authority by way of the unsaid, his looming presence demanding that the audience recognize and translate his unspoken words. Clinton, meanwhile, continued to speak in the manner prescribed by the debate, while her true meaning ("Back up, you creep") remained unsayable.

Power, according to Max Weber's (1969) classic definition, is one social actor's capacity to impose their own will on others. In the case of Trump and Clinton, Trump's presumed "masculine" dominance, his uncomfortable behavior, enabled him to impose onto Clinton the burden of either speaking out or remaining silent. Using bodily intimidation, Trump created a palpable instance of unsaid rhetoric to which Clinton was forced to respond, either by continuing to answer the debate question or by interrupting herself to confront Trump. Neither option could overturn the presumed hierarchy in which Clinton was marked subordinate as a woman. Clinton explained in her reflection: "Of course, had I told Trump off, he surely would have capitalized on it gleefully. A lot of people recoil from an angry woman, or even just a direct one" (2017, p. 137). Thus, by placing the burden of the unsaid on Clinton, given the language ideologies of their audience, Trump's behavior ensured that Clinton would remain in the disadvantaged rhetorical role.

Sociolinguist Victoria DeFrancisco (1991) demonstrates how the taciturn power of the unsaid expressed itself in many man-woman marital relationships in the late twentieth century. DeFrancisco found that in conversations between husbands and wives, wives tended to talk more, but husbands often did not engage the topics of conversation raised by their wives. Husbands' decisions to remain silent rather than respond to their wives' words – a rhetorical exhibition of the husbands' disinterest, or perhaps proof that they weren't listening at all – stripped these women of linguistic power even while they were speaking. Meanwhile, the husbands, although less likely to speak, were more likely to interrupt their wives and to set conversation topics. These husbands exercised linguistic power both by speech and by silence, both by the ideas they spoke and by those they left unsaid. While DeFrancisco's findings are certainly not true of all marriages (contemporary or otherwise), they illustrate how the unsaid operates differently for those in power than for those who are subordinate.

One common example of the power of the unsaid to enact and enforce social power is the relational move called "the silent treatment." By refusing to engage certain topics, or to engage in conversation at all, a person whose engagement is expected or desired can create discomfort through absence. Richard J. Watts writes, "inter-turn silences, particularly those of more than 1.7 seconds' duration, contribute in significant ways to the acquisition or loss of discourse status" (1997, p. 110). This power move often originates from authority figures like police officers, courtroom judges, and bosses, as Glenn (2004, p. 33) observes:

> The highway patrol officer's and the judge's silences extend much longer than 1.7 seconds, enhancing the status they already hold. But theirs is a situational (as well as institutional) silence, one that is always expected despite (or because of) the discomfort it causes others. Other authority figures, however, exert silence-as-control when silence is neither expected nor appropriate. Now while these uses of silence may be unintentional or unconscious, they, nevertheless, keep the subordinate figures in their place, particularly if theirs or the authority-figure's status is unresolved. . . .
> No matter what the situation, gendered power differentials – or gendered attempts at equilibrium – are played out with language and silence whenever a boss and an employee are involved and especially when the interactive silences are prolonged (longer than 1.7 seconds). Whether intermittent or constant, such silent treatment is torturous.

Yet the possibilities of the silent treatment are not monolithic, as Himika Bhattacharya (2009) demonstrates in her study of Indian women's performed silences. One of Bhattarcharya's interviewees, a woman named Laxmi, wields the silent treatment as a tool against oppression. After being raped and then forced to marry her attacker, Laxmi maintains her dignity by refusing to speak to her husband more than necessary. She comes from a higher caste than he does, a fact she will not allow him to forget, and thus she wields her silence as a constant reminder of his social inferiority to her; she will not even eat with him. Although she is in many ways marked subordinate and therefore feminine, her higher caste provides an alternative form of masculine power, subverting the perceived femininity of her sexed body in a patriarchal society. This gendered struggle for power is thus negotiated entirely within the realm of the unsaid. The masculine unsaid and the subordinate unsaid are always in tension with each other, sometimes trading places, sometimes subverted by leakages between the two.

The Subordinate Unsaid

Whenever I ask a question in public, at faculty senate or at a national meeting, I am nervous. My voice quavers, my heart beats fast, my entire body shakes.

As an undergraduate, I would sit in classes, whether large or small, and when the teacher asked a question I would think of the answer but then go on to think, "Oh, that can't be right." When someone else would say what I was thinking – or something worse – I would always think somehow that it was just an accident that I'd thought the same thing. I spoke little if anything during all my undergrad classes, even my English classes.

(cited in Glenn, 2004, p. 43)

These words are taken from an anonymous interview with a highly successful white female professor. When her ideas remain unsaid, her decision to leave them unsaid reflects her perception of her own inferiority, belying her academic status and her apparent empowerment. She relates an internalized sense of subordination rooted in how society has interpreted her woman's body as feminized and therefore less powerful.

The presumption of gendered subordination that motivates the unsaid can be rooted in a variety of factors: sexed body, of course, but also race, class, sexuality, and much more. Often these factors themselves remain unsaid, yet their relevance to the foreclosure of discourse is inescapable, as another anonymous interviewee (who now holds a PhD) explains (cited in Glenn, 2004, p. 44):

When I was an undergraduate at Cleveland State, I had a course in eighteenth-century British Literature. I don't remember the exact question I asked, but the professor was lecturing, and I raised my hand and asked something. He looked at me with that look that says, "Why do they let you stupid bracketed in here?" And then he almost literally said it: "You have asked a non-question. If you could read and use the dictionary, you wouldn't have to ask such a question."

From that day forward, I never asked another question in his class. I never said anything to anyone. I was the only person of African descent in the class and that made me unsure of myself. The thing that I used to get me through that class and all the others was this: "I know I ain't stupid. These white folks ain't no better than me. I know I can read and write." As for that class, I struggled to get a C and was glad to get it – and get out.

For this interviewee, her race threatened to feminize her in the eyes of her professor. Though she resisted, this feminization did cast all her future potential insights in that class into the realm of the unsaid. And unfortunately, not everyone who encounters the kind of hostility this woman did will be able to respond with the same fortitude. For some, the choice to leave their insights unsaid after being received poorly by authority figures becomes a rationale for permanent silence regarding certain topics.

Even men who belong to racial or sexual minorities, or to lower classes or socioeconomic statuses, are prone to being gendered feminine in the way they are relegated to the realm of the unsaid. Consider the adolescent recollections of Gregory Coles (2017, p. 12) upon realizing that he was gay within a discursive community that lacked such a category for Christians like himself:

If I had been reserved and private about my sexuality before, this revelation sealed my lips even tighter. I knew next to nothing about homosexuality, but I knew it was a topic reserved for hushed tones and sorrowful eyes. It wasn't something nice Christian boys like me talked about, not something they should need or want to understand.

The absence of a familiar narrative to fit within can often become a source of silencing. And when familiar narratives are constructed and advanced only by the masculine gendered and powerful, those attempting to speak from the margins may find themselves caught within a web of foreclosures that renders any meaningful speech impossible:

[T]here were all sorts of fears to keep me quiet. What would my friends think, especially my male friends? Would they hold me at arm's length out of disdain, or perhaps with the best of intentions, to spare me the risk of falling in love with them? If I lost every opportunity for healthy same-sex intimacy, wouldn't that just make the problem worse?

And what about my leadership roles? I was leading worship and speaking about my faith in increasingly public contexts. Would I lose the ability to reach those people? Would I create a rift in my community, turn from a success story into a tragedy? . . ..

So I held my tongue and acted my way through college. It wasn't that I lied, mind you – I wouldn't have stood for that – but I spoke the truth strategically. I told the part of the story I was ready to tell and replaced the rest of it with tangents and big words and wide smiles. I learned to do what I had always longed to do: blend in. (Coles, 2017, p. 24)

In many ways, Coles inhabits a privileged position; he is a man, white, well educated, recognized as a leader within his religious community. Despite these privileges, however, his silence on the subject of his sexuality remains motivated by subordination. In fact, the tenuous nature of certain privileges – the threat of erasure once certain taboos have been spoken – creates a new kind of subordination, as the seeming inherency of masculine advantage is rendered fragile by the threat of queerness.

The subordinate unsaid is often characterized by the inability of those who inhabit it to define themselves. The very nature of their subordination remains unsaid, their inability to speak becoming itself unspeakable. One of Glenn's anonymous interviewees (cited in Glenn, 2004, p. 44) writes,

I feel compelled to provide a specific, traumatic event with much at stake materially, academically, or emotionally. But since frequent and quite vulgar attempts to silence me occur on a regular basis, I cannot draw on one specific incident. I am a Black male, and silencing, like police harassment, comes with the territory; besides, to draw on one incident might neutralize the gravity of the phenomenon.

My psychological, spiritual, and cultural health and survival depend, in part, on my ability to deflect the transgressions of singular instances of silencing, overcome them, when possible, and ultimately ignore or blunt the emotional and psychological sharpness of their effects – therein lies the rub. Escaping the shadow of a dominant discourse which allows others to consistently control or contain what Blackness and Black maleness means inside or outside the classroom seems to be a task of Sisyphean proportions. Of course, I intervene; of course, I interrogate; of course, I resist – but much too often, the final word, the final definition is left in the mouths of others.

When self-definition is cast into the realm of the unsaid and the unsayable, it creates a paradox of speech for the subordinated figure. Speech remains possible, physiologically speaking, yet the possibilities of speech are meaningfully foreclosed. This tension either remains unsaid or it is spoken and misunderstood, making its meaning impossible to communicate. This same interviewee (cited in Glenn, 2004, p. 45) continues:

To speak of this silencing is too often to risk being accused of a sort of racial paranoia; to complain about a shadow is to construct myself into a low intensity insanity in the eyes of others. Silencing's very nonspecificness, its insentientness, makes speaking of it dangerous, dangerous because the very speaking of it admits to vulnerability.

To speak of it (my shadow, my containment) now feels emancipatory, but only temporally, because tomorrow I will be contained again. And the residue of my temporary emancipation in this moment will linger with me, offering me further hope along with further frustration.

The unsayable, as this passage fittingly demonstrates, may be expressed through total silence, but it is not necessarily expressed this way. Rather, the deprivation of the subordinate unsaid is often accompanied by listeners' assumption that no speech is off-limits, that the unsayable does not exist.

What remains (or threatens to remain) unsaid, then, is the identification of the unsaid itself as extant and meaningful. The act of labeling an empty space and naming the presence of the unspeakable is a bold statement of its own, thus requiring that the one who identifies it have the capacity to speak. In a vicious cycle of silencing, those who lack the power to speak against their own subordination equally lack the power to name the unsaid; meanwhile, those empowered to name the unsaid have no need of it. In this sense, if power and powerlessness, speech and silence, were ever to become absolute realities, the goal of locating the unsaid would become a methodological impossibility, because those able to locate it would be those unable to speak of it, or those unable to be heard, once they did locate it. Scholars of the unsaid must always be attuned for the voices whose unspoken meanings are least evident, those voices closest to total powerlessness.

The Resistant Unsaid

For individuals feeling trapped within the subordinate unsaid, creating a path for outspoken resistance is perhaps the most apparent way to resist power structures. For example, we might consider Glenn's (2018) retelling of the public dispute between feminist writers Mary Daly and Audre Lorde about feminism and whiteness. After Daly published her book *Gyn/Ecology*, Lorde wrote a compelling letter to Daly pointing out that the authentic voices of women of color had been excluded from Daly's vision of womanhood. Instead of remaining silent, Lorde sets out to right this inequity by responding verbally to Daly, contributing to feminist discourse a perspective that had been previously left unsaid by Daly's work. Daly, eventually, responded with an apology. As Glenn argues, the feminist ideals of openness and listening were realized in this case only when a once-silenced voice was able to speak and, just as important, was listened to.

However, speech is not the only means of resistance that can occur from the margins. At times, when a mandate toward a certain kind of speech exists, the unsaid can become a means of resistance as well. After all, as Sara Ahmed observes, "under certain circumstances, speech might not be empowering, let alone sensible" (2010, p. xvi). We might think, for instance, of Arthur Miller's (1953) depiction of the Salem Witch Trials, *The Crucible*, which shows women accused of witchcraft being commanded to speak to confess their alleged misdeeds and name their fellow "witches." Those women who refuse to speak – who maintain their innocence by leaving their guilt unsaid – are presumed unrepentant and executed. Yet it is also these women who form the heart of the resistance to an abusive authority system. Their feminine refusal to speak in confession subverts the supposed weakness of femininity by redistributing the extant rhetorical power. Indeed, the play's most triumphant moment occurs when protagonist John Proctor joins these women in refusing to declare his alleged guilt, becoming part of a belligerently feminine resistance movement.

One space where the feminine unsaid often appears as a form of resistance is the political sphere. Political leaders from Queen Elizabeth I of England to Benazir Bhutto of Pakistan, Angela Merkel of Germany, and Megawati Sukarnoputri of Indonesia have all negotiated a complex balance of speaking and leaving things unsaid. As a head of state, each of these women is gendered masculine to some degree, yet she is also marked as feminine by her sexed body in a culture that regards women as inherently less powerful. In such a position, boldness and resistance to hierarchic norms may take on a variety of forms. Often these women violate a norm that presumes women's silence by means of their forceful and authoritative speech. At other times, however, these women tellingly refused certain forms of speech that were presumed or mandated by the systems of authority around them, employing so-called feminine silence as a tool of resistance.

Consider the case of Indonesia's first – and, to date, only – female president, Megawati Sukarnoputri. A formidable presence in Indonesian politics during the decline of long-standing dictator Suharto in the mid-1990s, Megawati staged her protest to the corruption of the Suharto regime by remaining silent when the political scene around her expected her to speak. As a result, her silence drew attention to itself, becoming an eloquent and uncensorable protest of the established political power system. Angus McIntyre describes Megawati's unspoken words as a kind of "sign language," a message which could be communicated only by being left unsaid: "Megawati became a mute symbol; or, rather, a symbol because she was mute, a sign for decency amid the abuse of power of the Suharto regime" (2000, p. 109). Daniel Ziv (2001) observes that newspapers during this period often equated Megawati's refusal to speak with her tenacity and endurance and that this perception contributed substantially to her public popularity. He notes, "to a point, at least, Megawati's silence has indeed seemed golden. The less exposed, the more revered" (2001, p. 86). Because speech was expected of her, demanded by a hegemonic system, Megawati's use of the unsaid became a channel of resistance.

The boundaries between masculinity and femininity, already fraught in any instance of the unsaid, are especially complex when the resistant unsaid is at work. The capacity to resist implies an expectation of speech, which often reflects a degree of imputed masculinity – that is, an assignation of some measure of dominance. In Megawati's case, her role as a political party chair and her status as the daughter of Indonesia's first president, Sukarno, mark her as a powerful figure who therefore inherits the masculine expectation of speech. Could Megawati have enacted the resistant unsaid without this expectation – or would her unspoken words have been ignored, like the silence of so many others, presumed to have no import or meaning? The potential for ambiguity and leakages between the categories of the masculine, subordinate, and resistant unsaid are necessary features of such a classification system. Attention to gendered power differentials does not guarantee an infallible means of determining where power exists or how it functions in the realm of the unsaid. Rather, such a system opens our eyes to rhetorical and interpretative nuances that might otherwise go unnoticed.

The leakages between gendered power and powerlessness in the resistant unsaid are beautifully modeled in the final pages of Kristin Hannah's best-selling 2015 novel *The Nightingale*. During the Second World War, Frenchwoman Vianne Mauriac is raped by a Nazi officer named Von Richter. Soon after Vianne realizes she is pregnant by Von Richter, the war ends and her husband Antoine returns home. Vianne lies to Antoine and tells him the child is his, never confessing the truth either to Antoine or to the son born by this pregnancy, Julien. When Julien finally confronts Vianne many years later about the secrets she has kept from him all his life, Vianne explains her decision to speak some of these secrets and to leave others unsaid:

I see the incredulity in my son's eyes and it makes me smile. Our children see us so imperfectly. . . .

"Did Dad know?" Julien asks.

"Your father . . . " I pause, draw in a breath. *Your father.* And there it is, the secret that made me bury it all.

I have spent a lifetime running from it, trying to forget, but now I see what a waste all that was.

Antoine was Julien's father in every way that mattered. It is not biology that determines fatherhood. It is love . . . .

I will tell my son my life story at last. There will be pain in remembering, but there will be joy, too.

"You'll tell me everything?"

"Almost everything," I say with a smile. "A Frenchwoman must have her secrets." And I will . . . I'll keep one secret. (2015, p. 438)

In one sense, Vianne's silence about Von Richter has been a form of the subordinate unsaid: after all, it is Von Richter's sexual violence against Vianne that has created the conditions for her silence. Initially, she is motivated to leave Julien's parentage unspoken because of her shame and her fear that Von Richter's biological "fatherhood" will supersede Antoine's actions as Julien's familial father.

Yet Vianne's final decision to "keep one secret" is no longer motivated by fear or subordination. Instead, she aligns her decision to stay quiet about Von Richter's sexual violence with her agency as a human being: "A Frenchwoman must have her secrets." Instead of pretending that she has no secrets left to keep from Julien, she draws his attention to the presence of a secret and then leaves that secret unspoken. By reframing the meaning of her secrecy, Vianne shifts the very nature of the unsaid. She ends the book with a declaration of hope enabled by this rhetorical revelation: "I know now what matters, and it is not what I have lost. It is my memories. Wounds heal. Love lasts. We remain" (2015, p. 438). The content of Vianne's unspoken words has not shifted, yet their rhetorical function has been transformed.

Conclusion

To gender the unsaid and the unsayable requires far more than simply recognizing the gender identities of those who subtly or conspicuously remain silent. Nor can the effect of a communicative absence be determined simply by noting the gendered power differentials that exist between rhetors of the unsaid. Rather, as we have proposed here, gender attunes us to the ever-negotiated interplay among body, authority, society, and rhetorical possibility. Whether the unsaid functions as masculine/dominant, feminine/subordinate, or resistant, it is always and inescapably functioning as gendered. Rhetorical possibility is determined by the grammar of rhetorical power – "who may speak, who may listen or who will agree to listen, and what can be said" (Glenn, 1997, pp. 1–2) – in concert with or in contradiction to the expectations of language ideologies. To see rhetorical possibility, or impossibility, is to see the power differentials of gender.

In arguing for the utility of the masculine unsaid, the subordinate unsaid, and the resistant unsaid as valuable classifications for developing a comprehensive methodology of the unsaid, our intention is not to posit these categories either as comprehensive within themselves or as neatly discrete from one another. Rather, as we have shown, the various expressions of gendered power differentials within the realm of the unsaid are in constant engagement and renegotiation with one another. The framework we offer is thus not delimiting but heuristic. It is a way of locating deeply meaningful silences that might have gone unnoticed, a way of understanding how seemingly equivalent iterations of the unsaid will function in dramatically different ways according to the gendered power differentials of those who remain silent and those who receive this unsaid rhetoric.

In light of this framework, scholars of the unsaid would do well to consider the impact of three gendered factors upon our qualitative data. First, we must consider how the language ideologies of a given community – the expectations for speech or silence according to subject identity – are predicated upon differentials in power, whether those differentials are actively performed or merely presumed in the instance of the unsaid. Second, as the possibilities of language in each community become apparent, we must differentiate between that which is left purposefully unsaid and that which has been rendered (or gendered) unsayable by dominant discourses. Finally, we must recognize the leakages between power and powerlessness that are enacted by resistance, allowing that regardless of subject position or gendering, the unsaid is always rife with multiplicities of potential. Attuning to gender within the unsaid and the unsayable will not answer with finality all the methodological problems that arise in such studies. But gender is, at least, a necessary place to begin.

References

Acheson, K. (2008). Silence as gesture: Rethinking the nature of communicative silences. *Communication Theory, 18*, 535–555.

Ahmed, S. (2010). Foreword: Secrets and silence in feminist research. In R. Ryan-Flood & R. Gill (Eds.), *Secrecy and silence in the research process: Feminist reflections* (pp. xvi–xxi). London: Routledge

Bhattacharya, H. (2009). Performing silence: Gender, violence, and resistance in women's narratives from Lahaul, India. *Qualitative Inquiry, 15*(2), 359–371.

Bokser, J. K. (2006). The persuasion of Esther: A nun's model of silent, seductive, violent rhetoric. In P. Bizzell (Ed.), *Rhetorical agendas: Political, ethical, spiritual* (pp. 303–308). Mahwah, NJ: Erlbaum.

Booth, E. T., & Spencer, L. G. (2016). Sitting in silence: Managing aural body rhetoric in public restrooms. *Communication Studies, 67*(2), 209–226.

Brown, M. T. (2009). LGBT aging and rhetorical silence. *Sexuality Research and Social Policy: Journal of NSRC, 6*(4), 65–78.

Butler, J. (1993). *Bodies that matter*. New York: Routledge.

Cliff, M. (1978). Notes on speechlessness. *Sinister Wisdom, 5*: 5–9.

Clinton, H. R. (2017). *What happened*. New York: Simon & Schuster.

CNN. (2018, March 24). Emma Gonzalez: Fight for your lives [Television broadcast]. Atlanta, GA: Turner Broadcasting System. Retrieved from www.cnn.com/videos/us/2018/03/24/emma-gonzalez-full-speech-march-for-our-lives.cnn

Coles, G. (2017). *Single, gay, Christian: A personal journey of faith and sexual identity*. Downers Grove, IL: InterVarsity Press.

de Certeau, M. (1984). *The practice of everyday life*. (S. Rendall, Trans.). Berkeley: University of California Press.

de Lauretis, T. (1987). *Technologies of gender: Essays on theory, film, and fiction*. Bloomington: Indiana University Press.

DeFrancisco, V. L. (1991). The sounds of silence: How men silence women in marital relations. *Discourse and Society 2*, 413–423.

Enoch, J. (2008). *Refiguring rhetorical education: Women teaching African American, Native American, and Chicano/a students, 1865–1911*. Carbondale: Southern Illinois University Press.

Epstein, C. F. (1988). *Deceptive distinctions: Sex, gender, and the social order*. New Haven: Yale University Press.

Farmer, F. (2001). *Saying and silence: Listening to composition with Bakhtin*. Logan: Utah State University Press.

Fausto-Sterling, A. (1993, March 12). How many sexes are there? *New York Times*, p. A29. Retrieved from www.nytimes.com/1993/03/12/opinion/how-many-sexes-are-there.html

Fredriksen-Goldsen, K. I., Lindhorst, T., Kemp, S. P., & Walters, K. L. (2009). 'My ever dear': Social work's 'lesbian' foremothers; A call for scholarship. *Affilia, 24*(3), 325–336.

Gal, S. (1991). Between speech and silence: The problematics of research on language and gender. In M. di Leonardo (Ed.), *Gender at the crossroads of knowledge: Feminist anthropology in the postmodern era* (pp. 175–203). Berkeley: University of California Press.

Glenn, C. (1997). *Rhetoric retold: Regendering the tradition from antiquity through the Renaissance*. Carbondale: Southern Illinois University Press.

Glenn, C. (2004). *Unspoken: A rhetoric of silence*. Carbondale: Southern Illinois University Press.

Glenn, C. (2018). *Rhetorical feminism and this thing called hope*. Carbondale: Southern Illinois University Press.

Glenn, C., & Ratcliffe, K. (Eds.). (2011). *Silence and listening as rhetorical arts*. Carbondale: Southern Illinois University Press

Hannah, K. (2015). *The nightingale*. New York: St. Martin's Press

Johnson, N. (2002). *Gender and rhetorical space in American life, 1886–1910*. Carbondale: Southern Illinois University Press.

Knowles, A. (2015). The gender of silence: Irigaray on the measureless measure. *The Journal of Speculative Philosophy, 29*(3), 302–313.

Laqueur, T. (1990). *Making sex*. Cambridge, MA: Harvard University Press.

Mao, L., & Young, M. (Eds.). (2008). *Representations: Doing Asian American rhetoric*. Logan: Utah State University Press.

McIntyre, A. (2000). Megawati Sukarnoputri: From president's daughter to vice president. *Bulletin of Concerned Asian Scholars, 32*(1–2), 105–112.

Miller, A. (1953). *The crucible: A play in four acts*. New York: Viking Press.

Mills, J. (2006). Talking about silence: Gender and the construction of multilingual identities. *International Journal of Bilingualism, 10*(1), 1–16.

Montoya, M. E. (2000). Silence and silencing: Their centripetal and centrifugal forces in legal communication, pedagogy and discourse. *University of Michigan Journal of Law Reform, 33*(3), 263–328.

Rowe, A. C., & Malhotra, S. (2013). Still the silence: Feminist reflections at the edges of sound. In S. Malhotra & A. C. Rowe (Eds.), *Silence, feminism, power: Reflections at the edges of sound* (pp. 1–22). New York: Palgrave Macmillan.

Royster, J. J., & Kirsch, G. E. (2012). *Feminist rhetorical practices: New horizons for rhetoric, composition, and literacy studies.* Carbondale: Southern Illinois University Press.

Ryan-Flood, R., & Gill, R. (Eds.). (2010). *Secrecy and silence in the research process: Feminist reflections.* London: Routledge.

Scott, J. W. (1988). *Gender and the politics of history.* New York: Columbia University Press.

Silverstein, M. (1979). Language structure and linguistic ideology. In P. Clyne, W. Hanks, & C. Hofbauer (Eds.), *The Elements* (pp. 193–248). Chicago: Chicago Linguistic Society.

Trinh, T. M. (1986/1987). Difference: "A special Third World women issue." *Discourse, 8,* pp. 11–37.

Vernant, Jean-Pierre. (1982). *The origins of Greek thought.* Ithaca: Cornell University Press. (Original work published 1962)

Wang. B. (2008). Rereading Sui Sin Far: A rhetoric of defiance. In L. Mao & M. Young (Eds.), *Representations: Doing Asian American rhetoric* (pp. 244–265). Logan: Utah State University Press.

Watts, R. J. (1997). Silence and the acquisition of status in verbal interaction. In A. Jaworski (Ed.), *Silence: Interdisciplinary perspectives* (pp. 87–116). Berlin: Mouton de Gruyter.

Weber, M. (1969). *The theory of social and economic organization* (A. M. Henderson & T. Parsons, Trans.). New York: Free Press.

Ziv, D. (2001). Populist perceptions and perceptions of populism in Indonesia: The case of Megawati Soekarnoputri. *South East Asia Research, 9*(1), pp. 73–88.

9   The Language Ideology of Silence and Silencing in Public Discourse
Claims to Silencing as Metadiscursive Moves in German Anti-Political Correctness Discourse

Melani Schröter

The present chapter looks at silence through the lens of metadiscourse. The contribution of this chapter to the volume is that it points out how silence can be grasped analytically by studying metadiscourse about it. In doing so, it is also concerned with language ideology. I will argue that metadiscourse is indicative of attitudes towards or beliefs about the discursive phenomenon that is the object of metadiscourse, in this case silence and silencing. By way of a sample empirical analysis which illustrates the approach and the involved language ideological stances, I will deal with the anti–political correctness (anti-pc) discourse – a transnational discursive phenomenon since the 1990s that continues to cluster around language taboos, hate speech, (un)sayability, access to and limitations of public discourse, freedom of opinion, denial of voice and representation, silencing and censorship. Hence, aspects of silence, or more particularly silencing, loom large in anti-political correctness discourse, and the shape and idea of public discourse itself are invoked and negotiated here with a view on voice as a condition for democracy (cf. Couldry, 2010). Since it will be impossible within the scope of this chapter to cover various appropriations of anti-pc, I will focus on the German context, which to my mind is as good an example as any other. Having said this, it is likely that anti-pc debates in some other countries rest on similar premises and discursive strategies as laid out in the following, so that this chapter should provide useful aspects to consider and adapt for researchers concerned with other societies and languages.

I will maintain in this chapter that the unsaid becomes utilised in anti-political correctness discourse as a discursive strategy. The unsaid features in anti-political correctness discourse as something that (epistemologically) can be said, and that (socio-politically) wants, warrants or even needs saying but is prevented from being said through language taboos, silencing or even censorship. Within this context, or pretext, what is claimed to be unsaid more often than not does get said, or if not at least a case is made for the legitimacy of it being said. Anti-pc refers to established links between public discourse and democratic representation, so that claims about the legitimacy of the unsaid entail both the grievance and the illegitimacy of being silenced. We are therefore dealing with the more particular notions of silencing, taboo and censorship rather than silence more broadly. Silence can be a result of silencing as well as of deliberate choice – or both, in cases of, for example, self-censorship for not wanting to take risks or 'rock the boat' by breaking a taboo or whistle-blowing. Taboos can have the effect of silencing (cf. Zerubavel, 2006), as well as social marginalisation 'determined by the order of discourse that neither affords salience to certain points of view, nor resonance for voices from groups that are not perceived to be proper, or entitled, or participating speakers' (Schröter & Taylor, 2018, p. 9; cf. Achino-Loeb, 2006). Censorship (cf. Anthonissen, 2003; Galasiński, 2003) would involve powerful actors who have resources at their disposal to limit and suppress speech by others. All of these (taboos, silencing through marginalisation, censorship) are claimed by anti-political correctness discourse to be applied through political correctness. The salience of anti-political correctness discourses in Germany and probably elsewhere lies in the way in which silence and silencing are at odds with public discourse in post-war democracy, which I will discuss in the following.

Silence at Odds with Public Discourse

Since the spread of mass media in the twentieth century and online communication in the twenty-first century, silence has become at odds with public and political discourse. It has been shown for the German context that, historically, overt silence was a tool of wielding power in the seventeenth century (Benthien, 2006) and a means to avoid political conflict in the nineteenth century (Owzar, 2006). Proverbs about silence contain a sediment of language attitudes which suggests a positive view on silence as protection of valuable information (Spitznagel & Reiners, 1998). However, increasingly since the twentieth century, politicians and public figures are expected to provide a constant flow of and availability for communication. In this context, their silence would be viewed as problematic (Schröter, 2013). While mass media sustain and fuel this development, democratic governance with its requirements of public deliberation, transparency and accountability is at the heart of the valuation of communication and the problematising of silence.

Germany makes a good case for observing this development, since after the Nazi dictatorship, the occupation governments considered it of particular importance that the Germans relearn and engage with democratic debate (Verheyen, 2010). The parliamentary committee that worked out the new constitution of the post-war West German Federal Republic constantly emphasised the role and value of democratic debate (Kilian, 1997). It is perhaps not surprising that one of the most influential thinkers on the ethics of public deliberation, Jürgen Habermas, emerged from a West German post-war context. The generational revolt of 1968, which was sustained in various ways by social actors of the radical and political left, problematised the silence about the Nazi past, in particular about the Holocaust, and furthered the valuation of discussion, debate and public democratic deliberation (Kämper, 2012; Scharloth, 2011; Verheyen, 2010). An increasingly critical, sceptical (von Hodenberg, 2006) or at times even cynical journalism frequently puts politicians on the spot, ready to scandalise any obvious attempts at keeping silent or evading (Bull, 2003; Clayman, 2007). The popularisation of psychology and psychotherapy might have sustained the sceptical view on silence as a result of the valuation of communication as a means to solve personal and interpersonal problems (Kämper, 2002; Peters, 1999) and, increasingly, as a valuable professional skill (Cameron, 2000).

What is more, this political, cultural and intellectual context has led to increasing public language awareness (cf. Chouliaraki & Fairclough's 1999 notion of increasing reflexivity), so much so that 'metalinguistic sensitivity is, in a certain sense, a hallmark of contemporary social life' (Coupland & Jaworski, 2004, p. 6). Critical language awareness has, therefore, 'arisen in response to the growing importance of linguistic gatekeeping, i.e. an increasing number of individuals and institutions spelling out desirable or required versions of communication in various contexts' (Coupland & Jaworski, 2004, p. 39). The way people express themselves, especially in public and in the face of possibly multiplied audiences, has come under scrutiny because the way we talk is regarded as indicative of our attitudes and ideological positions. Again, Germany's Nazi past has influenced the reflection on the relationship between language and ideology there (cf. Sandkühler, 2008) and provides drastic examples of silencing and censorship. Post-structuralist approaches to language and discourse and in particular Foucault's thinking about the relationship among power, knowledge and discourse proved influential in seeing 'the order of discourse' as a modern manifestation of power beyond physical coercion. This theorising of discourse sheds a light on the marginalisation of groups or viewpoints going along with lack of voice and silencing.

These factors suggest a language ideology in public discourse which entails a negative view on silence and silencing. Silence is seen as not conducive to democratic governance, and mass media increase the need for and expectations of communication. The link made between language use and ideology leads to an increasing language awareness which means that people can be held to account for what they (do not) say, or how. Discourse is seen as constituting and enshrining power relations in societies, and silence is seen as indicative of a lack of power and/or as a result of silencing.

It is important to outline these factors, if only briefly, to understand the anti–political correctness discourse, the most salient language ideological debate of recent decades. The present-day German anti-political correctness discourse evolves mainly around claims by the New Right to have been silenced in a left-liberal discourse hegemony. I will describe anti-political correctness discourse as a language ideological debate and claims to have been silenced as strategic metadiscursive moves which seek to shift public discourse to gain legitimacy for the New Right's ideological positions and, most of all, to delegitimise the left, which is framed as censoring other views.

These strategies rely on the negative evaluation of silence and on the link between power and silencing. In its aim to undermine the political left, the New Right profits from the fact that the negative evaluation of silence, the valuation of discussion in a comprehensively accessible public sphere and the link between language and ideology as well as between power and silencing have been introduced by the political and intellectual left and sustained by a broader left-liberal milieu (cf. Black, 1988). This way, the New Right can undermine the left by suggesting a reversal – left-liberals proclaim openness and discourse accessibility for all, but are in fact, as a hegemonic force, silencing 'the majority' of 'ordinary people'.

Before I proceed to discussing the German anti-political correctness discourse as a language ideological debate and to providing examples for the metadiscursive moves around silence and silencing on which this debate rests, I will briefly outline what investigating metadiscourse can bring to the study of silence.

Metadiscourse and Language Ideology

Verschueren (1985) in his study of *What People Say They Do With Words* looks at 'linguistic action verbials', i.e. expressions in the lexical and idiomatic inventory used to describe the performance of a number of linguistic actions, including a chapter on silence. Through surveying such expressions, he is able to show how speakers conceptualise silence, e.g. different kinds of silence, characteristics of silence and whether silences are more or less deliberate as well as reasons for deliberate silences. It is interesting to note that the inventory of metalinguistic references to silence already provides some clues as to how speakers conceive of it. However, I am not concerned with an inventory of metalinguistic reference, but with metadiscourse, i.e. recurring references to instances of silence or silencing in their discursive contexts. Since 'the social meaning of communicative forms can never be taken as natural and transparent but must always be examined as cultural construction' (Woolard, 1998, p. 36), metalinguistic comments and metadiscourses provide particular insight into the process of construction and meaning making. As Coupland and Jaworski (2004, p. 26) argue, 'The "meta" dimension of language in use points us precisely to an interaction between socially structured meanings and values for talk and their activation in local contexts under local contingencies.' It therefore seems worthwhile to look at discourses *about* silence to understand how speakers make sense of silence, what it means to discourse participants, how they refer to or purport silences and at how silence and/or its appropriateness or legitimacy is assessed. All of this gives us clues about the language ideology of silence.

In Schröter (2013), I look at metadiscourse about politicians' silences in three instances from German public discourse, two involving political scandals and as a third case the metadiscourse about Angela Merkel's handling of silence. These analyses show that metadiscourse about silence provides rich data for studying the language ideology of silence in political discourse. I argue that silence manifests phenomenologically through disappointed expectations of speech. Thus, whenever politicians' silences are referred to in metadiscourse, this can be seen as indicative of a disappointed expectation of speech. Moreover, often the reasons for why speech was expected and, hence, the grounds on which silence gets noted were explicated in the metadiscourse about these silences, which reveals language ideological stances towards silence.

Woolard (1998) sees language ideologies as explicit or implicit representations 'that construe the intersection of language and human beings in a social world' (p. 20), specifying that ideologies of language are not about language alone. She continues, 'Rather, they envision and enact ties of language to identity, to aesthetics, to morality, and to epistemology' (p. 20). In language ideological debates, 'language is central as a topic, a motif, a target' and 'language ideologies are being articulated, formed, amended, enforced' (Blommaert, 1999, p. 1). They 'develop against a wider socio-political and historical horizon of relationships of power, forms of discrimination, social engineering, nation-building and so forth' (p. 2). Blommaert argues in favour of a better understanding 'of the precise role played by language ideologies in more general sociopolitical developments, conflicts and struggles' (p. 2), in this case, the language ideology of silence.

Elsewhere Blommaert (2005) also argues that research of language-in-society should 'start from the observation that language matters to people' and that 'we need to find out *how* language [and silence] matters to people' (p. 14; italics in the original). To investigate language ideological debates, a Critical Discourse Analysis (CDA) of such debates and meta-discourses seems useful for its attention to socio-political context as well as power and ideology in discourse. The present chapter aligns with the Discourse Historical Approach to CDA that emphasises macro-topic relatedness, pluri-perspectivity and argumentativity (cf. Reisigl & Wodak, 2009). I will discuss later how the German anti-pc debate is related to politically relevant issues such as national identity, multicultur-alism, feminism and different political stances taken on these matters. I will also refer to other texts surrounding the more in-depth case study, to point out interdiscursivity and also different perspectives involved in the discourse. I will look at recurrent arguments put forward by Germany's New Right in anti-political correctness discourse and at their implications for the ongoing language ideological debate.

I maintain that anti-political correctness discourse is a language ideo-logical debate and that a critical stance towards silence in public and political discourse is at the heart of it and in fact is exploited in this discourse. Blommaert asserts that debates 'are excellent linguistic-ethnographic targets ..., they produce discourses and metadiscourses' and constitute 'moments of textual formation and transformation, in which minority views can be transformed into majority views and vice versa ... and in which socio-political alliances are shaped or altered in discourse' (1999, p. 10); they thereby give us analytical access to studying processes of discursive change.

Metadiscourse can be indicative of discursive change but can also aim at discursive change. I see claims by the New Right to be silenced as strategic metadiscursive moves that are aimed at discursive change – essentially to make certain propositions more acceptable by instantly moving criticism of them into a metadiscursive realm in which the issue is not what has been said. Rather, a straw man claim of not being allowed to say it (while saying it) is set up, followed by a display of outrage at such censorship and delegitimising the purported censor as outlined in Wodak's (2015) 'right wing perpetuum mobile': it starts with a provocation, followed by denial and claimed victimhood for being accused as well as for being denied freedom of speech. Thus, the frame gets shifted to trigger a debate about political correctness which distracts from and helps in evading the original issue. Erdl (2004) similarly main-tains that the discourse about political correctness needs to be seen as a manoeuvre of discursive diversion rather than a serious discussion about what is (not) permissible to say in public discourse. Anti-political correctness discourse has established a topos of silencing which relies on the negative associations with silence in public discourse. Anti-political correctness discourse is a language ideological debate, at the heart of which is not language (or the absence of it) per se, but issues of society, national identity and power (cf. Woolard, 1998).

The New Right, Anti-Political Correctness and the Nazi Past

In the following, I would like to draw together what was outlined so far by looking at examples from German anti-political correctness discourse as a language ideological debate which is part of a broader social conflict which in the German case is very much about national identity and national integrity. The latter refers to the problematisation of a loss of national sovereignty and the favouring of an ethnically homogenous society. Regarding the former, the relevance of how to deal with the Nazi past for German national identity can hardly be overestimated, and it is particularly debates about 'the politics of the past' in which anti-political correctness discourse featured and has reoccurred by now for decades.

All of these issues are central to the New Right in Germany as a diverse political movement which became tangible during the 1980s. It puts emphasis on distancing itself from National Socialism while perpetuating a nationalist and ethnopluralist discourse and endorses the notion of cultural hegemony as a way of acquiring power. The appropriation of Gramsci's notion of cultural hegemony by Alain de Benoist was influential in Germany and forms the basis for an increasing challenge by the New Right of anything that is associated with left-liberal politics which, as it perpetuates, have been hegemonic in Germany since 1968, such as feminism, ecological politics, multiculturalism and ethnic diversity, as well as a politics of the past that acknowledges German guilt and responsibility in particular for the Holocaust.

According to Staas (2017), the term 'political correctness' featured in German newspapers for the first time in 1991, subsequently referred to interchangeably in English, or with the English acronym 'pc', or in German (*politische Korrektheit*; adjective: *politisch korrekt*). Initially, the references were limited to reporting about debates on US university campuses. However, in 1993 Dieter E. Zimmer published an essay in *Die Zeit*, again referring to US universities, but claiming that a similar cultural-political climate existed in Germany. From there it did not take long for the term to gain ground.

The way in which the notion of pc was taken up in the framework of an emerging anti-political correctness discourse is illustrated through a flurry of book publications in 1995 and 1996 relating to German political correctness, mostly with a negative view of pc either as ridiculous and futile language policing (Röhl, 1995) or as dangerous anti-democratic censorship (Behrens & von Rimscha, 1995; Groth, 1996). Political correctness was predominantly regarded in a negative light, but initially, as Erdl (2004) meticulously demonstrates, the term was used in a broad variety of contexts and related to various topics, most frequently to political issues around minority and identity politics. However, increasingly, anti-political correctness discourse became a domain of and central to the discourse of the New Right. Opposed politics of multiculturalism, EU integration, feminism, environmentalism and not least regarding the Nazi past are dismissed as politically correct, and anti-political correctness discourse became the main vehicle in which these issues could be linked with one another as well as with the left.

Since the arrival of the label 'political correctness' in the early 1990s, anti-political correctness discourse reliably resurfaces in every debate that ensues about controversial statements about the Nazi past and in particular about the historical singularity and memorialisation of the Holocaust. At the heart of these controversies are attempts by the New Right to hegemonise a historical narrative that puts the Holocaust in a context of, or to even frame it as a reaction to, other historical atrocities and to thereby relativise it, so as to relieve Germany from a specific legacy of guilt. German culture and politics of memorialising the Holocaust are seen as a constant painful reminder, a constant demand of shame, an obstacle to a 'healthy' collective self-confidence and self-understanding as a 'normal' country among others. It is also seen as a tabooing of German victimhood, to the extent that the existence of a radical(ised) right is blamed on the purported negation of a positive German national identity and the silencing of German suffering.

The first big public debate about dealing with the Nazi past into which the anti-political correctness discourse was fully inscribed occurred in 1998, triggered by a speech by renowned author Martin Walser who argued against what he viewed as ritualisation and lip-servicing of public commemoration and claimed that what he sees as the constant reminder of the Holocaust was exploited for present purposes and that Auschwitz was used as a means to intimidate and as a moral bludgeon (see Niven [2001] regarding the implications of Walser's speech for German 'politics of the past'). He also called the Holocaust Monument in Berlin a 'monumentalization of our disgrace' (Walser, 1998, p. 3). Mittmann (2008) sees the Walser debate as the point at which it becomes obvious that the New Right pursued a strategy of taboo breaking to shift the boundaries of sayability and to ensure acceptance via a campaign to safeguard the endangered freedom of opinion. The debate was considered so salient that just like previous ones and later ones, it was documented in book form shortly after it occurred (Schirrmacher, 1999). The following quotes (all translated from the original German by me) are taken from Schirrmacher's documentation, which contains letters by members of the public to both Martin Walser and Ignatz Bubis (the then-chairman of the Council of German Jews, who publicly condemned Walser's speech) as well as newspaper articles. I will in the following refer to the page numbers in the documentation in which these were published, rather than quoting the (partly untitled) material in this collection as individual texts.

First of all, it is worthwhile noticing that Walser himself indicates a gesture of taboo breaking in his speech by stating 'now I tremble with my own audacity when I say: Auschwitz is not suited to become a routine threat, a means of intimidation or moral bludgeon' (Walser, 1998, p. 3). Consequently, reactions to the speech praise Walser's courage and emphasise the risks that he took; his 'straightforwardness, openness and courage is incredibly moving' as he 'pursues his point with honesty and even under risk' (Schirrmacher, 1999, p. 29f.); he 'dared the utmost' by speaking the 'truth' (p. 76) and he was admired for resisting 'this control' (p. 195), for protesting 'against the enforcement of political correctness' (p. 33) and for taking 'a walk along the thin line which separates what you can and cannot say in this country when it comes to ritualization and instrumentalisation of the Holocaust. . . . Knowing too well which dangers he would face' (pp. 55f.).

These quotes illustrate that by 1998, anti-pc topoi were established which purport that public discourse is a space controlled by leftist liberals who will lash out at anyone 'speaking truths', which will 'trigger the rituals of indignation of leftist do-gooders . . ., the mechanisms of ostracization in the dictatorship of opinions through "political correctness"' (Schirrmacher 1999, p. 86). Furthermore, some contributions accuse 'the left' of having dropped out of dialogue mode: 'there is no listening anymore, but there is only ready-to-shoot-attention to see if the obligatory code words are placed' (Schirrmacher 1999, p. 59); the left purportedly demand 'the correct Nazi crimes memorisation formulae' (p. 81) and 'specific circles' 'deliberately use the term Auschwitz as a knockout argument' (p. 190).

Last but not least, critical as well as endorsing reactions reflect that Walser's speech is seen as a discursive intervention aimed at, or with the possible consequence of, change. Critical reactions to the speech accuse Walser himself of 'moving it [Auschwitz] into the realm of the utterly unspeakable' (Schirrmacher 1999, p. 82), thereby attempting to silence the past; 'the prize winning author demanded no less than the end of the public debate about the Holocaust' (p. 49), and of operating within the same parameters that he criticises since 'at the same time he caters for the media mechanisms of provocation, taboo breaking and outrage' (p. 82). More neutral reactions endorse the debate as worthwhile, as any debate will be a healthy sign of democracy (pp. 182, 199), while other contributions explicitly endorse a discursive shift that they see going along with it:

Therefore it is absolutely necessary that persons of integrity turn against paying the demanded 'lip service'. . . . This is the only way to avoid an exploitation of this climate . . . by those from the far right corner who will never learn. (Schirrmacher 1999, p. 161)

A lot of people in Germany have probably been waiting, and we have to thank him for pulling this topic away from the extreme right. In a way, he has made it socially acceptable and therefore accessible for democratic spheres who have been waiting for it. (Schirrmacher 1999, p. 183)

These quotes celebrate the prospect of far right issues becoming 'less far right' by being pulled into the centre by persons of good social standing (such as Walser and not, for example, militant Neo-Nazis). This notion of 'not leaving certain issues' to the far right, the claimed need to disassociate them from the far right and move them to a centre which the speaker claims to inhabit also reoccurs in later debates. It is as though the centre is imagined as a boat on the sea from which a rope is thrown to pull something heavy towards it, but only the object is conceived to be moving, not the boat – when it is more likely that the boat would move, too. However, pulling the boat, i.e. moving the centre to the right by tying it to far right propositions, might just be the aim of the New Right.

Mittmann (2008) notes how at this point the anti-political correctness discourse starts to operate with reversal, i.e. associating the 'politically correct left' (which would traditionally be most critical of the Nazi dictatorship) and its purported censorship with the Nazi dictatorship and positioning those who perpetuate anti-political correctness discourse as victims of this censorship who therefore also cannot themselves be associated with Nazism.

It is useful to provide this brief insight into this first debate relating to the Nazi past into which an anti-political correctness discourse, which was by then established and appropriated by the New Right, was fully inscribed. Several of the threads outlined earlier, such as the courage needed to speak out and the risk of telling truths in the face of attempts of silencing, pc as dictatorship and pc victims as victims of dictatorship as well as not leaving issues to the far right reoccur in later debates, as I will show below. The case that I am going to discuss also illustrates an intensification of the anti-political correctness discourse which has taken place since the Walser-Bubis debate in that anti-political correctness discourse becomes salient enough for the New Right to sustain entire book publications based on retaliating anti-political correctness discourse by self-declared pc victims. The example of Eva Herman was chosen because it illustrates such an intensification, because it is generally illustrative of the German anti-political correctness discourse by attacking 'the hegemonic left' and claiming to be silenced and also because it has received little attention as an instance of German anti-political correctness discourse.

New Right Anti-Political Correctness Discourse: The Case of Eva Herman

In 2007, the prominent German TV news journalist and talk show host Eva Herman, who had by that point published a couple of anti-feminist books that demanded a 'return' of German women to relishing mother-hood and family values, was publicly noted to have stated that through the condemnation of the Nazi past by the 1968 generational revolt, things that were positive, such as family values, were also discredited and abolished. She made this remark in a rather complex sentence structure produced in oral speech in reply to a question at a press conference in September 2007, and it was widely understood that she endorsed the family politics of the Nazis, which she did in fact briefly deal with and condemn in one of her books (Herman, 2006). At the press conference and in her book that was introduced at that conference (Herman, 2007), she also explicitly distanced herself from any radical ideologies, left or right. However, her remark was scandalised and widely covered in the media as an endorsement of Nazi family politics; as a consequence, she lost her job as a talk show presenter for the North German Public Broadcasting Service. In her account of the affair (Herman, 2010), she maintains that in her remark, she lamented the loss of family values that existed before, during and after National Socialism which if anything were perverted during the Third Reich. This perversion of values and traditions in her view led to the dismissal of family values through the social changes around and following 1968. The latter is her main focus of criticism, in particular, the second wave of German feminism in the 1970s and its purported focus on women's self-realisation at the expense of the needs of children. In October 2007, Eva Herman was invited to a popular talk show with a view on discussing her remarks about the Nazi past. The show provided air space for her to admit that she made a mistake or did not express herself clearly or, failing that, for her to be associated with endorsing Nazi family politics. She stubbornly denied the former, and she did not successfully manage to untie herself from the latter during the show but rather added a couple of problematic statements such as that it was dangerous in Germany to say anything about the past at all. This led to the dismissal of her as a guest by the host before the scheduled end of the show, which again triggered media reporting about this TV scandal. In this context, Jörg Thomann writes in the *Frankfurter Allgemeine Zeitung* (2007) that '[n]ow at the latest, Eva Herman has become a martyr of all those who are convinced that there is no right to free speech in this country.'

The attempts to associate Eva Herman with an endorsement of the Third Reich were vehemently rejected by herself and to some extent missed the point. Rather than trying to associate her with 'Old Nazism', it might have been more interesting to explore the ways in which she writes herself into the discourse of the New Right: with her creation of a catastrophic demographic scenario in which the Germans are dying out because women have been brainwashed to focus on their careers; with her condemnation of the 1968 generational revolt and in particular the feminist movement of the 1970s; and not least with pursuing an anti-political correctness discourse to legitimise her own stance and to delegitimise criticism of her anti-feminist and anti-1968 discourse. A prominent female public figure with a highly successful media career, educated and middle class, she provided a wealth of authoritative reference for the anti-feminist discourse of the New Right. Following the scandalisation of her remarks and positioning herself as pc victim, she subsequently wrote two retaliating media-critical books (Herman 2010, 2012) that were published with the *Kopp* publishing house, which hosts many other publications by the New Right. This move, to publish a retaliating anti-pc book in reply to scandalisation and criticism, was repeated later by Thilo Sarrazin (Sarrazin 2014). The occurrence of retaliating anti-pc publications indicates in my view not only the degree to which anti-pc topoi have become a widespread and widely accessible argumentative resource in public discourse, but also a radicalisation and intensification of the fight against the purported left-liberal cultural hegemony.

Unlike Sarrazin's anti-political correctness book published four years later, in Eva Herman's first retaliating book *Die Wahrheit und ihr Preis. Meinung, Macht und Medien* (2010; translates: The price of truth. Opinion, power and the media), anti-political correctness discourse is not foregrounded. The book reads as a partly personal, partly factual account of the origin and scandalisation of her remarks, up to a detailed, nearly line-by-line account of the talk show from which she was dismissed. She describes the effect that the affair had on her and provides quotes from correspondence, newspaper articles and statements by her lawyers. However, anti-political correctness discourse threads through the entire book, which I am going to show in the following. Before I proceed, it is worthwhile mentioning that her own publication was preceded by an anti-pc book dealing with the newspaper reporting about her which is dubbed a 'media witch hunt' in the title of the book, published by Arne Hoffmann (2007) in the New Right *Lichtschlag* publishing house, from which Eva Herman herself also gratefully quotes (pp. 42, 161). The following quotes from her own book (2010) are my translations.

In her retaliating book, Eva Herman maintains that media and politics in Germany work hand in hand to silence certain issues and voices that are trying to bring these issues to light. With regard to politics, she purports the political will for women to be in gainful employment and the creation of nursery provision for children at a large scale: 'that without criticism and without discussion, the federal republic has entered a path of mass provision of nurseries that could hardly be questioned anymore' (p. 56). She also detects the political will to implement a policy of gender mainstreaming, which she calls 'the largest and most dangerous re-education programme of mankind' (p. 46). She sees these politics as a result of the power and influence of the 1970s' feminists. She states, 'Germany's chief feminist [Alice Schwarzer] reconstructed the country for decades as the principal team leader and has turned it into the globalized gender mainstream with some cunning finger tricks' (p. 104). She expresses admiration for a professor whom she quotes, referring to feminists as 'stalinist lesbocrats' (p. 87), without distancing herself in any way from his choice of words. Thus, she refers to the 'public manipulation through politics and media in the past forty years' (p. 242) (i.e. since the 1970s) and a 'devious politics' which steers people's lives 'more and more into realms which are highly dangerous for freedom' (p. 114):

And many times I asked myself in despair which invisible, dark and paralysing force must lie over our country so that no one dared anymore to discuss entirely natural matters such as being a mother and having children. (p. 51)

She sees the media as working along these political premises which were brought about by feminism. The media partake in silencing any voices that stray away from this line, and she positions herself as such a critical voice:

But once you understand that my arguments not only go against the views of certain feminists, but that also the political mainstream cannot relate to a differentiated view on motherhood …, then you can also assume a political interest in not supporting any voices who state the opposite. (p. 72)

The media only focus on women's emancipation and self-realisation (pp. 102, 207); they silence the question of children's needs (p. 207) and thus 'there are a lot of issues that we urgently need to talk about since the mainstream media hardly provide any information about them' (p. 227).

The media therefore neglect their democratic function of providing mul-
tifaceted, non-partisan information. The media have a 'huge responsibility', but journalists do not live up to it by 'selling their own sad lifestyles as
the only truth, as mainstream opinion, as politically correct formula'
(p. 107).

Eva Herman also positions herself as a victim of silencing. First, she was
meant to remain politically neutral while she was still a newsreader at
a prestigious public broadcasting news show, and she saw this as
a limitation to pursuing her topic, so she gave up the job: 'Do I really have
to sing the common politically correct song . . . ? Shall I remain silent . . . so as
to keep my job?' (p. 21) Later in the book, she refers to these limitations as
'Auftrittsverbot' (p. 157), a term also, though not exclusively, associated
with the prohibition of performances by Jewish artists in the Third
Reich. Second, she portrays herself as ostracised by a misinformed and
misquoting press following her original scandalous remark: 'And if you say
the word mother these days, you must be a Nazi! . . . The most important
aim of this kind of reporting seems to be that the story appears interesting
from the outside and that outlet and author will shine in a politically correct
light. Marketable conclusion: Eva Herman is a Nazi! We are not!' (p. 105).
Third, as a consequence, she lost her job as a talk show host: 'And this state
has decided to pursue mass provision of nurseries . . . against which I clearly
and publicly position myself. Have I become a kind of regime critic? Is this
the reason why the North German Broadcasting Service wanted to take me
off the programme? That would be claiming too much honour, would it
not?' (p. 155). Last but not least, the talk show that she was invited to as
a guest was set up as a public tribunal to finish her off: 'I cannot get rid of the
feeling that a well prepared cooperation is happening here, or how is this
"court situation" to be explained? Am I accused of a crime? It seems so!'
(p. 191). She uses metaphors of inquisition (witch hunt, p. 39), incrimina-
tion and in particular hunting. She sees herself subjected to a hunt by a pack
(pp. 73, 82, 86, 91, 94, 99 and more). She also positions herself as a martyr
who has become the bearer of a divine ordeal (pp. 82, 86, 114, 154), and she
sees others as profiteers or exploiters of her downfall (pp. 121, 159f.).

However, she also positions herself as speaking on behalf of
a substantial number of ordinary people by constructing an opposition between public and published opinion: the latter tugs along
political preferences and premises, seemingly disassociated from the
former. The former expresses itself in letters and emails that Eva
Herman receives. However, ordinary people have no voice in the
public sphere and are too intimidated to speak their minds. Eva
Herman, as a public figure, provides them with such a voice and takes
the blame for it, acting on their behalf: 'the many letters and emails

which I receive daily, in which women, mothers as well as grandmothers, but also men thank me for my courage to talk aloud about all this' (p. 28); 'I encountered thousands of people, personally or in writing, who were glad that someone with a prominent name publicly addressed this problem, when they hardly dared to open their mouths anymore' (p. 53). She also suggests that people in the media sphere are detached from ordinary people and look down on them with arrogance: 'The people sitting out there in front of the screen are not as you seem to want them to be, which is numb, stupid and insensitive' (p. 218). Moreover, the media people are in the minority and the ordinary people are in the majority. Therefore, the German public sphere is undemocratically constituted in that a self-catering, navel-gazing minority dismisses the pressing concerns of the majority:

However, I know loads of these women. They write to me, they come to my public talks. And it is not a rare occurrence that they would cry with relief that someone understands, or even takes up the fight for them. Oh, why would I want to continue discussion with these vain media people here who only sit on their sparkly cloud and not even try to understand others, who are, by the way and in contrast to them, in the overwhelming majority! (p. 205)

Towards the end of the book, Eva Herman puts her hope in the delimitation of the public sphere through online communication (pp. 259f.). She pursues this point further in a subsequent book publication with the same publisher, *Das Medienkartell. Wie wir täglich getäuscht werden* (2012; translates: The Media Cartel, How we are deceived on a daily basis). The purported opposition between public and published opinion, elite self-interest and silenced majority and the prospect of a 'democratisation of the public sphere' through online communication are threads in the discourse of the New Right. For example, the New Right publisher André Lichtschlag makes the same points in an interview with the New Right weekly magazine *Junge Freiheit* (Schwarz, 2009) and Frauke Petry, then chairwomen of the New Right political party *Alternative für Deutschland*, writes a celebratory comment for the same newspaper (2016) in which she frames the election of Donald Trump as a victory for the silent majority.

During the talk show from which she was dismissed, towards the end Eva Herman also demands the safeguarding of the issue of motherhood and family values from occupation by the radical right. She quotes herself in her book saying:

It bears one great danger: If it is not possible anymore in our democracy to talk about these things. ... Then we really play into the hands of the right, because nobody cares about these things anymore ... (p. 210). Then they will claim this territory for themselves, because nobody else cares. (p. 211)

Thus, silencing her and the points that she makes means leaving an empty space that can be occupied by the right. It is not straightforward to see why it would be dangerous to leave this issue to the right – it can only mean that Eva Herman is convinced that she is in the centre, and not allowing her to occupy the territory and thereby to incorporate it into the centre would leave it to the right and make the right more popular. It either does not occur to her or she is trying to blur that she already pursues a discourse of the right – the New Right, not Old Nazi – and actively helps construct and popularise it. This becomes even clearer with the following last point in my analysis of Eva Herman's anti-political correctness discourse.

Finally, Eva Herman engages in an attempt to reverse the association with the Third Reich by claiming that she herself criticised Nazi family politics for advocating a separation of the children from their mothers, and that current feminists advocated such a separation (pp. 45, 109). She quotes another professor who criticises the way in which she was dealt with as a 'Säuberungsaktion' – 'cleansing operation', a Nazi euphemism pertaining to the forced removal of Jews and other people in German-occupied territories – and who furthers the reversal by claiming that especially the Jewish associations in Germany would be the last to want to tolerate such a development (p. 133). Eva Herman puts herself in a line with previous other pc victims 'all of whom, like me, were because of some quotes, speeches or reports that were purportedly not "politically correct" at times in a murderous way like poor animals hunted up and down the country' (p. 259). This, then, leads her onto a remarkable reversal of historical legacy and responsibility:

> The way in which dissidents were being dealt with should be a warning to us and sharpen our perception. Because we Germans just are a society with an extremely loaded, difficult past, in which life and death were decided upon with murderous actions, cynicism and deeply hurtful arrogance. ... We do not only carry this heavy guilt, we are also responsible for looking very closely at facts in the future, before we collectively judge and eliminate so-called dissidents. (p. 259)

This is a particularly problematic statement not only because some of the pc victims named by Eva Herman quite clearly pursued a revisionist agenda, and not only because she claims that political correctness is currently undermining the lessons to be learned from the past, but also because she claims that pc and its purported advocates are repeating the crimes of the past, and thus she appears on a par with victims of the Nazi regime. This Third Reich perpetrator-victim reversal is again a typical feature of revisionist and New Right discourse (cf. Wodak, 2015, p. 16).

Conclusion

In this chapter, it was my aim to describe anti-political correctness discourse as a language ideological debate through which the New Right seeks to gain acceptance for controversial propositions, and to show that silence and silencing are at the heart of this debate. The strategic metadiscursive moves of claiming to be silenced are a central means by the New Right to attempt such discursive shifts and to battle the purported left-liberal discourse hegemony. Claims to be silenced are particularly useful in this context for a number of reasons. First, left-liberal thinking about public discourse and with it the problematisation of silence is turned against the left: those on the left are purportedly the ones who do not adhere to the ethics of public deliberation – they close off and control the public sphere, and they actively silence others. They are the (political and media) elite who impede ordinary people's right to freedom of speech, and they have the power via discursive hegemony to do so, while members of the New Right are the underdogs who speak uncomfortable, but necessary truths. The left is therefore framed to be acting against its own premises. Thus, second, claims to be silenced delegitimise the left as undemocratic censors and legitimise the New Right as courageous taboo breakers who at times do so at considerable cost, but out of strong conviction. They thereby turn into the regime critics who the left has taught us to admire – although they supposedly have 'the silent majority' behind them. Third, anti-political correctness discourse is a metadiscourse that diverts any debate away from content into the meta-zone of who is (not) allowed to say what. Any criticism of problematic propositions is slotted into this metadiscourse and delegitimised as undemocratic censorship, making it more difficult to debate the proposition as such.

What this aims to show, in the framework of the present volume, is on the one hand that a contextualised analysis of metadiscourse, as suggested by Blommaert (1999) and Coupland and Jaworski (2004), is useful for studying language ideological debates as described by Woolard (1998), and that such an approach can, and perhaps should, be extended to include not only debates about phenomenologically manifest uses or misuses of language but also discourses about silence and silencing. On the other hand, for those already interested in silence, this shows that studying metadiscourse can be a fruitful way into empirical analysis. First, it circumnavigates the methodological difficulty, especially when dealing with public or political discourse, to identify silence because it allows studying references to perceived silences which can more easily form the basis of empirical textual analyses (see, however, Schröter & Taylor, 2018, for further and different methodological suggestions). However, metadiscourse is not just a stopgap; it also allows, second, the study of the norms and expectations or, here, the ideological conflict surrounding silence (or silencing) (Schröter, 2013) and therefore allows a more in-depth understanding of meanings assigned to silence, or the basis on which (in-)accessibility of discourse is claimed. Third, studying metadiscourse might provide access to effects that, for example, ostentatious silences have, which tend to draw attention to them (cf., e.g. Garbutt, 2018; Thurlow & Moshin, 2018;), or as in the cases described here, the salience of claims to being silenced, which are based on democratic ideals about participation in public discourse and aim to trigger ethical concern or moral outrage.

References

Achino-Loeb, M.-L. (2006). *Silence: The currency of power.* New York; Oxford: Berghahn.

Anthonissen, C. (2003). Challenging media censoring. In J. Martin & R. Wodak (Eds.), *Re/reading the past. Critical and functional perspectives on time and value* (pp. 91–111). Amsterdam; Philadelphia: John Benjamins.

Behrens, M., & von Rimscha, R. (1995). *Politische Korrektheit in Deutschland. Eine Gefahr für die Demokratie.* Bonn: Bouvier.

Benthien, C. (2006). *Barockes Schweigen. Rhetorik und Performativität des Sprachlosen im 17. Jahrhundert.* München: Fink.

Black, E. (1988). Secrecy and disclosure as rhetorical forms. *Quarterly Journal of Speech, 74*(2), 133–150.

Blommaert, J. (Ed.). (1999). *Language ideological debates.* Berlin; New York: Mouton de Gruyter.

Blommaert, J. (2005). *Discourse. A critical introduction.* Cambridge: Cambridge University Press.

Bull, P. (2003). *The microanalysis of political discourse. Claptrap and ambiguity.* London; New York: Routledge.

Cameron, D. (2000). *Good to talk? Living and working in a communication culture.* London; Thousand Oaks; New Delhi: Sage.

Chouliaraki, L. & Fairclough, N. (1999). *Discourse in late modernity.* Edinburgh: Edinburgh University Press.

Clayman, S. (2007). Speaking on behalf of the public in broadcast news interviews. In E. Holt & R. Clift (Eds.), *Reporting talk. Reported speech in interaction* (pp. 221–243). Cambridge: Cambridge University Press.

Couldry, N. (2010). *Why voice matters. Culture and politics after neoliberalism.* Los Angeles: Sage.

Coupland, N., & Jaworski, A. (2004). Sociolinguistic perspectives on metalanguage: Reflexivity, evaluation and ideology. In A. Jaworski, N. Coupland & D. Galasiński (Eds.), *Metalanguage. Social and ideological perspectives* (pp. 15–51). Berlin: Mouton de Gruyter.

Erdl, M. F. (2004). *Die Legende von der Politischen Korrektheit. Zur Erfolgsgeschichte eines importierten Mythos.* Bielefeld: transcript.

Galasiński, D. (2003). Silencing by law. The 1981 Polish 'performances and publications control act'. In L. Thiesmeyer (Ed.), *Discourse and silencing. Representation and the language of displacement* (pp. 211–232). Amsterdam: John Benjamins.

Garbutt, J. (2018). The use of no comment by suspects in police interviews. In M. Schröter & C. Taylor (Eds.), *Exploring silence and absence in discourse. Empirical approaches* (pp. 329–357). Basingstoke: Palgrave Macmillan.

Groth, K. J. (1996). *Die Diktatur der Guten. Political correctness.* München: Herbig.

Herman, E. (2006). *Das Eva-Prinzip.* München; Zürich: Pendo.

Herman, E. (2007). *Das Prinzip Arche Noah.* Münche; Zürich: Pendo.

Herman, E. (2010). *Die Wahrheit und ihr Preis: Meinung, Macht und Medien.* Rottenburg: Kopp.

Herman, E. (2012). *Das Medienkartell: Wie wir täglich getäuscht werden.* Rottenburg: Kopp.

Hoffmann, A. (2007). *Der Fall Eva Herman. Hexenjagd in den Medien.* Grevenbroich: Lichtschlag.

Kailitz, S. (2008).Die politische Deutungskultur der Bundesrepublik Deutschland im Spiegel des 'Historikerstreits'. In S. Kailitz (Ed.), *Die Gegenwart der Vergangenheit. Der 'Historikerstreit und die deutsche Geschichtspolitik'* (pp. 14–37). Wiesbaden: VS Verlag für Sozialwissenschaften.

Kämper, H. (2002). Sigmund Freuds Sprachdenken. Ein Beitrag zur Sprachbewusstseinsgeschichte. In D. Cherubim, K. Jakob & A. Linke (Eds.), *Neue deutsche Sprachgeschichte. Mentalitäts-, kultur- und sozialgeschichtliche Zusammenhänge* (pp. 239–251). Berlin; New York: de Gruyter.

Kämper, H. (2012). *Aspekte des Demokratiediskurses der späten 1960er Jahre. Konstellationen – Kontexte – Konzepte.* Berlin; Boston: de Gruyter.

Kilian, J. (1997). *Demokratische Sprache zwischen Tradition und Neuanfang. Am Beispiel des Grundrechte-Diskurses 1948/49.* Tübingen: Niemeyer.

Mittmann, T. (2008). Vom 'Historikerstreit' zum 'Fall Hohmann': Kontroverse Diskussionen um Political Correctness seit Ende der 1980er Jahre. In L. Hölscher (Ed.), *Political Correctness. Der sprachpolitische Streit um die nationalsozialistischen Verbrechen* (pp. 60–105). Göttingen: Wallstein.

Niven, B. (2001). *Facing the Nazi past. United Germany and the legacy of the Third Reich.* London: Routledge.

Owzar, A. (2006). *Reden ist Silber, Schweigen ist Gold. Konfliktmanagement im Alltag des wilhelminischen Obrigkeitsstaats.* Konstanz: Universitätsverlag Konstanz.

Peters, J.D. (1999). *Speaking into the air. A history of the idea of communication.* Chicago: University of Chicago Press.

184   *Melani Schröter*

Petry, F. (2016, November 9). Die Political Correctness ist am Ende. *Junge Welt.* Retrieved from https://jungefreiheit.de/debatte/kommentar/2016/die-political-correctness-ist-am-ende/

Reisigl, M., & Wodak, R. (2009). The discourse-historical approach (DHA). In R. Wodak & M. Reisigl (Eds.), *Methods of critical discourse analysis* (2nd ed., pp. 87–121). London: Sage.

Röhl, K. 1995. *Deutsches Phrasenlexikon. Politisch korrekt von A bis Z.* Berlin: Ullstein.

Sandkühler, G. (2008). Die sprachpolitische Auseinandersetzung: Historische und politische Grundlagen der Political Correctness in der frühen Bundesrepublik. In L. Hölscher (Ed.), *Political Correctness. Der sprachpolitische Streit um die nationalsozialistischen Verbrechen* (pp. 18–59). Göttingen: Wallstein.

Sarrazin, T. (2014). *Der Neue Tugendterror. Über die Grenzen der Meinungsfreiheit in Deutschland.* Stuttgart: Deutsche Verlagsanstalt.

Scharloth, J. (2011). *1968 – Eine Kommunikationsgeschichte.* München: Fink.

Schirrmacher, F. (Ed.). (1999). *Die Walser-Bubis Debatte.* Frankfurt am Main: Insel.

Schröter, M. (2013). *Silence and concealment in political discourse.* Amsterdam: John Benjamins.

Schröter, M., & Taylor, C. (2018). Introduction. In M. Schröter & C. Taylor (Eds.), *Exploring silence and absence in discourse: Empirical approaches* (pp. 1–21). Basingstoke: Palgrave Macmillan.

Schwarz, M. (2009, October 17). 'Wie moderner Terrorismus' Interview with André Lichtschlag. *Junge Freiheit.* Retrieved from https://jungefreiheit.de/debatte/interview/2009/wie-moderner-terrorismus

Spitznagel, A., & Reiners, B. (1998).Geheimhaltung in der Folklore und persönliche Geheimhaltungserfahrung (pp. 109–138). In A. Spitznagel (Ed.), *Geheimnis und Geheimhaltung. Erscheinungsformen – Funktionen – Konsequenzen.* Göttingen: Hogrefe.

Staas, C. (2017, February 1). Political correctness. Vom Medianphantom zum rechten Totschlagargument. Die sonderbare Geschichte der Political Correctness. *Die Zeit.* Retrieved from www.zeit.wde/2017/04/politicial-correct ness-populismus-afd-zensur

Thomann, J. (2007, October 10). Rausschmiss bei Kerner. Wie Eva Herman den Fernsehtod starb. *Frankfurter Allgemeine Zeitung.* Retrieved from www.faz.net/aktuell/feuilleton/debatten/rausschmiss-bei-kerner-wie-eva-herman-den-fern sehtod-starb-1490687.html

Thurlow, C., & Moshin, J. (2018). What the f#'$!: Policing and performing the unmentionable in the news. In M. Schröter & C. Taylor (Eds.), Exploring silence and absence in discourse: Empirical approaches (pp. 305–328). Basingstoke: Palgrave Macmillan.

Verheyen, N. (2010). *Diskussionslust. Eine Kulturgeschichte des 'besseren Arguments' in Westdeutschland.* Göttingen: Vandenhoek & Ruprecht.

Verschueren, J. (1985). *What people say they do with words.* Norwood, NJ: Ablex.

Von Hodenberg, C. (2006). *Konsens und Krise. Eine Geschichte der westdeutschen Medienöffentlichkeit 1945–1973.* Göttingen: Wallstein.

Walser, M. (1998, October 11). Experiences while composing a Sunday speech. Retrieved from *German history in documents and images*, http://germanhistory docs.ghi-dc.org/sub_document.cfm?document_id=3426

Wodak, R. (2015). *The politics of fear. What right-wing populist discourses mean.* London: Sage.

Woolard, K. A. (1998). Introduction: Language ideology as a field of inquiry. In B. B. Schieffelin, K. A. Woolard & P. V. Kroskrity (Eds.), *Language ideologies: Practice and theory* (pp.20–86). Oxford: Oxford University Press.

Zerubavel, E. (2006). *The elephant in the room. Silence and denial in everyday life.* Oxford: Oxford University Press.

Zimmer, D. E. (1993, October 22). PC oder: Da hört die Gemütlichkeit auf. *Die Zeit.* Retrieved from www.zeit.de/1993/43/pc-oder-da-hoert-die-gemuetlich keit-auf

10   Propaganda by Omission: The Case of Topical Silence

Tom Huckin

As all the chapters of this book attest, much human communication occurs not through what is said but what is *not* said. Political discourse, including propaganda, is no different. Politicians, public officials, journalists, special interest groups, and others who use political discourse do so in ways that foreground certain information while backgrounding – or concealing altogether – other information. Such selectivity is of course inherent to all discourse, but when it is used to manipulate entire populations it carries special power. In many cases, such manipulation constitutes a form of propaganda, defined as follows:

Propaganda is **false or misleading** information or ideas addressed to a **mass audience** by parties who thereby gain **advantage**. Propaganda is created and disseminated **systematically** and **does not invite critical analysis or response**. (Huckin, 2016, p. 126)

Shanahan's (2001) *Propaganda without Propagandists* provides an important amplification, stating, "[propaganda is] a form of communication in which specific interests achieve aims through *covert* and perhaps unconscious manipulation of social structure and communication systems" (p. 2, emphasis mine).

Thesis: Although propaganda is typically thought of as something created through written or spoken words or images (e.g., inflammatory Nazi posters or speeches), it can also occur through the *absence* of such stimuli, or what I call "propaganda-by-omission" (see Shanahan's use of the word *covert*). The purpose of this chapter is to illustrate an important way in which this occurs. My particular focus will be on what I call "topical silences," that is, those instances where the failure to address subtopics relevant to a certain topic can skew the recipient's understanding of that topic in a propagandistic way. Such omissions create, I will argue, a common and particularly potent form of propaganda in contemporary civic discourse.

186

Topical Silences

Imagine a televised campaign speech by a politician advocating lower taxes but failing to mention the adverse consequences of such a policy. Such a speech, I maintain, would be propagandistic because it satisfies the five requirements listed in my definition. It (1) is misleading in its one-sidedness, (2) is addressed to a mass audience, (3) is meant to be advantageous to the speaker, (4) is done systematically, and (5) does not invite critical reflection. More to the point, the manipulation involved is *covert*, as the audience is never made aware of alternatives or downsides to the speaker's point of view.

Such covert silences – or what I am calling "topical silences" – are especially potent precisely because they escape the attention of many if not most audience members. Instead, the audience's attention is being drawn to the (one-sided) information the speaker presents and favors. Given no options to choose from, many audience members will be induced to "go with the flow" and agree with the speaker's pitch, especially if it conforms to their own beliefs. In short, they are being manipulated covertly, making resistance or even curiosity difficult unless they are unusually skeptical.

Note: Topical silences are not the only kinds of manipulative omissions. In Huckin (2010), I identify and illustrate five other types of silence as well: conventional, discreet, lexical, implicational, and presuppositional. But, as I argue there, because topical silences are the least easily detectable, they are the most rhetorically potent.

Brief Review of Literature on Propaganda

Although the use of the term *propaganda* goes back to 1622 and the Roman Catholic Church's crusade against the Reformation, modern propaganda in its largely negative sense dates only from the First World War. Both sides in that war used blatant propaganda to influence public opinion in countries around the world, including posters, leaflets, radio broadcasts, postcards, and news reports and editorials. Propaganda-by-omission occurred largely through the censoring of ideas deemed not conducive to the war effort. A number of prominent public intellectuals, among them the great social activist Jane Addams, took particular exception to such censorship. In speech after speech Addams argued that the militarists who were running the war effort (on both sides) were using censorship to prevent citizens from even considering peaceful options. Such peace-seeking citizens are "denied all journalistic expression," she said, "while the war spirit is continually fed by the outrages of war" (Grate, 2016, p. 64).

Another critic of the government's propagandistic censorship was the great American journalist Walter Lippmann. A pioneer in the study of modern propaganda, Lippmann was among the first to note the power of topical silences:

> Without some form of censorship, propaganda in the strict sense of the word is impossible. In order to conduct a propaganda there must be some barrier between the public and the event. Access to the real environment must be limited, before anyone can create a pseudo-environment that he thinks wise or desirable. For while people who have direct access can misconceive what they see, no one else can decide how they shall misconceive it, unless he can decide where they shall look, and at what. (Lippmann, 1922, p. 28)

In general, analysts of propaganda over the years have focused more on its visible and audible manifestations than on its invisible, inaudible ones. But there are notable exceptions, including the following.

In a chapter of *Brave New World Revisited* titled, "Propaganda in a Democratic Society," Aldous Huxley laments how citizens are increasingly subjected to mass media distractions from reality:

> In their propaganda today's dictators rely for the most part on repetition, suppression and rationalizations – the repetition of catchwords which they wish to be accepted as true, the suppression of facts which they wish to be ignored, the arousal and rationalization of passions which may be used in the interests of the Party or the State. As the art and science of manipulation come to be better understood, the dictators of the future will doubtless learn to combine these techniques with the non-stop distractions which, in the West, are now threatening to drown in a sea of irrelevance the rational propaganda essential to the maintenance of individual liberty and the survival of democratic institutions. (Huxley, 1960, pp. 29–30)

Huxley's contrastive reference to "the repetition of catchwords which they wish to be accepted as true" and "the suppression of facts which they wish to be ignored" captures the chiaroscuro nature of propaganda-by-omission.

Social psychologists Anthony Pratkanis and Elliot Aronson, in *The Age of Propaganda* (1992, 2001), touch on propaganda-by-omission in discussing why certain stories are covered and many others are not. Not unlike Huxley, they attribute it to entertainment value in a world where entertainment is accorded high value. In their words:

> If you want access to the mass media, be entertaining. Such coverage does not present a balanced or complete picture of what is happening in the world, not because the people who run the news media are evil and necessarily trying to manipulate us but simply because they are trying to entertain us. And, in trying to entertain us, *they oversimplify and thus unwittingly influence our opinions about the world we live in.* (2001, pp. 276–277; my emphasis)

Anthony DiMaggio in *Mass Media, Mass Propaganda* (2008) describes at some length the phenomenon of self-censorship in corporate journalism. In a chapter titled "All the News that's Fit to Omit," DiMaggio argues that journalists are generally aware of the power structures, ideological leanings, and reward systems in a corporate-owned news organization and take care not to go against the system. He argues, "for censorship to be truly effective, it requires that journalists not only tolerate, but embrace the legitimacy and validity of conventional doctrines that thrive within the media establishment and American elite culture" (p. 45). In other words, by excluding information that goes against the grain of political and cultural orthodoxy, journalists effectively create propaganda-by-omission.

For many students of propaganda, the most path-breaking analysis of the subject is that of Edward Herman and Noam Chomsky's *Manufacturing Consent: The Political Economy of the Mass Media* (2002). In this classic work, the authors describe how the corporate-owned news media evaluate potential stories according to the corporation's economic interests. In particular, they posit the operation of five distinct "filters" through which any candidate news story must proceed: (1) "size, ownership, and profit orientation of the mass media" (p. 3); (2) "the advertising license to do business" (p. 14); (3) "sourcing mass-media news" (p. 18); (4) "flak and the enforcers" (p. 26); and (5) "anticommunism as a control mechanism" (p. 29). That is, to appear in print news must be aligned with the interests of the corporation's owners and advertisers, must accord with the opinions of mainstream "experts," must not incite sabotage from outside detractors, and must conform to an ideological master frame such as anticommunism. As a result of such "filtration," important information can be excluded from publication, producing a slanted story line that constitutes propaganda-by-omission:

> The five filters narrow the range of news that passes through the gates, and even more sharply limit what can become "big news," subject to sustained news campaigns. By definition, news from primary establishment sources meets one major filter requirement. Messages from and about dissidents and weak, unorganized individuals and groups, domestic and foreign, are at an initial disadvantage in sourcing costs and credibility, and they often do not comport with the ideology or interests of the gatekeepers and other powerful parties that influence the filtering process. (Herman & Chomsky, 2002, p. 31)

To support their argument, Herman and Chomsky make essential use of what I refer to as topical silences, that is, omissions of information (or subtopics) pertinent to the topic at hand. In section 3.7, "Quantitative Evidence of Systematic Media Bias," for example, they compare *New*

York Times coverage of two contrasting 1984 Central American elections, those of El Salvador and Nicaragua. El Salvador was a US vassal state, while Nicaragua under Sandinista rule was deemed a "communist threat." Herman and Chomsky's propaganda model predicted that the two elections would receive radically different coverage in the US corporate-owned mainstream news media. To test this prediction, the authors first studied official US government discourse about the two elections to see what US "agendas" might be operating in the two cases – that is, slanted coverage created by the omission of certain relevant subtopics. Then they examined twenty-eight *New York Times* articles about El Salvador and twenty-one *New York Times* articles about Nicaragua published shortly before each election.

In their analysis, Herman and Chomsky looked specifically for certain subtopics relevant, in different ways, to Central American elections. For example, they predicted that an establishment US newspaper like the *New York Times* when covering elections under an allied government like that of El Salvador would focus on favorable subtopics such as "democratic purpose and hopes" or "personalities and political infighting," whereas when talking about a hostile government like Nicaragua's it would focus instead on unfavorable subtopics like "(lack of) press freedom" and "public relations purpose." A count of such subtopics supported the authors' predictions. Coverage of the El Salvador elections focused heavily on favorable subtopics, giving only minimal attention to unfavorable ones, while coverage of the Nicaragua elections did just the opposite (pp. 132–136).

In a study of my own (Huckin, 2002), I took a similar but even more detailed approach. Concerned about the growing problem of homelessness in the United States, I was curious to know how it was being addressed in major US newspapers. Using the word "homeless" as a search term, I scanned the Academic Universe database of all national and regional US newspapers for all articles, editorials, and so on published during an entire month on the topic of human homelessness in the United States. This produced a study corpus of 163 documents containing 100,264 words. By eyeballing the corpus and reading scholarly treatments of the topic, I was able to create a list of 52 subtopics divided into four groupings ("causes," "effects," "public responses," and "demographics"). Each of the subtopics was then weighted according to frequency of occurrence and degree of textual foregrounding (position in text). This yielded a master list, which I then used to compare two editorials, one published in a progressive newspaper, the other in a conservative one. Out of all the 52 subtopics each editorialist had available, each addressed only a subset of about 40 percent, specifically those that contributed to their favored political slant; all other subtopics were ignored/omitted. Although editorials as a genre are not expected to be neutral or entirely balanced, they *are* expected to be fair. By completely excluding relevant but unsupportive information, each of these editorials exemplified propaganda-by-omission.

Brief Review of Literature on Audience Reception

Much of the literature on propaganda focuses more on its production than its reception. In so doing, it assumes that the audience is basically passive, unwittingly victimized by the propagandist. Such an assumption can reflect a traditional/formalist view of reading and listening according to which people construct meaning in "bottom-up" fashion by putting together basic units (sounds, words) to form larger ones. Such a procedure, if followed fully, puts the reader or listener entirely at the mercy of the text producer. Anything unsaid or unwritten is not even considered, which makes it easy for a propagandist to conceal alternative ideas and make a one-sided appeal.

Alternatively, a reader's or listener's comprehension can be seen as guided by higher-level knowledge structures called "schemata" (Rumelhart, 1980) or "frames" (Lakoff, 2004; Minsky, 1975) that develop out of life experience. Once such a schema or frame is activated in the reader's or listener's mind, it facilitates the processing of lower-level details, even to the point of "filling in" missing details. Thus reading and listening are both "bottom-up" and "top-down" activities. Under this cognitivist conception, the propagandist can still exercise control over the audience by triggering schemata that serve their particular interests (and block out competing schemata).

An example of such manipulation can be found in spinmeister Frank Luntz's creation of the term *death tax* for a tax levied on estates when they are passed on to heirs (Luntz, 2007). Legally referred to as an "estate tax" or "inheritance tax," this levy typically applies not to all estates but only to highly valued ones, a tiny percentage of all estates. The genius of Luntz's use of the term *death tax* is that it obscures via omission that last detail. In so doing it leads people to think that the tax applies to everyone who dies – including, ultimately, themselves. In cognitive-theoretical terms, by activating the powerful "death" schema, the propagandist conceals a key detail about monetary levels (a less-powerful schema), thereby misleading their audience. Studies indicate that this re-labeling of the tax has had the desired effect on many American voters (Sperling, 2017).

In contrast to both of the previous models, reader-response theory attributes considerable interpretive power to the reader/listener/viewer.

Meaning is not entirely "in the text" but rather arises out of the interaction between the text and its interpreter, with the latter drawing idiosyncratically on their life experience (Rosenblatt, 1938) or on the beliefs of their interpretive community (Fish, 1980). To some degree, such freedom on the part of the interpreter challenges, of course, the power of the propagandist. Still, interpretation even under this approach begins with a text of some kind, be it visual or aural. And when it comes to textual omissions, there is no "text" to trigger a reader's (perhaps idiosyncratic) response. If the omission itself goes unnoticed, there would be even less reason for a reader to construct some alternative interpretation.

In my own 2002 study discussed earlier, I claimed that ideology-driven selectivity likely has an impact on many readers: I (Huckin, 2002, pp. 365–366) argue as follows:

[T]extual foregrounding and backgrounding have been shown to have clear cognitive effects on readers (Loftus, 1975; Meyer, 1975) and manipulative textual silences are the ultimate form of backgrounding. By remaining out of sight, the subtopics concealed by such silences simply do not enter the mind of a compliant reader. Only critically minded readers will resist the temptation to "go along."

Of course, people vary greatly in their receptivity to information depending on their interest in the subject matter, their education, their world knowledge, their inclination to be skeptical, their training in critical thinking, their biases and emotional investments, and other individual variables. Although many readers/listeners/viewers may be persuaded by propaganda, others may be resistant. The point is that under any theoretical model of audience reception, topical silences present perhaps the greatest challenge to any reader/listener/viewer, even critically minded ones, simply because there is nothing overt to trigger a critical response. In contrast to overt propaganda, which *instructs* its audience what to think and do, propaganda-by-omission plays on its audience's existing beliefs, short-circuiting critical questioning. It is for these reasons that topical silences are among the most potent weapons in a propagandist's arsenal.

Methodology

In line with tenets of interpretive social science (Bevir, 2010) and inductive discourse analysis (Barton, 2002), the procedure I use to identify propagandistic topical silences consists of several steps (cf. Huckin, 2002): (1) *Selection of a type of communication (or genre)* designed for a mass audience; this includes analysis of the genre and its affordances and constraints (Berkenkotter & Huckin, 1995). (2) *Selection of an appropriate topic*, one that appears to have some impact on the general society. Normally this will be a topic with which the investigator already has some familiarity and one that the investigator feels comfortable pursuing. (3) *Wide reading about the topic.* Because propagandistic topical silences are based on deliberate omission of relevant subtopics, the analyst needs to develop a sense of what those subtopics are. That requires the perusal of diverse sources of information, resulting in a set of candidate subtopics (i.e., universe of discourse) about the general topic. (4) *Tentative claim.* Based on one's wide reading, the investigator notices certain subtopics left untreated in particular texts about the general topic. If there seems to be some pattern to these omissions, the investigator posits an interesting claim about it subject to confirmation or refutation. (5) *Creation of a study corpus.* The analyst creates a corpus of texts suitable to impartial testing of the claim. (6) *Detailed examination.* Each text is examined to see what subtopics are included and excluded. (7) *Pattern analysis.* The patterns of inclusion and exclusion are analyzed with regard to supporting or disconfirming the claim.

The example discussed next pertained to a high-profile topic (the North Korean crisis) given extensive albeit superficial attention in the US corporate-owned news media. I read widely about the topic, using a variety of sources including scholarly books and papers, government documents, respected independent news sites, television and radio interviews with experts, etc. Meanwhile, I was noting on a daily basis how the topic was being treated in mainstream news outlets such as the *New York Times*, Associated Press, *Salt Lake Tribune*, and *ABC World News Tonight*. By drawing on all of this information, I arrived at a working hypothesis, namely that *the US mainstream news media routinely omit key information from their coverage of the North Korean crisis, producing a one-sided narrative that constitutes a form of propaganda through omission.*

An Example: North Korea

Genre Selection

I chose to work with newspaper articles (reports, editorials, etc.) for study for two reasons. First, this genre has traditionally been the primary means of informing the American public about important events in any kind of depth. Second, in contrast to television, radio, or internet news tweets, newspaper articles often give a journalist enough space to go into some depth about important issues, including contrasting points of view.

Topic Selection

I chose to focus on North Korea because, at the time of my study (June 2017 to January 2018), North Korea's accelerated development of its nuclear weapons program was consistently a headline story in the American press. Kim Jong-Un, the North Korean president, was bragging that his country had developed powerful nuclear bombs and the capability of sending nuclear-tipped ballistic missiles to targets as far away as the United States. Donald Trump, in his first year as US president, was making bellicose threats in response. It was an increasingly dangerous situation, and I couldn't help but notice that the national newspaper articles I was reading on a daily basis, despite the affordances of the genre, were consistently presenting only a US viewpoint that depicted Kim as some sort of madman whose actions were entirely irrational. That blatant imbalance not only supported my tentative study hypothesis but also encouraged me to study the topic in depth.

Wide Reading

North Korea has been an important part of American history ever since World War II. When the war came to an end, Soviet forces in the North and American forces in the South occupied the Korean Peninsula, with the 38th parallel serving as a dividing line. National hero Kim Il Sung (Kim Jong-Un's grandfather) emerged as leader in the North; Syngman Rhee was installed by the United States as a puppet leader in the South. Civil war erupted in June 1950, with North Korean forces invading the South and occupying some 95 percent of the entire peninsula (Lankov, 2013); but in September of that year, US forces intervened and quickly pushed the North Koreans back well north of the 38th parallel. Chinese forces then entered the war, restoring the 38th parallel as the dividing line between North and South Korea. The war raged on for two and a half more years and included saturation bombing of the North by the United States. According to historian Bruce Cumings, "What hardly any Americans know or remember is that we carpet-bombed the North for three years with next to no concern for civilian casualties" (Cumings, 2010, p. 149). In fact, the United States dropped 635,000 tons of bombs and 32,557 tons of napalm on North Korea – more than in the entire Pacific theater during World War II. The United States made no distinction between military and civilian targets – it was wholesale slaughter and destruction. The targets included hydroelectric dams, water supplies, bridges, schools, population centers, factories, etc. According to Gen. Curtis LeMay, US/UN forces killed more than 20 percent of the population, or well over 2 million people, mostly civilians (Kohn & Harahan, 1988, p. 88). Memories of that experience are still seared into North Korea's living history today.

In July 1953, the two sides agreed to a cease-fire. But on numerous occasions since then, the United States has refused to negotiate a peace treaty and the two sides are still technically at war. The United States has had more than 30,000 troops stationed at ten permanent bases in South Korea and has conducted annual naval exercises off the North Korean coast. In 1994, the two sides signed an "Agreed Framework" that relaxed tensions and opened the way to negotiations. In 2003, however, the Bush administration renewed US threats toward North Korea, labeling it part of the "Axis of Evil" along with Iraq and Iran. In response, Pyongyang announced its withdrawal from the Nuclear Nonproliferation Treaty that it had signed in 1985.

This historical background gives rise to some alternative interpretations of North Korea's recent actions. For one, it could well be that Supreme Leader Kim Jong Il observed how Saddam Hussein's lack of a nuclear deterrent led to his demise, and he was determined not to make the same mistake: to protect himself and his country he restarted the country's nuclear program (Polk, 2017). His son, Kim Jong Un, may have learned a similar lesson in observing what happened to Libya after it abandoned its weapons of mass destruction program: NATO forces orchestrated by the United States attacked the country and its leader, Moammar Ghaddafi, was brutally murdered. Indeed, according to historian Andrei Lankov, who has studied North Korea for more than thirty years, Kim understands that having nuclear weapons is likely the best defense against an attack by the United States (Lankov, 2013, p. 149). On this interpretation, the recent acceleration of North Korea's nuclear weapons development could be seen as, in part, a self-defensive measure taken in response to a hawkish new administration in Washington (Wright, 2017). As former US president (and successful negotiator with North Korea) Jimmy Carter recently said, "What the North Koreans have wanted for a long time is just assurance confirmed by the Six Powers Agreement – with China and Russia and Japan and South Korea and so forth – that the United States will not attack North Korea as long as North Korea stays at peace with its neighbors" (Page, 2018).

Alternatively, North Korea's nuclear weapons buildup could be due to a more general assertion of the country's independence not only from the United States but also from all the other actors in the region. As historian Paul French (2014, p. 417) noted in a comprehensive study published prior to this latest nuclear weapons buildup:

The primacy of the armed forces has been a guiding philosophy of the regime from the start; the guerrilla tradition that liberated, defended and established the country has continued to loom large over the national culture. North Korean propaganda constantly refers to external threats; this bolsters the patriotic nationalism, which in turn reinforces the regime. Nuclear weapons, WMDs and CBWs are the culmination of this – a "deterrent" against attack and annihilation; symbols of independence, modernity and success that physically demonstrate the primacy of the Military First line. The links between the military and the wider economy are fundamental.

Or it could be some combination of motives, including other, less obvious ones. The point is that little of this history is mentioned in mainstream US news reporting. Through such omission, the news media effectively frame Pyongyang's nuclear and ballistic missile activities as purely offensive in nature rather than as the self-defensive and/or patriotic measures they could well be. Haunted by the horror-filled memories of the Korean War and confronted ever since by the world's most powerful and aggressive military, North Korea's leaders have had every reason to be anxious about their security (Boardman, 2017; Lankov, 2013). Yet US reporting about the situation routinely ignores this possible perspective from Pyongyang and only presents the mainstream Western one.

So the United States and the broader Western public is left in the dark about North Korea's possible motives for pursuing its nuclear program. There are significant omissions on the US side as well, which contribute to the propagandistic nature of the reporting. We have already pointed to several: North Korea's inclusion in Bush's Axis of Evil, the execution of Saddam Hussein, and the killing of Moammar Ghaddafi. While all three of these historical events could well be relevant to Kim Jong-Un's thinking, they are rarely mentioned in US news reports about the current situation. And there are other omissions as well. For example, since the Korean War armistice in 1953, the United States has attacked numerous countries including Cuba, Vietnam, Cambodia, Laos, Haiti, Grenada, Iraq, Libya, Nicaragua, Panama, Afghanistan, and Syria, among others (Blum, 2004). The US military has long conducted provocative actions toward North Korea, including annual joint naval exercises off the North Korean coast and frequent practice bombing runs from a US air base in Guam. The US military is currently at war in seven nations and has Special Operations forces in 142 others (Turse, 2018). Such facts could well explain North Korea's decision to accelerate development of its nuclear program, yet they are rarely mentioned in US news reports.

Tentative Claim

I claim that, in effect, the US mainstream news media coverage of the US–North Korea conflict fits the definition of "propaganda," specifically propaganda-by-omission: it is *misleading* in its one-sidedness and omission of historical context; it is *addressed to a mass audience* by news corporations who *gain advantage* by pandering to that audience's patriotism; it is created and disseminated *systematically*; and it *does not invite critical analysis or response*. The reportage is propagandistic especially on two distinct grounds: (1) it fails to mention the sixty-eight-year history of US–North Korean antagonism, especially the war of 1950–1953; and (2) it fails to mention President Kim's possible concern about meeting the same fate as Iraq's Saddam and Libya's Ghaddafi were he to give up his nuclear arsenal (Basu, 2017).

Study Corpus To test this claim, I accessed ProQuest's USNewstream database and randomly selected four days' worth of US news coverage published in mainstream US newspapers over a period of four months. Those days turned out to be November 3, 2017; December 9, 2017; January 1, 2018; and March 3, 2018. Using only news stories and editorials that mentioned "North Korea" at least twice, I ended up with a study corpus of forty-nine documents totaling 42,961 words.

Detailed Examination Of the forty-nine documents that were examined, forty-six supported my claim. Those news reports contained no mention at all of the sixty-eight-year history of US–North Korean antagonism, Kim's fear of suffering the same fate as Saddam and Ghaddafi, or North Korea's tradition of independence. The three exceptions were all lengthy editorials, not news reports. And they were only partial exceptions in that they all mentioned Kim's and North Korea's fear of being attacked by the United States but did not include any discussion of the horrors North Korea suffered at the hands of the United States during the 1950–1953 war. Notably, the most comprehensive of these three exceptions was a long editorial published on March 3, 2018, in a second-tier outlet with no national profile, the *Hartford Courant*; it was written not by an American but by a high-ranking official of the Chinese government.

Pattern Analysis All forty-nine of these newspaper articles depicted North Korea as a threat to the United States and its allies. In those cases where blame for the tensions was attributed to one side or the other, North Korea was held responsible. Although President Trump promised to wreak nuclear devastation on North Korea – "fire and fury like the world has never seen" (Warrick, 2017), in these articles there was little discussion of the risk of harm to North Korea and its people. Rather, emphasis was consistently placed on the risk of harm to the United States and its allies. Of particular significance to the present discussion was the omission of any historical context about North Korea or about US military aggression toward other countries. And there was no speculation of any complexity about President Kim's possible motives.

Not surprisingly, public opinion polls in the United States consistently participate in this propaganda campaign and reflect its efficacy. Although North Korea has not attacked another country since 1950 while the United States has attacked numerous countries in that time, public opinion polls in the United States have consistently asked questions about North Korea being "a threat" while not asking the same question of the United States. And roughly three-fourths of the respondents consistently deem North Korea to be a threat, not only to its neighbors but also to America (PollingReport.com, 2018).

Conclusion   On the assumption that this random selection of newspaper articles is representative of US mainstream news coverage of the recent US–North Korea confrontation, I claim that such coverage is propagandistic. The propaganda occurs not through words or images but through their absence – specifically the omitting of relevant information about North Korea that would allow American readers to make more informed judgments about the situation. As a result of these omissions, the newspaper coverage as a whole fits our working definition of "propaganda": it is *systematically misleading* and *does not invite critical analysis or response* (at least not from the *mass audience* to whom it is directed). As for *parties who thereby gain advantage,* see the following discussion.

Discussion

What is the absence doing? Political discourse generally operates on at least two distinct levels: (1) that of some particular policy or set of policies and (2) that of some broader ideology. Propaganda is no different. Typically deployed in support of some specific interest, propaganda simultaneously draws on and promotes a more general underlying political ideology. As the French propaganda theorist Jacques Ellul says in his classic 1965 treatise, *Propaganda,* a key condition for the development of propaganda is "the prevalence of strong myths and ideologies in a society" (p. 116).

These societal myths and ideologies simultaneously enable the propaganda and are reinforced by it.

To see this, let us consider the example discussed. The omission of information about North Korea's modern history, in particular about past US aggression against that country and others, has allowed the US news media to depict the United States as an altruistic defender of South Korea and Japan and the North Korean regime as an unhinged threat to those countries and to the United States itself. That story line has become a journalistic cliché repeated over and over by news outlets across the land to a patriotic audience receptive to it. This narrative draws on and reinforces a more general ideology – namely, that of an America that is always well intentioned and benign in its dealings with other countries, an America that's "exceptional" (Jouet, 2017; Pease, 2009). In the words of President George W. Bush, "Our nation is the greatest force for good in history" (Johnson, 2004, p. 1). Historian Richard T. Hughes, in *Myths America Lives By*, refers to it as "the myth of the Innocent Nation," asserting that although it is "grounded in self-delusion," it is widely subscribed to by the American public and "is therefore, in many ways, the most powerful myth of all" (2003, p. 8). (In contrast, a 2013 poll of 67,806 respondents in sixty-five countries by WIN/ Gallup International found that the United States was considered "the most dangerous threat to world peace" of any country in the world, a finding supported in a similar Pew Research poll in 2017 [Zuesse, 2017].)

In other words, propaganda-by-omission reinforces a prevailing mythology that benefits powerful forces behind the scenes. By omitting information about North Korea's history and culture and reasonable speculation about Kim's possible motives, the news coverage reinforces nationalistic myths about American benevolence vis-à-vis other countries. By omitting the dark side of American foreign policy and history, it promotes an uncritical attitude in the general public that serves the status quo and its beneficiaries, especially those in power. Most obviously, such whitewashing benefits what President Eisenhower called in his 1961 Farewell Speech "the military-industrial complex," a major component of the US economy and a significant financial contributor to prominent politicians. As we saw in the case of the Iraq invasion, it facilitates whatever military action the US political establishment might choose to take. And it promotes an uncritical patriotism in the general populace that dampens social unrest (Parenti, 1994).

It is worth noting that none of these effects is necessarily "intentional" in the traditional sense of the word, i.e., deliberately or consciously planned on the part of the individual journalist. As Herman and Chomsky (2002) describe in their five-filter model noted earlier, most professional journalists operate within commercial and sociopolitical cultures that exercise constant influence on what they produce (see also Parenti, 1993). Thus, their writing reflects what I have referred to elsewhere (Huckin 2002) as "dispersed intentionality," where, for example, the individual journalist crafting a report or editorial unconsciously adheres to the ideological leanings of that news outlet's owners and editors. Indeed, the pressures of news production coupled with a journalist's embeddedness in the larger society may well dissipate intentionality even further, to nation-level doctrines (cf. Shanahan's reference to "unconscious manipulation of social structure and communication systems" [2001, p. 2]). All of these forces conspire, in a sense, to foster conformity to a power-driven status quo and its prevailing orthodoxy of opinion.

Conclusion

In analyzing public discourse for possible propagandistic content, one should always avoid assuming that there is some countervailing "truth." The goal of propaganda analysis is not to reveal some truth but rather to simply interrogate truth claims that appear to be false or misleading. Currently, in American political discourse, it is commonplace to read allegations that certain news reports are propaganda or, as President Trump calls it, "fake news." Because they make overt claims, such reports can be checked for factuality by specialized websites such as politifact.c om and snopes.com.

Propaganda-by-omission is different. It is largely impervious to such fact checking – precisely because it does not present any facts. Instead, it misleads the public by concealing important information. In some cases, such concealment is easily detected and thus ineffective. For example, advertisements routinely omit any information not favorable to the product they are promoting, yet most consumers expect such bias and are not deceived by it. But when it comes to national and world issues, the situation is very different. First of all, many if not most citizens have considerable trust in mainstream news sources; second, many lack sufficient world knowledge to challenge the veracity of reports from such sources anyway; and finally, many lack the time or resources or inclination to research such issues. Under these circumstances, propagandists in the news media can put forth stories about important issues that are one-sided yet not perceived as such. They do this, I argue, mainly by relying on unspoken presuppositions about the world that have long been propagated in that culture – in some cases to the point of being deeply incorporated into that culture's myths and ideologies.

Thus, propaganda-by-omission operates on at least two levels. First, on the surface level, certain relevant information is routinely and systematically omitted from breaking news coverage. Because the resulting story accords with audience members' ideological worldview, they do not notice the omissions that helped create it. Consequently, they perceive the report to be accurate and complete when in fact it is not. In this way, they are being systematically misled, i.e., propagandized. Second, when similarly truncated stories accumulate over time, each based on a similar worldview and its ideological presuppositions, that underlying worldview itself is reinforced as "common sense." To the extent that those myths and ideologies are unfounded, they are propagandistic. Recalling the definition we started out with, I claim such reporting is propagandistic because it (1) is *misleading*, (2) is addressed to a *mass audience*, (3) *advantages certain parties*, (4) is done *systematically*, and (5) *does not invite critical analysis or response*.

In the case of North Korea, for example, the US mainstream media have consistently followed a simplistic story line about that country's "threatening actions" without considering any North Korean perspective, including the possibly defensive nature of its actions and the long history behind them. Such reportage exemplifies propaganda-by-omission, I claim, on both of the levels just described. By giving only a US perspective, it is propagandistically one-sided. And by presupposing an overly positive worldview of US ideology and foreign policy, it is propagandistic on a deeper level.

On the Matter of "Truth"

Propaganda by its very nature is untruthful or at least deceptive. In the definition cited at the beginning of this chapter, we called it information that is "false or misleading." The aim of propaganda analysis, therefore, is to cast light on cases where news reports or other examples of mass communication are deemed to be untruthful. With overt propaganda, that project is usually straightforward: the analyst consults respected authorities on the subject and finds the claims do not hold up. Propaganda-by-omission is more challenging, since the deception is only indirect. Instead of debunking truth claims, the goal of the analyst is simply to describe how the deception occurs. If that involves posing alternative accounts, as I have done here, those alternatives do not have to be "true" in some absolute sense; they need only be *plausible* – i.e., have sufficient factual grounding along with a coherent counter-narrative – to raise appropriate questions about the standard account.

Take-Home Lessons for Researchers

The main takeaway from this study is that propaganda-by-omission is a phenomenon of entire discourses, not just of individual texts. While methodical research can identify omissions in isolated texts (e.g., Huckin, 2002; O'Halloran, 2003), labeling such omissions as "propagandistic" should only be done via reference to some broader body of texts. To "see" what was potentially missing from a news report about North Korea, in particular, I had to imagine what sort of information *could* have been included but was not. That step should not be speculative; rather, it should be based on valid criteria for inclusion.

One such criterion is that of *genre,* or text-type, since each genre has its own particular affordances and constraints. In the case of news reports, a key affordance is found in journalism's *raison d'être:* "The primary purpose of journalism is to provide citizens with the information they need to be free and self-governing" (Kovach & Rosenstiel, 2001, p. 17). Such a dictum implies that news reporting has an obligation to provide accurate and comprehensive information – including, to a reasonable extent, "both sides of the story." Yet, in following the North Korea saga, I kept noticing that only one side of the story was given a voice; in many of those cases, I could not detect any genre-based constraint preventing mention of "the other side." This apparent violation of journalism's primary purpose is what aroused my curiosity and led to this study.

But how typical were these violations? Were they just aberrations that I happened to have noticed, or were they part of a systematic *pattern?* To answer that question, I decided to create a corpus of randomly selected texts addressing the topic in question. That step, as I hope I have shown, confirmed that these omissions were not exceptional but systematic.

That led me to ponder why professional journalists would systematically omit important, relevant information in their reporting about such a topic. I thus engaged in wide reading and reflection on topics such as American ideology, American society, American politics, modern journalism, and military history. That led to my understanding of how these omissions were not only systematic but also how they created genuine propaganda.

Take-Home Lessons for Citizens

The foregoing describes how topical silences can be identified in news media discourse. The process as illustrated here is rather painstaking, necessarily so for scholarly standards. But the identification of propagandistic absences should not be just an academic exercise. Rather, in a democratic society it should be a routine activity practiced by all citizens, for two reasons: first, propaganda is typically used by those having disproportionate, undemocratic power – power that in a democratic society should always be challenged. Second, democracy is based on the citizenry's informed understanding of important issues, and to the extent that citizens are misled by propaganda, such understanding is undermined.

This begs the question, how can overburdened, harried citizens make the detection of propagandistic absences a routine activity? The answer, I believe, lies in the deployment of two cornerstones of critical thinking, namely skepticism and subject matter knowledge. First, one should be *skeptical* about the validity of the claims and motives of the author/ speaker. Such skepticism is a general habit of mind that should be cultivated through education and practice. Second, one must have sufficient *knowledge* about the topic to detect what's been left unsaid. That requires both curiosity and good sources of information. To quote again finally Professor Ellul: "A high intelligence, a broad culture, a constant exercise of the critical faculties, and full and objective information are the best weapons against propaganda" (1965, p. 111).

References

Barton, E. (2002). Inductive discourse analysis. In E. Barton & G. Stygall (Eds.), *Discourse studies in composition* (pp. 19–42). Cresskill, NJ: Hampton.

Basu, K. (2017). The North Korean missile crisis. *Project Syndicate*. Retrieved from www.project-syndicate.org/commentary/north-korea-nuclear-threat-game-theory-by-kaushik-basu-2017-07?barrier=accessreg

Berkenkotter, C., & Huckin, T. (1995). *Genre knowledge in disciplinary communication: Cognition/culture/power*. Hillsdale, NJ: Lawrence Erlbaum.

Bevir, M. (2010). *Democratic governance*. Princeton, NJ: Princeton University Press.

Blum, W. (2004). *Killing hope: US Military and CIA interventions since World War II*. Monroe, ME: Common Courage.

Boardman, W. (2017, July 8). North Korea does not threaten world peace, the US does. *Reader Supported News*. Retrieved from https://readersupportednews.org/opinion2/277-75/44563-focus-north-korea-does-not-threaten-world-peace-the-us-does

Chomsky, N. (1989). *Necessary illusions: Thought control in democratic societies*. Boston: South End.

Cumings, B. (2010). *The Korean War: A history*. New York: Modern Library.

DiMaggio, A. (2008). *Mass media, mass propaganda*. Lanham, MD: Lexington.

Ellul, J. (1965). *Propaganda: The formation of men's attitudes*. New York: Vintage.

Fish, S. (1980). *Is there a text in this class?* Cambridge, MA: Harvard University Press.

French, P. (2014). *North Korea: State of paranoia*. London; New York: Zed.

Grate, L. (2016). Jane Addams: A foe of rhetorics of control. In G. L. Henderson & M. J. Braun (Eds.), *Propaganda and rhetoric in democracy* (pp. 51–71). Carbondale: Southern Illinois University Press.

Herman, E., & Chomsky, N. (2002). *Manufacturing consent: The political economy of the mass media*. New York: Pantheon.

Huckin, T. (2002). Textual silence and the discourse of homelessness. *Discourse & Society, 13*(3), 347–372.

Huckin, T. (2010). On textual silences, large and small. In C. Bazerman et al. (Eds.), *Traditions of writing research* (pp. 419–431). London; New York: Routledge.

Huckin, T. (2016). Propaganda defined. In G. L. Henderson & M. J. Braun (Eds.), *Propaganda and rhetoric in democracy: History, theory, analysis* (pp. 118–136). Carbondale: Southern Illinois University Press.

Hughes, R. (2003). *Myths America lives by*. Urbana; Chicago: University of Illinois Press.

Huxley, A. (1960). *Brave New World & Brave New World revisited*. New York: Harper & Row.

Johnson, C. (2004). *The sorrows of empire: Militarism, secrecy, and the end of the republic*. New York: Metropolitan.

Jouet, M. (2017). *Exceptional America*. Berkeley: University of California Press.

Kohn, R., & Harahan, J. (Eds.). (1988). *Strategic air warfare*. Washington, DC: Office of Air Force History, United States Air Force.

Kovach, B., & Rosenstiel, T. (2001). *The elements of journalism: What newspeople should know and the public should expect*. New York: Three Rivers.

Lakoff, G. (2004). *Don't think of an elephant: Know your values and frame the debate*. White River Junction, VT: Chelsea Green.

Lankov, A. (2013). *The real North Korea: Life and politics in the failed Stalinist utopia*. Oxford: Oxford University Press.

Lippmann, W. (1922). *Public opinion*. New York: Free Press.

Loftus, E. (1975). Leading questions and the eyewitness report. *Cognitive Psychology, 7*, 560–572.

Luntz, F. (2007). *Words that work: It's not what you say, it's what people hear*. New York: Hyperion.

Meyer, B. J. F. (1975). *The organization of prose and its effects on memory*. Amsterdam: North-Holland.

Minsky, M. (1975). A framework for representing knowledge. In P. Winston (Ed.), *The psychology of computer vision* (pp. 211–277). New York: McGraw-Hill.

O'Halloran, K. (2003). *Critical discourse analysis and language cognition*. Edinburgh: Edinburgh University Press.

Page, S. (2018, March 18). Jimmy Carter: Trump's decision to hire John Bolton is "a disaster for our country." *USA Today*. Retrieved from www.usatoday.com/videos/news/2018/03/26/jimmy-carter-calls-trumps-decision-hire-bolton-disaster-our-country/33298463/

Parenti, M. (1993). *Inventing reality: The politics of the news media*. New York: St. Martin's Press.

Parenti, M. (1994). *Land of idols: Political mythology in America*. New York: St. Martin's Press.

Pease, D. E. (2009). *The new American exceptionalism*. Minneapolis: University of Minnesota Press.

Polk, W. R. (2017, September 4). How history explains the Korean crisis. Cons ortiumnews.com. Retrieved from https://consortiumnews.com/2017/08/28/ho w-history-explains-the-korean-crisis/

PollingReport.com. (2018). Korea: North and South. Retrieved from www.pol lingreport.com/korea.htm

Pratkanis, A., & Aronson, E. (2001). *Age of propaganda*. New York: Freeman.

Rosenblatt, L. (1938). *Literature as exploration*. New York: Appleton-Century.

Rumelhart, D. (1980). Schemata: The building blocks of cognition. In R. Spiro et al. (Eds.), *Theoretical issues in reading comprehension* (pp. 33–58). Hillsdale, NJ: Lawrence Erlbaum.

Shanahan, J. (2001) *Propaganda without propagandists? Six case studies in US propaganda*. Cresskill, NJ: Hampton.

Sperling, G. (2017, April 25). Don't cut the estate tax – raise it. *The Atlantic*. Retrieved from www.theatlantic.com/business/archive/2017/04/estate-tax/ 524250/

Turse, N. (2018). Donald Trump's first year sets record for US Special Ops. TomDispatch.com. Retrieved from www.tomdispatch.com/blog/176363/

Warrick, J. (2017, August 8). North Korea now making missile-ready nuclear weapons, U.S. analysts say. *Chicago Tribune*, p. A1. Retrieved from www.chi cagotribune.com/news/nationworld/ct-north-korea-nuclear-missiles-2017080 8-story.html

Wright, A. (2017). US experts say North Korean leadership may be ruthless and reckless, but they are not crazy. *Common Dreams*. Retrieved from www.com mondreams.org/views/2017/07/14/us-experts-say-north-korean-leadership-m ay-be-ruthless-and-reckless-they-are-not

Zuesse, E. (2017, July 8). Polls: US is "the greatest threat to peace in the world today." *Strategic Culture Foundation*. Retrieved from www.strategic-culture.org/ news/2017/08/07/polls-us-greatest-threat-to-peace-world-today.html

11   Silencing Whistleblowers

C. Fred Alford

> They wouldn't talk with me about it, and they wouldn't
> talk with me about not talking about it. –
>
> A whistleblower

The silence of whistleblowers is the consequence of organizational power. It is not merely the absence of voice, but the destruction of voice. The result is that while most whistleblowers are not actually silent, their voice often has the quality of an endless monologue. Silencing is a political act, not just the exertion of power, but the exercise of power, a demonstration. The audience is the other members of the organization, and beyond. Silence is not just the absence of voice. It is the marginalization of the whistleblower, in which they become invisible as well as inaudible.

In theory, it is almost impossible to prove that silence and silencing exist. How does one prove the absence of an absence? In practice, it is not so difficult, as the epigraph of this chapter reveals. The most obvious is refusing to talk about the unethical or illegal acts the whistleblower has brought to light, and in many cases refusing to talk about not talking about it. The absence of dialogue does not demonstrate silencing; the destruction of dialogue does. Silencing is not about not talking. It is about the eradication of that place from which the whistleblower could be heard. It is about the destruction of words, as in George Orwell's Newspeak, particularly words that invoke moral responsibilities.

In the language of narratology, as the study of narrative is called, silencing occurs when the organization refuses to respond at the same diegetic level as the whistleblower. That is a fancy way of saying that the whistleblower wants to talk about the organization and its mission, and the organization responds with claims about the emotional or moral competence of the whistleblower.

One can tell one's story only if the one who reads or hears it shares the terms of the discourse. The failure or refusal of others to share the terms of the discourse is a powerful, subtle, and probably the most common way in which families and organizations silence their members. In both cases, diagnosis turns actors into patients. Michel Foucault (1979) was not wrong when he argued that today discipline is practiced as diagnosis. Diagnosis is silencing.

I have spent years talking with whistleblowers, attending their support groups, going on a week-long retreat with them, and sitting down to coffee with several dozen (Alford, 2001). I continue to receive emails and telephone calls from troubled whistleblowers. Some of this more recent experience is included in this text. All unattributed quotations come from experience. All whistleblower names are pseudonyms.

I would not call what I do interviewing. I would call it listening and interpretation. This often means that I too am not at the same diegetic level as the whistleblower. The whistleblower wants to talk about what the organization did. I want to know how the whistleblower responded, how they felt. Do I too participate in silencing the whistleblower? I do not think so, because not silencing would become the equivalent of hearing people exactly how they want to be heard. That is both impossible and undesirable. Still, silencing is not as clear-cut as whether the actor has a voice or no voice. What is clear is that if no one listens, then the voice is silenced. As one whistleblower put it in an email:

A whistleblower on government contract fraud is most akin to the tree that falls in the forest trapping an animal of nature with no one around – the falling actually occurred and the animal dies, but no one listened, no one helped the animal, and the cycle continues.

There is often a tone of desperate sadness and confusion in the communications that I receive from whistleblowers. Silencing is not just silence; it can drive a whistleblower to desperate acts. These acts, rather than the ethical or legal issue raised by the whistleblower, become the grounds of termination. Among the whistleblowers I studied, the average length of time between speaking out and losing one's job was about two years, long enough to separate the retaliation from the act of whistleblowing. The organization has a long memory.

Silencing is not just a refusal to listen. It extends to the attempt to make people invisible as well as inaudible, as if they did not exist. This is generally the goal of the large organization confronting a whistleblower. The real tragedy is how fellow workers frequently cooperate in this disappearance, presumably out of fear of losing their own jobs. My hypothesis, which I am unable to prove here, is that this fear has a more primitive basis in the silencing that takes place in families and school. Everything you really need to know about silencing you learned before you were seven years old, even if it takes a lifetime to remember, and most never do. Silencing is about exclusion from the group, whether it is the family, playgroup, or whatever. We think we are a lot more independent than we are, and aspects of our culture make it worse.

I spoke to a few South Korean whistleblowers as part of a larger research project on Korean values (Alford, 1999). Koreans are said to be a group-culture; the group is everything, the individual nothing. In fact, Koreans are far more aware of what they are willing to give up to belong – more groupish than North Americans perhaps, but also more aware of their own groupishness. Our ideology of individualism makes our willingness to sacrifice ourselves to the group less visible, but no less powerful. It is one reason most whistleblowers are so surprised at the extent of their exclusion, not just from the organization but also from the company of former friends and colleagues. They have crossed a boundary no one wants to admit – most people's willingness to do anything to belong. The power of silencing rests on the power of exclusion, something so terrifying we are reluctant to know it.

In the end, mine is not a study of whistleblowers, but of how organizations act to silence their members. Silence does not always mean that silencing occurred. However, among the whistleblowers I studied it generally does. Silencing involves pushing whistleblowers to the margins of society. This is easier than it seems. Work is where most of us get the money to live on, including the money to pay the mortgage, buy health insurance, pay for college, and prepare for retirement. Somewhere between one-half and two-thirds of the whistleblowers lose their jobs, according to several studies (Glazer & Glazer, 1989, pp. 206–207; Miethe, 1999, pp. 77–78; Rothschild & Miethe, 1996, pp. 15–16;). At least one study, however, has found significantly less retaliation (Miceli & Near, 1992, pp. 226–227). As might be expected, most of the difference depends on who and how one counts (Miethe, 1999, pp. 73–78). It also depends on the size and composition of the population studied. One study that directly addresses my concerns, "When you talk and talk and nobody listens," has a sample size of one (Bjørkelo et al., 2008).

Among the whistleblowers who lose their jobs, more than half will lose their homes and marriages. Whistleblowers frequently become obsessed with their cases and often turn to alcohol or drugs, generally for a limited period. People like this do not make good marriage partners, particularly when the marriage is shaky to begin with. My more limited survey (several dozen whistleblowers) fits this generalization. One reason to look at whistleblowers is that we see the brutality of silence up close. Silence has the power to make people disappear: not just from the group but also from themselves. People begin to doubt their own experiences. One of the few virtues of a harsh organizational response is that it tells people that what they saw and said was real, even as organizations work hard to deny it, basing their retaliation on other causes. This is why the lag time between whistleblowing and firing is so long.

Whistleblower Narratives

Whistleblowers have only their narratives. They need someone to talk with, someone to hear the narrative and so help the whistleblowers make it their own. Narrative is framed and formed as it enters discourse, for narrative means story, and we tell stories in the hope that they will be listened to. In the absence of a discursive frame, narrative tends to turn in on itself, which generally means that it becomes repetitive, like a snake chasing its tale, an endless saga of humiliations. Many whistleblowers talk about their experience in ways that resemble a monologue, as if they were already used to being ignored.

We may tell our own stories, but we cannot tell them to ourselves. We can tell them only if others are prepared to hear them in something resembling the terms in which they are told. What happens when the terms we most value are not recognized by the world? What happens when principles for which one has ruined one's life are regarded by others as mere words?

Neither whistleblowers nor the rest of us live in a world of wall-to-wall narrative. The whistleblower's narrative is not arrested because all narratives are arrested. The whistleblower's narrative is arrested because the whistleblower has had experiences that cannot be framed and formed within the resources of common narrative. These last remarks may seem obvious. They are aimed at those academics who write as if narratives live a life of their own.

Silencing and the Limits of Common Narrative

Silencing is the destruction of narrative, the story we tell ourselves and others about the meaning of our lives. This silencing can be as crude and brutal as O'Brien's torturing Winston Smith in *Nineteen eighty-four*, but in the world of the whistleblower it is subtler. Lawrence Langer writes about survivors of the Holocaust. While their suffering was orders of magnitude more intense than that suffered by whistleblowers, the same principle applies. Langer notes, "our ability to gain access to these narratives depends on what we are prepared to forsake to listen to them" (Langer, 1991, p. 195). This applies not only to those who listen to whistleblowers but even more to the whistleblowers themselves.

The silencing that most bedevils whistleblowers is self-silencing, in which they cannot believe that what happened to them was real. "I know they fired me for speaking out," said one, "but sometimes I don't believe it myself. Sometimes I believe what they said, that I was the liar." While it is difficult to compare the silencing of whistleblowers to other acts of silencing, one possibility suggests itself. What we most want in all the world is that goodness and power be one. That is the definition of God, and it is why some abused children would rather blame themselves than their parents (Hazzard et al., 1995). The organization certainly is not God, and it is not a parent, but the organization looms large in the lives of many. Some come to doubt themselves rather than the organization, part of a lifelong habit.

What must whistleblowers give up to hear their story? The truths of common narrative, such as "the little man who stood up against the big corporation and won" is a common narrative. Common narratives are like clichés, worn and out-of-context truths, insufficiently complex to account for experience. What does common narrative consist of? Here is a partial listing:

> That the individual matters.
> That law and justice can be relied on.
> That the purpose of law is to remove the caprice of powerful individuals.
> That ours is a government of laws, not men.
> That the individual will not be sacrificed for the sake of the group.
> That loyalty is not equivalent to the herd instinct.
> That one's friends will remain loyal even if one's colleagues do not.
> That the organization is not fundamentally immoral.
> That it makes sense to stand up and do the right thing. (Take this literally, that it "makes sense" means that it is a comprehensible activity.)
> That someone, somewhere, who is in charge knows, cares, and will do the right thing.
> That the truth matters, and someone will want to know it.
> That if one is right and persistent, things will turn out for the best in the end.
> That even if they do not, other people will know and understand.
> That the family is a haven in a heartless world. Spouses and children will not abandon you in your hour of need.
> That someone will want to hear your story.
> That the individual can know the truth about all this and not become merely cynical, cynical unto death.

Without giving up the common narrative, whistleblowers can hardly believe themselves. Unable to do so, whistleblowers are less convincing to others. Common narrative is not only the enemy of truth, but it is also the most effective means of silencing another, one in which whistleblowers must give up almost everything they believed to hear themselves speak. Not all whistleblowers can do that. Like some abused children, they would rather not believe themselves. Not only is it hard to come to terms with these truths, but when one finally does it seems one is left with nothing. Consider the case of Joseph Rose, who exposed the Associated Milk Producers' illegal contributions to Nixon's reelection campaign:

I believe I can make a contribution to the young people in this country by continuing to respond with a strong warning that all of the public utterances of corporations, and indeed, our own government concerning "courage, integrity, loyalty, honesty, and duty" are nothing but the sheerest hogwash. (Glazer & Glazer, 1989, p. 223)

How in the world could one want to teach this to schoolchildren and not be possessed by cynicism? Rose would teach a lesson as bitter as his heart.

"Knowledge as Disaster"

The term "knowledge as disaster" is Maurice Blanchot's (1995), and it should be taken literally: not knowledge of the disaster, but knowledge as disaster because it cannot be contained within existing frames and forms of experience, including common narrative. A simple example of what may seem a less than disastrous experience may help to explain.

Mike Quint was an engineer who exposed defects and cover-ups in the construction of tunnels to be used by Los Angeles Metro Rail. Since Los Angeles is the site of frequent earthquakes, shortcuts in building the tunnels endangered hundreds of lives. Though Quint was eventually fired from the construction management company that oversaw the building of the tunnels, he persisted in his letter-writing campaign about defects and cover-ups in the Metro Rail tunnels. As a result, the construction management company was removed from the project, the tunnel contractor performed remedial work taking eight months, and several employees of the Los Angeles Metro Rail went to jail. Quint takes little satisfaction in his victory. Not only does he say he would not do it again, but he has turned into something of a zombie on his new job. Whistleblowing "has reduced my trust and faith in people and in our justice system. . . . I [now] expect fewer benefits from work, and perform my duties as directed, with fewer questions of decisions or procedures"

(Miethe, 1999, pp. 161–62). One study of Norwegian whistleblowers found less retaliation, but the same lack of satisfaction with work after whistleblowing (Skivenes & Trygstad, 2010).

Trust and faith in people: these are simple words, but what if they really mean something? For some, the earth moves when they discover that people in authority routinely lie and that those who work for them routinely cover up. Once one knows this, or rather once one feels this knowledge in one's bones, one lives in a new world. Some people remain aliens in the new world forever. Maybe they like it that way. Maybe they have no choice. Would one want to go so far as to say that Quint was silenced by the world he discovered, the world of lies behind words like "trust" and "faith"? One would not ordinarily call that silenced, for Quint has silenced himself. But if the world turns out not to be the world he thought he was living in, then perhaps he has been silenced by the corruption he found there. He won, but in doing so he has silenced his own voice in grief and anger. Silence *is* the way he grieves; silence is the way he expresses his anger at this corrupt world.

"My case is not grievable," said Bob Warren. He meant that it was not subject to further grievance procedures, but one might think about it another way. Bob could not feel the appropriate grief because he would have to learn too much about what he knew. That is what "knowledge as disaster" really means. Often, I felt as though the endless monologues of travails by some whistleblowers were a way of not having to stop and feel the grief of loss, not just of their job, home, and family but also of the new job that many had given themselves as a professional whistleblower. However, I did not subject the whistleblowers to paper and pencil tests designed to uncover silent grief, and I would not have done so even if I could. My feeling of their grief remains a feeling.

Whistleblowers Transgress Sacred Boundaries

What would political theory look like from the perspective of one who has been pushed not just out of the organization but also halfway out of society, ending up with no career, no savings, no house, and no family? What would political theory look like to Al Ripskis, a whistleblower who says, "It's a hell of a commentary on our contemporary society when you must be ready to become an insolvent pariah if you want to live up to your own ethical standards" (Glazer & Glazer, 1989, p. 207).

The organization, almost any large organization, acts as if it lives in a perfectly Hobbesian world: the goal is autarky, and it is achieved via transgression. The organization secures its boundaries only by transgressing the boundaries of others, lest it be transgressed against. In this regard, it is misleading to suggest that the whistleblower sets truth against loyalty. This suggests an image of the organization that is too passive and static. The real opposition is between individual and collective transgression. Will or will not the individual be available for the act of collective transgression?

In such a world, the most terrifying thought is that representatives of the outside are on the inside, traitors in our midst. The whistleblower becomes an insidious disease, a boundary violator. The anthropologist Mary Douglas (1966) uses the term "slimy" to capture the fear of one who will not stay in their place, or rather, one whose place we do not even know. It is what every organization is most afraid of: that someone inside represents the interests of the outside, that the organization cannot control its own boundaries, that it does not even know them. The former president of General Motors, James Roche, expressed this fear when he said the following:

Some of the enemies of business now encourage an employee to be disloyal to the enterprise. They want to create suspicion and disharmony, and pry into the proprietary interest of the business. However, this is labeled – industrial espionage, whistleblowing or professional responsibility – it is another tactic for spreading disunity and creating conflict. (Clark, 1997, p. 1071)

If this is how the leaders of organization think, then it is not hard to understand why whistleblowers are poison to the organization, and why they must be silenced. To allow them voice threatens organizational power, which ultimately depends on controlling the conditions of exit. *Exit, voice, and loyalty* is a classic work by Albert O. Hirschman (1970) on the individual and the organization, stating the choices faced by those who work there. The mistake Hirschman makes, at least as far as whistleblowers are concerned, is assuming that exit will be noticed, and voice heard. The power of the organization would render the individual invisible and silent, which is why organizations generally come down so hard on whistleblowers, often out of proportion to the threat they pose to the organization. The threat is not just over a matter of policy or practice; it is to the very idea of organization.

If whistleblowers are scapegoats, then they are *pharmakos*, an ancient Greek term that means both poison and cure, as well as scapegoat. As *pharmakos*, the whistleblower is poison to the unity of the organization, which wants to obliterate every reminder that the organization has obligations to those outside it. Organizational thinking is fundamentally primitive (Bion, 1998). The whistleblowers are cure to the degree they can give voice to the values and needs of those outside the organization. That is the voice that the organization would silence.

Construction and Discipline of the Whistleblower

"All people need is a civics lesson," says Ralph Nader. He is responding to those who say we need a new political theory to explain the fate of the whistleblower. If Nader is correct, the civics lesson we require is like nothing anyone ever learned in high school.

What would a civics lesson from Michel Foucault look like? Though there are more recent theorists, Foucault remains one of the most influential social theorists of the day. Among his most influential ideas is that social control in the contemporary world is exerted not as raw power, but as discipline. This is the perspective I have adopted here (Foucault, 1979).

The power that disciplines the whistleblower, Foucault might say, has less to do with the organization's ability to fire the whistleblower than one might suppose. That is merely power's most obvious expression, its last and most visible eruption. Power works in more intimate and subtle ways in the modern world, isolating the insubordinate one from their fellows by diagnosing them as abnormal or disturbed. Foucault (1979) calls this "disciplinary power," which casts the gaze of the entire organization on the whistleblower, almost as though the organization were a physician, treating the whistleblower not as someone who has challenged the power of the organization but as one who is sick, ill, morally suspect, criminal, or disturbed, and so must be isolated from those who are normal.

Disciplinary power makes of the whistleblower a patient, though we must understand that term in its broadest sense: one whose flawed perceptions of reality are the result of a moral or emotional illness and who must be reformed by power, lest their symptoms prove catching. Under discipline, there can be no political or ethical discourse. Any talking that takes place with the patient is strictly instrumental, aimed at controlling the patient through categorization and labeling. Ideally the patient accepts the label. This too is silencing. As one whistleblower said:

> The psychiatrist they sent me to said I was suffering from a histrionic personality disorder. I think that meant I needed to show off. No one else but a show-off would have gone to talk with that environmental group about what we were doing. Well, you know what. I believed them. I really did. For years I believed them . . . sometimes I still do. A little bit, sometimes.

"Nuts and sluts" is what many whistleblowers call this familiar strategy, by which their claims are ignored by finding the whistleblower to be emotionally disturbed or morally suspect. Anita Hill, who challenged the fitness of Supreme Court Justice Clarence Thomas at his confirmation hearings, is the most famous nut and slut in recent years. David Brock (1993) called her that in *The real Anita Hill: The untold story*, a hatchet job that he has since recanted, at least in part. Daniel Ellsberg might have been neutralized in this way had Nixon's plumbers not bungled their burglary of Ellsberg's psychiatrist's office. In high-stakes court cases, it is common for the organization's lawyers to hire private detectives to probe every aspect of a whistleblower's life. Today few records are unavailable. Until a few years ago, the easiest way to get rid of a federal employee was to send them to a government psychologist who would find them psychologically unfit for duty. Today some whistleblowers report that Employee Assistance Programs, which provide a therapist paid for by the organization, have taken over this disciplinary function.

Of all the things that make whistleblowers crazy, the most maddening is the unwillingness of the organization to listen to them. To listen would be to recognize the whistleblower as an individual with a political or ethical claim on the organization. To listen would be to recognize the whistleblower as a political actor, not a patient. To listen would be to participate in a dialogue and, to that degree at least, make the whistleblower's claim real – not necessarily true, but about something real. It is this that must be denied in the first place, and it is this that disciplinary power aims at: the transformation of actors into patients and politics into discipline. Disciplinary power aims to make ethical discourse impossible:

I told them they didn't need to fire me. I'd quit. I had my letter of resignation in my hand. All they had to do was listen to what I had to say and see my evidence. I'd have cleaned out my cubicle that afternoon. But they refused to listen. No one would even talk with me about it. They wouldn't talk with me period. It took them three years to get rid of me. And they're still paying for it.

Rather than listen to Tim Fuchs, his company paid him off with a bonus and early retirement, even if it took the threat of a lawsuit to get them to do it. It was my impression that Fuchs would have sacrificed the money in a minute to be heard, but when I asked him he only smiled.

The discipline that Foucault writes about works through expert knowledge, the knowledge that can diagnose a political protest as an expression of illness or a concern with ethics as a sign of emotional immaturity and maladaptation. In a word, discipline works through diagnosis. Though this diagnosis is often psychiatric or moral, it may also be judicial, as in "you do not have standing to sue, as your act does not fall under the purview of legally protected behavior." Sometimes diagnosis is bureaucratic, as in "that is not your department and hence not your proper concern." At its heart, diagnosis is concerned with the discipline of categories, under which people and things are classified so that they may be subject to expert knowledge. Experts do not talk with their

subjects; they diagnose them, even when the diagnostic language is judicial, bureaucratic, or social scientific.

It is the autonomous ethical individual who is the real threat to the
organization, and the law finds little room for such people. Or rather, it
finds room for them as an idea in such a way as to render the individual
behind the idea expendable, often because they do not fall under
a protected class of actors or acts. In whistleblower protection legislation,
process rules (Alford, 2016).

Theory of Silence and Silencing

All social organization, says Zygmunt Bauman (1989),

consists in subjecting the conduct of its units to either instrumental or
procedural criteria of evaluation. More importantly still, it consists in dele-
galizing all other criteria, and first and foremost such standards as may
render behaviour of units resilient to uniformizing pressures and thus autonomous vis-à-vis the collective purpose of the organization (which, from the
organizational point of view, makes them unpredictable and potentially de-
stabilizing). ... *All social organization consists therefore in neutralizing the
disruptive and deregulating impact of moral behavior.* (pp. 213–15, emphasis
mine)

The best way to disrupt immoral behavior is not to discuss it and not to
discuss not discussing it. Then it does not exist. Right?

Talking about what we are doing is not just talking about process and
procedures, how we are going to do it. Talking about what we are doing
means talking about how what we do affects others, as well as ourselves.
Talking about what we are doing puts our actions in the larger context of
their influence on a world of others. Talking about what we are doing
makes these others present, as though they were represented in the
discussion.

Talking about what we are doing, and to whom, requires discourse, as
people take turns talking and listening, perhaps even listening to what
others are saying. Jürgen Habermas (1984) makes this the mark of communicative rationality, the rationality of the lifeworld, as opposed to the
rationality of science and technology, what Bauman (1989) calls instrumental or procedural criteria of evaluation.

Silencing occurs in the worlds of science and technology too. There are
many stories of scientists who were silenced, which means not being
published in scientific journals, because the paradigm shift they proposed
was threatening and unthinkable, which means it must not be made more
real in discourse (Siler, Kirby, & Bero, 2015). Talking about it would
recognize its potential to be real.

Nevertheless, most silencing occurs in what Habermas calls the life-world, the world of everyday life in homes and organizations. The silencing can range from a slap across the face (or worse) to the transformation of discourse into diagnosis in the organization or law courts. Silencing makes the other person invisible. Seeing and talking are inseparable in discourse, even if seeing just means recognition of the other's existence.

Mine is not a "should" statement; it is an "is" statement. I am not arguing that the organization should care about others outside the organization, only that talking about what one is doing means talking about the effects of one's acts on those outside of (as well as within) the organization and whether these effects are good or bad, right or wrong.

We live in a moral world, not because people are good, or because people always think morally about what they are doing, but because as human beings the categories of right and wrong are part of our natural moral environment. To talk about what one is doing requires someone else to listen. Not listening means silencing because it means that dialogue is impossible. To be refused participation in dialogue is to be rendered extinct.

Mine is an attempt to use general social theory to explain whistleblowing. If the reader is interested in a more thorough study of the whistleblowing literature itself, then *Evolution of whistleblowing studies* by Culiberg and Mihilic (2017) is probably the place to begin.

Talking with Oneself?

The reader might respond to all this with the argument that people can talk with themselves. "Thought" is the term Hannah Arendt (1978) gives to Socrates's inner dialogue, his conversation with himself. Writing about Socrates's refusal to inflict an injustice for fear of damaging his relationship with himself, Arendt refers to the soundless dialogue (*eme emautō*) between me and myself (Theaetetus, 189e, Sophist 263e). Unlike Hippias, who cannot bear to talk with himself, Socrates listens to the other fellow who is waiting at home for him, his internal partner. If Socrates has done something that is shameful, his internal partner will not let him rest in peace. She notes, "later times have given the fellow who awaits Socrates in his home the name of 'conscience'" (Arendt, 1978, part 1, p. 190).

It is Arendt's almost desperate hope that a thoughtful person's ability to be dissatisfied with the self with whom they are living might serve as an antidote to evil and a source of goodness. During what Arendt calls "boundary situations" and "special emergencies," the internal dialogue becomes impossible to continue unless the thoughtful one acts in the world to bring the selves back into a friendly relationship. Generally, one does this, says Arendt, by saying "no."

Natan Sharansky, a Soviet refusenik, spent nine years in prison during the 1970s and 1980s, much of it in solitary confinement. In *Fear no evil* (1998), his account of his years in prison, Sharansky writes that he would sometimes summon up the image of his wife, Avital, and have conversations with her. She became his invisible partner in resistance. In reality, she was already in Israel, working for his release, and he received occasional messages from her.

Sharansky was in some ways exceptional, in some ways not. Those who refuse on the grounds of ideological or religious conviction almost always rely on a group of supporters, even if the one who says "no" is physically isolated. Few whistleblowers share these circumstances. Few act in the name of religious or ideological conviction, especially one shared with other activists. The whistleblower is almost always alone. Among the chief surprises and tribulations suffered by whistleblowers is the turning away of former friends and colleagues. "I expected my boss to retaliate," said one whistleblower, "I didn't expect my colleagues at work to pretend I didn't exist." These colleagues were men and women with whom he had spent more time with than his family over the past few years: "Some would cross the hall when they saw me coming; others would look away." None would take his telephone calls. Even his minister refused to support him, saying he did not know the whole story.

Studies of shunning may be helpful here (Harper, 2013). Shunning is not the most aggressive form of silencing, but for many it is the most hurtful, especially when it involves whistleblowers' friends, or those they thought of as friends. We do not know the extent of our fear and subservience until we are faced with a pariah in our midst. The ability of the organization to make a pariah out of any of its members tells every member that they too can be rendered invisible. Silence need not be actual silence, though that is its more common form among former co-workers and friends. Discipline is also silencing, rendering the content of what the whistleblower says a symptom of an underlying disorder. When co-workers cooperate in silencing, we learn that the power to disappear someone includes anyone. If we are in any way self-aware, we learn the extent of our own moral cowardice, a cowardice that has a real basis in the organization's control of a worker's income, health insurance, and ability to pay the mortgage and keep their family together.

Silencing Is More Than Scapegoating

Silence is not bad; often it is good. It is in silence that we hear ourselves think and ideally talk with one's self as Socrates did. He was a friend to himself. Silence can be active, shutting out a world of noise. But while silence can be good, silencing is almost always bad. Whether by parents or a large organization, silencing is an expression of power. One of the interesting things about whistleblowers is that they render the power to silence visible. What is not quite so visible is the way in which discipline legitimates silencing. It is not hard to find, however, if one knows where to look.

The silence imposed by the large organization is experienced by the whistleblower as anger, alienation, and the experience of being lost in space. Daniel Ellsberg, the whistleblower who leaked the Pentagon Papers, said that his former friends and colleagues regarded him with neither admiration nor censure but with wonder, as though he were a space-walking astronaut who had cut his lifeline to the mother ship (personal communication). What was this mother ship? Was it the academic-military-industrial complex, the system, the organization? Call it what you will, it is not so much a precise concept as an overwhelming feeling. It is this feeling that many employees would do anything to avoid, perhaps because it recalls other absences, other voids, including those experienced as a child.

While the silencing of the whistleblower is not hard to find, more difficult is the line between permissible and impermissible speech. One would expect to find a difference in punishment between the whistle-blower who went to the boss' boss and the whistleblower who went straight to the media. One stayed in house; the other went outside. In fact, there is almost no difference. Among the whistleblowers I studied, there was no difference at all. In either case, one has identified oneself as someone whose loyalties lie elsewhere, and that is enough. Other studies have found a measurable difference; external whistle-blowers suffer more (Dworkin & Baucus, 1998). Nevertheless, the difference is less than one might expect. It serves the organization's purpose to keep the boundaries of retaliation fuzzy, as it keeps employees who might be thinking about saying something unsure of what might happen. In this regard, the most important thing to know about whistleblowers is that they serve not so much as scapegoats as living demonstrations of how readily someone can be pushed to the margin of society.

What happens to the whistleblower who is pushed to the margins of society? Many languish there. Some find another way of being. But the cost remains, and it can be measured not only in silence but also in the rationing of speech. Joe Wahlreich values silence more since he came to terms with being fired for speaking out:

You know what's different now? It's a funny thing, a little thing really, but it feels like a big one. I can't make small talk anymore. When I hear someone saying the little things people say every day, I get impatient. I want to say to them, "Look, open your eyes. People around you are living in hell, and you don't even notice." I was in hell and no one noticed. I didn't either, not for years. You can't get out of Hell until you know you're there.

For Joe, silence is a place to listen to the pain of others, as well as a way of saying that he has seen behind the veil. Or as another whistleblower put it, "I have seen the truth and the truth has made me odd" (Smith, 1997, quoting Flannery O'Connor).

And what is this truth? The truth is stated by Bauman, "all social organization consists therefore in neutralizing the disruptive and deregulating impact of moral behavior" (1989, p. 215). Silencing is one way organizations do this, and it easy to overlook its refined brutality. Listening to the stories of whistleblowers, we are reminded.

Suggestions for Future Qualitative Research on Silence

A couple of ethical issues require further discussion. One of the mysteries of whistleblowing is why whistleblowers do it in the first place. Qualitative research seems best suited to uncovering the motivation, but a word of caution is in order. Originally, I thought I wanted to know why whistleblowers did it. I suggest some possibilities in my book on the topic (Alford, 2001). However, the more I asked, the more I felt that I had become an unwitting partner in the discipline of the whistleblower. In the end, the question is not whistleblower psychology, but the ways in which organizations silence whistleblowers.

The alliance between researcher and whistleblower (or almost anyone in a vulnerable position) is always a misalliance. Whistleblowers want their stories told, while the researcher wants to know how organizations silence their members. It is not the same story, and researchers should state that they are not there to tell the whistleblower's story, but to understand how organizations silence their members. Janet Malcolm (1990) has written poignantly about this misalliance. Her subjects are different, but the issue is the same.

I cannot emphasize enough that I did not "interview" my subjects, or at least that was not my primary research method. I listened to them talk with one another: at the whistleblowers' support group and at a gathering at a retreat for stressed-out whistleblowers. Interviewing is itself at risk of becoming a mode of silencing. Interviewers have their perspectives, hypotheses, and so forth. Listening to whistleblowers talk among themselves raised issues and questions I had never considered.

At the same time, it is worth emphasizing that the whistleblower's presentation of self, as Erving Goffman (1959) called it, takes place in every social interaction. It is also a form of silencing, including self-silencing, as whistleblowers decide to present themselves in a particular way: victim, warrior, survivor, etc. It is worth listening to what is not being said and asking questions about it. The best way of listening to what is not being said (a form of self-silencing) is to listen to lots of whistleblowers (or other subjects), as different whistleblowers presented different faces to the interviewer, and each whistleblower has many faces, just as each individual does. The context in which the listening occurs makes a difference. Listening to whistleblowers speak among themselves for more than a year brought out more faces than a single interview.

Finally, the question arises about the relationship between silence and Foucault's concept of discipline. Silence is not lack of speech. Silence is the inability to frame and form one's narrative so that it is part of a relationship with the listener(s). Destructive silence occurs when others refuse to participate in any frame or form of discourse. Destructive silence has more to do with the unwillingness of others to listen than an inability to speak. Like most social activities, speech takes at least two people to participate.

References

Alford, C. F. (1999). *Think no evil: Korean values in the age of globalization.* Ithaca, NY: Cornell University Press.

Alford, C. F. (2001). *Whistleblowers: Broken lives and organizational power.* Ithaca, NY: Cornell University Press.

Alford, C. F. (2016). Whistleblower protection policy. In S. Schechter (Ed.), *Encyclopedia of American governance* (vol. 5, pp. 295–299). Detroit, MI: Macmillan Reference.

Arendt, H. (1978). *The life of the mind,* part 1. New York: Harcourt Brace.

Bal, M. (1997). *Narratology: Introduction to the theory of narrative* (2nd ed.). Toronto: University of Toronto Press.

Bauman, Z. (1989). *Modernity and the Holocaust.* Ithaca, NY: Cornell University Press.

Bion, W. R. (1998). *Experiences in groups and other papers.* London: Routledge.

Bjørkelo, B., Ryberg, W., Matthiesen, S. B., & Einarsen, S. (2008). When you talk and talk and nobody listens: A mixed method case study of whistleblowing and its consequences. *International Journal of Organisational Behaviour, 13*(2), 18–40.

Blanchot, M. (1995). *The writing of the disaster.* (A. Smock, Trans.) Lincoln: University of Nebraska Press.

Brock, D. (1993). *The real Anita Hill: The untold story.* New York: Free Press.

Clark, C. (1997). Whistleblowers. *CQ Researcher, 7,* 1057–1080.

Culiberg, C., & Mihelic, K. M. (2017). The evolution of whistleblower studies: A critical review and research agenda. *Journal of Business Ethics, 146,* 787–803.

Douglas, M. (1966). *Purity and danger: An analysis of concepts of pollution and taboo.* Harmondsworth, UK: Penguin.

Dworkin T. M., & Baucus, M. (1998). Internal vs external whistleblowers: A comparison of whistleblower processes. *Journal of Business Ethics, 17,* 1281–1298.

Foucault, M. (1979). *Discipline and punish: The birth of the prison.* (A. Sheridan, Trans.) New York: Vintage Books.

Glazer, M. P., & Glazer, P. M. (1989). *The whistleblowers.* New York: Basic Books.

Goffman, E. (1959). *The presentation of self in everyday life.* New York: Anchor.

Habermas, J. (1984). *The theory of communicative action,* 2 vols. (T. McCarthy, Trans.) Boston: Beacon Press.

Harper, J. (2013). The silence of shunning: A conversation with Kipling Williams. *Psychology Today.* Retrieved from www.psychologytoday.com/blog/beyond-bu llying/201309/the-silence-shunning-conversation-kipling-williams

Hazzard, A., Celano, M., Gould, J., Lawry, S., & Webb, C. (1995). Predicting symptomatology and self-blame among child sex abuse victims. *Child Abuse and Neglect, 19*(6), 707–714.

Hirschman, A. O. (1970). *Exit, voice, and loyalty: Responses to decline in firms, organizations, and states.* Cambridge, MA: Harvard University Press.

Kish-Gephart, J. J., Detert, J., Trevino, L., & Edmondson, A. (2009). Silenced by fear: The nature, sources, and consequences of fear at work. In B. M. Staw & A. P. Brief (Eds.), *Research in organizational behavior* (Vol. 29, pp. 163–193).

Langer, L. (1991). *Holocaust testimonies: The ruins of memory.* New Haven: Yale University Press.

Malcolm, J. (1990). *The journalist and the murderer.* New York: Vintage.

Miceli, M., & Near, J. (1992). *Blowing the whistle: The organizational and legal implications for companies and employees.* New York: Lexington Books.

Miethe, T. (1999). *Whistleblowing at work: Tough choices in exposing fraud, waste, and abuse on the job.* Boulder, CO: Westview Press.

Orwell, G. (1949). *Nineteen eighty-four.* New York: Signet.

Rothschild, J., & Miethe, T. (1996). *Keeping organizations true to their purposes: The role of whistleblowing in organizational accountability and effectiveness.* Aspen Institute.

Sharansky, N. (1998). *Fear no evil.* New York: Public Affairs.

Siler, K., Kirby, L., & Bero, L. (2015). Measuring the effectiveness of scientific gatekeeping. *Proceedings of the National Academy of Sciences* (Vol. 12, pp. 360–365). Retrieved from www.pnas.org/content/112/2/360.full

Skivenes, M., & Trygstad, S. (2010). When whistleblowing works: The Norwegian case. *Human Relations, 63*(7), 1071–1097.

Smith, R. J. (1997). "The general's conscience: Why nuclear warrior George Lee Butler changed his mind." *Washington Post Magazine,* December 7. Retrieved from www.timeshighereducation.com/news/most-cited-authors . . . /405956 .article

12 Between Sound and Silence: The Inaudible and the Unsayable in the History of the First World War

Jay Winter

We historians of the Great War must acknowledge all the things we cannot hear. The cacophony of the Great War cannot be recaptured. The sheer terror of combat and the array of weapons deployed in it raise problems for those attempting to write its auditory history. We have vast archives of images and words to enable us to write the visual, the verbal, the documentary, the epistolary, and the literary history of the war. Abundant artefacts form the basis of the history of the material culture of the conflict. But the history of sound and the audible world at war is another, more difficult, matter.

Museum curators and designers of historical exhibitions are particularly vulnerable to the need to provide what is termed "total immersion" including ambient sound to aid visitors in traversing the space of historical representation they provide. In most cases, they give the visitor the mistaken impression that they can enter the auditory landscape of war. This chapter offers reasons why sound effects distort history and why silence is a better way of representing the collective violence of war.

This field is in no sense empty. Scholars have explored musical composition and performance (Kennedy, 2014), soldiers' entertainments (Fuller, 1990), the development of jazz (Gioia, 1997), and the world of popular songs (Hanheide & Helms, 2013) and their dissemination through the global gramophone industry (Martland, 2013), and they have benefited from the collection of voice recordings of contemporaries both in the war period and long after the Armistice (Grant & Hanna, 2014). There are as well archives of interviews of the children and grandchildren of the soldiers of 1914–1918. But these efforts are merely the beginnings of a history that may never be realized. The sounds of war on both the front and the home front are very remote from us. Some are irretrievable, given the passage of four generations between wartime and our time.

The unheard is the sister of the unsaid. The French language recognizes this in the word *malentendu*, which means misunderstood, but which also means badly heard. Those who speak believe there is someone somewhere who either intends to or is able to hear them. Otherwise, why speak at all? In a book on the unsaid, silence must be given its due.

One solution is to paraphrase Wittgenstein and say "of that which one can never hear, thereof one must be silent." This chapter takes a different tack. Silence is not simply the absence of sound. It is a language of memory in its own right; when used carefully, it can provide a better, more authentic, more honest, approach to the past than can special effects meant to approximate what the past sounded like. This chapter explores the dialectic between silence and sound in the auditory history of the Great War and in its representation in contemporary museums.

It does so from the perspective of a cultural historian, whose task is to investigate past and present cultural practices. Representing war in museums and in other media is one such practice. Probing its history may yield not a theory of silence but insights into the ways in which attending to silence deepens our understanding of both a time of world war a century ago and of our own times today.

Silence in the Historial de la Grande Guerre, Péronne, Somme, France

In 1992, a new museum of the Great War, the Historial de la Grande Guerre, opened in what had been German headquarters during the Battle of the Somme in 1916. I was one of the team that designed the museum. This level of participation is highly unusual and was the result of an agreement struck with the main figure in the administration of the Department of the Somme, Max Lejeune. In 1986, he asked me to serve as the British historian in a project for which he had already secured the participation of two distinguished historians, Jean-Jacques Becker of Paris, Nanterre University, and Wolfgang Mommsen of the University of Düsseldorf. I agreed, with one proviso: that the Department of the Somme create and fund a research center of the best historians of the Great War worldwide. My aim was to make the design of the museum a reflection of then-current historical scholarship. Lejeune agreed and, with his blessing, we worked together with museographers over a period of six years to design the museum, which opened in 1992. We chose the name the Historial de la Grande Guerre as a neologism, reflecting how we intended to make the museum a commemorative site, a place for collective memory, and a historical site, a place for scholarly reflection.

The striking achievement of the Historial de la Grande Guerre is its use of the horizontal axis to organize objects and the space of representation. The vertical – the stance of masculine prowess and of hope for the future – is the conventional dimension governing the design of war museums. In contrast, the horizontal axis is the posture of mourning, the downward gaze of those registering the unalterable reality of mass death in wartime. Forcing the visitors to look down required placing objects on the floor, or indeed, a bit under floor level. This made sense with respect to a museum of the Great War, since most soldiers survived by digging holes in the ground and staying below ground level. Snipers and trench artillery made standing up suicidal. Going underground was not a choice but a necessity.

During the six years it took to design the museum, I recall no single discussion among the planners in which anyone advocated the introduction of ambient sound in the museum. It was simply taken for granted by all of us on the design team that there was a need for enhancing the visitor's experience through sound. A film for all visitors in the audio-visual hall of the museum made dramatic use of Britten's *War Requiem* and the thin voice of a British soldier of the Great War, Harry Fellowes, in its presentation of the Battle of the Somme. But that hall, cut off from the rest, was the exception. In my recollection, the sound of footsteps on the highly polished wood floors was all that we intended to puncture the silence of the museum space we constructed (Winter, 2000).

The main idea behind this approach was to depart from the representational strategy of the "Somme experience" in the Imperial War Museum, which suggested that visitors (in some way) could enter the battlefield and the trenches and savor the sounds and senses of trench warfare. Our intent was the opposite: no "immersion experience" (Stogner, 2011) for us; no support whatsoever for the notion that visitors to the museum could really return to the past, in some updated version of Ranke's epithet that it is possible (and necessary) to know the past as it really was, *wie es eigentlich gewesen war*. Such positivism had long since faded away; consequently, the Historial offered a new approach to representing war, one that made demands on visitors to pose for themselves the question, "Is it even possible to represent the Great War?"

Since the opening of the Historial de la Grande Guerre in 1992, museums at Ypres and Meaux have amplified the use of sound, with more high-tech gadgets and strategies than in the old Imperial War Museum. What is wrong with their approach? They use sound in an intrusive and *dirigiste* manner. In designing the Historial, we rejected using ambient sound and music to tell the public how and what they ought to feel about the war. I still believe this is the right way to proceed.

Figure 12.1 Objects in a *fosse*, or dugout, representing German trenches in the First World War. (Photograph by Jay Winter)

And yet we must recognize that our approach is the outlier, the exception in the world of war museums. Silence is rare in this domain.

In the Historial, we use silence to suggest that in a profound sense modern, industrialized war is beyond representation. War and combat are limit experiences; we cannot pretend that we can come along and just join the lived experience of the soldiers of the Great War when we visit the Somme in general or the Historial in particular. Instead, the Historial, in its austerity, presents silently the case that it is impossible to enter the world of war as if we were entering a neighbor's home. What we can do is find its traces, its remains, and its documents and try to put them together in the best way we can. But that is far from facile realism, the stage design of those who still believe that visitors to a museum can relive the past, *wie es eigentlich gewesen war.*

The alterity, the otherness of modern war is the problem. That is why in the *fosses* the objects soldiers had in their kits are placed in unrealistic symmetrical order, as in a Mondrian painting, and on white, entirely clean displays (Figure 12.1). Silence reinforces the aura of these *fosses* and etches in the minds of visitors their resemblance to archeological sites or graves. Thus, silence becomes the sound of horizontality, the key to our approach to the representation of war.

In effect, silence cautions the visitor against facile sentimentality or easy identification with those who went through the war. Sound shortens, frequently in a cheap and unacceptable way, the distance between the present and our violent past. With sound, the strangeness of war diminishes and ultimately disappears.

Starting from this statement that silence is better than sound in the effort to represent war, I want to relate the unheard, the ambient silence of the museum, to the unsaid. To do so, I suggest that there are two kinds of silence – the descriptive and the performative, and that understanding performative silence enables us to recapture many of the silent sounds of the war and its aftermath. I shall try to separate these silences by their domain, where they arise, why they arise, and how long they last.

The third part of this chapter examines the claim that the study of silence still leaves much of the auditory history of the war beyond us, in an ontological no man's land. If this argument is correct, then now 100 years after the Armistice, it behooves us to swallow a very large dose of humility in our claim to present any kind of complete history of the war.

Performative Silence

The silence present in the Historial is performative rather than descriptive. This distinction derives directly from J. L. Austin's (1962) theory of speech acts, *How to do things with words*. Following Austin, I urge you to consider the way we do things with silence (Winter, 2010).

Simply put, the silence men and women brought back from war had many different meanings. These survivors time and again brought us what I term "performative non-speech acts." By that term, I follow Austin, who posited that there are speech acts that are constitutive rather than descriptive; they establish the condition of which they speak rather than describe it. I go one step further than Austin and suggest that there are performative non-speech acts through which some people tell us about war beyond words (Winter, 2017).

I want to elaborate this approach to silence a bit more fully before turning to instances directly arising from the Great War. In short, there are three kinds of silence. The first is of those who cannot speak or those who believe or who truly have no one to listen to them. The second group is the taciturn: those who do not want to speak to anyone. The third is those who are selectively taciturn, those who refuse to speak about certain subjects, either privately or publicly. In all three cases, silence is neither forgetting nor oblivion. Silence is a language of memory.

In most cases, silence is a social phenomenon, a social space created by men and women who believe that they cannot and should not speak about certain things. Taboos apply here. Those who break the silence pay a price for doing so. And yet, when silence is broken, the unsayable becomes visible, and open to discussion or dispute. All silences have half-lives. They never last forever and, in many cases, are lucky if they last a lifetime.

Silence operates in four domains. They occupy different social spaces, in which there is what Plato called a space of memory, the *topos*, and a trace of memory, the *eikon*. Performative silence, like memory, is always socially constructed; it emerges out of decisions groups of people take to make some things unsayable.

The first such space is liturgical. The *topos* is the church and the *eikon* is the holy text. In all religious practices of which I am familiar, the problem of theodicy has no answer. If God is all good, then how did evil get into the world? The silence of God is a common refrain, one that gestures toward the doubts and anguish of those who want to believe despite stubborn facts about the way the world is and what war does to human beings.

Politics is the second domain we examine. Here the *topos* is the state and the *eikon* the law. Political silences exist when groups of people decide to bury the traces of their inglorious acts. These gestures toward purity are ubiquitous and almost always fail. Many entail the need to defend foundation myths against the test of history; we will hear more on this later.

Essentialist silences exist when a particular group, in our case soldiers, claims that they and only they have the right to speak about war. Only they know of what they speak, and the rest of us should simply remain silent. This romantic notion of experience, ingested viscerally, has bonded soldiers and ex-soldiers for generations. One consequence is an unavoidable tendency to misogyny among such defenders of the holy fraternity of men of arms. Here there are numerous topoi, including veterans' associations or other sites of camaraderie, and multiple *eikons*, including memoirs and memorials.

The fourth social domain of silence is familiar to us all. Family silences enable family members to go on living with one another despite dreadful and intolerable actions by one or all of them. In a sense, all families are defined by their silences, their secrets kept away from the outside world.

Silence has other domains, but the four we discuss here have left substantial traces out of which a history of the practice of silence can be written. Together, they locate silence within social networks that, in the twentieth century, reach very substantial parts of the population.

This framework is in no sense arcane. Some such non-speech acts are relatively well known. The two-minute silence on Armistice Day or Remembrance Sunday is one of them. Liturgical approaches to mourning those who die in war are full of silences, since such losses profoundly challenge our sense of meaning or order or justice, or the succession of generations.

Other silences are political in character. For instance, the Museum of Memory in Santiago de Chile is eloquent about the victims of the Pinochet regime but totally silent on the perpetrators, many of whom are still alive and unlikely to answer for their crimes. The museum performs the instability of the regime and its unwillingness to face its recent past. There is still an embargo in Spain on calling to account those guilty of war crimes committed during and after the Spanish Civil War. These cruelties are beyond words (and punishment) because people chose to put them there. Still other silences are essentialist, in that they are based on a claim that only those who have been there could or should talk about war. This turn of mind has blocked the participation of women in conversations about war for generations.

Finally, there are family silences that are kept by fathers and mothers, sisters and brothers, to enable family life to go on, by not facing terrible memories of war and what family members did in it. Repression, in these situations, almost always fails. Silence is by no means forgetting. Failing to speak or to permit conversations on war (among other subjects) postpones, rather than prevents, their arrival in what is sayable. The unsaid is a state of affairs wherein everyone knows what no one says. The unsaid can be voiced at the speed of sound. All it takes is for someone to have the courage to say what everyone already knows.

Silences of the Great War

The liturgical silences of the Great War emerged right at its outset. Here was a conflict that pitted Catholic against Catholic, Protestant against Protestant, Jew against Jew, and Muslim against Muslim all over the world. Transnational religions faced fratricide without much theological armor to defend them. Claiming God for one side or the other was both commonplace and ridiculous. Thus, churches and churchmen blended silence on theology with as much pastoral compassion as they could muster.

The need for churchmen to help the millions in mourning put them in a predicament. They could hardly "explain" the carnage as God's will and, by doing so, answer the plea of bereaved parents for some accounting of the death of their sons, brothers, husbands, fathers. In this regard, spiritualism, the belief in communication with the dead, offered more than the churches did, and millions of people all over the world bypassed the churches in their anguish over the fate of the fallen (Winter, 1995).

Some theologians recognized the dilemma by rethinking their principles. Karl Barth published his *Epistles to the Romans* in Switzerland in 1916 to break the silence of his fellow churchmen (Barth, 1968). His aim, he said, was to sound a bell that would awaken Christians to their faith at a time when church leaders mouthed shibboleths, clichés, or turned silent. Martin Buber and Franz Rosenzweig decided to translate the Bible from Hebrew to German and thereby reconfigured much Jewish thought on fundamental theological questions. But they were the exceptions. Most believers took the road to silence and stayed there.

The political silences of the war are legion. Many of them arise from the demands of those constructing foundation myths about their national histories. It is hardly surprising that the creation of the Turkish state was a tale told without reference to the crimes committed in the course of its birth. It mattered not that the Ottoman Empire, led by the Young Turks, carried out the Armenian genocide. The project of national liberation was then, and is still now, sacred and, therefore, incompatible with the truth that genocide and ethnic cleansing were essential elements in the story (Winter, 2017). The parallels with the North American genocide committed on Native Americans and the British genocide committed on the Aboriginal population of Australia are evident and have taken centuries to break through the cover of silence.

In the case of Australia, we should attend to another political silence. The expeditionary force sent from down under to Gallipoli and the Western front was called the "Anzacs," Australian and New Zealand Army Corps. The night and day of the landing at Gallipoli, April 24–25 are sacred days in the Australian calendar. In all the services and parades I have attended, no one seems to hear the silence embedded within the word "Anzac"; that is, no one notices that the New Zealanders have disappeared. Anzacs are Australians, or rather Australians in the making, emerging as a nation through their heroism and the shedding of blood. The same is true, though less striking, in New Zealand, reinforcing the view that national myths cannot be plural. There is room for only one nation on the head of the pin of foundation myths.

Political silences abound in Eastern Europe too. Reborn nations like that of the Poles are silent on the participation of their men in the armies of the Russian, German, and Austro-Hungarian armies, but quite vocal on the men who fought in the civil war from 1918 to 1921, out of which emerged the Second Polish Republic. The viciousness of the civil war in Ukraine, Byellorussia, and the Baltic states after the First World War is also hidden from publics told much about their enslavement under the Soviet Union. And the very existence of the bloody Finnish civil war in

1918–1919, where most of those who died were killed after hostilities were over, has been kept underground until the recent past. Even now, the story remains a hidden one (Lehto-Hoogendorn, 2000).

Soldiers' gatherings were the sites of mutual recognition, the rekindling of old friendships, and the feeling that only "we" know what war is. With the dying off of the front generation, this fraternity has all but disappeared. In contrast, the veil on family histories in wartime is being lifted progressively due to the successful public solicitation of family archives during the centenary of the outbreak of the Great War. What they will show is anybody's guess, but at least they will go beyond the conventional accounts of loyal peasants and workers to give us a glimpse of the world of hardship and worry families in wartime endured.

Beyond Silence?

If I am right in my claim that silence is performative, then the four categories I have outlined – the liturgical, the political, the essentialist, and the familial – are the domains in which the unsaid is performed. But it is important to move to the second claim I make, which is that the unheard is cognate with the unsaid. To be unable to hear a voice, or to choose not to hear a voice, is to reduce and at times to destroy its social character. Voices need audiences, which in turn need to have the capacity and the opportunity to listen and to witnesses. Without these capacities and opportunities, the unheard and the unsaid are one.

In conclusion, I want to examine the claim that while performative silence tells us much about war, we are still severely limited in what we, 100 years after the Armistice, can say about the Great War.

The instances I cite are among those that require us to recognize major lacunae in our representations of war, not because we have no evidence but because the scale of warfare – reflected in the very name the Great War, meaning not a very big war, but one that went beyond all previous military conflicts – was so vast and revolutionary as to make representation either very difficult or impossible. There are many ways to illustrate the limits of our auditory archive of the war. Consider first the record offered by a seismograph (Figure 12.2). It shows the moment when the Armistice took effect at 11 a.m. on November 11, 1918. We see to the left a visual reproduction of artillery shelling continuing until the very last moment; then comes the silence of the guns. What did it sound like to move into silence? Those alive at the time have not left us evidence to answer this question; hence, we can only wonder as to the nature, fifty months after the outbreak of the war, of a long and unbroken silence.

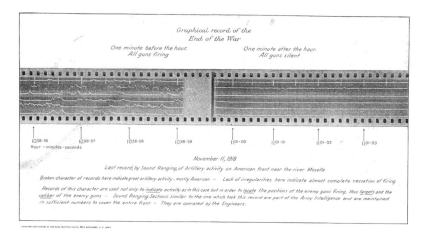

Figure 12.2 The end of the war: A seismograph of the cessation of artillery fire on November 11, 1918.

All histories refer to other canonical moments in the history of the war, but they have left no audible trace. We have propaganda images of what a revolution was supposed to look like, but not the sound of power changing hands. When Lenin and Trotsky awoke in the Smolny Institute, the day after their seizure of power, surprised at still being alive, what did the city sound like? Here again, we face a paucity of contemporary sources or survivors.

One of the most deleterious consequences of the Great War was the way it obliterated the distinction between civilian and military targets. This degeneration of warfare was most explicit in the decision of the triumvirate who ran the war in Constantinople to expel the entire Armenian population of Anatolia from their homes and into the Mesopotamian desert. What is the sound of a whole village, a whole world, marching to its death? We have images of the columns of women and children on the move, but no direct knowledge of what it sounded like.

Attacking civilians – including neutrals – in ocean-going vessels was an integral part of the German war effort in the Great War. What did a massive passenger liner sound like when it went down? In 1915, when the torpedoes struck the *Lusitania*'s hull, what did the passengers and the crew hear? Survivors' recollections tell us almost nothing about this. Here is an iconic moment to which everyone refers but for which there is no trace of evidence at all.

Other revolutionary developments in the war were equally difficult to render in auditory form. One was the use of poison gas in trench warfare by the German army in Ypres in April 1915. This practice was taken up by all combatants thereafter. By 1918, one out of every four shells was a gas shell. We have accounts of the sizzle of gas delivered by shells, but no idea whatsoever of the cacophony of fumbling attempts to fit on gas masks, or the cries of those who failed to do so.

Gas terrified but it did not kill large numbers of men. Much more lethal than gas warfare were the months' long offensives of 1916, which produced for the first time in history, casualty rates in excess of 1 million men. Here is a revolutionary event in the history of war. But what did the opening of the Battle of Verdun sound like? Or the seven-days' bombardment on the Somme in late June 1916, or the opening of the Michael offensive in March 1918? Metaphors fail, as will any attempt to recreate the sound in an "immersion experience" museum.

Explosives were used not only on land and in the air but also under the ground. Huge mines were dug and deployed on the Western front. What did the "tap-tap-tap" of tunnelers working under La Boisselle on the Somme or in other sectors sound like to the German soldiers above them? We can see official footage of the destruction wrought by these mines, but we have no idea of the roar of death and destruction accompanying them.

Other facets of the war are beyond representation, in part because of the paucity of evidence that has survived. The Great War was a horse-drawn war; more than 10 million horses were mobilized between 1914 and 1918. And yet we have no idea as to what a wounded horse sounded like to the men, mostly farmers, a few yards away in the trenches, compelled to listen to its cries. Can we ever know? Can we ever represent this kind of suffering in either prose or in a museum space?

We have already referred to the difficulty of hearing what it was like when the Armistice stopped the guns on November 11, 1918. But the real end of the war on the Western front came six months later. The war was brought to a formal end in diplomatic proceedings starting in Versailles and reaching its high point during the signing ceremony of June 28, 1919. What sound accompanied the entry of the German delegation to the Hall of Mirrors, faced first by the *Gueules cassées*, disfigured veterans put there by French Premier Georges Clemenceau to shock them, and then by the victorious delegations? Were there gasps of shock? Cries for revenge? Sighs of relief? No one knows.

In all these instances, fundamental features of the Great War are beyond our capacity to represent them in any realistic or complete way.

That is why those who believe in the immersion experience of museum design are most deluded. They invent sounds when silence is all we have and persuade visitors to take the ersatz for the real.

In sum, it makes sense at this point in the centenary commemoration of the 1914–1918 conflict to reflect on the inaudible as the unknowable. Only with a full sense of the limitations both of our auditory archives and of what can be represented honestly can we begin to offer guidance on the experience of war to readers, students, or visitors to historical museums. This is a lesson in humility that all scholars exploring qualitative research should ponder.

For all these reasons, we need to leave unsaid that which is false or invented or commercially effective and stage-managed in our museums and other public representations of war. Fake noise is fake history. Only when we realize this simple truth can we serve the very large population of people who seek a deeper understanding of a war whose destructive force shaped the world in which we live.

References

Austin, J. L. (1962). *How to do things with words: The William James Lectures delivered at Harvard University in 1955.* London: Oxford University Press.

Barth, K. (Ed.). (1968). *Epistle to the Romans.* Oxford: Oxford University Press.

Fuller, J. C. (1990). *Popular entertainment and troop morale in the British and Dominion armies.* Oxford: Berg Books.

Gioia, T. (1997). *The history of jazz.* New York: Oxford University Press.

Grant, P., & Hanna, E. (2014). Music and remembrance: Britain and the First World War. In B. Ziino (Ed.), *Remembering the Great War* (pp. 110–126). London: Routledge.

Hanheide, S., & Helms, D. (Eds.). (2013). Musik bezieht Stellung. In *Funktionalisierungen der musik im Ersten Weltkrieg.* Osnabruck: Universitätsverlag Osnabruck.

Kennedy, K. (2014). A music of grief: Classical music and the First World War. *International Affairs, 90*(2), 379–395.

Lehto-Hoogendorn, M. (2000). The persistence of a painful past: The Finnish Civil War of 1918. *The Masaryk Journal, 3*(1), 83–94.

Martland, P. (2013). *Recording history: The British record industry 1881–1931.* Landham, MD: Scarecrow.

Stogner, M. B. (2011). The immersive cultural museum experience – creating context and story with new media technology. *The International Journal of the Inclusive Museum iii, 3*(3), 117–130.

Winter, J. M. (1995). *Sites of memory, sites of mourning: The Great War in European cultural history* (chap. 3). Cambridge: Cambridge University Press.

Winter, J. M. (2000). Public history and the 'Historial' project 1986–1998. In S. Blowen, M. Demossier, & J. Picard (Eds.), *Recollections of France:*

Memories, identities and heritage in contemporary France (pp. 52–67). Oxford: Berghahn Books.

Winter, J. M. (2010). Thinking about silence. In E. Ben Zeev, R. Ginio, & J. M. Winter (Eds.), *Shadows of war: A social history of silence in the twentieth century* (pp. 1–30). Cambridge: Cambridge University Press.

Winter, J. M. (2017). *War beyond words: Languages of remembrance from the Great War to the present* (esp. chap. 7). Cambridge: Cambridge University Press.

13   Affect and the Unsaid: Silences, Impasses, and Testimonies to Trauma

Michael Richardson and Kyla Allison

Trauma and the unsaid are intimately entangled. Trauma is precisely that which refuses to be rendered into language and in doing so resists finding a place in our narrative of self. Splinters of experiential time, the remnants of violence and abuse, or the sheer force of accident itself slip into the skin and are carried in the body, asserting their presence with ferocity when the body moves just so, when the world arrives at just this angle, or when the body of another is encountered in just this way. In Cathy Caruth's famous formulation, "trauma is not locatable in the simple violent or original event in an individual's past, but rather in the way that its very unassimilated nature – the way it was precisely not known in the first instance – returns to haunt the survivor later on." It is "the story of a wound that cries out, that addresses us in the attempt to tell us of a reality or truth that is not otherwise available" (1996, p. 4). In this well-worn definition, a foundational one within trauma studies in the humanities, trauma resides in paradox, defined by the way it is both known and not known – and by what can and cannot be said. Much of what surrounds trauma is also bound up with silence: diffuse yet intractable impasses to expression and action, the limits of testimony in accounting for experience, and cultures of not speaking and so not knowing and not acting.

And yet the body is so much more than voice or its silence. The body's capacity to express and to make manifest its defining experiences continually exceeds language and its limitations. The body is affected and affecting, moved and moving, even when it cannot or will not speak in words (Manning, 2013; Spinoza, 1677). Rather than ask what words are absent in the event of the unsaid, we might instead explore what the body expresses and what it experiences, how rupture and disjuncture emerge in gesture or sensation, how power that silences and the power of silence contend with each other in complex and perhaps impossible to untangle ways. In this chapter, we sketch an affective approach to understanding, researching, and writing the unsaid. Our intention is not so much a comprehensive account or singular methodology, but rather an unfolding

236

of potentials for how silence might speak without words. We proceed in three parts. In the first section, "Affect Theory and the Unsaid," we offer a necessarily brief account of affect studies in the humanities and explain their value in the qualitative study of silence, particularly in the context of trauma. Then, our collective voice becomes singular as we each set out affective methodologies that move along resonant yet divergent paths. Each of us grapples differently with the tension between writing as a distinctly linguistic mode of expression and the unsaid as precisely that which is not speech. Neither seeks to escape or elide this paradox, but rather to deploy voice, register, and style in ways that attend to the tensions inherent to communicating the unsaid in writing. In "Affective Witnessing and the Unsaid of Torture," Richardson considers how affect theory intervenes in traditional accounts of trauma in the humanities, outlining a theory of affective witnessing to the silences of political violence. Moving from the third person to the intimacy of the first, in "Silence and the Affects of the Impasse," Allison sets out a visceral account of relations between silence and the body in the unsaid of sexual abuse, exploring the problem of writing in the face of blockages to speaking. We rejoin our voices in the final section to consider in more general terms what affective methodologies might bring to qualitative research into the unsaid.

Affect Theory and the Unsaid

In the humanities, affect theory refers to a heterogeneous, interdisciplinary body of thought that provides critical vocabularies, concepts, and insights into embodied experience. Unlike phenomenological, psychoanalytic, or psychological approaches to understanding bodily experience, affect theory emphasizes the relations between bodies and between bodies and worlds. To be affected, in the most straightforward sense, is to be moved in response to someone or something (Shouse, 2005). In general terms, affect theory seeks not only to account for the complex, changeable, visceral, and autonomous ways in which bodies are moved but also how atmospheres are formed, meanings are coalesced, moods are shifted, and changes of state are registered. In describing the field in their oft-cited introduction to *The affect theory reader*, Melissa Gregg and Greg Seigworth (2010, p. 5) identify at least eight distinct currents of contemporary affect theory but note that the two most influential are "Silvan Tomkins's psychobiology of differential affects and Gilles Deleuze's Spinozist ethology of bodily capacities." While the former focuses on discrete and precognitive bodily responses to stimuli, the latter emphasizes the forces and capacities of bodies. Both strands have value for thinking, researching, and writing the unsaid because each concerns the body, expression, and capacity for action independent of language, but without excluding language's effects, significance, or capacity for making meaning.

For Silvan Tomkins, an American developmental psychologist, affects are precognitive bodily responses that take specific forms; they are "the primary motivational system in human beings [and] the primitive gods within the individual" (1995, p. 57). Affects arrive in the body through encounters – exposed as false before another, the face blushes before one feels shame – and so while they are discrete biological phenomena in Tomkins's (1963) work, they are also constitutively relational. Crucially, this expressive-responsive dynamic occurs before cognitive recognition. While hearing or seeing certain words might induce an affective response and affect might be present in speech, affective experience is itself constitutively distinct from language. For Tomkins, as we develop from infancy into adulthood, our bodies develop "scripts" for managing the unbidden arrival of the affective, for turning unruly affect into containable, personal, and recognizable emotions that can be accounted for in words, whether to oneself or another. Tomkins's approach to affect thus describes experience outside or alongside language but also encompasses the transition from the unsaid to the sayable. Drawing on this understanding of bodily specific, relational, and yet pre-linguistic experience, feminist scholars have used his work as the conceptual foundation for the analysis of literary texts (Tomkins, 1995), interpersonal dynamics (Brennan, 2004), media contagion (Gibbs, 2001), and other phenomena in which silence can play a significant role.

Within the strand of affect theory descended from Spinoza and then Deleuze, relationality and bodily capacity are foregrounded over biological response. Writing in the seventeenth century, Spinoza sought to escape Cartesian dualism by rearticulating beingness as unfolding through the body's capacity to affect or be affected by the world. In contemporary affect theory, this notion has been taken up most influentially by Brian Massumi. For Massumi (1995, p. 88), affect is "unqualified" intensity, irreducible to the discrete, biological phenomena of Tomkins. Affect in this reading is the autonomous force of relation between bodies in encounter with each other and the world. As such, affect-as-intensity offers a means of conceptualizing the macro and micro forces at work in movements and modulations of bodies: it provides a mode of understanding what happens between one person and another, for instance, when words fail, fall short, or cannot be uttered. Because this conception of affect situates it *between bodies* rather than *within or on the surface of any given body*, it accounts for flows and forces of relation that occur via technological mediation and in fluid, mutable, and diffuse forms. Videos that "go viral" on social media, for example, might do so without what drives that virality ever really entering into language: there is simply a charge, a burst of intensity that shifts one's state in such a way that one smiles or reels in shock (Munster, 2013). From a methodological standpoint, affect-as-intensity provides a language for the absence of language, for those moments when *something else* is going on with or without language: what we might call the force of the unsaid.

Affect theory thus provides an alternative methodological standpoint for conceptualizing and researching the silent and unsaid precisely because its point of emphasis is not language but the body – and not the body alone, but the body "webbed in its relations" (Gregg & Seigworth, 2010, p. 3). As the chapters collected in this volume make clear, the unsaid takes many forms and arises in varied, finely textured circumstances. Things go unsaid in the everyday, in professional contexts, in situations of oppression and hope and ambivalence. What goes unsaid is often carried in the body, but also in the body's movement through its environments, alongside and in response to other bodies. Within the humanities, the turn to affect has facilitated research into experiences, events, and modes of representation in which speech is only one factor among many or even absent entirely. This is precisely why affect theory has a particular resonance when applied to trauma. Its resistance to language, both in the event of its occurrence and its belated return, calls for methodological frameworks that attend to the spectrum of experience and its manifestations. For traumatized bodies or bodies that encounter the traumatic in more mediated, diffuse, and fluid ways, the unsaid can be both radically affecting and deeply affective. Traumatic affect emphasizes the affectivity of trauma itself and the capacity to encounter the traumatic in ways that are affecting without being traumatizing (Atkinson & Richardson, 2013).

Since affect describes bodily intensities and changes in state, for the crowding of potentials that both open and foreclose what the body might do, it offers generative means of thinking and researching bodies that fall or are rendered silent. Yet affect is not oppositional to language – far from it. As Massumi (2015, p. 213) points out, "it primes and stokes language's singular ability to exceed the given (its power to fabulate)." Poet and academic Denise Riley (2005, p. 1) makes a similar point far more viscerally, writing of the "forcible affect of language which courses like blood through its speakers." So too the work of Anna Gibbs (2003), Meera Atkinson (2017), one of the present authors (Richardson, 2013, 2016), and other scholar-practitioners, all of which makes clear that the affective dynamics of what cannot, should not, or might not be said can resonate in powerful ways with what *does* enter language. Indeed, it is the capacity of affect to gesture beyond but with, through, and alongside words that makes recognizing its presence so crucial to understanding the unsaid.

How all this plays out in practice is no simple matter. As Britta Timm Knudsen and Carsten Stage (2015, p. 2) ask, "How do you identify affective processes and discuss their social consequences through qualitative research strategies if affect is bodily, fleeting, and immaterial and always in between entities or nodes?" Rather than assert a prescriptive set of techniques, Knudsen and Stage suggest the need for meeting challenges: developing starting points, collecting or producing embodied data, and tracing affects empirically. In the two sections that follow, we seek to enact writing practices that respond in different ways to these three challenges in the context of the unsaid. That this should necessarily be undertaken *in writing* complicates matters because writing, or at least these writings, are not silent. Yet, for us, writing is at the heart of method. With Anna Gibbs (2015, p. 224), we recognize that writing

cannot be a methodological "tool" in any simple sense. It is, rather, a process, implicitly dialogical, in conversation with the world, with other writing, and, reflexively, with itself. It is this very means of procedure – a turning and returning – that characterizes it as an affective methodology.

This chapter, then, cannot offer a toolkit, nor can it prove out the methodological value of affect in researching the unsaid. What it can do is gesture toward the potential of an affective approach to silence, a gesture enacted as much (or more!) in the practice and performance of writing as in the elucidation of theory or precision of critique. Each in our different ways, from our positions as bystander and survivor, can seek to write generatively and productively, attendant to shifts in bodily state, to macro and micro changes in relations between one body and another, or between a body and an event, or body and media. What follows is not the last word but might be taken as two starting points chosen from among countless possibilities, two movements to embody the data of experience and to trace in writing the effects of silence, the unsaid, and the traumatic.

Affective Witnessing and the Unsaid of Torture (Richardson)

Torture and language are bound up with each other in complex, seemingly intractable ways. In her seminal work on the subject, *The body in pain*, Elaine Scarry (1985, p. 4) writes that torture's "pain does not simply resist language but actively destroys it." In the act of torture, pain overwhelms the capacity to speak, even as torture demands that words be uttered. Thus, the victim who wishes to confess or reveal cannot do so, and the torture must continue. This is torture's paradox: the demand that the body speak from within pain that renders speech impossible. For the torturer, this injurious combination of the exhortation and eradication of speech is precisely the point: it is what instantiates their power and that of the state on whose behalf they torture. As Scarry (p. 29) famously puts it, torture's pain is "world-destroying" for its victims, because the impossibility of speaking – even silently to one's self – destroys the capacity to bring the world into being through language. For Scarry, this quality is inherent to all acts of torture but is also necessarily reflected in literary works that seek to grapple with this particular form of violence and thus with its paradoxical, destructive relationship to language. In short, torture violently exposes the limits of signification, with consequences for how we understand the act itself and representations of it. How, in the face of pain that erases language, can language account for such pain? How can the experience of the subject be understood when both world and speech are destroyed? The challenge of answering is compounded by the enduring silencing that can occur in the return of the event as trauma, which resists or rejects representation in its belated arrival, a rupturing of experience caught out of time (Caruth, 1996; Herman, 1992; Ojeda, 2008). Torture thus places the relationship between language and experience under remarkable pressure. To bear witness to torture is to confront the limitations of language in particular and representation in general to do justice to the experience, both in its occurrence and in its rippling aftermath.

Affect theory offers an alternative line of inquiry into this site of aporia and paradox in the relation of language to experience. Rather than ask what disappears or becomes unrepresentable in the aporia between the traumatic event and language, we might instead analyze what the traumatic does to the relation between language and event, between representation and the unrepresentable. What, in other words, is the bodily force of the falling short of signification? How are events *affectively witnessed*? Deploying an affective approach to torture and its traumas has consequences for understanding the event in its occurrence and in works of literature, film, and art that address torture. Doing so does not mean abandoning or dismissing the textual, psychoanalytic, and sociocultural approaches adopted by Scarry, Caruth, or other scholars of torture, trauma, and violence. Rather, an affective methodology of addressing torture seeks to evoke what sits alongside such accounts and to attend to the intensities of experience and relationality precisely in the bodily, worldly, and communicative ways in which they fall into aporia, paradox, and absence. As Massumi (2011) has argued, relations of non-relation can possess a forceful intensity. Put differently, there is something intensely moving in the ungraspable itself. This intensity is not concerned with language as such, but with the body that carries the incapacity to speak and the affects of that incapacity, how they shape and reshape the world through which the body moves, and the other bodies that it encounters. Between speech and silence, affect can account for bodily experiences without fixing it within the domain of the representational or signifying.

Affective intensities bind the tortured and the torturer, generating an enduring relationality that leaves each changed in different yet inextricably entangled ways. Consider the tortures committed by the United States after 9/11. As in so much torture, agents of the state exploited not only the language constitutive of being in the world but also affectivity itself. Waterboarding is not only about reducing the body to bare, unspeaking life but also about collapsing experience into the intense, fearful horror of death's arrival. Detainees stripped naked, paraded before others, or forced into human pyramids are not only shamed before others but also feel shame in "witnessing the abuse of others, and knowing how utterly dishonored they felt," to quote ex-Guantanamo detainee Moazzam Begg (2008, p. 112). In these and countless other instances, affects resonate, modulate, and amplify between bodies, forming intensities between tortured and torturer that can implicate one body in that of the other (Richardson, 2016). The task of affective analysis is to find traces of those relations in the stories, images, and imaginings of survivors, perpetrators, and bystanders and to compose modes of understanding their dynamics. To begin to account for the tortures of the war on terror in terms of affect might thus entail the examination of interrogator memoirs, legal memoranda, human rights testimonies, and detainee poetry – or it might involve interviews and other such empirical study. The precise objects are not predetermined: affective research methodologies are emergent from the sites in which research is located.

Applied to literary, cinematic, and other forms of cultural witnessing of torture, an affective methodology attends to the minor and the gestural; to the falling short of language and the movement of bodies; to intensities that resist, refute, or refuse the play of meaning as such. In the context of literature, this means being alive to those moments of intensity within the text, when the writing calls forth something that it cannot contain – or when the reading body has no choice but to respond. In her influential book with Dori Laub, Shoshana Felman (Felman & Laub, 1992, p. 5) asks how literature might "bridge, speak over, the collapse of bridges, and yet narrate at the same time the process and event of the collapse." To approach the unsaid in its most injurious, enduring, and resistant forms is to confront directly this problem of finding language for that for which language falls short. In seeing torture on screen or reading it on a page, affect theory enables the unsaid to retain its silence, since silence can be an essential mode of resistance to torture, but at the same time to express itself through bodily intensity, caught in time and webbed in a set of complex, uncertain, and even contradictory modes of relation.

Absences work in just this way in *Negative publicity: Artefacts of extraordinary rendition* (2015), an art-book collaboration between photographer Edmund Clark and human rights researcher Crofton Black, which uses the resonance among documentary evidence, short essays, and photographs of emptied sites and spaces to testify to torture and rendition. While the written reportage, documentary records, and photographs of US "black sites" across the globe can be productively read in multiple ways, an affective methodology of the unsaid attends both to the absence of bodies and to the resonant, gestural, and fleeting affectivity of negative spaces. As I have shown in more detail elsewhere (Richardson, 2017), the journalistic facticity of the writing, the unsettling mundanity of the photographs, and the bureaucratic documents that evidence fragments of the carceral network built after 9/11 all work together to arrange and structure traumatic affect, the disappearance of bodies, and the absence of accountability. Divided into chapters that each center on a different site within the carceral network of US torture and rendition, the book assembles, for example, photographs of the offices of an aviation company in North Carolina, the swimming pool of the hotel in which a rendition crew stayed in Mallorca, and the Milan street from which a Muslim man was kidnapped, surveillance camera maps, excerpts from arrest warrants, and testimony from a torture survivor. The absence of bodies in the images speaks to the silence to which the book is addressed: the absence of witnesses to events of kidnapping and torture.

What is left of the events? Who can still speak to their meaning? What words might be erased, lost, or simply unavailable? In *Negative publicity*, it is the accumulation of intensities within and between the images that gives the inability to provide definitive answer an affective forcefulness. Here, the disappearance of bodies, their rendering into torture, is witnessed through affective traces that are marshalled by the photographs themselves (unadorned, naturalistic, attentive to shades of light and dark) and their resonance with bare documentary evidence, essayistic commentary, and the occasional personal testimony. More than simply referencing one another, each element of the work – the images and texts, but also their aesthetics and contents – vibrate conjunctively, "a concatenation in which affect resonates with like affect, so as to link otherwise unrelated scenes without producing articulable meaning" (Gibbs, 2013, p. 133). Assembled together, these elements constitute affective arrangements, "heterogeneous ensembles of diverse materials forming a local layout that operates as a dynamic formation, comprising persons, things, artefacts, spaces, discourses, behaviors and expressions in a characteristic mode of composition and dynamic relatedness" (Slaby, Mühlhoff, & Wüschner, 2017, p. 2). This dynamic assemblage is not confined either to the content or the formal aesthetic of the text but also concerns its materiality and, crucially, the encounter of the reader with it. While *Negative publicity* bears witness to torture and rendition in the war on terror, it does so *to* the reader – and the forcefulness of that communicative dynamic is a necessary dimension to the methodology of affective witnessing that I have proposed here. For some, this inclusion of the reader and the experiencing of reading within the frame of analysis raises red flags, but as an aesthetic methodology affective witnessing cannot avoid such entanglements. Just as in phenomenological, reader response, and poststructuralist techniques of analysis, affective methodologies can only go so far in extricating the affected reader from the milieu of the text. If works such as *Negative publicity* are indeed forms of bearing witness, what affect makes possible is critical recognition and evocation of the resonance of absence, the forcefulness of what goes unsaid, falls silent, or simply resides outside language.

Torture is a limit case for bodily violence and its relationship to expression, as the brief excursion into Scarry's work at the top of this section attested. Like rape, sexual assault, and other violent acts, torture produces specific sequelae and cannot simply be conflated with all other traumatic experience. Yet what torture shares with other forms of trauma is the intense duress it places on the intersection of language, body, and experience. Affect provides a conceptual vocabulary for the circulation of trauma and absence in much more fluid, nuanced, and ambivalent contexts. As an embodied research methodology, affective witnessing responds to the problem of the aporia or gap in knowing that marks the limit of the relation between language and the world it describes. It insists on the bodily intensity of the unsaid and unsayable as an expression of experience and offers a critical framework for thinking about the capacity of the epistemological gap between language and experience to act upon bodies, worlds, texts, and events in meaningful ways.

Silence and the Affects of the Impasse (Allison)

From the multitude of allegations of sexual abuse leveled at Harvey Weinstein over 2017, it is possible to see that the traumatic unsaid takes on new and particular forms when it moves in, on, and between new and different bodies. In the bodies of feminist theory and women's lived experience, it can sit differently; but regardless of how it sits, it is a needling pain, one that differs in intensity dependent on how we move. Through making visible, political, and theoretical the otherwise unsaid experiences of women's oppression, feminism has begun the work of excision to remove this pain. One of the places where the unsaid intrudes upon our bodies to produce particularly sharp pain-spasms is in those moments after experiencing sexual abuse, when confiding, disclosing, and accusing are meant to be acts of healing, but which so easily become injurious to the already vulnerable. By the end of 2017, at least fifty women are known to have accused Weinstein of various forms of sexual misconduct (Davies & Khomami, 2017). This seemingly sudden out-pouring has raised a lot of questions: Why didn't those involved accuse him earlier, and why don't women speak out about sexual abuse more frequently in general? How are we to understand this silence? As a product of material structures of power? As the ruptured silence of trauma? Or simply as fear itself? Whatever factors we might point to, the presence of a certain affectivity is undeniable. An affectivity that entails a way of relating to the world that shapes the way we articulate our experiences. This affectivity is that of a blockage, an impasse. It is a bodily blockage to speaking. It is the repeated folding of injury in on itself, multiple times. The impasse faced by many of the Weinstein accusers, and indeed many victims of sexual abuse, is one wherein the presence of the potential for future injury at the hands of a patriarchal legal system, those they confide in, or the person they are accusing (among others) is felt before it is actually experienced. It is an encountering of the affectivity of hurt before it is a lived reality. The relational potential – the "what if?" – creates an impasse wherein the experience of future trauma is ever pre-sent, and ever silencing. The methodology enacted here seeks to address this problem of the unsaid in women's experience and to provide a vocabulary for the unspeakable that enables and encourages speaking out. Women carry the unsaid in a particular way, and as such it has to be unraveled and theorized in a way that is particular to them.

What is proposed here will not be a complete or holistic solution to accounting for the unsaid as it relates to feminist theory, or to sexual abuse. Rather, this methodological approach focuses on three trajec-tories: making the personal theoretical, reparative reading, and reparative writing. Each trajectory is part of a process designed to create a framework for thinking through and writing about the unsaid: taking on the unsaid as a feminist problem with the understanding that it is particularly pertinent to the experience of sexual abuse. This passage purposely moves from third-party reflection on Weinstein to a personal methodology-in-action. This approach is driven by language or, more precisely, the problem of language and what escapes it. It is inextricable from a practice of writing that tries to capture the unsaid, situated in a world in which women have consistently been unable to speak out about their sexual abuse at the hands of men like Weinstein. It is the practice of a woman theorizing how to write the unsaid as an act of speaking out itself, as I occupy the position of both author and survivor. In doing so, I break with the (masculine) traditions within academia, I ignore the notion that my emotional attachment to the unsaid is an impediment to this work, and I shun the logic that tries to keep survivors of sexual abuse from naming themselves as such. This practice of writing acknowledges that I have a particular and important relationship to the unsaid as a survivor of sexual abuse, and that the way that I will theorize it is particular and important because of this. This writing is doing the affective work of capturing the unsaid in a specific way. This writing is speaking out.

Because the nature and form of this writing have arisen due to the nature and form of women's experiences of the unsaid, it can best be understood as a methodological bricolage. The foundational layer of this bricolage is Eve Kosofsky Sedgwick's (2003) notion of "reparative reading." Following Sedgwick, I propose a move against the grain of "paranoid reading," or reading that suspects the text of having hidden meanings that only the critic can uncover, toward a process of reading texts and experiences more organically. The speaking out of the Weinstein accusers, for example, should not be approached with the suspicion that we may already know where research on it will "lead" us. The process of researching should consider texts and case studies somewhat congruently with the process of healing – an unforeseen weaving together of fresh skin cells that may leave a scar in a variety of shapes and sizes, or perhaps no scar at all. It is constantly changing, and changeable. Healed skin can vary widely in appearance and texture, depending on the variables within the healing process itself: rough and raised, faint and smooth. When skin thatches itself back into repair, the pattern changes. We cannot assume what a scar will look like after years of fading and aging by simply looking at the initial injury. To abandon my bodily imagery for a moment: we cannot assume what we may find out about sexual abuse from the experiences of the Weinstein accusers before researching has begun. We do not know what kind of mark, if any, the healing process may yet leave.

Louisette Geiss explains what Weinstein did to her during an interview with the *Washington Post* with relative calmness. Her words have an understandable air of rehearsal about them. Understandable, as by using limited expression she may escape the labels and misogynistic language that surrounds "emotional women." Only once during the entire interview do her words appear to flounder, when she states that she was thankful "to get out, as you know, un-, un- . . . Well, I wasn't hurt. He didn't get to hurt me anymore. Physically. Obviously, emotionally, he hurt me quite a bit" (Kindy & O'Conner, 2017). In this moment, she fidgets more. She appears more uncomfortable. Of all the things she speaks about regarding Weinstein during this interview, she appears to struggle the most with describing the *potential* hurt that could have been hers. She seems unable to find the language to describe the "un" of her experience. The unspeakable clings to this moment. Many of the Weinstein accusers claim that they felt like they could not speak about what he had done to them for various reasons (Lee, 2017; Moloshok, 2017; Weaver, Ellis-Petersen, & Khomami, 2017). Geiss herself has previously been quoted saying, "I never thought I would have the chance to stand up against Harvey Weinstein" (Patten, 2017). "Standing up" appears as speaking out. The inability to speak out makes standing up impossible. The unspeakable and unsayable manifest as an oppressive structure that hinders the ability of women to achieve equal treatment either socially or legally. Working with affective and affected methodologies is working to bring the "un" of women's experience into language. It teases out the personal affectivity that the "un" refers to. It is creating a vocabulary that includes the "un" and makes loud those personal and silent experiences.

The personal and intimate places my writing sometimes explores throughout proposing this methodological framework takes its cues from Helene Cixous's (1976) notion of *l'ecriture feminine*, with the intention of decentering masculine forms of writing. It is intentionally disruptive of academic writerly norms, favoring the playful language that affect theory seemingly lends itself to. "Lends itself to" in the sense that intensities of experience are at once attached to and simultaneously disconnected from the body, allowing my writing to dance around and between these foundations. This approach to affect is messy, as it does not devote itself to one particular thread of affect theory. I prefer to stitch together different strands of thinking around affect throughout this work, creating a patchwork of ideas and concepts. This approach draws on the work of my co-author Richardson, as he suggests that this non-purist movement between thinkings on affect allows for a "focus on the productive potential of affect," noting that this is best thought of as the practice of creating "new constellations of concepts that do something for our understanding of, working with, or relation to, the world" (Richardson, 2016, p. 37). The methodology proposed here intends something similar, although perhaps these creations of mine are better thought of in tangible terms – a rough patchwork quilt, a collage of magazine clippings, and lumpy glue;

something with texture, recognizable by touch – something that stays closer to the skin.

Indeed, I am writing close "to the skin," as suggested by Sara Ahmed in her book *Living a feminist life* (2017, p. 10). I take seriously her suggestion that "the personal is theoretical" (p. 10), and this obfuscation of the two is shown not only in that I suggest we draw on personal experience as a type of text but also in the way my words stick to the skin. To my skin. I write against the traditional notion of "objectivity" often reinforced in academia by inserting myself into these words. Again, here I am entangling myself within reparative reading, as I am not an outsider to these texts or to this theory – I am enmeshed within them. "We might then have to drag theory back, to bring theory back to life," writes Ahmed (p. 10). I attempt this proposition throughout this methodological proposition not only by dragging my theory through living, bodily language – language that moves into theory like air into expectant lungs – but also through the proposal that we write and read our experience as a type of text, each example of which will force theory into the everyday. That is, the remarkably unremarkable experiences of gendered harassment and assault that we may experience, and which I cannot here pretend to divorce from the Weinstein example that prompted this methodological proposition.

The form of writing-as-research that I propose sympathizes with Alcoff and Gray's (1993) conception of survivor discourse, as they note that the potentially disruptive allegations of sexual abuse are often recuperated and disarmed by dominant discourses. Of particular note is their critique of "confessionals," wherein a confessor and a mediator (or mediators) who by dint of a presupposed (but nonexistent) objectivity to the situation are granted the ability to interpret and rearticulate a woman's experiences back to her in such a way that robs her "speaking out" of its transgressive potential (p. 272). They also note that transgressive and potentially disruptive moments are most likely to happen during horizontal dialogue between sexual abuse survivors (p. 278). This approach also intersects with the documented notion that many women do not feel comfortable describing and recounting their experiences of rape as "rape," for fear that the criminal justice system will not believe them (McGregor, 2005, p. 5), or out of fear that they will be found culpable and blamed for the events, as has been the case historically (Albin, 1977, p. 427), and whereby oppressive structures work to ensure that "not only the testimony but the person herself is smeared" (Gilmore, 2017, p. 2). That is, in identifying herself as a victim "a woman puts herself in the midst of confused and conflicting discourses that can … undermine her own understanding of the sexual events that she tries to master through the evaluation of rape" (Hengehold, 2000, p. 189). Through an intentional obfuscation of myself and other writers and researchers as objective mediators, this methodology attempts to eschew some of the complications that can be experienced by women who are deemed "victims," "survivors," or "liars." It intends to allow a certain freedom from rigid or hierarchical ways of thinking through these experiences. I insert the personal into this methodology and into this writing in a purposeful attempt to blur these lines. Writing our lived experiences into theory, breaking the boundary between myself as survivor and myself as researcher, disempowering myself as interpreter of others' experience while simultaneously empowering myself as "experienced" – these are all intentional moves attempting to create a methodology that somewhat breaks the confessional structure of victim, expert, and judge.

Writing this way becomes intentionally compositional at points in sympathy with my experiences of sexual abuse and in sympathy with the experiences of other women. I write a sense of bodily vulnerability into this methodology intentionally because of this. Although the vulnerability I write into my theory is not necessarily of a sexual or gendered nature, it is reflective of the vulnerability within the examples I have used here and my desire to examine them, and patriarchy more generally, as wounds that need fixing. This writing makes affectively real my desire to use these unsaid impasses for healing purposes. I am turning reparative reading into reparative writing, although perhaps in a much more literal sense of the word. The body becomes a canvas throughout this methodology on which I write repair. I am making the deeply personal theoretical, and in doing so I am hoping to clean each unsaid impasse like a wound and lay down the stitches that can promote future healing.

Toward Affective Methodologies of the Unsaid

The unsaid is a changeable thing. It can be fractured or fluid, formless or rigid. Although it moves differently across torture, sexual abuse, and other forms of trauma, it often carries with it rupture and impasse. It can *be* both rupture and impasse. In focusing on the corporeal, affective components of the unsaid, we recognize the way that specific silences make new meanings and mean new things according to their affective arrangements. This means that in proposing affective methodologies of the unsaid, we have entangled ourselves within varying intensities of experience and within the (in)expression of these intensities by bodies and language. Our intention here has not been to provide a singular way to theorize and write about the unsaid but rather to call attention to the necessity of diverse ways of doing so, and to the potential for particular modes of writing to produce research that attends to the corporeal dimensions of silence. What we have sketched here are some of the messy processes that are necessary to pull the unsaid and its affects into closer proximity to language – and critical language in particular – without flattening out experience or ignoring its textures. This process entails the acknowledgment that such methodologies are inherently open ended and necessarily changeable.

In acknowledging this, perhaps affective methodologies of the unsaid are better thought of as seedlings. Given fertile ground and nourishment, they grow and flourish in unexpected ways. Within the critical research practices of the humanities, affective methodologies are necessarily concerned with language – with bringing the unsaid into the domain of critical thought and critical analysis without eradicating its force, the sheer potency of unspeaking silence as it occurs in the world. As such, affective methodologies cannot be stable, monolithic structures that entrap the unsaid and fill in the blanks of its silence. Our separate voices in this chapter demonstrate two of the forms such a methodology might take – and the differences between them. Torture and sexual abuse are not the same thing, or not necessarily so. Their forms and impacts are distinct, even if they can overlap in certain circumstances. Their traumas – their silences and their enduring wounds – are their own. As one methodology wraps itself around the force of absence itself, around the deliberate erasure of language that is at the heart of torture, so the other eases its way into silences more diffuse, impasses more uncertain and everyday, to tease out the shape of not speaking out in response to sexual harassment and assault.

For some researchers, theorizing the unsaid through two separate (and yet resonant) affective methodologies may seem counterintuitive. Bringing the unsaid into language may seem more the domain of linguistics and discourse, while affect may appear more entangled with the body. What these two illustrations of affective methodologies do through writing *into* the unspeakable and unsayable experiences of torture and sexual abuse is highlight the radical intimacy of affect and language. This intimacy is born from the relationship between bodily experience and how those experiences create silences. Recognizing this, we urge qualitative researchers to consider the affective potentialities of language in their writing and its limits in the words of others that they encounter. Pay particular attention to this relationship in approaching the unsaid in its countless forms yet seek to write into and through these silences affectively. It is this searching after language, alongside a keen awareness of its bodily limits, that provides the nuance necessary to evoke the unsaid, its uncomfortableness, its context, its potentially transgressive ruptures, and its bodily comportments. Aestheticized writing does something affectively that other forms of writing do not, even if in doing so it risks aestheticizing the unsaid itself. As such, it is not the sole possible or necessary response to silence and the unsaid. But it does allow the attuned and attentive researcher to tease out otherwise unexaminable elements of the unsaid.

Affective methodologies can reshape themselves around the unsaid, with the particularities of this reshaping forming the methodological core, the shoot that springs from the seed. In this way, our methodological propositions are reflective of the adaptable heterogeneity of affect theory itself. Our methodologies unfurl in the writing, manifesting in the written work itself because we cannot write the methodology without – partially, incompletely – writing the research. And, at the same time, what we cannot write about the unsaid is almost as pertinent to these methodologies as what we have articulated. If affect theory offers a critical and conceptual vocabulary for embodied experience in all its relationality, affective methodologies are themselves necessarily contingent and mutable. Affect theory asks us to attend to the minor as well as the gestural, the bodily and the incorporeal, and is what our methodologies seek to do as they conceptualize, engage, and make material the unsaid, the silenced, and the silent.

References

Ahmed, S. (2017). *Living a feminist life*. Durham; London: Duke University Press.

Alcoff, L., & Gray, L. (1993). Survivor discourse: Transgression or Recuperation? *Signs*, *18*(2), 260–290.

Atkinson, M. (2017). *The poetics of transgenerational trauma*. New York: Bloomsbury Academic.

Atkinson, M., & Richardson, M. (Eds.). (2013). *Traumatic affect*. Newcastle upon Tyne: Cambridge Scholars Press.

Begg, M. (2008). *Enemy combatant: A British Muslim's journey to Guantánamo and back*. London: Pocket Books.

Black, C., & Clark, E. (2015). *Negative publicity: Artefacts of extraordinary rendition*. New York: Aperture Foundation.

Brennan, T. (2004). *The transmission of affect*. Ithaca, NY: Cornell University Press.

Caruth, C. (1996). *Unclaimed experience: Trauma, narrative, and history*. Baltimore: The Johns Hopkins University Press.

Cixous, H. (1976). The laugh of the Medusa. *Signs*, *1*(4), 875–893.

Davies, C., & Khomami, N. (2017, October 22). Harvey Weinstein: A list of the women who have accused him. *The Guardian*. Retrieved from www.theguardian.com/film/2017/oct/11/the-allegations-against-harvey-weinstein-what-we-know-so-far

Felman, S., & Laub, D. (1992). *Testimony: Crises of witnessing in literature, psychoanalysis, and history.* New York: Routledge.

Gibbs, A. (2001). Contagious feelings: Pauline Hanson and the epidemiology of affect. *Australian Humanities Review, 24.* Retrieved from http://australianhuma nitiesreview.org/2001/12/01/contagious-feelings-pauline-hanson-and-the-epi demiology-of-affect/

Gibbs, A. (2003). Writing and the flesh of others. *Australian Feminist Studies, 18,* 309–319.

Gibbs, A. (2013). Apparently unrelated: Affective resonance, concatenation, and traumatic circuitry in the terrain of the everyday. In M. Atkinson & M. Richardson (Eds.), *Traumatic affect* (pp. 129–147). Cambridge: Cambridge Scholars Press.

Gibbs, A. (2015). Writing as method: Attunement, resonance, and rhythm. In B. T. Knudsen & C. Stage (Eds.), *Affective methodologies* (pp. 222–236). London: Palgrave Macmillan.

Gilmore, L. (2017). *Tainted witness.* New York: Columbia University Press. Retrieved from https://doi.org/10.7312/gilm17714

Gregg, M., & Seigworth, G. J. (2010). An inventory of shimmers. In M. Gregg & G. J. Seigworth (Eds.), *The affect theory reader* (pp. 1–25). Durham, NC: Duke University Press.

Hengehold, L. (2000). Remapping the event: Institutional discourses and the trauma of rape. *Signs, 26*(1), 189–214.

Herman, J. L. (1992). *Trauma and recovery.* New York: BasicBooks.

Kindy, K., & O'Conner, E. (2017). Former actress Louisette Geiss on her encounter with Harvey Weinstein. Retrieved from www.washingtonpost.com/ video/entertainment/former-actress-louisette-geiss-on-her-encounter-with-har vey-weinstein/2017/10/14/ad80806a-b06b-11e7-9b93-b97043e57a22_video .html

Knudsen, B. T., & Stage, C. (Eds.). (2015). *Affective methodologies.* London: Palgrave Macmillan UK. Retrieved from https://doi.org/10.1057/ 9781137483195

Lee, B. (2017, December 14). Salma Hayek claims that Harvey Weinstein threatened to kill her. *The Guardian.* Retrieved from www.theguardian.com/fi lm/2017/dec/13/salma-hayek-claims-harvey-weinstein-threatened-to-kill-her

Manning, E. (2013). *Always more than one: Individuation's dance.* Durham, NC: Duke University Press.

Massumi, B. (1995). The autonomy of affect. *Cultural Critique, 31,* 83–109. Retrieved from https://doi.org/10.2307/1354446

Massumi, B. (2011). *Semblance and event: Activist philosophy and the occurrent arts.* Cambridge, MA: The MIT Press.

Massumi, B. (2015). *The politics of affect.* Cambridge: Polity.

McGregor, J. (2005). *Is it rape?: On acquaintance rape and taking women's consent seriously.* Hampshire; Burlington: Ashgate Publishing.

Moloshok, D. (2017, October 21). "Don't be so naive": Lupita Nyong'o says Weinstein offered to help her career for sex [Text]. Retrieved from www.abc .net.au/news/2017-10-21/lupita-nyongo-says-weinstein-offered-to-help-her-career-for-sex/9072346

Munster, A. (2013). *An aesthesia of networks: Conjunctive experience in art and technology.* Cambridge, MA: MIT Press.

Ojeda, A. E. (2008). *The trauma of psychological torture.* Westport, CT: Praeger.

Patten, D. (2017). Harvey Weinstein accused of sexual harassing actress at Sundance 2008. *Deadline.* Retrieved from http://deadline.com/2017/10/har vey-weinstein-accuser-louisette-giess-speaks-gloria-allred-sexual-harassment-1202185460/

Richardson, M. (2013). Writing trauma: Affected in the act. *New Writing, 10*(2), 154–162. Retrieved from https://doi.org/10.1080/14790726.2012.725748

Richardson, M. (2016). *Gestures of testimony: Torture, trauma, and affect in literature.* New York: Bloomsbury Academic. Retrieved from http://ebookcen tral.proquest.com/lib/unsw/detail.action?docID=4528278

Richardson, M. (2017). Resonances of the negative: Traumatic affect and empty spaces of writing. *Text Journal, Special Issue 42,* 1–12. Retrieved from www.te xtjournal.com.au/speciss/issue42/Richardson.pdf

Riley, D. (2005). *Impersonal passion: Language as affect.* Durham, NC: Duke University Press.

Scarry, E. (1985). *The body in pain: The making and unmaking of the world.* New York: Oxford University Press.

Shouse, E. (2005). Feeling, emotion, affect. *M/C Journal, 8.* Retrieved from http:// journal.media-culture.org.au/0512/03-shouse.php

Slaby, J., Mühlhoff, R., & Wüschner, P. (2017). Affective arrangements. *Emotion Review,* 1–10. Retrieved from https://doi.org/10.1177/1754073917722214

Spinoza, B. (1677). *The ethics and selected letters.* (S. Shirley, Trans.). London: Hackett Publishing Company.

Tomkins, S. S. (1963). *Affect, imagery, consciousness* (Vols. 1–4). New York; London: Springer & Tavistock.

Tomkins, S. S. (1995). *Shame and its sisters: A Silvan Tomkins reader.* Durham, NC: Duke University Press.

Weaver, M., Ellis-Petersen, H., & Khomami, N. (2017). Cara Delevingne says Harvey Weinstein tried to make her kiss woman. *The Guardian.* Retrieved from www.theguardian.com/film/2017/oct/10/georgina-chapman-harvey-wein stein-wife-split

14 The Unsaid and the Unheard
Acknowledgement, Accountability and Recognition in the Face of Silence

Stephen Frosh

Murmurs

If there is anything that can be learnt from John Cage's (1952) 'silent' composition *4'33"*, it is that silence is unattainable. Indeed, that seems to be part of the point: ironic and mischievous as the piece may be, if an audience behaves itself and enters into the game without mockery, it finds itself directed to all the 'unnoticed' noises around it. We might call these the 'murmurs of reality', which various interventions try to silence: for instance, voice and music, the twin soundtracks of life; but also the city and nature, the inescapable noises all around; even, in the psychoanalytic consulting room, the noise of breathing, of expelling air and with it the effort laboriously to manufacture meaning out of nonsense, words from the shapeless abyss. Speaking can be a way of warding off the noisy murmurs from which everything develops. The beginning out of which things are formed is not silence; it is not as if there is an absent nothingness or non-being potential which is activated only when the first word is spoken. Silence is an *intervention* in the noise that is always there, in the endless regime of sound making, of spluttering and coughing, of sighing and singing, which constitutes the nature of both the human subject and the world. Perhaps intuitively, the first Jewish translator of the Bible into English, Abraham Benisch, realised this when he translated the Hebrew word at the start of Genesis, '*Tehom*', unusually as 'murmuring deep': 'the earth was desolate and void, and darkness was upon the face of the murmuring deep' (Rosenbaum & Silbermann, 1973, p. 2). Avivah Zornberg (2009), who takes the phrase 'The Murmuring Deep' as the title of her book on the 'Biblical Unconscious', elaborates on its resonance:

This poetic reading conveys some of the complex harmonics of *tehom*: the Hebrew roots *hamam, hamah, hom* cover meanings like *humming, murmuring, cooing, groaning, tumult, music, restlessness, stirring, panic*. A large register of tones and sounds and movements. (p. xx)

254

God's first creative act is not to distinguish between light and dark as ordinarily thought, but between this shapeless murmuring with its echoing depths and overlapping tones, and the organised speech that makes something of it. If God says, 'Let there be light', it is not in a voice that suddenly animates silence, but rather as one that carves out a space in an already overcrowded terrain. Noise is all around. Slavoj Žižek (2006, p. 154) comments,

> The primordial fact is not Silence (waiting to be broken by the divine Word) but Noise, the confused murmur of the Real in which there is not yet any distinction between figure and background. The first creative act is therefore to *create silence* – it is not that silence is broken, but silence itself breaks, interrupts, the continuous murmur of the Real, thus opening up a clearing in which words can be spoken. There is no speech proper without this background of silence.

Yet whilst it is exactly the case that there is always noise and that the symbolising intervention is to shape and order this noise, to select out of it some sounds that can be heard and used (as speech, as music) and to exclude others that are nothing more than a 'confused' or confusing murmur (or racket), the act that Žižek calls 'creating silence' is not straightforward. It is not really that silence is created, but rather that an act of *silencing* takes place, in which the continual background murmur of the Real is diverted by the construction of – let us call it – the Symbolic, here coded as 'a clearing in which words can be spoken'. The murmur exists first; then there is speech and from this comes creation; the murmur is quietened and its soft and shimmering resonances – *humming, murmuring, cooing, groaning, tumult, music, restlessness, stirring, panic* – are hidden, maybe even repressed. The act of speech is an act of exclusion; all the alternatives that might have come first (music before light, cooing in the dark, restlessness) are placed 'under the bar' of the signifying, 'let there be light'.

Silence is not something original, but it is produced by the action of a masterful pronouncement that shapes or represses the original murmur; the act is not one of creating the nothingness implied by silence but instead is one of exclusion. This is evoked in the Biblical translation, but it is also echoed in the actions of human subjects, not so much mimicking the divine as enforcing the boundaries of what can be heard, and what has to remain unspoken. In a tentatively desacralised world, the murmuring deep is a human production, with its own distinct hum and tumult and its patterns of sensitivity and violence. Revisiting her earlier ethnography on the legacies of violence directed at women during the Partition of India in 1947, Veena Das writes about one of her 'subjects',

Manjit, in terms that offer a warning to researchers but also to all witnesses of fragmentary testimonies:

> What I found compelling in my relations with Manjit was her recognition that her violation was of an order that the whole principle of life stood violated and that to put it back into words could not be done except with extreme hesitation. Hence the boundaries she had created between saying and showing could not be crossed by careless invitations to conversation such as: Tell me what happened. (Das, 2007, p. 92)

'Extreme hesitation' in enunciating the violation accompanying dehumanisation is what characterises the speech of one who is trying to recover a recognisable life; that is, the words will not flow, but they are nevertheless there, just about, always perhaps failing but never completely lost. 'Careless invitations to conversation' will not access them. More generally, speech always excludes, without ever rendering completely silent the material that it refuses to allow into consciousness. This last point is significant methodologically: the murmuring deep remains, even if it is subjugated and often hard to hear. Its legacy is found in those experiences that seem to slip away just when we are about to speak (of) them, in the way speech runs up against its own limitations. Sometimes this produces what we might call a 'genuine' silence, this time a speaking silence rather than a silenced murmur. This happens when it feels like there is nothing left to say, or nothing that seems right to say, or when it is only possible to hint and edge towards the thing that remains unsaid as a way of evoking it in its smoky form, knowing that it is inexpressible in its fullness. Silence at these points is a statement of the limits of hegemonic speech and the demand for something more or something else to take place – a demand that is met in the psychoanalytic domain by listening and reflecting, by introspecting and acknowledging the impossibility of completely taking away someone's pain. But in this regard, this kind of silence is another form of speaking or murmuring: it is itself a positive statement, not an absence. It is a demand for recognition, a calling-out for some kind of response. In the vocabulary that I hope to develop shortly, it is a request for a kind of *witnessing* that can embrace the suffering subject even if what that subject wishes to communicate is hard to bear. Silence of this sort is a mode of resistance to hegemonic speech, whether or not consciously adopted as such.

Witnessing

There is something else to be recovered here: that the murmuring is *embodied*. '*Humming, murmuring, cooing, groaning, tumult, music, restlessness, stirring, panic'*: these are sounds generated in and by the body, *lived* sounds. They are not just background noises: it is not possible to hum or coo, to groan or feel restless and panicky or even to make tumult and music without some physicality, some inhabiting process. This suggests that murmuring may indeed be 'silent' in relation to verbal speech, but it also has its own language of expressiveness that either accompanies speech or may break through it to enrich or even undermine it. A restless or tumultuous response is a murmur suggesting something wrong; it fills the silence with its own message. Not being linguistic, it inhabits the act of breathing and being, and in the materiality of its presentation it especially indicates the spaces – the 'clearing' – in which witnessing needs to take place. This is a complex issue that will take some unpacking, but the first point is obvious: speech and sound are not the same thing. The speech of the subject lies over the murmuring deep in which something else is sounding. In response, the subject who receives this speech – the listener or witness – might be tempted to speak over it, to convert it quickly into an interpretable message, into words: 'tell me what happened'. However, what the murmur insists upon is that there is a need for this witness to hold counsel, to retain the possibility of 'being silent', of not rushing in with speech when one is in the position of having to listen. This necessary requirement if one is to witness something of significance has its own poetic sound:

> The one who understands is not extracting the abstract form out of the tone, the rhythm, and the cadences – the noise internal to the utterance, the cacophony internal to the emission of the message. He or she is also listening to that internal noise – the rasping or smouldering breath, the hyperventilating or somnolent lungs, the rumblings and internal echoes – in which the message is particularized and materialized and in which the empirical reality of something indefinitely discernible, encountered in the path of one's own life, is referred to and communicated. With this internal noise it is the other, in his or her materiality, that stands forth and stands apart making appeals and demands. The other is not simply the recurrent function of appealing to and contesting me; he or she is an empirically discernible vulnerability and intrusion. (Lingis, 1994, p.91)

The noise, the murmur, in this passage from Alphonso Lingis's (1994) *The community of those who have nothing in common* is both what is listened to and what listeners offer through their silence: a passage of being (Lingis's focus is on accompanying someone who is dying) in which one person stays alongside another, silent in the matter of speech, yet in a kind of noisy murmur of association and communication. Lingis continues,

> We communicate to one another the light our eyes know, the ground that sustains our postures, and the air and the warmth with which we speak. We face one

another as condensations of earth, light, air, and warmth, and orient one another in the elemental in a primary communication. (Lingis, 1994, p.122)

The 'elemental' is closely connected to the 'murmur'; witnessing of this kind requires reversing the silencing process, so that this murmur of elemental identification and concern can find its (predominantly non-linguistic) voice.

Is the suffering other here, who needs the kind of witnessing that is usually crowded out by speech, a traumatised subject? There is certainly a sense of violence around when the 'colonising' tendency of speech predominates – 'I will speak to you, I will speak for you' – and the speaking voice of the traumatised subject is itself silenced. For Jessica Benjamin, who has written extensively on witnessing, the question of violence relates closely to a psychoanalytic ethic of recognition and an awareness of the peculiar situation of psychoanalysts as those who become involved with suffering by virtue of their role or, perhaps, 'calling'. The analyst, come what may, stirs up hurt through the analytic demand that what is most damaged and fragile in us is also what must become present in the analysis. As a consequence, the analyst has a responsibility to observe and take some kind of ownership over that hurt. Once called into being as an analyst, the analyst is required to become engaged. Despite not having caused the hurt in the first instance, or no more than any other 'citizen', one might say, the analyst will be responsible for what happens next, for whether or not it can be remedied. A failure to notice, to recognise the subject's suffering – which at times can be performed as a mishearing of 'silence' as implying that there is nothing that needs speaking about – constitutes a further perpetration of violence, this time on the part of the analyst. From here, Benjamin's account of witnessing takes shape: the witness is one who is called upon to listen and to speak out, for whatever reason. Neglecting to do so, backing away, refusing to hear and take some kind of action constitute 'failed witnessing', the loss of that third space that could make change possible. And failed witnessing is itself a perpetuation of violence. Here is one of Benjamin's most compelling accounts of this, in the context of psychoanalysis and of the Israel-Palestine tragedy:

Being the failed witness or abandoning bystander can ... be collapsed into appearing to be the abuser or injurer – both being forms of betrayal and resulting in mystification, which involves deep injury to the sense of self. ... Even if bystander and abuser were originally distinct positions at the time of historical injury, in re-enactments the violent erasure and mental evacuation of the other's experience of fear and pain often feels commensurate with the violence of the act. Thus denial or refusal to witness can have a retraumatizing effect. (Benjamin, 2016, p. 14)

Benjamin's analysis is directed both towards psychoanalysts and others in a position of professional responsibility for receiving traumatic tales, and to political situations in which the witnessing other – for instance, the international community – refuses to hear what the victim is saying. Taking the psychosocial situation at its fullest, it is a statement of how failures of witnessing are also modes of silencing, something which historically is a very familiar tale. For instance, the story of how Holocaust victims did not speak about their suffering until the 1960s or later is not quite true to what happened, which is that many of them did speak – for example, through extensive writings in Polish and Yiddish at the end of the 1940s and early 1950s – but the problem was that there was little response to this speaking, and their voices dried up (Cesarani & Levene, 2002). The broader issue refers to the widespread, and psychoanalytically underpinned, idea that trauma produces silence, that by definition a traumatic experience is one that cannot be symbolised – and indeed that it is the lack of symbolisation that gives the trauma its continued hold over the psyche (in the case of the individual) or the society (in the case of suppressed, unspoken events). Holocaust witnessing is taken as a paradigm of such supposedly 'impossible' situations of testimony. The trauma that is being testified to is assumed to be so immense as to be unsymbolisable and hence inarticulable, a view that has been taken up strongly by Giorgio Agamben (2002) and others in their versions of the idea that the true witnesses of the concentration camps, the *Musselmänner*, are precisely those unable to testify to what went on there. But is it actually the case that trauma is not speakable? Given how widespread discourses of trauma are, how much we seem to live in a 'trauma culture' (Luckhurst, 2008), the claim that trauma is unsymbolisable seems to lack credibility – indeed, talk about trauma is apparently unceasing. Yet this does not mean that it is heard; instead, it could be that the reason why trauma is spoken about so much is precisely that it is never properly 'decoded'; it never finds its place of rest. After examining the evidence for this, Thomas Trezise (2013, p. 211) writes: 'The routinely repeated claim that the traumatic experience of the Holocaust is unrepresentable or unspeakable appears to stand in for a refusal to listen.' This is precisely the dynamic of *silencing*, rather than silence. It may be impossible ever to complete the task of listening, but this does not mean that trauma is inexpressible or that it cannot be witnessed; it just describes the difficulty that people in the position of listener have in holding themselves together sufficiently to allow the speaking to occur. Such listening requires a kind of self-censorship, a quieting of the impulse to speak too soon; and it also requires a capacity to stay with the other and to allow what is seeking expression to emerge.

Witnessing of the kind evoked here, which means active participation in acknowledgement of hurt and destructiveness, has parallels with the situation of receiving testimony about trauma because in both situations, failed witnessing – the act of turning away and not listening – adds to or perhaps even reproduces the original trauma. 'The attachment to the failed witness ruptures even as the confidence in one's own sense of self crumbles', writes Benjamin (2016, p. 14). This suggests that failed witnesses are especially culpable because they offer the promise or hope of recognition but turn out not to be really present or available. There is also an issue about *Nachträglichkeit*: that is, the original trauma gathers excessive, additional or maybe sometimes even formative meaning through the failed witnessing. Primo Levi's (1988) famous dream of surviving Auschwitz but then having his story discounted haunts the discussion here: the trauma could be contained, perhaps, but is instead revived through the failure of listening by the witness to the testimony. Even though it is crucial to retain a differentiation between perpetrators and witnesses or bystanders, this brings into play the distinction between a witness who perpetuates suffering and one who enables something healing to occur. And the situation is made more difficult if the witness is either implicated in the suffering in the first place (for example, as the descendant of a perpetrator) or a 'victim' of a parallel situation which floods back into awareness when witnessing. Benjamin classes this under the heading of 'only one may live', indexing the fantasy that allowing for the other's suffering somehow disallows one's own. She thinks that this has to do with the listener's adoption of the victim position, something very regularly observed in politicised situations of violence. Benjamin (2016, p. 7) writes, 'Our identification with the suffering of others can be interfered with by the identity of victimhood, in which a dissociated fear of forfeiting recognition plays a great role.' If we are 'victims' too, it is very hard to maintain the position of witnessing, hard to acknowledge others' hurt, especially that hurt to which we have contributed or are currently contributing.

Acknowledgement

If the issue of silence is really one of *silencing*, then the methodological question is how to create a process through which the 'hesitant' murmur of a kind of non-linguistic, subjugated 'truth' can be allowed expression. In the individual case, this involves a delicacy of listening in which the struggle is to balance over-involvement with the speaking subject with a turning away that is equally rejecting. Whilst the former is potentially a form of colonisation in which the listener says immediately, 'I know how you feel . . . it happened to me too', so blocking the possibility of under-standing the speaker's specific experience, the latter is a more explicit avoidance ('this is too hard to hear'). Trezise (2013) defines this balance as a 'paradox':

[T]he first person of testimonial memoir represents not so much a place one might occupy, as a site of tension between the speaker who says 'I' and second persons who, as potential first persons, are invited to identify with the speaker and yet simultaneously forbidden to do so, since identification can obliterate the differ-ence between survivor and nonsurvivor and hence renew, in effect, the silence that the survivor seeks to break. (p. 80)

The delicacy here is of maintaining an 'impossible' balance between overfull listening and repudiation. The impossibility is, however, part of the point, revealing the necessary failure of coming to terms with suffer-ing. There is a reason why the murmur is not articulated clearly: it is genuinely something that stands outside the discursive possibilities of ordinary speech. Yet the failure to witness effectively can also be a matter of shame and motivated avoidance; as a response to this, it can turn into a repudiation of the legitimacy of the demand for recognition by a victim or survivor. This is part of the dynamic whereby the idea that trauma survivors cannot speak of their experience (so in a sense it is their 'problem') can function as a way of excusing the failure to listen.

Some of the tension around witnessing and silence has to do with responsibility for current hurts, but some of it connects with historical violence and has fuelled interventions such as truth commissions and more psychoanalytically structured encounters between historically opposed groups. As many have noted, these encounters can be very fraught (Ehrlich et al., 2009; Davids, 2016). It is not as if the historical damage lies silent, put to rest. It reverberates, keeps coming back, needs addressing in each generation as if it is an implacable ghost, however much one tries either to resolve it or escape from it. There is, of course, an enormous literature on transgenerational haunting, much of it to do with the history of trauma as it resurges from one period of time to another, with the victims usually the focus. Some of this literature, additionally, deals with the legacy of perpetrators; given the enormity of the cata-strophe and the deep relevance it had to the history of psychoanalysis, it is not surprising that much of this has been in relation to the legacy of Nazism, from the Mitscherlichs' (1967) *Inability to mourn* to examina-tions of how the corruption of German psychoanalysis during the Third Reich has affected later generations of analysts (Frosh, 2005). This material raises many issues, including how the legacy of silence about the Nazi period affected subsequent generations of Germans. It is also clear that there are ways of speaking about suffering – particularly one's own suffering – that aim at silencing the suffering of others, and that sometimes this can be motivated by a wish, whether conscious or not, to be relieved of responsibility for that suffering. For instance, in his book mixing memoir, psychoanalysis and historical analysis, Roger Frie (2017) describes how after the Second World War Germans found ways of speaking about their experiences that effectively displaced the narrative of suffering from the victims of Nazism to the Germans themselves, in a manner relevant to Benjamin's claims about competitive victimhood mentioned earlier:

> Germans have always talked about their suffering. … The focus on their own suffering meant that there was little motivation to address participation in and support for an immoral regime or its genocidal policies. It was certainly easier to identify as sufferers and victims than to experience guilt and shame for being perpetrators. The local histories of the time reflect this dynamic and concentrated on suffering, not on the complicated entanglements in the regime. Until the early 1970s commemorations of the Second World War bombing raids referred to Germans as victims, free of any historical or moral considerations. (Frie, 2017, pp. 104–105)

Frie goes on to discuss the emergence of a literature and cultural awareness of the suffering of Germans during and after the war, especially of those who were children in that time and therefore could not be held responsible for what happened. He notes the generally psychoanalytic frame of much of this awareness, in that it argues that only by acknowledging the suffering might it be possible for later generations to come to terms with their inherited past. Nevertheless, even if this argument has force, he asks whether this has also turned into a way of exculpating the Germans, prioritising their own suffering and equalising it with that of their victims. That is to say, whilst at the individual level it may be necessary to make it possible for silenced suffering and shame to be articulated and acknowledged, at the social level this might also be a way of denying responsibility. Frie writes,

> The difficulty is that an understanding of trauma and memory derived from a focus on the individual easily neglects the social contexts in which memory is generated. It can also overlook the political forces that shape German responses to the wartime years. Indeed, the very language used to name the traumatic experiences of children of war belongs to the larger cultural and politicized memory discourse. (Frie, 2017, p. 134)

This raises questions about the relationship between individual and social responsibility, as well as about individual and social silences. What seems logical is that under certain social conditions, individuals can take up the kind of listening stance described here with greater or lesser degrees of ease, or as less or more active stances of resistance. In a situation of social denial, which is effectively what Frie presents as happening in post-war Germany (the periodisation of this being long – at least into the 1980s), acknowledging one's own connection to violence, whether direct or indirect, is correspondingly more difficult. Speaking out can be experienced as an act of betrayal of one's community, just as keeping silent betrays the victims. Different kinds of silence and silencing are at work here: the silence of perpetrators, the silencing of victims; the silence of a society with something to be ashamed of or to hide, the silencing of those within it who would wish to speak up; the silence of the present, the silencing of the past.

Gabriele Schwab (2010) writes about the experience of being a German child, post-Holocaust, trying to find out what happened in her German-American family and consequently finding herself always pointing to the unsettling truth behind a façade of conformity and colla-boration. In her thinking, the act of silence or silencing is a profoundly moral and implicating one:

Most of my life, I hated being German. When I tried to bring up the topic of the Holocaust at home, my parents called me a '*Nestbeschmutzer*', a term referring to a bird that soils its own nest. The first time I tried to write about my experiences of growing up in postwar Germany was in high school after I learned about the Holocaust. The urge to pursue this project has been on my mind ever since, but like most Germans of my generation, I was for a long time too scared and in other ways not yet ready to face the challenge. For decades, I couldn't bring myself to come near the topic. It was too close to a home that was not home. Of course, this avoidance was also an involuntary participation in Germany's silencing of the Holocaust, and as such an unwitting collusion with the parental generation. I can now see the kind of public and personal silencing I experienced, and the censoring of my own voice, as a form of magical thinking in which, rather than conjuring and believing in a wishful reality, one attempts to make something unbearable simply go away. (Schwab, 2010, pp. 5–6)

Using the general narrative theme of 'haunting', Schwab considers the position of being a child of Nazi perpetrators, and more generally of a Nazi society, in relation to unworked-through guilt. Amongst the core issues here is the question of how it is that something that troubles one generation is experienced as real and personal in a later one. In the passage just quoted, Schwab describes her parents' active and explicit policy of silencing her as a '*Nestbeschmutzer*'. This would relatively easily explain the self-censorship and avoidance of a topic that would put both her and her parents to shame, and undoubtedly provoke conflict. The naming of her silence as 'an unwitting collusion with the parental generation' both locates the ultimate responsibility with these parents and their generation and acknowledges how the silence of the later generation, however easy it might be to understand in terms of parent-child dynamics, perpetuates the injustice and hence the lack of recognition of suffering that continues to shame the whole society. It also shows how an 'implicated witness' – that is, someone who is linked in some way to an injustice that they were not responsible for (Schwab is not of the generation of the Holocaust) yet is marked by – might have to engage in a highly assertive process of enlightenment and resistance. Implicated witnesses feel, and arguably have, a responsibility to speak out against the silence because the silence is operating 'in their name', even if they have not themselves signed on to it. Whilst this makes complex the link between individual and social – how can someone be responsible for something over which they had no control? – it accurately reflects both a set of ethical concerns (those who live in the shadow of an event need to speak about it, even if they had no part in it) and psychological realities (each of us is marked by the actions of those to whom we are close, even if we had no part in those actions, or even reject them). Speaking out against the injunction to be silent becomes an important project, which is not to say that its acute difficulty should not also be acknowledged, nor that – as Ahmed (2004, paragraph 52) comments in relation to the 'non-performativity of anti-racism' – there is no danger that 'the investment in saying as if saying was doing can actually extend rather than challenge racism'. This kind of self-validating project of apparent speaking can be part of the problem when contesting socially structured silences of which one is a beneficiary; but again, there is a responsibility towards acknowledgement here that has to be accepted, however hard it is to do so with integrity.

Whilst the *'Nestbeschmutzer'* example is one of explicit silencing, Schwab is also concerned with how later generations are haunted by the experiences of their predecessors when the silencing is not so active or, rather, when the silence is not even acknowledged. This has some resonances with the psychoanalytic notion of melancholia, particularly in the version that, building on Freud (1917), sees melancholia as a kind of failed mourning that preserves the lost 'object' as an unconscious reality precisely because it denies either that the object was lost or that it was loved in the first place (Butler, 1997; Frosh, 2013). The melancholic object shadows the psyche because it has never been put to rest; its alienating effect is the result of its being internalised without ever being integrated into the subject's psyche. On a social scale, it could be argued that the depravities of 'empire' function like this in a postcolonial world, in which it is no longer legitimate to celebrate imperialism yet the damage done in its name is also not acknowledged and brought to life so that it can be repaired (Gilroy, 2004). It could also be argued, in the current context, that the Jews of Europe function as such a melancholic object for European society as a whole, and for Germany in particular: Europe's lost Jews are not properly mourned by those who damaged and destroyed them, and responsibility for their excision from Europe is never fully assumed. This means they continue to haunt the environment, resurfacing as anti-Semitism itself continues to resurface, appearing as Holocaust denial and also various ways of shifting responsibility but also, more simply, as an unmourned loss (Schmukalla, 2018). The relationship between denial of loss, melancholia, and haunting is close here: the first causes the second, which materialises as a form of the third. Like many writers in this arena, Schwab (2010) integrates this awareness with Abraham and Torok's (1994) notion of the 'crypt' as that psychic and social domain that both hides something away and secretly attracts attention to it. A crypt is a secret place, but it is also in some ways always in view; the point is precisely that access to it is denied (its message is 'encrypted'), yet this very act excites interest and promotes attempts to find out what it hides. For Schwab, this is why the secrets entrusted to the crypt always seem to leak out:

It is the children or descendants . . . who will be haunted by what is buried in this tomb, even if they do not know of its existence or contents and even if the history that produced the ghost is shrouded in silence. Often the tomb is a familial one, organized around family secrets shared by parents and perhaps grandparents but fearfully guarded from the children. It is through the unconscious transmission of disavowed familial dynamics that one generation affects another generation's unconscious. (Schwab, 2010, p. 4)

The 'unconscious transmission of disavowed familial dynamics' seems here to be not so much hidden but rather the observable 'return of the repressed' – ways in which the silence of the first generation haunts later ones, puzzling them and calling out for some kind of solution. Schwab is quite explicit that the 'secrets' at the heart of the crypt are shared between some people ('parents and perhaps grandparents'), making the silencing process a conspiracy against the children. But even without this overt conspiracy, one can see how the existence of a secret, a silence where there should be speech, is itself a way of calling out. If this incitement to explore is itself repressed, then the next generation also becomes a carrier of the secret, knowing that something troubling has been passed on but unable to articulate what it is. If the incitement is allowed to work, then there is more likelihood of antagonism and the kind of violent rejection of the previous generation that was visible for a while in the Germany of the

1960s and 1970s. There can therefore be dramatic consequences as the hidden past continues to infect the present, mystifying it at the same time as announcing that something is terribly wrong. When there is shame attached, perhaps the process is even more potent. 'Silencing these violent and shameful histories', writes Schwab (2010, p. 49), 'casts them outside the continuity of psychic life but, unintegrated and unassimilated, they eat away at this continuity from within. Lives become shadow lives, simulacra of a hollowed-out normality.' It is hard to imagine a clearer evocation of melancholia, and hard too to see how one might recover from such a position.

Breaking the Silence

Failures of listening and speaking are at the source of silence, which in this chapter has been rendered as a process of *silencing* the murmur that is always there, a murmur that testifies to what is not symbolised and especially to hurts and processes of victimisation. Encrypted knowledge is still knowledge, even if it is only the knowledge of a kind of absence of knowledge: what happened, how could it have happened, what role did this or that person have, what has happened to prevent it being spoken about, how did we not know, what did we do in order not to know? These are both personal and social questions that explore issues of acknowledgement and responsibility and also point to ways in which we might approach listening to the ongoing murmur, even in the face of extensive efforts to silence it. Let me finish with one small, public example. In a university hall, a distinguished white academic has presented an account of some powerful research that traces the genealogy of British slave owners and the compensation paid to them after the abolition of slavery, compensation that is now revealed to be scandalous. In the discussion, a young black woman notes that there are good records of these slave owners: we know their names, their possessions, their homes, their income and who their parents were and what happened to their children. The young woman asks how she can trace her own ancestors who, so far as she knows, were slaves. There is, it seems, no way to do this: except in rare instances, there are no records that individualise such people. The victims disappear; the perpetrators remain. The young woman says that she feels 'hollowed out' by this. I take this to mean that she is made to feel empty by this absence of knowledge, this silent history which she experiences as a removal or killing of her being. If there is a chain of tradition, hers is anonymised; if there are ghosts waiting for recognition and recompense, hers are unnameable and lost. If, indeed, we think of the psyche as necessarily inhabited by those who have come before, by what

we have taken in from them, how we identify with them, their characteristics, their loves and hates, their quirks and ideals, then the absence of
recognition of these ancestors – especially of victimised ghosts, which
therefore have a claim on us – leaves the psyche itself depleted, hollowed
out. This is, indeed, the right term, and in the moment of enunciation in
that university hall, it seemed to pierce any complacency and even to turn
anger at the scandal of compensation for the loss of slaves (when the slaves
themselves were not compensated) into an access of grief.

I am interested here not so much in my own response to the young
woman's intervention, which was a mix of sympathy and shame, but
rather in what the conditions were that allowed this electrifying
moment to surface. (I cannot be sure that it was electrifying for
everyone, but a lot of responses after the event suggested that my
sense of it was widely shared.) One feature was that the supposed
safe space of academic encounter, which in reality is usually not safe
at all but is characterised by competitiveness, precarity and intellectual violence, was on this evening made more tangibly safe by
a process of chairing and encouragement that allowed and validated
tentative voices, uncertain ones, to get heard. Taking time, allowing
slowness, offering space for speech and a reception especially by the
person chairing the event who was not afraid to echo, to acknowledge
and identify with what was being said. 'Hollowed out, exactly sister':
not taking over her words, but amplifying them enough to let them
breathe, to allow their harmonics and associations to be heard – once
again, '*humming, murmuring, cooing, groaning, tumult, music, restlessness, stirring, panic*'. This time, it is these murmuring sounds that are
allowed to surface and find their harmonics explicitly in the space of
a surround of like-minded people who are held together by the
possibility of expressing something. The lack of past recognition,
the troubled wanderings of an unsettled ghost, one whose name is
lost but who still can find a way of being heard, centuries later,
through the unhappiness but also the courage of someone who can
speak of the experience of being hollowed out – of finding a murmur
rising from within that has no real shape but yet expresses something – an austere and devastated realisation ('hollow') but one which
frames the silence in words that are both cogent and a carrier for
feeling. Something in the enunciation and its reception allowed it to
take flight, so that the continuing silence – the unnamed ancestors –
could be heard by a community, even a fleeting and transient one,
and memorialised and made real. The traces of this silence were
embodied in the young woman, felt as a living absence that articulated itself in a way that could not be refused, could no longer be

denied. It would be good, I think, if we could manage this more often.

What can we learn from all this as researchers? I am reluctant to offer simple 'take home' lessons. The field is too complex, the nuances of the work too subtle. Returning to Veena Das's (2007) injunction, it is clear that the simple request 'tell me what happened' is insufficient, one more likely under some circumstances – circumstances of affective signifi-cance – to create rather than refuse silence. Nevertheless, Das goes on to say (p. 94): 'Words can show one's numbed relation to life just as gesture can tell us what forms of life, what forms of dying, become the soil on which words can grow or not.' That is, if one observes the 'showing' nature of words, not just cataloguing the themes contained in them, but allowing oneself to experience what they do, it might become possible to open oneself out *as a researcher* to the life being conveyed, to the difficult elements, the hollows and hesitations, that the speaker is beginning in however stammering a way to express. This is not the same as fully grasping them, but it is also not to stand in mystical awe at something inexpressible. In his work on trauma and history, Dominic LaCapra (2001) acknowledges the difficulty of witnessing trauma fully but never-theless insists on the importance of a mode of empathic responsiveness that is still part of 'working-through', that still involves thinking and acknowledgement of both the limits of understanding and the need to try to understand. 'One's own unsettled response to another's unsettle-ment can never be entirely under control', he writes (p. 103), 'but it may be affected by one's active awareness of, and need to come to terms with, certain problems related to one's implication in, or transferential relation to, charged, value-related events and those involved in them.' Reflecting on our own position as witnesses, on what we are implicated in and what calls to us from the silenced yet murmuring speech of the other, is part of our practical and ethical responsibility and a way in which we might begin to hear what is otherwise unsaid.

References

Abraham, N., & Torok, M. (1994). *The shell and the kernel: Renewals of psychoanalysis*. Chicago: University of Chicago Press.
Agamben, G. (2002). *Remnants of Auschwitz*. New York: Zone Books.
Ahmed, S. (2004). Declarations of whiteness: The non-performativity of anti-racism. *Borderlands, 3*(2). Retrieved from www.borderlands.net.au/vol3n o2_2004/ahmed_declarations.htm
Ahmed, S. (2010). *The promise of happiness*. Durham, NC: Duke University Press.
Benjamin, J. (2016). Non-violence as respect for all suffering: Thoughts inspired by Eyad El Sarraj. *Psychoanalysis, Culture & Society, 21*(1), 5–20.

Butler, J. (1997). *The psychic life of power.* Stanford: Stanford University Press.

Cage, J. (1952). *4'3".* (Musical composition)

Cesarani, D., & Levine, P. (2002). *Bystanders to the Holocaust: A re-evaluation.* London: Routledge.

Das, V. (2007). *Life and* words: *Violence and the descent into the ordinary.* Berkeley: University of California Press.

Davids, M. F. (2016). Psychoanalysis and Palestine-Israel: A personal angle. *Psychoanalysis, Culture & Society, 21,* 41–58.

Erlich, H. S., Erlich-Ginor, M., & Beland, H. (2009). *Fed with tears, poisoned with milk: Germans and Israelis, the past in the present.* Giessen: Psychosozial-Verlag.

Freud, S. (1917). Mourning and melancholia. *The standard edition of the complete psychological works of Sigmund Freud, volume xiv (1914–1916): On the history of the psycho-analytic movement, Papers on metapsychology and other works,* pp. 237–258. London: Hogarth Press.

Frie, R. (2017). *Not in my family.* Oxford: Oxford University Press.

Frosh, S. (2005). *Hate and the Jewish science.* London: Palgrave.

Frosh, S. (2013). *Hauntings: Psychoanalysis and ghostly transmissions.* London: Palgrave.

Gilroy, P. (2004) *After empire: Melancholia or convivial culture?* London: Routledge.

LaCapra, D. (2001). *Writing history, writing trauma.* Baltimore: Johns Hopkins University Press.

Levi, P. (1988). *The drowned and the saved.* New York: Simon and Schuster.

Lingis, A. (1994). *The community of those who have nothing in common.* Indianapolis: Indiana University Press.

Luckhurst, R. (2008). *The trauma question.* London: Routledge.

Mitscherlich, A., & Mitscherlich, M. (1967, German original). *Inability to mourn.* New York: Grove Press, 1984.

Rosenbaum, M., & Silbermann, A. (1973). *Pentateuch with Rashi's commentary: Genesis.* New York: Hebrew Publishing Company.

Schmukalla, M. (2018). *Artistic ruptures and their 'Communist' ghosts.* Unpublished PhD thesis, Birkbeck, University of London.

Schwab, G. (2010). *Haunting legacies: Violent histories and transgenerational trauma.* New York: Columbia University Press.

Trezise, T. (2013). *Witnessing witnessing: On the reception of Holocaust survivor testimony.* New York: Fordham.

Žižek, S. (2006). *The parallax view.* Cambridge, MA: MIT Press.

Zornberg, A. (2009). *The murmuring deep.* New York: Schocken.

15   Conclusion: Topographies of the Said and Unsaid

Kevin Durrheim and Amy Jo Murray

Signs of Silence

Human activity is at once both expressive and repressive. Every utterance that is made and every act that is performed leaves something else unsaid or undone (Billig, 1999; Zerubavel, 2006). Sometimes these unsaid or undone possibilities become evident to people in a setting. When they do, they become hearable silences, the subject matter of this volume. Qualitative studies of silence focus analytic attention on these absences that arise at the intersection between speaking and hearing. What makes something heard when it was not said? How can silence be spoken? By whom? And what can hearers do? How do they keep silent, collude, or speak about the silence? What happens when particular silences – themes, topics, voices – become entrenched in relationships or in society at large? And what happens when collective silences are broken?

In this concluding chapter, we consider the interactional dynamics of silences between speakers and hearers. As researchers, interaction is all we have at our disposal. Studies of silence lack firm empirical footing because the unsaid is absent by definition, and not directly verifiable. The detection of silence is always, in the first instance, a subjective impression and a private determination. One gets the sense of a silence. Silence is heard! Silence is felt! These impressions are recognizable silences, even if the absence is not easily defined or described (Ephratt, 2008). Like all psychological concepts, such hearings are in need of "outward criteria" – a shared language – if they are to be codified and confirmed (Wittgenstein, 1953, § 580). Without a shared language of silence, private experiences are easily denied or attributed to the interests and investments of the hearer – such as the lone crazy whistleblower (Alford, Chapter 11, this volume), or the self-interested political or social class (e.g., Schröter, Chapter 9, this volume).[1]

Rather than treating the ambiguity and slipperiness of silence (Jaworski, 1993; Rappert & Bauchspies, 2014; Schröter, 2013) as an impediment, qualitative researchers recognize that it is precisely these properties that lend absence its haunting quality and are a necessary part of how silences function rhetorically and ideologically. The chapters in this book have offered the qualitative researcher a rich compendium of signs of silence, which are entry points to analysis. We might not be able to put our finger on the unsaid itself, but the unsaid can become evident in: the use of "figured language" (Billig & Marinho, Chapter 1); refusals to listen and social/moral exclusion (Alford, Chapter 11; Opotow, Ilyes, & Fine, Chapter 6); gendered ways of narrating (Fivush & Pasupathi, Chapter 7); conversational breaches and code words (Sue & Robertson, Chapter 4); the language of implication, euphemism, and hesitation and generic formulations (Zerubavel, Chapter 3); topical omissions (Huckin, Chapter 10); conversational redirection (Toerien & Jackson, Chapter 2); looming presences across contexts (Murray & Lambert, Chapter 5); quiet resistances across power differentials (Coles & Glenn, Chapter 8; Murray & Lambert, Chapter 5); traumatic returns and affective impasses (Richardson & Allison, Chapter 13); the use of sound and silence in representation (Winter, Chapter 12); failed witnessing (Frosh, Chapter 14); and language ideologies that regulate what should and should not be said (Schröter, Chapter 9).

The shared language of silence that the chapters describe includes the discursive formulations, ethnomethods, and moves that make the absence evident. In this regard, the turn to silence by qualitative researchers should not be seen as a turn away from discourse. We do not aim to clean the mantelpiece of qualitative research of the accumulating discourses and repertoires that have been stacked upon it, stripping it bare to leave absence as the sole object of contemplation. On the contrary, we want to rearrange the objects so that the spaces between them are also revealed as meaningful artifacts, constituted in negative by arts of indirection, suppression, evasion, circumnavigation, and so on. We want to connect absences and presences, the said and the unsaid. This focus on discourse and interaction does not mean that qualitative studies of silence disregard systemic concepts such as norms, situations, institutions, and ideologies. Studies of silence are ideological analyses because it is only against the shared background of social life that silences can be spoken or heard at all. Social conventions and expectations for conduct make the unsaid noticeably, observably, or relevantly absent so that a silence may be hearable. As Schröter and Taylor (2018) proclaim in their recent book on the subject, silence becomes evident in "disappointed *expectation*" (our emphasis).

Situational norms make expected actions "significantly" (Billing & Marinho, Chapter 1) or "relevantly" (Toerien & Jackson, Chapter 2) absent. Chapters have considered, for example, the looming possibility of a mental health diagnosis (Toerien & Jackson, Chapter 2); the absence of applause at the conclusion of a speech (Billig & Marinho, Chapter 1); refusing to talk about racism in the face of discrimination (Sue & Robertson, Chapter 4); how we narrate our stories in particularly gendered ways (Fivush & Pasupathi, Chapter 7); and inequalities that haunt intimate relationships (Murray & Lambert, Chapter 5). Institutional, national, and interactional norms and social conventions make particular expectations salient in situated interaction. These affect what can be said or done, how, by whom, and to what effect.

Unfulfilled expectations may also take shape against the backdrop of recognizable investments of the actors. On the one extreme, these are collective ideological interests, for example, in nationalism, racism, sexism, or heteronormativity (Billig & Marinho, Chapter 1; Coles & Glenn, Chapter 8; Murray & Lambert, Chapter 5; Sue & Robertson, Chapter 4; Zerubavel, Chapter 3) or the avoidance, re-presentation, or omission of topics in the media (Huckin, Chapter 10; Schröter, Chapter 9). At the other extreme, the investments in avoidance may be deeply personal, as is the case when veterans refuse to talk about the war (Winter, Chapter 12), trauma and torture victims remain painfully silent about their experiences (Frosh, Chapter 14; Richardson & Allison, Chapter 13), and those on the margins of society are silenced when the powerful refuse to listen (Alford, Chapter 11; Coles & Glenn, Chapter 8). Finally, unfulfilled expectations may be evident in the exercise of power via law and procedure (Opotow, Ilyes, & Fine, Chapter 6). Norms and investments can either arise informally or be institutionalized as policies that are administered and policed. The regulation of silence is most clearly apparent in the courts, but as Opotow and her colleagues (Chapter 6) argue, disciplinary knowledge in the sciences also functions to discredit and silence some knowledge.

This concluding chapter aims to set these signs of silence in the interactive contexts from which they emerge. In so doing, we develop an understanding of some of the connections implicated in silences, between speaking and hearing, between presences and absences, between concrete actions and their generative contexts, and between individual and collective agents. It is an ambitious task that we hope to accomplish by developing a topographical metaphor for thinking about these connections. We develop an appreciation of the discursive structuring of the said and unsaid and the way these structures arise from but also give shape to social interaction by imagining routines of speaking as paths traversing a discursive terrain of absences and presences.

Discourse, Silence, and Joint Action

How does social life progress? How do argument and conversation move from speaker to speaker and from topic to topic? What trajectory will they follow and how will the process unfold? Samuel Johnson (1818, p. 12) tells us that the term "discourse" comes into the English language from the Latin, *discurrere*, meaning "to run hither and thither." The word denotes progressive action, an idiosyncratic running about. However, discourse is dialogical "joint action" (Blumer, 1969; Shotter, 1993). Johnson recognizes this too, quoting Glanville's definition of discourse as "the act of the mind which *connects* propositions" (Johnson, 1818, p. 12, italics added). Narratives, conversations, and arguments flow from point to point, topic to topic across turns of speaking subjects, each contribution meaningfully connected to its predecessor and pushing the whole in a singular direction. Fifty years of research in conversation analysis shows that the process is organized and can flow with some predictability as unfolding sequences of action, with each turn responsive to and displaying understanding of prior talk (Schegloff, 2007). Of course, participants can also display their misunderstandings, and the discourse will take its twists and turns as it makes room for and accommodates the unexpected, correction, reversal, retreat, and repair (see Schegloff, 1992).

Discursive presences and absences meet each other at these points of connection. Each utterance or performance fills a void of expectation created by the preceding turn. Sometimes conventional responses – e.g., answers to questions, return greetings – might not be forthcoming, leaving a noticeable absence (see Schegloff, 2007, pp. 19–20). On other occasions, subsequent turns might only incompletely fill the void of expectation (answering a question with a question, a half-hearted greeting), leaving a "murmur" (Frosh, Chapter 14) of unfulfilled possibility. Both the said and unsaid thus mark the path of discursive wandering, giving it a singular trajectory. If each contribution, each utterance or performance, is an act of exclusion of actions not being performed, then it is at these points of connection where silence may be evident as an unfulfilled expectation. Silence is marked by troubled connections – hesitation, repair, avoidance, redirection, audible silence, anger, justification, surprise, contradiction, argument, and so on – but it can also lie camouflaged in the ordinariness of conversational routine.

Blumer (1969, p. 18) described discursive joint action as "unprescribed conduct." It is unprescribed both because each participant is free to make their own contribution at each point in the interaction and because the destination to which the whole progresses is emergent.

Unprescribed conduct takes the form of discourse that moves hither and thither. The progression of discourse – and the absences embedded in that discourse – depends partly on how individual contributors may enter into social life, navigating between the said and unsaid, to make a contribution. Blumer observes that each contribution to joint action must be "formed anew" as participants "build up their lines of action to fit them to one another" (p. 18).

How then may participants fit their lines of action together to form seamless joint wholes when failure is always an imminent possibility? Studies of discourse suggest that they do so by making choices that resolve tensions among discursive investments, conventions, and situational demands. Sequence organization and the conversational apparatus of turn taking and repair provide the interactional framework for exercise of choices about what to do and what to say at each point (Sacks, Schegloff, & Jefferson, 1974; Schegloff, 1992). In addition, in topical talk, speakers also build on existing discursive resources. Potter and Wetherell (1987) usefully describe these as interpretive repertoires, the recognizable lexicon, metaphors, and tropes that are culturally available for talking about a subject. This is resonant of Foucault's definition of discourse as a "group of statements that belong to a single system of formation" (1972, p. 121). There is a family resemblance among the statements that make up, for example, clinical discourse, psychiatric discourse, or economic discourse; meaningful contributions to conversation are established by articulating familiar objects, subjects, and relations in ways that are intelligible in that discourse (see Fairclough, 1992; Parker, 1992).

However, as the chapters in this book have shown, such discursive formations not only include statements; they also exclude statements. Interpretive repertoires and discourses contain silences. For example, medical discourse, which made pain a spectacle – "look in order to know, to show in order to teach" – was premised on a violent silencing of the "sick body that demands to be comforted" (Foucault, 1973, p. 84). Every social act takes place in an existing symbolic, pragmatic, and ideological landscape that includes recognizable interpretive repertoires and routines of speaking but also has its silences, taboos, and repressed themes. Consequently, participation in discursive joint action depends on recognizing where you are in this landscape of established discursive presence and absence and knowing how to move forward. Participants need to recognize what kinds of absences are likely to be noticed as significantly and relevantly absent at any point, and whether these will be considered acceptable or treated as accountable, potentially resulting in interactional trouble.

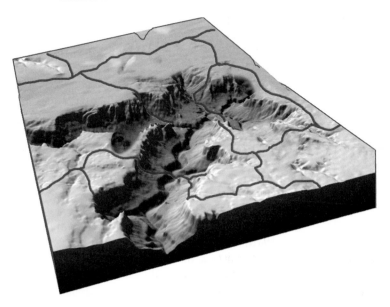

Figure 15.1 Topographical map of the said and unsaid

We might imagine this discursive terrain as a topographical map of the said and the unsaid, much like the paths that navigate the elevations and contours of a topographical map of discursive possibilities (see Figure 15.1). These discursive possibilities can be visualized on a terrain that is structured around collective presences and absences, the sayable and unsayable, the doable and the undoable, cultural taboos and prescriptions. When we hike in the wilderness, we use trails and paths that help us navigate through wild terrains. The path is defined by its edges, by the spaces just beside and beyond it that are not part of the trail but are working to constitute the trail. The edge of the path is not definite nor is its course set in stone. As we walk, we may see old paths, overgrown, and no longer in use. We may see new paths emerging, where grass has been trampled down by feet looking for sure footing. We are aware of dangers or difficulties in the terrain by seeing how the paths contour around them. We can see where there are directions that the path could have taken to avoid a gully or a cliff but yet did not. The terrain is the vast "argumentative fabric" (Laclau 1993, cited by Wetherell, 1998, p. 393; 2001) of discourse that we use to construct our realities and navigate through life. We can imagine the edges of paths and the potential paths as representing the unsaid. The unsaid exists on the edges of the said and beyond. The unsaid are the paths that are not there, but that could have been had a different bearing been used to satisfy alternative interests. The said – that which we can talk about in polite conversation – is defined by that which goes unsaid, which could compromise and shift the path and its course.

The chapters of this book have reminded us that the discursive fabric is woven from both the said and the unsaid. It contains silences and taboos as well as topics that are (almost) imperative to speak. Each occasion of joint action traverses this terrain via a network of paths and routes that have already been carved into the landscape. Conversational routines are almost habitual, and they circumnavigate taboos and rudeness as a matter of routine, just as paths avoid cliffs and gullies and make their way carefully through steep or treacherous terrain. Our feet can slip off the path as we step into the unsaid but we quickly regain our footing. The path keeps us safe. The path keeps us together. The path keeps us moving toward a goal that has been marked out by others before us. Collectively, we keep these paths well worn and in common use. The unsaid is made evident as the said winds around it, cuts through it, and avoids it to prevent breaking up the group on our journey as a collaborating society, collectively avoiding those terrains that may trouble a hegemonic journey.

The topographical metaphor shows that the said and unsaid are continually brushing up against one another, are kept in place by human activity, and are historical products, always open to change if someone is prepared to do the "work" of beating a new path. Studies of racial discourse illustrate this well. Racism is both a present absence and an absent presence in many societies. Speaking out against racism is a powerful imperative. We might say that there is an antiracist discourse at work. This discourse is evident by familiar tropes such as "we are all equal," "race is a social construction," "apartheid is racism," and so on. But the discourse also renders explicit racial discrimination and crude racial stereotyping taboos. Antiracist discourse is characterized by presences and absences. And yet, despite the wide acceptance of this discourse, racism and racial stereotyping persist. There are routines for implicitly invoking stereotypes of even the most despicable kind (Durrheim, 2012, 2017), and explicit antiracism may implicitly echo unspoken taboos. For example, when the South African Human Rights Commission states the antiracist morality explicitly – "There can never be any context in which the use of the K-word is acceptable" (Times Media Digital, 2017, par 1) – they rouse interest and conjure in the imagination the encrypted content of the K-word. Uttering the K-word would breach the norm, but the signification of blackness and the history of racism are routinely invoked by the use of the term "K-word."

In the first instance, fitting lines of joint action together to make points of connection requires locating oneself in an existing topography of the said and unsaid and moving along paths of discursive convention. Culturally competent members take this landscape for granted as they follow the routines of their culture. Hidden silences become evident where interaction is ruptured by a troubled connection, such as a misjudged racist expression or unintended slip of the tongue. Such breaches of convention are not judged merely as misunderstandings but as moral failures. It is not simply a matter of a failure to correctly follow a rule that is prescribed by commonly accepted discourse. Rather, such failures reveal flawed choices, even flawed personalities or groups. Like all contributions to discursive joint action, such choices are always consequential. They move the discourse forward, creating new contexts for subsequent turns and silences.

Accountable Conduct

The previous section considered how points of connection are made in social interaction by conforming to discursive conventions. Discursive conventions are thus reproduced by "the forcible citation of a norm" (Butler, 1993, p. 232). However, fitting lines of action to one another (Blumer, 1969) is not simply an act of conformity. In this section, we show how consideration must also be given to context and how, ultimately, the norms and conventions of conduct are worked out together by participants in the situation.

Participants in social life need to do more than conform to norms and follow routines, "re-citing" established discourses and maintaining their silences (Butler, 1993). Each line of action needs to fit the emerging trajectory of interaction in conventional ways, but it also needs to fit the developing situation. Each situation may share recognizable features with other situations, but every situation is unique and if norms are to be applied, they must be applied – to use Garfinkel's memorable expression – "for another first time" (cited in Heritage, 1984, p. 122). Participants are tasked with working out together what norms apply here, what routines to follow, what performances to enact, what discourses to recite, and what (of course) should remain unsaid. Norms, routines, and conventions do not function as rules that dictate how people will act in any situation. There is always room for maneuvering, choice, and agency as participants work out which norms and conventions apply in any particular situation, what silences need to be maintained, and how these themes should be properly expressed or repressed.

Derek Edwards's (1997) theory of discourse can help us understand how normative structures such as illustrated in Figure 15.1 may function in non-deterministic ways to propel joint action. He builds on the work of ethnomethodology and conversation analysis, arguing that actions do "not so much obey as orient to norms" (p. 7), and that "participants bring actions under the auspices of norms and rules" (p. 18). It is a subtle but profound shift in emphasis. Norms, routines, conventions, and discourses do not govern behavior, providing behind-the-scenes direction for speaking or keeping silent about a topic. Rather, they are taken into account in the arrangement and enactment of behaviors, and they are used as interpretive resources by recipients/hearers of actions. People can choose to deviate from the norm if they wish, but they do so knowing that the norm may be used to understand their actions as deviant (see, e.g., Heritage's 1984, account of greetings, pp. 106–110).

It is not necessary for the actor to consciously narrate each move before action, quietly saying to themselves, "say this, don't say that." Rather, performances are undertaken "designedly" so that they can be recognized for what they are, thereby averting even needing to account for them in many/most cases. However, if an account is needed, norms and shared meanings would be handy resources for formulating explanations, reformulations, excuses, and so on. Of course, the norms themselves would be constructed in this process of accounting, and their place and formulation in this sequence of interactions would itself be a gesture eliciting a response. Actions thus knit together situations and norms, adapting norms to specific situations, and adapting situations to specific norms, creating – along the way – something altogether new, but at the same time, altogether familiar: "another first time," in the sense suggested earlier.

Situational norms and conventions are thus established retrospectively. They form in the wake of actions. As responses, actions give recognition to the norms that apply by the way they treat immediately preceding turns, either aligning with (endorsing), refining, or rejecting these (Schegloff, 2007). Each act in the sequence will be designedly normative, conventional, or even counter-normative, but its fate depends on its reception. For example, the uttering of a crude racial stereotype does not necessarily contravene a racism taboo. What counts as a contravention and receives the label "racism" is a "collaborative accomplishment" (Condor et al., 2006). The status of an utterance as racist "ultimately depends upon its acceptance or rejection on the part of an audience" (Condor et al., 2006, p. 458). If the audience allows an utterance to pass without comment or resistance, the speaker and audience have collaboratively defined and given substance to the norms that apply in this situation – what can be spoken and what should remain unsaid. If the utterance receives an objection – using an "antiracist" norm to treat the utterance as (possibly) racist – it might be qualified or retracted as the situational norms that apply here and now are worked out (see, e.g., Burford-Rice & Augoustinos, 2018; Stokoe, 2015; Whitehead, 2015). Responses that allow previous contributions to pass without trouble have the effect of both rendering previous action creditable and giving substance to the norms that apply to this case and in this situation (cf. Schegloff, 1992, p. 1331). Whitehead (2018, p. 288) describes this as "participant-administered" accountability because it is the participants themselves – the speakers and hearers – who together decide what is or is not acceptable in any situation.

Accountable conduct is any contribution to social life that fits into developing lines of joint action and takes them further. On the other hand, participant-administered accountability becomes troubled when contributions to joint action are criticized, rejected, or ignored. The chapters of this book have shown that participant-administered accountability is developed both via the propositional content of utterances as well as the taboos, absences, and silent themes that remain unsaid. Discourse may gesture toward unsaid shared knowledge, invoking it implicitly or, if the content is especially toxic, accountability will be developed by avoiding it altogether, by tiptoeing around the proverbial elephant in the room or by refusing to hear that which is troubling.

Accountability may also be managed by topicalizing silence. The fine line between what may be conventionally said (by whom) and what should remain unsaid can be negotiated by "metadiscursive moves" (Schröter, Chapter 9), which topicalize silence and comment on its desirability. A host of idioms provides conventional means for doing so. For example, the colloquialism "Silence is golden" valorizes silence and can be employed to regulate social interaction, as in the belief that "children should be seen and not heard" or the now-defunct proverb "silence is a woman's best garment." Both of these explicitly prescribe silence for categories of people in lower hierarchical positions (women, children), and thus treating "speaking" ("not-silence") as a privilege of categories higher in the hierarchy. In the process of topicalizing silence, unsaid themes of privilege and misogyny may be brought to light. Repressed topics can be dredged up to the surface of social interaction, where they can be put to work in redirecting joint action, constructing situations, and formulating accountable conduct. In Chapter 9, Schröter shows how right-wing discourse in Europe has been emboldened by calling out the silencing powers of antiracist norms, and in the process breathing new life into the repressed values of the Nazi past.

Of course, hearing silences may be as blameworthy as holding them. Speaking the unspeakable can be morally objectionable, rude, politically incorrect, and even pornographic. Moreover, the tenuous empirical grounds of exposed absences can place the hearer in the difficult position of having to support their claims; such tenuous and blameworthy utterances further expose the hearer to personal attributions of mental or moral deficiencies and unwholesome interests or self-ascribed moral superiority. This is apparently what happens to whistleblowers who, as Alford (Chapter 11) shows, experience "knowledge as disaster" by telling secrets and speaking the unsaid and who end up shut out of social life, talking to themselves with no one to listen.

There is a warning lesson here for those who want to call out the elephant in the room. There is a warning also for qualitative studies of silence. Speaking of a silence is an accountable act, subject to the same felicity conditions as other utterances and performances. There might be methodological criteria for identifying and exposing silences but each unsilencing is an act of accountable conduct that will help to shape the emerging situation, and whose reception will instantiate the norms that are applicable there. Constructing silence is thus no different from any other kind of social construction: it is an occasioned and interested social act that must attend to the rhetorical demands of justification and criticism; it plays its part in helping to fashion the emerging social situation. Speaking of silence – calling it out – is always a choice and as such is always also an act of exclusion that is itself silencing. Speaking about silence is thus a political and accountable act – whether it is done by participants or researchers, however well intended.

Collective Silences and Social Change

In the previous section, we considered discursive silences from the point of view of conversational utterances that unfold dialogically in the sequence of turns between speaking subjects. But, of course, as illustrated by the path metaphor of Figure 15.1, the said and unsaid together constitute a collective discursive environment that is produced and shared by members of a community. The conversational failures and achievements we discussed in the previous section – (not) speaking, (not) hearing, speaking silence, and speaking of silence – are individual acts that adhere or fail to adhere to the conventional paths on the shared landscape of the said and unsaid. These individual acts form part of a collective pattern of silence and silencing (Murray & Durrheim, 2018). The rare occasions when the Mexicans that Sue studied acknowledged racism were breaches of a shared norm of racism disavowal (see Sue & Robertson, Chapter 4) that attracted censure and made visible the collective routines of racism avoidance. Likewise, when Gabriele Schwab's parents called her a *"Nestbeschmutzer"* for talking about the Holocaust at the dinner table (see Frosh, Chapter 14), they were acting like many others Germans of that generation, enforcing a collective taboo, each in the privacy of their own home. When the judge in the case presented by Opotow, Ilyes and Fine (Chapter 6) ruled that facilitated communication was impermissible, she relied on legal precedents and conventions of disciplinary knowledge. Fivush and Pasupathi (Chapter 7) show that silences are communicated early in life by parents whose interaction with boys and girls reflect shared "master narratives" that "privilege the expression and elaboration of emotional experience for women" and silence "emotional expressivity and vulnerability for men." In our path metaphor, these are examples of people being kept from "stepping off the path" and of the responses and interactional troubles that can follow such "missteps" of keeping silent, speaking a silence, or speaking about silence. These are the actions that keep the path in good repair (cf. Heritage, 1984, p. 210) and make it difficult – but, as noted later, not impossible – to beat new paths. Although each act of holding or breaking the silence occurs as a concrete instance, collectively these conventions keep shared repressions encrypted.

Social change occurs when individual instances of speaking the unspoken become part of a new collective consciousness, or when new topics enter collective taboos. The paths represented in Figure 15.1 are malleable and plastic. Untamed veld of the unsaid can become well-worn paths of acceptable expression, and topics that are speakable at one point in time may become avoided or unused, falling away into a wilderness of the unsaid. But this does not happen by one or a few people saying the unsayable; it requires many people to tread there for a new path to be forged, and similarly an old path becoming overgrown requires that it becomes conventional not to follow it. Billig (1999) describes such a change when he suggests that the "topic of race today has slid into the seat vacated by sexuality" (p. 259). The twentieth century saw the progressive undoing of Victorian taboos of talking about sex at the same time that uninhibited anti-Semitism and racism became unspeakable in polite society. Such changes can happen rapidly when people are swept along by new conventions of speaking the unsayable or silencing what had once been sayable. This appears to be happening in Europe and the United States today, where views about foreigners – that for a generation were unspeakable echoes of Nazism – have started to become defensible once again (Durrheim et al., 2018; Schröter, Chapter 9).

The links between agentic individual acts of silencing and the collective structures of the unsaid are dialectical rather than causal. The discursive topography of the said and unsaid needs to be taken into account as preexisting norms, as interacting agents "build up their lines of action to fit them to one another" (Blumer, 1969, p. 18). Individual acts are thus "prospectively adjusted to norms," orienting to them. However, it is only in their acceptance or rejection that actions become "retrospectively productive of norms" that apply in any particular situation (cf. Durrheim, Quayle, & Dixon, 2016, p. 22). It is only through these interactive processes of enactment and reception – taking norms into account and recognizing them – that the topography and routines of the said and unsaid become visible. To the extent that actions (individually and collectively) stop being designed and interpreted in light of them, they effectively ceases to exist. So, the topography is (re)constituted, in emergent form, in the actions it informs.

The concept of "stigmergy" describes the dialectical mechanism by which collective silences arise from discursive expressions. Stigmergy describes the self-organizing "formation, acquisition, mediation, transmission and dissemination of knowledge in complex communities" (Marsh & Onof, 2008, p. 1; see also Heylighten, 2016) – including its absences – via the effect that social interactions have on the environment. The concept was developed to explain the emergence of collective intelligence in interacting networks of simple agents. Ants, for example, follow a simple rule in their search for food: "go where others have gone." Each ant leaves a small pheromone trace as it moves, and a second ant will strengthen the mark at places where paths intersect, establishing more attractive places for further ants to pass through. Collectively, then, ants build complex dendritic trails that merge into paths that become dynamic life-giving arteries for the colony (Helbing et al., 1997). Importantly, no command center is required for networks of interacting individuals to act intelligently to produce intricately designed and functional emergent structures. Individual acts make small changes to the environment that provide the basis for self-organizing collective behavior and emergent structures that can dynamically respond to big environmental changes, such as the depletion of a food source.

The same happens with human trails (see Figure 15.2). As people move to their destinations, they affect their environment, making small changes that facilitate travel for others. At first these changes are barely perceptible, but they eventually result in paths which may become deeply inscribed, attractive routes or may vanish if they no longer serve human needs (Goldstone & Roberts, 2006; Helbing et al., 1997, 2001). Human trails are emergent self-organizing phenomena that can be reproduced in

Figure 15.2a Trail system on the university campus of Brasilia (Reproduced with kind permission by Klaus Humpert.)

multi-agent simulations where each agent has its own destination, but all follow the very simple rule, preferring to walk on ground that has been previously trod (Helbing et al., 1997). As paths emerge, they become self-reinforcing, representing a collective intelligence of embodied purpose and efficiency that can persist across generations. (See Figures 15.2a and 15.2b.)

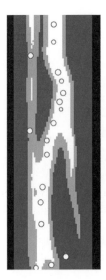

Figure 15.2b Stigmertic simulation of trail formation (Helbing et al.,
1997)

The concept of stigmergy and the metaphor of paths help us understand the self-organizing emergence of the unsaid in collective discourse. What is customary – the contoured paths of discourse – has
the power to "routinely create the unsaid" (Billig, 1999, p. 67), the
grassy patches outside the paths. Silence is "contoured by language"
(Schlant, 1999, p. 1). These untrod "hinterlands" are created as by-
products of stigmergic activity, but – equally – individual acts are
motivated by hinterland avoidance; collectively such acts define and
thoroughly constitute the paths of routine and conventional presences.
The unsaid arises from collective discourse and then gives shape to
routines of joint action. The whole worked landscape of crisscrossing
routes – both physical and discursive – is an emergent, dynamic, self-
organizing intelligence. Like paths, discursive topographies of the said
and unsaid arise "without any common planning or direct communication among the users" (Helbing et al., 1997, p. 56). But once in
existence, the said and the unsaid are mutually reproducing. Every
action or performance demarcates absent possibilities, which gain
shape and potency. The said and unsaid are emergent structures,
kept in place by actions that take coordinates from the normative
contours and moral/accountable beacons of what can be said or

must remain unsaid with degrees of compulsion and by the antici-
pated or actual trouble associated with saying the unsayable.
Stigmergic landscapes embody collective intelligence. Paths provide direction and purpose because they are the result of purposeful
action. If you find a path when you are lost in the veld, you can be
reassured that you are going somewhere, even if you still do not
know where you are. Unwalked places, in contrast, signal danger
and the possibility of getting hopelessly lost. In a similar way, the
discursive routines of the said represent safe grounds for accountable
conduct, whereas those who venture into the unsaid risk being
misunderstood or worse (Alford, Chapter 11; Coles & Glenn,
Chapter 8; Murray & Lambert, Chapter 5). It is always possible,
of course, to voice the unsaid, and sometimes it becomes necessary
to break conventions. These pioneering acts have potential to
change landscapes, creating new routines of the said and unsaid,
as is shown by Schröter's (Chapter 9) examination of anti-political
correctness discourse. Discursive paths provide a preexisting framework for human action, but they are entirely dependent on the
action that they spawn for their existence. They evolve, change,
and disappear as human needs change.

Unconscious Awareness and Qualitative Studies of Silence

Thus far we have depicted discourse as emergent and self-organizing joint
action that goes hither and thither over a landscape of the said and unsaid.
It is neither governed by rules nor driven by intentions, but it progresses
via participant-administered accountability. As individual contributions
join their lines of action together, they not only take their bearings from
the discursive landscape (Figure 15.1), but they also affect the landscape,
leaving an impression of what constitutes accountable conduct. Then by
the "general principle that activity often begets more activity" (Goldstone
& Roberts, 2006, p. 44), others develop a preference to act accountably
by similar means.

But this topographical metaphor begs the question about the nature of
the "landscape" that affects and is affected by discourse and its silences.
Ant and human trails form on the environment of physical surfaces. But
on what environment does discursive activity leave a trace? Following
Laclau (1993) and Wetherell (2001), we have treated discourse as a vast
argumentative texture, like a cloth or fabric with threads "woven through
the whole" (Wetherell, 2001, p. 389). This formulation nicely captures
the idea that any instance of discursive absence we find is connected to the

whole and runs, as a strand in cloth, through many other contexts. However, the metaphor treats the discursive topography and its paths as preformed and static and fails to capture the dynamics and emergence of stigmergic environments.

In developing a "stigmergic conception of social cognition," Marsh and Onof (2008, p. 144) argue that the concept of a connectionist "extended mind" is the "only plausible model currently on offer that can accommodate the dynamic tacit dimension of the acquisition and perpetuation of social knowledge." This extended mind is composed of networks of interacting individuals, brains and bodies, technologies, and artifacts through which knowledge and affect flow and are stored. Each act of accountable conduct leaves an impression in the network of connections between humans and humans and between humans and things. These impressions are instantiations of relationships that pass though participant-administered accountability and flow through the social network as media representations or as individual and collective habits, skills, or mores. This is the dynamical, embodied, extended, distributed, and situated environment on which individual acts of discourse leave their traces of the said and unsaid, and onto which are inscribed the said and unsaid.

Billig and Marinho (Chapter 1) rightly refer to such impressions of discursive intelligence as "ideological habits." They are historical and collective ways of acting that have become habitual for individuals who are socialized in these contexts. They are also reproduced mechanically as representations. Ideological habits are both conscious and unconscious. They are unconscious in the sense that they are not "systematically planned in detail" in advance of the performance. Speakers do not necessarily identify unspeakable themes and ways of avoiding or expressing them in advance and then deliberately deploy pre-formulated expressions as they enter into joint action of social life. On the other hand, however, expressions and the silences they cover are never "accomplished by accident." The successful coordination of "precisely choreographed" discursive joint action betrays individual and collective awareness of social demands, accountability requirements, and possibilities of audience reactions (cf. Billig, 2006). Thus, Billig and Marinho (Chapter 1) conclude that "it is likely that there is a combination of awareness and unawareness" in all expression and silencing. They attribute this unconscious awareness to the "ideological background" that we have described here topographically as the emergent paths or routines of human conduct. These are inscribed on things and on flesh and made visible in artifacts and habits of conduct. This is reflected poignantly in Ernestine Schlant's analysis of the silences around the Holocaust and Jews in West German literature when she notes that "this silence was pervasive; it rested on unstated shared thinking, established unconscious bonds of complicity, and relied on code words for communication" (Schlant, 1999, p. 25).

The ideological background that accounts for the ideological habits of social interaction is the basis for any qualitative study of silence. Analysts have no means of entering the minds of the actors to tell whether they have intentionally kept some theme unsaid. Neither do they have to. All they need to do is show how interaction is collaboratively being kept on track, steered away from the unsayable (Billig, 2006). We study the details of this interaction, but the unconscious side of the unsaid means that "there can be no escape from the duty to interpret" (Billig & Marinho, Chapter 1). Analysts (like participants) will have to bring their own familiarity with the ideological landscape to bear in doing their work and in themselves entering the fray of social life. In so doing, they are able to "uncover the assumptions of our times" (Billig & Marinho, Chapter 1), which are the routines and exclusions that are allowed to pass through the fires of participant-administered account-ability. Qualitative studies of silence are thus able to reshape the ideolo-gical landscape as they challenge forms of accountability and create new habits of living and representing, leaving their own impressions in the stigmergic topographies of the said and unsaid.

The analysis we describe here takes its bearings from the routines and habits of social life. It seeks to describe the paths of the said and how these map out and keep out the hinterlands of the unsaid. We start at the conscious side of unconscious awareness, identifying absent themes from the presences that stand in their place.

But sometimes in life we have no choice but to start from the side of "socially reproduced unconsciousness" (Billig, 2006, p. 17). We find ourselves catapulted – by trauma, horror, or social exclusion – into the hinterlands of the unsaid and have to begin to find our bearings from there. Chapters by Richardson and Allison (Chapter 13), Winter (Chapter 12), Alford (Chapter 11), and Frosh (Chapter 14) show how the trauma of torture, war, and tyranny can produce experience that "refuses to be rendered into language" (Richardson & Allison, Chapter 13). The pain of torture and the horrors of war and tyranny are "world-destroying" (Scarry 1985, cited in Richardson & Allison, Chapter 13). The same appears to be true of social exclusion of the kind described by Alford (Chapter 11). The "disappearance" of the pathologized whistle-blower, bludgeoned by silence, leaves the individual world destroyed, without a recognizable language or way of entering properly into the social life of discursive joint action. The basis for silence here, in contrast to the earlier examples, is the lack of adequate discursive capacity, rather than (as earlier) moral proscriptions against the use of certain ways of speaking.

It is tempting to think of unconscious expressions – the murmuring, groaning, cooing (Frosh, Chapter 14) – as "pre-discursive" (e.g., Hook, 2006), imagining that they might speak the language of the body itself, of universal symbolism, or of raw experience. In our view, the pre-discursive does not lie outside of the terrain of the said and unsaid, in another world altogether. The problem is not a complete inability to respond but the impossibility of responding properly. The material left out of the response – the sounds of war, the terrible singularity and aloneness of trauma, cruelties beyond words, the horrors of tyranny both for perpetrators and survivors – cannot be done justice by the available means of representation, which tend to foreclose and misleadingly cover over the trauma by "speaking for it" (Frosh, Chapter 14). There is an inability to respond properly, to join lines of action together with the survivors of "limit experiences" (Winter, Chapter 12) with any authenticity. We cannot enter into the daily lived experiences and conditions of the subaltern, the oppressed, or the marginalized as if we can walk in their shoes. We cannot enter the world of war as if we were entering our neighbor's home. Nor can we enter the world of torture, abuse, or the Holocaust with "facile sentimentality of easy identification" (Winter, Chapter 12), or with the "colonizing tendency of speech" (Frosh, Chapter 14). The available discursive resources, fashioned as they are in social convention, are not adequate to the task of representing the singularity of world-destroying limit experiences.

But, even so, the sounds of the murmuring deep that Frosh (Chapter 14) describes – the "humming, murmuring, cooing, groaning, tumult, music, restlessness, stirring, panic" – are human productions and are part of the collectively manufactured stigmergic landscape of the said and unsaid. It might be encrypted knowledge, overshot with silence, as psychoanalytically informed clinical and literary studies of trauma have shown (e.g., Levine, 2014), but the knowledge that is communicated in these murmurings is "still knowledge of a kind" (Frosh, Chapter 14). It might not be possible – now – to enter into the discourse with these expressions, but there is always a hope that one could. Even though trauma, horror, and social exclusion catapult people into terrain unmarked by paths of convention, these paths constitute the terrain, and there is a hope that one might work one's way toward a path or perhaps find one inadvertently – like a lost hiker. Trauma and horror may not be speakable, but neither is their murmur an indecipherable cacophony. The tumult has recognizable notes, rhythms, and refrains. The margins between the well-trod paths of the said and the grassy hinterlands of the unsaid are shorelines of incoming and outgoing tides; dreams; premonitions; fleeting impressions; hauntings; transmissions; uncanny feelings; and, of course, murmurings, groanings, and cooings (cf. Frosh, 2012). The constitution of the said by the unsaid gives the murmurs of silence their shared, social, and ideological quality. These embodied murmurings have a haunting and melancholic quality as they "speak" from the hinterlands of the unsaid.

Listening to the murmuring deep requires a different approach and objective on the part of the qualitative researcher. Not all silences need to be spoken by the qualitative researcher. In the absence of a shared language, trauma may only be witnessed and acknowledged. Indeed it must be for its haunting power to dissipate (Frosh, Chapter 14). Rather than joining the discourse, qualitative researchers might here join the speaker or the community of speakers, accompanying them as witnessing listeners rather than speakers. Such accompaniments allow affect to flow through the listener. The objective of listening is not necessarily individualizing and therapeutic. Listening to survivors of trauma and exclusion can also be mobilizing and can facilitate the forging of new paths from the hinterlands of the unsaid to the well-trod ideological grounds of accountable conduct. This is well illustrated in the unsilencing methodologies that Richardson and Allison (Chapter 13) describe as "messy processes that are necessary to pull the unsaid and its affects into language ... without flattening out experience or ignoring its textures." Survivors of various forms of violence and other trauma may begin to forge solidarity through qualitative studies of silence that nurture recognition of shared experience. Qualitative studies of silence might tread some kind of middle ground along the lines of not speaking silences but still being able to speak *with* them.

Acknowledgments

The support of the DST-NRF Centre of Excellence in Human Development toward this research/activity is hereby acknowledged. Opinions expressed and conclusions arrived at are those of the author and are not necessarily to be attributed to the Centre of Excellence in Human Development.

We would like to thank Alistair Nixon for his help in designing the topographical image; Dirk Helbing and the American Physical Society for granting permission to reprint the path image and stigmergic simulation; and Klaus Humpert for giving us permission to reproduce his path image.

References

Billig, M. (1999). *Freudian repression: Conversation creating the unconscious.* Cambridge: Cambridge University Press.

Billig, M. (2006). A psychoanalytic discursive psychology: From consciousness to unconsciousness. *Discourse Studies, 8,* 17–24.

Blumer, H. (1969). *Symbolic interactionism: Perspective and method.* Berkeley: University of California Press.

Burford-Rice, R., & Augoustinos, M. (2018). "I didn't mean that: It was just a slip of the tongue": Racial slips and gaffes in the public arena. *British Journal of Social Psychology, 57,* 21–42.

Butler, J. (1993). *Bodies that matter: On the discursive limits of "sex."* New York: Routledge.

Condor, S., Figgou, L., Abell, J., Gibson, S., & Stevenson, C. (2006). "They're not racist . . . ": Prejudice denial, mitigation and suppression in dialogue. *British Journal of Social Psychology, 45,* 441–462.

Durrheim, K. (2012). Implicit prejudice in mind and interaction. In J. Dixon & M. Levine (Eds.), *Beyond the prejudice problematic* (pp. 179–199). Cambridge: Cambridge University Press.

Durrheim, K. (2017). Race trouble and the impossibility of non-racialism. *Critical Philosophy of Race, 5,* 320–338.

Durrheim, K., Quayle, M., & Dixon, J. (2016). The struggle for the nature of "prejudice": "Prejudice" expression as identity performance. *Political Psychology, 37,* 17–35.

Durrheim, K. Okuyan, M., Twali, M.S., García-Sánchez, W, Pereira, A., Portice, J.S., . . . & Keil, T. (2018). The interactional functions of racist discourse for mobilizing right-wing populism: The construction of identity and alliance in reactions to UKIP's Brexit "Breaking Point" campaign. *Journal of Community and Applied Social Psychology, 28*(6) 385–405.

Edwards, D. (1997). *Discourse and cognition.* London: Sage.

Ephratt, M. (2008). The functions of silence. *Journal of Pragmatics, 40,* 1909–1938.

Fairclough, N. (1992). *Discourse and social change.* Cambridge: Polity Press.

Foucault, M. (1972). *The archeology of knowledge and the discourse on language* (A. M. Sheridan Smith, Trans.). New York: Harper and Row.

Foucault, M. (1973). *The birth of the clinic: An archaeology of medical perception* (A. M. Sheridan Smith, Trans.). London: Routledge

Frosh, S. (2012). Hauntings: Psychoanalysis and ghostly transmission. *American Imago, 69,* 241–264.

Goldstone, R. L., & Roberts, M. E. (2006). Self-organized trail systems in groups of humans. *Complexity, 11,* 43–50.

Hook, D. (2006). "Pre-discursive" racism. *Journal of Community and Applied Social Psychology, 16,* 207–232.

Helbing, D., Schweitzer, F., Keltsch, J., & Molnár, P. (1997). Active walker model for the formation of human and animal trail systems. *Physical Review E, 56,* 2527–2539.

Helbing, D., Molnár, P., Farkas, I., & Bolay, K. (2001). Self-organizing pedestrian movement. *Environment and Planning B: Planning and Design*, *28*, 361–383.

Heritage, J. (1984). *Garfinkel and ethnomethodology*. Cambridge: Polity Press.

Heylighten, F. (2016). Stigmergy as a universal coordination mechanism I: Definition and components. *Cognitive Systems Research*, *38*, 4–13.

Jaworski, A. (1993). *Power of silence: Social and pragmatic perspectives*. Newbury Park, CA: Sage.

Johnson, S. (1818). *A dictionary of the English language; in which the words are deduced from their originals; and illustrated in their different significations, by examples from the best writers* (Vol. II). London: Longman, Hurst, Rees, Orme & Brown.

Laclau, E. (1993). Politics and the limits of modernity. In T. Docherty (Ed.), *Postmodernism: A reader*, pp. 329–344. London: Harvester Wheatsheaf.

Levine, H. B. (2014). Psychoanalysis and trauma. *Psychoanalytic Inquiry*, *34*, 214–224.

Marsh, L., & Onof, C. (2008). Stigmergic epistemology, stigmergic cognition. *Cognitive Systems Research*, *9*, 136–149

Murray, A. J., & Durrheim, K. (2018). "There was much that went unspoken": Maintaining racial hierarchies in South African paid domestic labour through the unsaid. *Ethnic and Racial Studies*, *doi* https://doi.org/10.1080/01419870.2018.1532096.

Parker, I. (1992). *Discourse dynamics: Critical analysis for social and individual psychology*. London: Routledge

Potter, J., & Wetherell, M. (1987). *Discourse and social psychology: Beyond attitudes and behaviour*. London: Sage.

Rappert, B., & Bauchspies, W. K. (2014). Introducing absence. *Social Epistemology*, *28*, 1–3.

Sacks, H., Schegloff, E. A., & Jefferson, G. (1974). A simplest systematics for the organization of turn taking in conversation. *Language*, *50*, 696–735.

Schegloff, E. A. (1992). Repair after next turn: The last structurally provided defense of intersubjectivity in conversation. *American Journal of Sociology*, *97* (5), 1295–1345.

Schegloff, E. A. (2007). *Sequence organization in interaction: A primer in conversation analysis*. Cambridge: Cambridge University Press.

Schlant, E. (1999). *The language of silence: West German literature and the Holocaust*. New York: Routledge.

Schröter, M. (2013). *Silence and concealment in political discourse*. Amsterdam: John Benjamins Publishing Company.

Schröter, M., & Taylor, C. (2018). Introduction. In M. Schröter & C. Taylor (Eds.), *Exploring silence and absence in discourse: Empirical approaches* (pp. 1–21). London: Palgrave Macmillan.

Shotter, J. (1993). *Conversational realities: Constructing life through language*. London: Sage.

Stokoe, E. (2015). Identifying and responding to possible -*isms* in institutional encounters: Alignment, impartiality and the implications for communication training. *Journal of Language and Social Psychology*, *34*, 427–445.

Times Media Digital (2017, June 9). Never use the "k-word": *HRC*. Retrieved from www.timeslive.co.za/news/south-africa/2017–06-09-never-ever-use-the-k-word-hrc/

Wetherell, M. (1998). Positioning and interpretative repertoires: Conversation analysis and post-structuralism in dialogue. *Discourse & Society*, *9*, 387–412.

Wetherell, M. (2001). Debates in discourse research. In M. Wetherell, S. Taylor, & S. J. Yates (Eds.), *Discourse theory and practice: A reader* (pp. 380–399). London: Sage.

Whitehead, K. A. (2015). Everyday antiracism in action: Preference organization in responses to racism. *Journal of Language and Social Psychology*, *34*, 374–389.

Whitehead, K. A. (2018). Managing the moral accountability of stereotyping. *Journal of Language and Social Psychology*, *37*, 288–309. doi:10.1177/0261927X17723679

Wittgenstein, L. (1953). *Philosophical investigations* (G.E.M. Anscombe, Trans.). Oxford: Blackwell.

Zerubavel, E. (2006). *The elephant in the room: Silence and denial in everyday life*. Oxford: Oxford University Press.

Note

1. In this chapter we reference contributions to this volume by citing the chapter author(s) and chapter number.

Index